Devotions for Couples on the Grow

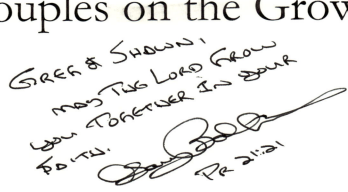

By Gary Baltrusch
with contributions by Glenda Baltrusch

PublishAmerica
Baltimore

© 2009 by Gary Baltrusch.
All rights reserved. No part of this book may be reproduced, stored in a retrieval system or transmitted in any form or by any means without the prior written permission of the publishers, except by a reviewer who may quote brief passages in a review to be printed in a newspaper, magazine or journal.

First printing

PublishAmerica has allowed this work to remain exactly as the author intended, verbatim, without editorial input.

Scripture taken from the HOLY BIBLE, NEW INTERNATIONAL VERSION ®. Copyright © 1973, 1978, 1984 by International Bible Society. Used by permission of Zondervan Publishing House. All rights reserved.

The "NIV" and "New International Version" trademarks are registered in the United States Patent and Trademark Office by International Bible Society. Use of either trademark requires the permission of International Bible Society.

ISBN: 978-1-61546-284-1
PUBLISHED BY PUBLISHAMERICA, LLLP
www.publishamerica.com
Baltimore

Printed in the United States of America

Dedication

In appreciation for all you taught me growing up, for the example of married family life you set, for the blessing of raising me in a Christian home, and keeping me in church and in the Lord, this book is dedicated to you, my parents, Paul and Delores Baltrusch.

Acknowledgments

Special thanks and appreciation to my Sweetheart, Glenda, for all her support and encouragement. My Love, I'm grateful for your ideas, your proofreading and editing, and the continual inspiration and heartening you've provided. You are truly the helpmate God had in mind when He created wives. I'm blessed beyond measure to have you as my covenant wife.

Thanks to my daughter Jackie for the good ideas, and scripture verses to incorporate the themes for them, and for her consistent encouragement.

You two made this project much easier. Blessings to you both.

Foreword

If you are looking for a lumbering, dull, daily devotional, don't read this book. It is neither lumbering nor dull. Your day will be brightened and your step quickened with these words for every day living. I was not surprised to hear that Gary & Glenda were still enlarging their circle of influence and stretching their ministry (Isaiah 54:2) with a new project; a book of daily devotions.

Our friendship began when God put us together as a ministry team. Later, God placed us on different paths, but always serving the Master and we occasionally get to share some precious time together.

Gary & Glenda are polished musicians and encouragers for those who seek comfort and healing during these difficult days. As their pastor for a few short years, I came to know their passion for the lost. Glenda is the only pianist I know that would leave the piano and platform, at the moment the music minister is ready to begin, to speak passionately to someone's lost condition. It is an inspiration to know a couple who have completely accepted the challenge to "follow me" (Lk 9:23).

Gary & Glenda are not just real; they are real "friends" of Jesus. Their music is a testimony of their lives, and the encouragement they bring to others through this journal is genuine.

James Wallis

Introduction

If you've been using couples devotionals to enhance your relationship, thank you for utilizing ours. If this is your first use of a book of daily devotions, welcome!

Step one is to make the commitment that you'll have these devotions together every single day, and let nothing stop you. It'll be worth the investment of time as you reap a harvest of blessings in your marriage.

Step two, of course, is to read the daily devotion together, out loud, and discuss anything you may have questions regarding, or want to comment about, with one another.

Step three is to pray together, again, doing so aloud. We find it's best if you both pray in turn. The prayer at the end of each day's devotion is just to get you started, so begin there, and continue with your own thanks, petitions, and requests.

As you journey through this year in devotions, you'll have the opportunity to clarify your beliefs, apply God's word to your lives, and become more solid in your faith. We pray God's richest blessings on you both as you spend these few moments together each day. You'll soon find you're a 'couple on the grow.'

Jan 1
Happy New Year

"So we make it our goal to please Him..." II Cor 5:9a

New years are a great time to renew our commitments and work on improvements in ourselves we've been putting off. Bear in mind, as we seek to grow in our walk, there are many behaviors, ways of thinking, goals and aspirations that we can change, or begin anew. It's like walking with Jesus. When we fail, when we stumble, if we'll turn to Him, He'll forgive us and we can start again.

Our counsel to you as you make new resolutions:

Don't set goals you know you can't possibly attain.

Do set goals that will stretch you.

Don't try to change your whole personality.

Do seek to improve one or two aspects that you feel aren't pleasing to Christ.

Don't try to change the way your spouse does things, or behaves.

Do learn new ways to live with them without frustration.

Don't start huge projects that you won't keep up with.

Do take on manageable portions of a large project.

Don't try to grow mature in your faith immediately.

Do grow a little every day.

Don't make your goal to read the whole bible every day, twice a day.

Do read a chapter, or part of a chapter every morning. Your whole day will be better, and your attitude will improve, along with your ability to handle the daily issues that occur.

Don't ignore the Lord as you go through your days.

Do spend time in His presence, every day, throughout your day.

Don't ignore your spouse and children as you get busy with work/projects.

Do keep in contact with them so they know they're important and loved.

Don't float through life without purpose.
Do live each day intentionally, deciding what's important and doing it.
Don't float through life without purpose.
Do live for and with Jesus intentionally!
Don't make excuses!
Do the right things!

Prayer: Holy Spirit, give me the goals and resolutions you want me to improve on. Help me to be consistent, and when I miss the mark, pick me up, and set me right back on the correct path...

Jan 2
Which Character Are You?

"My Dove...show me your face, let me hear your voice; for your voice is sweet, and your face is lovely." Song of Songs 2:14

Remember when you were first dating? You couldn't wait to see him/her; you thrilled at the sound of his/her voice. You were intent on acquainting yourself with the real heart of your love.

Back in the early days of radio and television, when radio shows, and then animated cartoons became the "entertainment" for a whole generation, there was one man who greased the wheels for much of the sound effects and voices. Mel Blanc was literally the voice of Warner Brothers cartoons, including voices of Bugs Bunny, Daffy Duck, Porky Pig, Yosemite Sam, Tweety, Sylvester, and many more. Most of us have had the opportunity to enjoy watching the antics of many of those characters. Mel could give each of them it's own voice.

Sometimes, we're just like that. We speak with any number of different voices. Sometimes we're the voice of husband or wife, sometimes child, sometimes friend, sometimes boss, sometimes lover, sometimes father or mother, sometimes Christian, sometimes hunting or shopping buddy, even sometimes reason. Isn't it interesting how we present different personas in different situations? It's important for our spouse and our family to be able to count on getting the straight, honest, loving truth from us. After all, one of the aspects they love about us is our character, not just being a character. With our family, with our husband or wife, no character facades are necessary! They'll love us best when they get the real voice.

Prayer: Dear Lord, help me to be genuine in my speech and actions. Give me the self-discipline to speak with my real voice...

Jan 3
How Shiny Is Your Armor?

"Husbands, in the same way be considerate as you live with your wives, and treat them with respect as the weaker partner and as heirs with you of the gracious gift of life…" I Pet 3:7a

Chivalry is dead! Well, sometimes it seems it's nearly dead. One of the casualties of the feminist movement has been the attitude of being a gentleman. From the rude retorts, the criticisms for stepping aside for a woman, the caustic assertions that a woman can do anything a man can, belligerent feminism has taken it's toll. Now, don't get me wrong, I believe in the workplace, if males and females do the same work, they should receive equivalent compensation. That's not what I'm talking about, though. I'm talking about social interaction.

Women still want a knight in shining armor. How can we be that for our wives? Just as importantly, how can we, as Christian men, set ourselves apart, make a positive difference in the eyes of a self centered, selfish, me first world? Well, I've found it's actually simple. Be Polite! The old fashioned virtues of being a gentleman show a different lifestyle like nothing else has in recent years. This can't be a superficial, I'll do it when people are watching project. It has to be a changed lifestyle, one we also do at home, and the thing is, it's so easy! For instance, here are a few simple ways to be "set apart":

Open the doors for your wife, or others when we have opportunity.
Refuse to walk in front of your wife.
Help your wife carrying her packages or things.
Hold her arm when crossing potentially treacherous ground.
Protect your wife, family, and the innocent.

See, being polite is just the golden rule put into practice. Once you make these things a habit in your life, it's just a continuous reward flow coming in, too. Your wife will appreciate you more. People will notice we're different, earning their good opinion. It gives us opportunities to set an example for Christ. Really, it's just putting other's needs first.

Prayer: Lord, have your Holy Spirit remind me to be polite, and gentlemanly in the way I treat others, so I can show them there's a difference having you in our lives...

Jan 4
Sugar and Spice and Everything Nice?

"Wives, in the same way be submissive to your husbands so that, if any of them do not believe the word, they may be won over without words by the behavior of their wives, when they see the purity and reverence of your lives." I Pet 3:1-2

You thought you skated by pretty smoothly yesterday, didn't you Wife? Fortunately (sometimes unfortunately), God's Word addresses issues for everyone.

This passage speaks to not only our behavior, but to our inner spirit. We know that out of the heart, the mouth speaks. Note in this verse, though, that it's done "without words". Ouch! How do we manage that?

First, let's deal with that tongue control issue. If you make a request of your husband, you've communicated your desire. If you tell him a second time, you've reminded him. If you've told him a third time, unless your husband is notoriously forgetful, you've crossed over the threshold into the realm of nagging. Sometimes we have to resign ourselves to the fact the he's just not going to do it. No amount of badgering will change that, and if it does, you've lost the war of resentment anyway.

Secondly, we must live in a pure and reverent manner. Our behavior has to show the peace and joy of Christ within. In a later devotion, we'll expand on the fruit of the spirit. As much as we can, we should minimize conflict. That doesn't mean issue avoidance, but it does lead to the purpose of peaceful resolutions to the problems we face together.

Thirdly, let's go beyond the verses above. In three and four, it talks about our beauty. It's to come from within. Now, the verse doesn't say not to wear nice clothing, or jewelry, or new hairdos. It only says our beauty shouldn't come from those things. Our beauty is an inner loveliness that virtually glows from within, from our gentle spirit and quiet, peaceful nature.

If we're going to speak, let's make it words of approval, open, respectful conversation, love, and affirmation.

Prayer: Father in Heaven, give me your grace to become the wife you intend for me to be…

Jan 5
Get a Streak Going

"It gave me great joy to have some brothers come and tell about your faithfulness to the truth and how you continue to walk in the truth." III Jn 3

When the kids were little, we used to play a game in the yard with a Frisbee. It was a simple game, but if you've played with a Frisbee, you know how tricky it is to catch it every time, especially for children. We kept score by how many times in a row we could throw and catch the Frisbee without a drop. How long could we keep the streak going? It was always exciting when we set a new record.

That kind of competitive game helps me keep doing the right things in life. For instance, we have a seventeen plus year streak going of having devotions together every day. Even when we've been physically separated, we still have devotions by phone each day. A little over two years ago (at this writing) I began a daily streak of reading my Bible every day. Prior to that, I always read in inconsistent streaks. It has helped me tremendously. Now, I'm the kind of person that, once I have a great streak going, I don't want to break it for any reason. This may seem a trivial way of keeping going, but the point is, it helps me do the right, consistent things in my life. Every day is a new record! You can laugh at my way of accomplishing these helpful habits, but it works!

Our goal is to be consistent and faithful in our walk in the truth. One of the ways we've found of keeping ourselves together, and our relationship vibrant, is by having devotions together every day. Like every couple, we've had our tough times. No relationship is all sweetness and light. This habit of devotions has sustained us through difficult situations that many, if not most couples, don't make it through. One or both of us just wouldn't let the streak break. Consequently, we're still here, better than ever, more in love than we could ever have imagined. We encourage you to do the same.

Now, get your streaks going!

Prayer: Gracious Lord, we know that we need to be in your Word, and that it will benefit us to have devotions consistently. We want our marriage to be all that you want it to be, so help us…

Jan 6
Are You Proud of Your Humility?

"'God opposes the proud but gives grace to the humble.' Submit yourselves, then, to God." Jas 4:6b-7a

Arrogance is not a virtue! We can all be a bit overweening in our estimation of ourselves at times. But it's noteworthy that God himself bragged about how humble Moses was. If we have to brag about ourselves, we're really just puffing ourselves up. The key to humility is in keeping the right perspective. So who are you?

You're a son/daughter of the Most High God, adopted into His family.

You're a prince/princess of the Blood (of Christ).

You're one with the responsibilities of royal blood.

You're an ambassador for Christ Jesus.

You're the servant of all.

You're a minister of the good news of Jesus.

Now, what does that all mean? It means we have no reason to hang our heads, or be embarrassed about who we are. Our Heavenly Dad is the Lord of heaven and earth. We are joint heirs with Jesus. Adopted brother/sister to Jesus Christ, the Messiah, the Savior of the world, the King of Kings, the Lord of Lords. We are those to whom the deposit of His Holy Spirit is given as a guarantee. We are the ones who bring the message of our king to those we communicate with. We have a mission to help those in need, to provide comfort and sustenance to those around us, to give encouragement and bolster flagging faith, to serve others in every way we can. We are His children, to whom He gives talents and abilities to use for Him.

Above all, we are humbly thankful to our Lord. Our position comes from His sacrifice, from His grace, from His love and mercy. It was nothing that we did, or attained on our own. We have every reason to be humble, and not a single one to be proud of. We owe all we are and all we have to Him!

Keep the correct perspective.

Prayer: Lord, show us who we are in you. Give us the perspective we need to walk humbly before you, giving you thanks in all things...

Jan 7
Be Prepared!

"Preach the Word; be prepared in season and out of season; correct, rebuke and encourage-with great patience and careful instruction." II Tim 4:2

When the new century was approaching the "experts" told us that we needed to prepare for the worst. Y2K could be the end of civilization as we know it. Computers wouldn't work, which would lead to worldwide disaster, transit systems shutting down, power companies stopping producing energy, banking systems in chaos. Stockpile plenty of food and heating oil, make sure your vehicles were full of fuel.

Now, you know the year 2000 came without so much as a blip, but that doesn't stop the media from going right on to the next impending calamity. Why? Because they sell news. The more sensational and frightening they can make it sound, the more people will listen to, or read, their news.

Don't get me wrong; we are supposed to stay prepared. Just not for every so-called impending disaster (although you could obviously make the case hell is one). We need to be prepared to explain the hope and salvation we have in Christ. Everyone tries to be ready for a Sunday school class or bible study they're going to teach. But how about Tuesday when we run into someone who starts questioning Christianity, or your particular church denomination. What about Friday when your friend asks you why you're so sure you're going to Heaven? It's not the expected that throws us, it's the unexpected. That's why it's important to be prepared at all times to give an account of the faith we hold. Have you thought about; do you know what you do believe?

Prayer: Heavenly Father, give us wisdom and knowledge as we study your word. Help us to be prepared at all times to explain, humbly and patiently, what we believe...

Jan 8
The Gift of Forgiveness

"...forgiving each other, just as in Christ God forgave you." Eph 4:32b

Forgiveness is a gift! It's the greatest gift we've received from the Lord. When you've been granted it from your spouse, or loved ones, you're grateful. It heals you. As important as that is, it's equally important to forgive others. That also heals you. It may help others that way too, but it's essential for our own heart and spirit.

When forgiveness is withheld, it may hurt the person to whom it's directed. But it harms the unforgiver much, much more. The grievance begins to fester, causing irritation, anger, and bitterness. That bitterness turns to spite, and then to hatred. What's worse, if it's directed at someone who really doesn't like you, they're probably glad you're miserable wallowing in your acrimony. It doesn't bother them at all. Often, though, the one you're upset with doesn't know it! They're not even troubled by it. And you carry around all that angst for nothing.

When we choose to let go of a grudge, it cleanses our heart and our mind. It frees us to think of wholesome things. We're no longer wasting valuable time and energy on something that enslaves our spirit. We can dwell on productive, positive attitudes that will bless us, and our family and friends.

So today, if you're holding a grudge, we encourage you to make the decision, and let it go. If it means apologizing to someone, then gear up your courage and do so. Forgiveness blesses both the forgiver, and the forgiven. This is also one of the most important lessons we can teach our kids. If you'll teach them to forgive, you'll give them one of the greatest blessings they'll ever receive in life. You'll have given them the gift of forgiveness.

Prayer: Dear Lord, we know you've forgiven us so much. We need to be like you, and forgive others too. Give us the courage to step out in obedience to your word…

Jan 9
Take the Test

"Examine yourselves to see whether you are in the faith; test yourselves…" II Cor 13:5a

Wise people often take a moment to step back and assess themselves, their goals, purpose, and accomplishments. It helps them to stay focused on the final result, and make sure they're staying on course as they work toward that end. Also, it allows them to make quick corrections when they get slightly off course.

When we built our house, we had a plan, a set of blueprints, a specific amount of money we could spend (a budget), and a timeline to complete the project. As we were building, we continued to check the blueprints to be sure our construction was accurate. We monitored our cash flow to verify we would have enough money to finish. We worked hard to complete the house within six months. By following our preset plans, reassessing every few weeks, and making adjustments, we were able to accomplish our task in the timeframe we had set for ourselves.

Our spiritual house is much the same. The bible is our blueprint for our spiritual, and thus our physical, journey through life. While we don't know the specific timeline, we realize that our journey should characterize continual growth and progress. To be sure we're growing, we have to look at where we began, and assess our mile markers along the way, making adjustments at regular intervals. If we don't examine ourselves, we really won't know where we are in the faith with any accuracy. Our goal is to grow and please our master, Jesus Christ. Far better we test ourselves, than to be tested by someone else. Plus, it's an open book test! So take the test!

Prayer: Father, move us to stay in your word, and examine ourselves in it's light. Help us to measure up to the bible…

Jan 10
Happy Troubles

"We also rejoice in our sufferings, because we know that suffering produces perseverance; perseverance, character; and character, hope." Rom 5:3b-4

"I just thank God for this flat tire. While changing it, I'm going to learn more perseverance. My character will improve. Hallelujah!"

"Thank you, Lord, for the dryer going out. What an opportunity to grow in perseverance while we look for one to replace it and search for the money to do so. How my character will improve, and I know I'll have hope."

"Glory to God, a tree fell on the house. Praise the Lord; it's actually three trees. Cutting up these limbs is going to cause real suffering, and bless God; I'll have to persevere. What character that'll build. I hope!"

Rejoicing in the face of adversity isn't as easy as it seems on paper, is it? In fact, it's extremely difficult, because our natural reaction is more likely for us to cuss or throw things. That never improves the situation, though, does it? If we're going to be obedient to scripture, we have to cause ourselves to rejoice, because we know God's word is true. Have you noticed that most of the instructions given us in the bible are contrary to our natural inclinations? The Lord wants us to intentionally do what he asks us to. That's how we grow in the faith; improve our actions to match His will. When we set our mind to achieving this growth, the Holy Spirit will nudge us continually in the right direction.

You know, you'll have to decide to rejoice in sufferings, because that's not our instinctive reaction.

Prayer: Gracious Lord, help me to hold my tongue and my hands and my feet when things go wrong. Give me your perspective in rejoicing over them, because we know they're given to help us grow in perseverance and character…

Jan 11
Stay One!

"And they shall become one flesh." Gen 2:24c

"The husband should fulfill his marital duty to his wife, and likewise the wife to her husband. The wife's body does not belong to her alone but also to her husband. In the same way, the husband's body does not belong to him alone but also to his wife. Do not deprive each other except by mutual consent and for a time, so that you may devote yourselves to prayer. Then come together again so that Satan will not tempt you because of your lack of self-control." I Cor 7:3-5

These passages are about our sexual intimacy as a married couple. God tells us that it's important for us to be active in our intimate life.

Too often, one partner or the other in a marriage is willing to use sex as a reward or punishment system. That's not God's purpose for us. The repercussions of using it are far reaching. If you withdraw from physical touch, you force your spouse to withdraw emotionally, which leads you to retaliatory silence, which leads your spouse to physical withdrawal from the living space for longer periods of time to avoid the tension, which leads to more anger and harsh words on your part, which leads your spouse to respond in kind, which leads you to increase ignoring him/her, which eventually leads your spouse to notice there are other people out there who treat them with a lot more kindness, which leads to… Well, you get the idea. You've seen it in other marriages.

It's so important to communicate physically, as this is one of our ultimate expressions of love in the marital partnership. Never, ever, use sex as a weapon in an argument. It's akin to calling names, or bringing up past mistakes. If you have to do that, you're not really trying to solve the issue, you're just trying to win the battle. And as is often the case, you may win the battle while losing the war. Peace will usually reign supreme in a home where there is good vocal communication, love and affection shown freely, and "fulfilling the marital duty" regularly.

    Besides. It's Fun!

    Prayer: Heavenly Father, thanks for giving us such a pleasant, fun way to express our love. Help us to never demean it by using it wrongly, but give us the freedom to enjoy our love with the joy you meant for us...

Jan 12
Focus

"Fix your thoughts on Jesus." Heb 3:1b

Is there anything more worth your attention, or more helpful to your life, than to stay focused on Jesus. Throughout the gospels, we have every example from him we need, to help us learn the most important aspects of our journey through life.

Sometimes on earth, we're blessed with a great picture of Christian living. Glenda's dad lived with us just over the last three years of his life. Dad had a brain tumor, and followed that with brain cancer. The latter part of his time with us, he really struggled with his illness, and his memory was much affected. At times, he thought he was somewhere else. But what I took away from the experience, and so admired about Dad, was his consummate devotion to Christ. He lived what he believed, even when he couldn't think clearly. Many nights, when I peeked into his bedroom to check on him, I'd catch him on his knees by the bed, praying for his family. He prayed out loud, naming them off. I was privileged to observe him reading his bible, even when he couldn't see it very well any longer. I watched his manners, his courtesy, his kindness, his willingness to help, to work, and his pure speech. He spent so much time with Jesus that he became quite like him.

When we fix our thoughts on Jesus, that's what happens to all of us. We become more and more like him. Dad wasn't perfect. None of us is. But he was as conformed to the image of Christ as anyone I've known. We're not instructed to emulate our Christian examples here on earth. We can glean some of what they've learned, though. Ultimately, we're to fix our thoughts on Jesus, the one whom our examples became like.

Prayer: Dear Father, give me the singleness of purpose to fix my thoughts on Jesus. Engrain on my heart and mind His ways, His speech, and His actions…

Jan 13
Nice Outfit

"Clothe yourselves with compassion, kindness, humility, gentleness and patience." Col 3:12b

A couple months ago, one of the men's clothing stores in our town went out of business. Being reasonably frugal (a good steward-lol), although I needed new suits, I didn't think I'd spend the money. As the closing time drew near, one day I went in to see what they had. Wow! Nice suits, really on sale. I bought two new suits, which would normally sell for about $800.00, for $109.00 and change, including tax. After getting the trousers cuffed, I'd spent a grand total of $138.00. Cool! I was able to get something I really needed, and save seven hundred bucks. We like that! God blessed us!

It's fun to be able to wear new clothes. They look great, haven't worn thin yet, and have a nice "crisp" feel. They make us feel sharp. Sometimes people notice our new duds. We appreciate compliments, don't we?

Today's verse means we put on, like a nice outfit, or new clothes, these attributes. They're far more important than good clothing, though, because they're a part of our character, our attitude. They allow us to treat people in a way that helps them, serves them, and shows them we love and care about them. Compassion helps us to sympathize with people without showing pity. With kindness we're able to do for others what they need without making them feel put off by it. Humility keeps the right perspective, realizing that it's God that has blessed us with the ability to help. Gentleness is the controlled strength to softly handle or approach their need without giving offense. Patience is required to give us the ability to see the real need, rather than rushing off on a perceived errand that may not exist, because we didn't wait and listen.

When we've clothed ourselves with compassion, kindness, humility, gentleness and patience, we're able to display a new suit, as it were. This suit clothes our temperament, our personality, our spirit, with a crisp, sharp, new look, that never wears thin, or ever gets old.

Prayer: Lord Jesus, give us these new clothes that we need. Clothe our lives with these virtues, and let us use them for you...

Jan 14
Primarily for Men—Be Strong

"Finally, be strong in the Lord and in his mighty power." Eph 6:10

Okay, let me get something off my chest. I'm *tired* of the sissification of Christian men. Somewhere along the line in the past two or three decades, we've lost our foundation of strength as men in the church. Even much of our contemporary music is just so *feminized*. Why do we have to sing love songs to Jesus that make us sound like a bunch of sissies? Nowhere in scripture does it talk about, or indicate in any way, that Jesus got in touch with his feminine side. Nowhere in God's word does it tell us to be effeminate in our worship, or our walk with Christ.

We have check blanks with a rose logo on them. A few years ago I checked out my purchases at our local Lowes Home Center, and the cashier saw the check and remarked "Oh, how nice, you must be in touch with your feminine side". Being a gentleman, I held my tongue. Now, I want you to know, I like roses, grow roses in our gardens to enjoy, and I picked out those checks. I'm not the least bit intimidated, or shaky in my self-confidence as a man. Ask my wife. But my first urge, when she made the comment, was to say, "yes, and someday perhaps you'll get in touch with yours". People's thinking has gotten so skewed.

This verse is the segue into putting on the full armor of God. I'm still one who believes that men are to be men, the foundation of strength for the family, protector of wife and children, provider of security, someone our loved ones can lean on, look to, and depend upon. It doesn't say, be strong. It says be strong *in the Lord*, and in *His* mighty power. I can be even stronger as a man when I have *His* strength and *His* power to call on. That doesn't mean we're to be rough, or gruff, or uncouth, and we'll talk about that in another devotion. It does mean we lean on Jesus Christ as the source of our strength, which gives us a far greater reservoir to draw from.

Prayer: Father in Heaven, give me your strength, and your mighty power as I lead my family spiritually, emotionally, and physically...

Jan 15
Distractions

"Martha was distracted by all the preparations that had to be made…Mary has chosen what is better, and it will not be taken away from her." Lk 10:40a &42b

We all know when company's coming, there are a million things to do. The rooms need to be picked up and dusted, the floors swept and vacuumed, the food prepared, the table must be set, the bathrooms have to be cleaned and stocked, and on and on. While these things are important, they're not the most important. We want the house to look nice, and for it to be clean. It can be embarrassing if there are cobwebs or dust bunnies found. We want to make our guests feel special by setting a nice table. Food is important at our house, just as it is in most. We never want anyone to leave our table unsatisfied. Then there are dishes to clean up and leftovers to put away. Sometimes we get so caught up in the preparation and work and cleanup that we miss the time together.

Company comes so we can visit. Our goal is to enjoy fellowship. Whether it's friends or family, interacting with people is what's vital. Sharing our lives together provides pleasant times for us all. We need to know what's going on in their lives, and they need to know what's happening in ours. That's how we maintain our relationships. Jesus knew that spending time together was much more important that fixing things up. And spending time with Jesus is the most crucial item of all. It's the basis, the foundation, of our entire life.

In our home, with our spouse, the same holds true. We can get so bogged down with all the chores that need to be done, we forget to spend quality time together, renewing and refreshing our love relationship. That needs to be done on a daily basis. Sometimes, you just have to leave some things undone. There are more important issues to attend to, and our spouse is one responsibility we just can't let slide. Choose and make time for what is better. It won't be taken away from you.

Prayer: Lord, help us to keep our priorities in order. Our love life is more important than anything else…

Jan 16
Found Wanting

"You have been weighed on the scales and found wanting." Dan 5:27

Even King Belshazzar answered to the Most High God. Even King Nebuchadnezzar before him ended up praising and glorifying the Lord.

These scales are the scales of justice. We often know what's right. We know the things we ought to do, but so often, in our arrogance, we just go our own way.

This is what Daniel, chapter five, says about King Belshazzar. "You have set yourself up against the Lord of heaven… You praised gods of silver and gold, of bronze, iron, wood and stone, which cannot see or hear or understand. But you did not honor the God who holds in his hand your life and all your ways." Dan 5:23a & c

We do not want to be found wanting when we're weighed on His scales. Let's be sure we walk obediently before the Lord of heaven and earth. Honor, worship, and praise should be on our lips for the Most High God, as we reverence him.

When King Nebuchadnezzar became too arrogant, and refused to acknowledge God, God himself humbled him, and stripped him of his power, and his sanity. When Nebuchadnezzar finally turned his eyes toward heaven, God restored his sanity, and then his kingdom.

Walk humbly before God, praise and exalt and glorify the King of heaven. Do the work of him who redeemed you unto Himself. Then when we're weighed on God's scales, we'll be found *worthy*, not *wanting*.

Prayer: Lord, we recognize you as the Most High God. Help us to be faithful, walking humbly before you in obedience…

Jan 17
What's Your Comfort Level?

"The man and his wife were both naked, and they felt no shame." Gen 2:25

This was in the garden, before the fall. It shows us what God's intent for us was, and in Christ, I believe, still is. In the beginning, there was no shame. There wasn't any sin yet! Sin has destroyed the openness present in original marriage. Let's delve into this a bit.

How open are we with each other in our marriage? Sometimes we can be quite comfortable with each other's nudity, but how comfortable are we with opening our hearts? Our love life goes far beyond the physical to the mental and emotional and spiritual. Many of us have little nooks and crannies inside that we don't want anyone to know, not even, or sometimes especially, our spouse. The more open and honest we are with each other, the more accepting and forgiving, the better our relationship will be. Here are some basics. Tell each other the truth. Not brutally, but gently. When you're told the truth, withhold any criticism or recriminations. If you react negatively, it's unlikely that your spouse is going to be willing to bare their heart to you. No one willingly does things that cause themselves' pain. The goal is to improve our lives, our love, and our relationship.

It's important that we be accountable to our spouse. If we don't give them permission to occasionally ask the hard questions, they can't help us. Be willing to tell the truth without shame. No one's perfect. We all have things we wish we hadn't done or said. But we can't go back in time and change them. We can learn from them, and resolve not to stumble that way again with God's help. Our spouse has our best interest at heart. We don't rejoice in demeaning our partner, rather we rejoice when we confess and correct errors. If you're not willing to bare your heart, you'll never realize the wonderful love life God wants for us.

Get naked without shame at your heart level. Live in the garden!

Prayer: Dear Father, help us to have the courage, and the resolve, to be open and honest with each other. Holy Spirit, hold our tongues when our spouse tells us intimate things, and let us use it for help and encouragement...

Jan 18
Shameless!

"Godly sorrow brings repentance that leads to salvation and leaves no regret," II Cor 7:10a

"If we confess our sins he is faithful and just and will forgive us our sins and purify us from all unrighteousness." I Jn 1:9

"For I will forgive their wickedness and will remember their sins no more." Heb 8:12

Yesterday we talked a little bit about shame, and about openness in our relationship. We'd like to develop this point more fully. Often, even as Christians, we tend to feel shame and guilt for things in the past that we've been forgiven of. Satan would like nothing better than for us to just remove ourselves from the battle because our past makes us unfit for the fight. But we need to look at ourselves through God's eyes, not Satan's.

These three verses mesh to form a great chain of thought. When we sin, the Holy Spirit convicts us of our sin. He makes us feel pain in our conscience to feel sorrow for what we've done. That Godly sorrow leads us to repent (turn away from sin), and leaves no regret. Now when we confess our sin to God, he forgives us. He purifies us. I love that. He makes us righteous (in correct, or right relationship with Him) through the blood of Christ. And God says He'll forgive us and He won't even *remember* our sin any more. He now sees us as pure and holy. If God isn't remembering it, if He's forgiven us so completely, then there's no reason for us to hold onto it, and carry a load of refuse we don't need.

When we accept God's forgiveness, we're under no obligation to feel guilt, or pain, or remorse, or shame any longer. Give it up! We're unable to forget the way He does, but we can renew our minds in thankfulness for our cleared, clean slate.

We're now shameless!

Prayer: Lord, thank you for the clean slate, the removal of our sin, and the pure heart you give us. Help us not to let the past get in the way of our future with you, and the work you have for us to do...

Jan 19
He's Alive!

"Do not be afraid. I am the First and the Last. I am the Living One; I was dead, and behold I am alive forever and ever! And I hold the keys of death and Hades." Rev 1:17b-18

Isn't it wonderful to know we serve a risen Savior? That does something for me. And it makes me smile every time I read the gospels. Don't you want to invite Jesus to every funeral? He was the *life* of the party. He never let a good wake stop him from *livening* things up! Just ask the widow's son, or Jairus' daughter, or Lazarus. Or Jesus himself! And when he raised Lazarus, do you notice how careful he was to call him by name, so the whole graveyard didn't come out? That's great!

He tells us not to be frightened. "I've always been here and I always will be." What do we have to be afraid of? Jesus holds the keys to death and Hell both. We can have every confidence in the one to whom we've given our trust. We've put our faith in the One who's always been and always will be. He's got power!

Now, how about this verse? "For God did not give us a spirit of timidity, but a spirit of power, of love and of self-discipline." II Tim 1:7 (We'll use this again later)

Think on that! He's alive! We're alive!

Prayer: Lord Jesus, we rejoice that you've risen, and that you live and reign with our Father on high. We thank you for the spirit of power in us…

Jan 20
We Have Confidence

"If our hearts do not condemn us, we have confidence before God and receive from him anything we ask, because we obey his commands and do what pleases him." I Jn 3:21-22

When I was I young and into my teen years, I never hesitated to go to Dad when I needed or wanted something. I trusted my dad to take care of me, and help me when I needed him. I also learned through the years what requests Dad would grant, and those that he'd refuse. When I went to Dad, I went with confidence, knowing he'd take care of me, or the issue, as the case might be.

All of us are like that. As we grow in our family, we're naturally ingrained with our parent's mindset, their thinking. We know if we ask for something outrageous, or frivolous, we aren't likely going to get it. Sometimes they'll give it just for fun. But if we ask for a legitimate need, it's normally given.

God's family is like our earthly families in a lot of ways (if you grew up in a semi-normal family). As we spend time with our Heavenly Dad, as we ask for things that he gives us, or refuses, we learn His mind. We learn His will, His heart. When we read and study God's word daily, when we spend time in His presence in prayer and worship, we gradually learn His will. We stop requesting things that are insignificant; we begin praying for Kingdom issues, and we have confidence as we pray His will. Our Heavenly Dad grants those things prayed according to *His* will. When we pray His heart, we please Him and we have confidence that He'll move to accomplish His purposes.

Know our Heavenly Dad. Have confidence.

Prayer: Heavenly Dad, we want to know you as completely as we can. Point out what you want us to learn in your word, so that when we pray, we pray your will...

Jan 21
Live by the Spirit—1

"So I say, live by the Spirit, and you will not gratify the desires of the sinful nature. But if you are led by the Spirit, you are not under law." Gal 5:16 & 18

What, exactly, does it mean to live by the Spirit? If we're led by the Spirit, how are we not under law?

Let's start with the law stuff. Most of my early years we were taught the don'ts. If you grew up in an evangelical church there were even more don'ts. Don't drink. Don't smoke. Don't go to movies. Don't gamble. Don't even play cards. Don't date. Don't kiss. Don't cuss. Don't chew. You've heard it. "We don't smoke or drink or cuss or chew, and we don't date the girls that do." Those were part and parcel of our modern day church law. Take the Ten Commandments and add as many more good ones as we can think of.

But that isn't God's purpose for us. He's given us the dos, and when we follow the Spirit, we're freed from the law. When we seek to follow God's will, the don'ts cease to have any meaning, because we're walking the Lord's path. We talk in a polite manner, we do the things that won't cause others to stumble, we'll find hobbies that are pleasing to our Heavenly Father, we're honest in our business dealings, we exhibit integrity in our commitments, we honor the Lord and our spouse in our relationships. As we live to please God, our desires for sinful things fade away. We're free when we walk worthy before Him, and as we find ways to please Him.

Now, *that's* livin'!

Prayer: Lord, teach us to live by the Spirit, so that in all things, and in all ways, we please you by our walk…

Jan 22
Living by the Spirit—2

"The acts of the sinful nature are obvious: sexual immorality, impurity and debauchery: idolatry and witchcraft: hatred, discord, jealousy, fits of rage, selfish ambition, dissensions, factions and envy: drunkenness, orgies, and the like. I warn you, as I did before, that whose who live like this will not inherit the kingdom of God." Gal 5:19-21

Yesterday we began studying living by the Spirit. This is interesting. First it tells us the acts of the sinful nature are obvious, and then Paul gives us a list just in case they're not as obvious to us as they ought to be.

We instinctively know most things that are sin. In other passages in the New Testament, we're told that, anything we do that doesn't come from faith is sin for us. One fact that springs from the list here is that if you're engaging in any of these practices, you're not living by the Spirit. It's pretty thorough too. We look at these practices and say, "well I'm not involved in sexual immorality, idolatry or witchcraft. I don't cause discord; I'm not selfish or jealous. Really? Do you look at even soft pornography? Do you have hobbies that take precedence over your service to the Lord? Do you criticize the Pastor, or Christians, and try to entice others to join you in your way of thinking? Do you wish you had what others have, or wish you looked as good, or had their perceived talents, or their kind of nice kids? Do you lose your temper and yell and throw things? When these occur, we're not walking in the Spirit. We're not living as God desires for us to.

We talked about the list of don'ts. This list is good, because we'll know we're living by the Spirit when they're absent from our lives.

Prayer: Lord, forgive us for the areas we've failed in. As we read this list, we see sins that we've engaged in, and we want to live by your Spirit…

Jan 23
Living by the Spirit—3

"But the fruit of the Spirit is love, joy, peace, patience, kindness, goodness, faithfulness, gentleness and self-control. Against such things there is no law. Since we live by the Spirit, let us keep in step with the Spirit." Gal 5:22-23, 25

Are you developing and nurturing the fruit of the Spirit in your life?

Love. The decision to do what's in the best interest of the other.

Joy. The inner feeling of well-being and contentment that comes from knowing God is in control.

Peace. That absence of strife or discord in our life. A sense of calm inside.

Patience. That virtue we want right now. The willingness to hang with something or someone without feeling or exhibiting frustration.

Kindness. Being polite to and for someone, refusing to be harsh or rude, but treating with softness.

Goodness. Doing the right thing, showing integrity in action, for others.

Faithfulness. Fulfilling our promises and commitments, honoring them in all our dealings.

Gentleness. Controlled strength! Often confused with weakness by those with little understanding.

Self-control. The self-discipline to stop when your nature would like to keep going.

When we develop this fruit in our lives, we're living by the Spirit. It frees us, not for sinful things, but from the desire to even do them. We're so focused on living in ways that please our Heavenly Father we don't even want to do those things that He calls sin.

When we exhibit the fruit, we're walking right in step with the Spirit.

Prayer: Dear Lord, help us to nurture the fruit of the Spirit in our lives. Bring to mind these virtues as we go through our day…

Jan 24
Who's Got Your Wallet?

"Remember this: Whoever sows sparingly will also reap sparingly, and whoever sows generously will also reap generously. Each man should give what he has decided in his heart to give, not reluctantly or under compulsion, for God loves a cheerful giver." II Cor 9:6-7

We grew up on farms in North and South Dakota. We learned early on that if you don't plant (sow) enough potatoes in the ground, you wouldn't harvest (reap) enough potatoes for the year. If you don't plant enough wheat seed in the spring, you won't have an abundant harvest of wheat in the autumn. Farmers over the centuries have learned the hard way that if you don't plant abundantly, you don't harvest abundantly.

That same principle applies in *every* area of our spiritual life. We tend to segment our lives into a lot of little compartments. But God doesn't look at life that way. He doesn't say "your work is separate from your Christianity, so you can behave any way you want". Nor does he say, "you can flirt when your husband isn't around". God doesn't say, "money you earn is yours alone to do with as you please". He holds the same standards all the time. There's no such thing as situational ethics in God's kingdom. When you're at work, God expects you to work and act and talk in ways that honor and glorify Him. Whether your spouse is around or not, God expects us to be faithful, and careful to behave in ways that our spouse would feel is appropriate and honors them. We work, not to spend on ourselves, but to take care of our families.

Part of sowing generously is to give to God's work, and to do so cheerfully. Often we're not willing to trust God with our money. But Malachi says we should bring the whole tithe (10 %) into the storehouse (His house), and He promises to bless us when we do. We're not under law, we should decide in our hearts what to give, and invest in God's kingdom work faithfully. We strip ourselves of God's harvest in our lives if we don't. If God doesn't have your wallet, he doesn't have your whole heart.

We'll take this up more fully another day. Remember this though. Good intentions don't matter when you don't act.

Sow generously, and you *will* reap generously!

Prayer: Heavenly Father, lay on our hearts the amount of money you want us to give to our church each week, and we'll be faithful to bring it. Bless us as we're faithful in this area...

Jan 25
The Cynic

"To the pure, all things are pure, but to those who are corrupted and do not believe, nothing is pure." Tit 1:15a

I think we all know people who seem to always doubt people's integrity, who have a tough time believing anything that doesn't fit their preconceived notions. Now, the question is, if you tell that person the truth, and they don't believe you, does that make it untrue? Of course not, but convincing them that it's the truth can be difficult, not to mention irritating. When that person thinks he/she's been short changed in a business transaction, even when you take them through step by step and show them they weren't, they still may not believe it. Does that mean they were cheated? No! They just think they were.

We tend to think that most people are similar to us. If we're honest, we trust that most people are honest. If we're kind and thoughtful, we have faith that most people are the same. If we deal with others with integrity, we count on them to do the same.

The reverse holds true, too. When we lie, we assume others do, also. When we cheat, we believe people do the same. When we try to pull a stunt on someone, we count on him or her to do the same if they can get away with it. How we see others, and their motives, tells more about us than it does them.

When we read in God's word that we're to be honest, and kind, and faithful, and gentle, and self-controlled, we're given the instructions about how we are to be. Not just how to act, but how to *be*. There's a difference. When we're obedient to His instructions, and we conform to his image, we become pure. To us then, all things are pure.

This verse tells us. How do you think? Pure, or corrupt?

Don't be a cynic. Be the Pure!

Prayer: Oh Lord, give us wisdom to understand your thinking, and help us to become pure, just as you are…

Jan 26
In His Presence

"Nothing in all creation is hidden from God's sight. Everything is uncovered and laid bare before the eyes of him to whom we must give account." Heb 4:13

We talk often about spending time in God's presence. Now, we're always in His presence. But that doesn't mean we're thinking about it, or acknowledging He's here with us. This verse reminds us, though, that nothing is hidden from God's sight. We may not be paying attention to Him, but He's paying attention to us.

Since everything is laid bare before Him, let's be sure we're living in obedience. Just like we try to do the things that we know please our Mom and Dad, we do those things that we know please our Heavenly Dad.

We enjoy spending time with people we really love. We look forward to when we can see them again, and visit and do things. We look with anticipation to the moment we hear their voice again.

It's time we spend more of our day with our attention on the Lord. There's such a sense of peace and well being when we're focused on Him. The fellowship with Him is so sweet, so neat. It blesses our spirit when we spend time with Him. And the Bible tells us He wants to fellowship with us. He has things He wants to tell us. He may even have hobbies He wants to do with you. By the way, did you know God loves to golf?

Spend time in His presence.

Prayer: Heavenly Dad, bring to our minds often that you want to spend time with us. Put us in the habit of focusing on you, of including you in our thinking...

Jan 27
Don't Accept Bondage

"Therefore do not let anyone judge you by what you eat or drink, or with regard to a religious festival, a New Moon celebration or a Sabbath day. These are a shadow of the things that were to come; the reality, however, is found in Christ." Col 2:16-17

It's a fact of life that we tend to avoid doing things that we're criticized for. We have to remember, though, that we're not under law, we're under Christ. Jesus is the reality. In Jesus, we're freed from sin and bondage, and folks, the law was bondage. It was given not to bring righteousness, but to show us we're sinners in need of a savior (Rom 3:20).

"You shouldn't drive so fast." "The speed limit is 60." "You still shouldn't drive that fast. It isn't safe." What do you do? When the nagger is along, you probably slow down. Why? Were you speeding? No, but you want to avoid conflict, so you slow down.

That's the type of thing this verse is speaking to. Don't let anyone judge you, or lay restrictions on you that have nothing to do with walking in the freedom we have in Christ.

We're no longer in bondage. Don't allow anyone to put you back in chains of don'ts. Stay free to "do unto others what you'd have them do unto you". We're freed from the sinful nature to do the good things of the Lord. That's the reality!

Stay free!

Prayer: Lord, you've called us to freedom. Help us to follow you, and not be restricted by others opinions…

Jan 28
Lifelong Favor

"Sing to the Lord, you saints of his; praise his holy name. For his anger lasts only a moment, but his favor lasts a lifetime." Ps 30:4-5a

When you put your trust in Jesus Christ as Lord and Savior, you became a saint. When the Bible talks about saints, it's not talking about someone the Roman Catholic Church has canonized as a Saint. It's talking about those who are believers in Jesus.

As saints, we're to sing to the Lord. That's part of our worship. We praise His holy name (Jesus). Worship is turning to God and acknowledging Him through music, praise, and prayer. We agree with Him that He is the Most High God, and we reverence Him for who He is, and for His love for us. Bless God by lifting up words of honor and thanks, glorifying Him and His attributes of majesty, holiness, purity, love, and grace to us.

We have so much to be thankful for. We know how ugly we are inside, how filthy in sin we've been. Despite that though, He sacrificed His son for us, paid the debt of our sin, and redeemed us to Himself. He's loved us! Because He loves us, He treats us as His children. We discipline our children when they misbehave. God disciplines us at times, because we are His children. His anger with us lasts only a moment though.

His favor lasts a lifetime! If you're his child, you're walking continuously in His *favor*. You can't walk out of it. Just like the gift of eternal life, we have His *favor* forever. That should really lift our spirits.

Ponder that for a while. Ruminate on what it means to have God's *favor*, now and always.

Prayer: Most High God, we give you praise and honor for making us your children, and we give you thanks for your lifelong favor…

Jan 29
Suitable

"But for the man no suitable helper was found… Then the Lord God made a woman from the part he had taken out of the man, and he brought her to the man." Gen 2:20d & 22

And the man said, "Wow!" Let's be honest men. Isn't that exactly what we said when we first saw our wives? I was struck by how astonishingly beautiful Glenda is. God has proven to me that He does great work in supplying suitable helpers for us men. We need to appreciate God's foresight, and appreciate the gift He's given us in our wife.

After I recovered from the initial amazement, I began to learn about this helpmate that was to become my wife. And she's become more than I ever envisioned. My imagination wasn't large enough to encompass what God was doing for me. He's provided a companion, a lover, a confidante, a soul mate, and outside of Jesus, the best friend I have, or could ever have foreseen. See, God gives us more than we could ask or imagine. And that's saying something, because I can imagine a lot. When God sees a lack in our lives, he provides what's needed to fill the gap.

Now, look at how this happened. God took a part from the man's side, and went away to create the woman. When He was done, he brought her to the man. Why? God was looking forward with anticipation to the man's reaction. He was gratified at Adam's great surprise. Can you see the look on Adam's face? God knew He'd done great work!

Women, you were created to be the suitable helpmate for your husband. That means your responsibility is to be the strength to his weakness, the complement to his gifts, the insight in the areas he misses. You are his love, his companion, his soul mate, his confidante, and his best friend. *You* are his completion. For you see, you *are* his suitable helpmate.

Prayer: Lord God, give us an appreciation for each other and help us to express it. We know you've designed us for one another…

Jan 30
One Thing I Know

"One thing I do know. I was blind but now I see." Jn 9:25b

So often when we think about witnessing for Christ we get intimidated, because we're not fluent, we don't know enough scripture, we might mess everything up, or say the wrong thing. But you know, you can testify to the one thing you know.

The blind man in this scripture when questioned by the Pharisees and religious leaders admitted he didn't know whether Jesus was saint or sinner, didn't know who he was or where he went. The one thing he confidently testified to was that he had always been *blind*, but now he could *see*!

Interestingly, this man must have looked different too. They couldn't even tell if this was actually the blind man they all knew, or knew of. They sent for the man's parents and brought them in to verify that this was really him.

We're like the blind man. From birth until Christ came into our lives, we were spiritually blind. When Jesus came in, He gave us spiritual sight. Like the blind man, we too can say, I was blind, but now I can see.

When we have the opportunity, all God wants us to do is testify to what He did for us. One thing I do know. I was blind but now I see.

Prayer: Father, give us confidence to speak boldly about what we know. You opened our eyes to truth…

Jan 31
Let Your Yes Be Yes

"Simply let your 'Yes' be 'Yes,' and your 'No, No'; anything beyond this comes from the evil one." Mt 5:37

One of our most popular songs is 'Let Your Yes Be Yes', based on this very scripture. Don't we always want to add verification, or maybe obfuscation, to our answers (I used those words here because Glenda didn't think I should use them in the song; she said it was too complicated. lol)? We seem to think it adds weight and evidence to our authenticity.

If you've been through an election, or listened to some celebrity trying to answer hard questions about something stupid they did, you know how people try to deceive us by the things they say, or the things they don't say. They vacillate about this, equivocate about that, exaggerate about the other, and prevaricate about another. They're just ducking, and dodging, and weaving all over the place trying to say something when they're just talking nonsense, doing their best to say nothing at all.

God calls us to tell it straight. No embellishments, no minimizing, just be open and honest, and let your 'yes' be 'yes,' and let your 'no' be no'. Since we're not in league with the evil one, we'll do it God's way.

Prayer: Lord, help us, always, to be straightforward when we give an answer. We want to please you with our speech...

Feb 1
How Do You Love Your Wife?

"Husbands, love your wives, just as Christ loved the church and gave himself up for her… In this same way, husbands ought to love their wives as their own bodies. He who loves his wife loves himself." Eph 5:25 & 28

As we can see from this scripture verse, love is more a decision meshed with action, than it is an emotion or a feeling. Christ gave himself up for us. He sacrificed! So often today, we see men who want to act as king of the hill, or spoiled little boy getting everything he wants. But we as men are called! This verse is addressed specifically to us as husbands. We're called to act in the best interests of our wives. Isn't it telling that these verses communicate that by loving our wives, we love ourselves? We're called to: Care for our wives.

Be the spiritual leader in our home.

Take our family to church.

Set an example of bible reading, prayer and devotion.

Feed our family.

Make sure they have clothes.

Be involved in their activities when appropriate.

Help our wife with chores that will please her.

Give her quality and quantity time. Neither is a substitute for the other.

Tell her how much we admire her beauty, how much we appreciate her.

Buy her little gifts from time to time.

The neat thing is, when you focus on your wife and family, an outpouring of blessings comes on *you*.

Prayer: Lord, forgive me when I'm self-centered. Help me to focus on being the kind of man you want me to be, being the husband you want me to be, and that my wife needs…

Feb 2
(Glenda)
Must We?

"Wives, submit to your husbands as to the Lord. For the husband is the head of the wife as Christ is the head of the church, his body, of which he is the Savior. Now as the church submits to Christ, so also wives should submit to their husbands in everything." Eph 5:22-24

Submit—there's that, shall we say, curious word again. Just how was it meant to be taken, how far should it be taken, and who wants to do it anyway?

Well, the godly woman of Proverbs, the wife of noble character, will want to take notice. She is the one whom her husband has full confidence in. He believes in her loyal attitude. He knows that if other people do not respect him, it is not because of his spouse. She is not talking behind his back and lowering people's opinions about him in any way. She understands that care is needed in their daily conversation, because her strong husband is, indeed, vulnerable; a snide comment, or a condescending attitude can sink him like a ship. She is careful to voice her thoughts in a peaceful manner. If he does not accept them, then the blame for the consequences, whether good or bad, lies squarely upon his shoulders.

Does he often make poor decisions? You probably can't change that. Keep him in prayer constantly and remember his good, thoughtful ones. He has to live with his mistakes or sins, too, and it doesn't help to point them out. They're obvious.

Also, we mustn't forget the part of this verse that says "as to the Lord". We don't need to feel guilty about revering our man. Sarah called Abraham, her husband, lord, and if you will notice, she had his complete loyalty. He greatly valued her opinions and gave heed to her requests.

God wants us to have a loving, committed marriage, and a peaceful, harmonious home for our children. Teach them to honor their father and obey him promptly. Show them that Daddy is the king of the castle. It has a domino effect. He will be grateful for you, and your children will bask in security.

In submission, you win!

Prayer: Dear Lord, give me the grace to lovingly submit whenever necessary, and to provide peace and stability in our home...

Feb 3
One Approved

"Do your best to present yourself to God as one approved, a workman who does not need to be ashamed and who correctly handles the word of truth." II Tim 2:15

Every so often you'll run into someone who says something about Christian beliefs that are just myths passed along through ignorance. "When you die you're going to get your wings and halo. You'll be an angel." Nope. That's not what the Bible says. "Cleanliness is next to godliness." No, it doesn't actually say that. "God helps those who help themselves." Sorry, it doesn't mention that either.

Now, some of these sayings are good principles, but they aren't scripture. We are instructed to work hard, we're taught to be clean, and we know we're going to heaven if we know Jesus Christ as Lord. But we're going as redeemed human believers in our own glorified body.

It's quite amazing to find out how many Christians don't know even some of the most basic tenets of His word. They've never actually sat down and read the Bible for themselves, let alone thought about the passages they read and how they apply to their daily life. They just go to church, listen to the sermon, take one or two things from it, and think they know what they believe. What we find is, they may know what they believe, but they don't really know why they believe it.

The question is, how can we handle the word of truth correctly? The obvious answer is, by knowing God's word. Friends, you cannot know God's word if you fail to read and study it. One of the reasons we continually encourage people to read the bible daily, and preferably in the morning, is because we see the results in our own lives, as well as in the lives of friends who do the same. Again we say, don't bite off more than you can consistently handle. Read a chapter or two, or half a chapter if that's all you can, but do it every morning. It'll change your understanding, you'll gain knowledge, you'll understand God's will, you'll know His principles, and you'll give yourself a joyful attitude. Then you'll know that when you speak a word, it's accurate. You've correctly handled the word of truth because you *know* His word.

Prayer: Dear Lord, help us consistently stay in scripture, so that when we speak our beliefs, it's based on your word...

Feb 4

The Dirt Won't Get Glovey

"Do not be misled: 'Bad company corrupts good character.' Come back to your senses as you ought, and stop sinning." I Cor 15:33-34a

Several years ago I heard a message by Pastor Chuck Swindall in which he used this illustration of the white glove test. The white glove test is where you clean everything spic and span and when you're finished, you put on a clean, white glove, and run your finger over the surfaces to see if the glove picks up dirt. Now, in this test, the glove gets dirty. The dirt never gets glovey.

The same thing tends to happen when we hang around bad, or ungodly friends. Instead of the sinful becoming good, or pure, we seem to compromise down toward their level. We may want to influence our unbelieving friends for Christ, but if we allow ourselves to do the same ungodly things they do, we're failing miserably. Only by refusing to compromise our standards do we lead our friends toward Christ. Not with show or fanfare, but humbly, quietly, and consistently taking a stand for Jesus.

This verse also points out that even Christians fall into sin. If they didn't, Paul wouldn't be telling us to come back to our senses. And that's exactly what happens when we slide into sin. We lose our senses. We lose our godly perspective. We rationalize why it's ok. We justify what we do by blaming someone else's failure for precipitating ours. If they hadn't done that, I wouldn't be doing this etc.

The fact is, there's no excuse for continuing to sin when you know in your heart it's wrong. If you're in a sin situation, it's time you come to your senses and stop sinning. Turn to the Lord and ask His forgiveness. Humbly seek the forgiveness of whom you're sinning against. It'll lift a burden from your life, and God will set your feet on the right path again.

To continue sinning will just pile up more and deeper consequences. And that's just plain stupid! Take it from one who knows.

Become the white glove once again. Dirt can't get glovey!

Prayer: Lord, forgive us when we sin. Set our feet on the right path. When we sin, bring us back to our senses, and clean us up for you…

Feb 5
Intercession

"I appeal to you for my son Onesimus, who became my son while I was in chains.

If he has done you any wrong or owes you anything, charge it to me."
Phm 10 & 18

Paul is interceding here for Onesimus. Onesimus was a slave who'd run away, and Paul was sending him back, but doing his best to make sure he would be welcomed, rather than punished. He knew he'd done wrong, but Paul is asking Philemon to forgive him, and welcome him as a brother in Christ, or barring that, charge whatever is owed to him, with the promise that Paul himself would pay it if necessary.

Have you ever done that for one of your children, or for your friend, or your brother or sister? When we know someone who's done wrong, and we love that person, and we believe they've repented, we want to minimize the consequences, because we trust that going forward, they won't repeat the mistake. We're willing to step out and risk our good name to intercede for our child, friend, brother or sister.

We have an advocate with the Heavenly Father when we're believers in Christ Jesus. Romans and Hebrews tell us Jesus intercedes for each of us. You have your own personal intercessor with the Father. When we fail, Jesus says, he/she's ok; he/she's one of mine. I've paid the penalty for that sin.

Doesn't that make you feel great? Jesus intercedes for us! Doesn't it make you want to make sure Jesus doesn't have to step up that way for us, just out of a heart of gratitude? If Jesus is going to intercede for us, we want it to be for positive things for the kingdom of heaven, for our growing spiritual life, or for granting our petitions for others.

Prayer: Lord Jesus, thank you for interceding for us. Lead us to also intercede for others…

Feb 6
In Harmony

"Live in harmony with one another; be sympathetic, love as brothers, be compassionate and humble. Do not repay evil with evil or insult with insult, but with blessing, because to this you were called so that you may inherit a blessing." I Pet 3:8-9

Being singers, we love great harmony. When those separate parts lock in together, the sound can be so thrilling it sends chills down your spine. In good harmony, sometimes one note will suspend. It sounds somewhat out of sync, but then it resolves into the major chord and brings a sense of relief, of rightness, and completeness. That's because the chord has become what it's supposed to be.

Life is like that. We're many parts, but we're called to be in harmony. When we are all in the right place, at the right time, doing the right thing, we're in harmony. But when we don't do what we ought to, or when we're missing, or go our own way, we end up with discord. Discord is when the parts don't fit together properly. In music it sounds awful. In life, it *is* awful, because it causes discomfort, frustration, and strife.

To be in harmony, we need to do what the verse tells us. Love as brothers, be compassionate, be sympathetic, and be humble. Bless others regardless of how they treat us. Sometimes we just have to be the bigger person. Because someone insults us or treats us badly doesn't mean we have to do the same. We can be better in Christ, and bless instead of curse. When we bless, we live in harmony. And for Gary & Glenda, that's a *good* thing!

Prayer: Heavenly Father, give us the self-discipline to live in harmony with others. Help us to always be a blessing...

Feb 7
Lover or Beloved?

Lover: "How beautiful you are, my darling!"
Beloved: "How handsome you are, my lover!"
Lover: "Your eyes are like doves."
Beloved: "Oh, how charming."
Lover: "Let me hear your voice; for your voice is sweet, and your face is lovely."
Beloved: "My lover is like a gazelle or a young stag."
Lover: "I will go the mountain of myrrh and to the hill of incense."
Beloved: "His left arm is under my head, and his right arm embraces me."
Lover: "All beautiful you are, my darling; there is no flaw in you."
Beloved: "I held him and would not let him go till I had brought him to my mother's house, to the room of the one who conceived me."
Lover: "Your two breasts are like two fawns."
Beloved: "My lover is mine and I am his."
Lover: "Your graceful legs are like jewels."
Beloved: "I have taken off my robe."
Lover: "I have gathered my myrrh with my spice."
Beloved: "Listen! My lover is knocking."
Lover: "I have eaten my honeycomb and my honey."
Beloved: "My heart began to pound for him."
Lover: "I have drunk my wine and my milk."
Beloved: "I arose to open for my lover."
Lover: "I have come into my garden, my bride."
Beloved: "I opened for my lover." Excerpts from Song of Songs

In case you haven't thought about it, Valentine's Day is coming up. Have you thought about and made preparations to enjoy the love and intimacy the Lord blessed us with?

Plan ahead to enjoy God's blessing, and to show love and appreciation for the partner He gave you.

Prayer: Lord, thank you for the gift of intimacy, and the examples of expression of it in your word. Allow us to enjoy your blessings fully...

Feb 8
Serve Others

"Each one should use whatever gift he has received to serve others, faithfully administering God's grace in it's various forms." I Pet 4:10

Notice this doesn't say, "if you've received gifts", it assumes you have. Do you know why? Because you have! All of us receive gifts and abilities from God and they're to be used faithfully to administer God's grace.

Two things are at work here. First, we're to have a servant's heart. We know from other scriptures that we're to serve those around us. In fact, Jesus said, "Whoever would be greatest among you must be the servant of all". When we serve others, we exhibit humility, God's love, His care, and His kindness. That's administering God's grace. It blesses the heart of God. We serve by caring for, or meeting, other people's needs.

Secondly, we're called to be faithful. Use your gift(s) consistently to bless your brothers and sisters. Not much is more trying than having someone responsible to do a task in the church who frequently bails out, misses, or just doesn't do what's needed. The same holds true in the workplace, or in the home. We need to be faithful to be used by God. You're not administering His grace in the form you have to offer if you don't *do* it. If you're in the choir, be there to rehearse, and to sing for worship. If you're an usher, then ush. Be there to fulfill your responsibility. If you're to greet at the front door, be there early and greet. If you teach, then study, prepare, and teach as interestingly as you can. If you work in the kitchen, then cook and clean up. If you're the janitor, clean diligently and be sure the facilities are ready. If you're the pastor, pastor, and for heaven's sake, be there for services, studied up, prayed up, and ready to exhort the saints—lol.

Serving others isn't something we think, or are. It's something we *do*!

Prayer: Lord, help us to be diligent, consistent, and faithful in using our gifts for you…

Feb 9
Tame That Tongue

"No man can tame the tongue. It is a restless evil... Out of the same mouth come praise and cursing. My brothers, this should not be." Jas 3:8a & 10

Ladies, don't think this isn't speaking to you just because it says no *man* can tame the tongue. We know from experience that this is a problem we all struggle with.

"Sticks and stones can break my bones, but words will never hurt me." A quaint old saying which is, unfortunately, absolutely wrong! Nothing has the ability to cause us more pain than harsh words. Nothing cuts us to the quick like a nasty personal comment. Nothing ruins a relationship like gossip. This is one of, if not the, most important things we must do as Christians. We need, through the Holy Spirit's help, to take control of our tongues.

How are we to do this? First, we know that "out of the heart the mouth speaks". Let's fill our hearts with the things of the Lord. When we're filled with God's love, word, and grace, that's exactly what we'll speak.

Secondly, we have to exercise self-discipline. Have the patience not to speak without thinking first. When we were in high school (yes, they had them then), there was a quote that began going around. "Start brain before engaging mouth." That's still great advice. Resolve not to say things that you'll regret later. Don't say anything that will come back to bite you. If you want to say something just to hurt your partner, *don't say it*. You'll be thankful later that you didn't. Nothing kills romantic love like criticism.

God's word tells us to use our tongues to build each other up, to encourage one another. Nowhere is that more important than in our marriage, with our spouse. Men, if you tell your wife how lovely she is, she'll respond with warmth, even if she doesn't really believe you. If you point out that she's growing cellulite, she'll respond coldly from pain. Women, if you point out your husband's chest sliding down to his waist, don't expect warm fuzzies. If you compliment him on how adept he is at something, or how handsome you find him, he'll respond with warm gratitude, even if he doesn't believe *you*.

With our tongues, we can bless, or we can crush. Choose! Tame that tongue.

Prayer: Holy Spirit, take control of our tongues. Bring to our remembrance that we need to think before we speak...

Feb 10
Being One in Spirit and Purpose

"If you have any encouragement from being united with Christ, if any comfort from his love, if any fellowship with the Spirit, if any tenderness and compassion, then make my joy complete by being like-minded, having the same love, being one in spirit and purpose. Do nothing out of selfish ambition or vain conceit, but in humility consider others better than yourselves. Each of you should look not only to your own interest, but also to the interests of others." Php 2:1-4

We've been inundated in the past several years with self help books, looking out for number one style philosophies, and how to get ahead ideas. This should come as no surprise from the world, because, they not only don't, but can't, have the mind of Christ. What's alarming is how these ideas have crept into the church. If we're going to eliminate these pervasive, corrupt thoughts from the body of believers, we're going to have to actively adhere to scriptural values and principles. We have to keep in mind that, *we're not number one*. Our spouse is. Our brother/sister in Christ is. Our neighbor is.

We *are* united with Christ, therefore, we *do* have encouragement in Him, we *have* comfort in His love, and we *have* fellowship with the Holy Spirit, because He lives within us. We *are* people of tenderness and compassion.

This passage is directed to us for the fellowship of believers as a whole. But, buddy, it starts in our marriage, and our home. Because we're in Christ, we have the same love, one spirit, and one purpose. Because we love our spouse, we don't just act out of selfish desires, we look for ways to take care of our partner. We humbly seek ways to bless our wife/husband, striving to bless them and bring them happiness. Even in the church, and in the world, we look to care not just for our interests. We consider what's in the best interest of others.

We act this way because, as husband and wife, we're like-minded, being one in spirit and purpose.

Prayer: Heavenly Father, help us to be considerate of those around us, seeking to bless others in all we do…

Feb 11
Are You Reaching Maturity?

"Therefore let us leave the elementary teachings about Christ and go on to maturity." Heb 6:1a

When our children are little, we wish they'd stay that way. We love how cuddly they are, how cute, and how innocent. As they grow, we get to a point where we'd like them to stop being so childish! Then we realize they're growing up too fast, and we'd like to have them stay in that loveable teen time. But they continue to mature until we're proud of the young adult they've become.

Now, deep down, we really don't expect or want them to stay children. It's unnatural. But you know, the same holds true in our Christian walk. We enter God's family as a babe in Christ. Just as we grow in our natural, physical life, in our spiritual life we grow as well. Sadly, though, some believers' growth is stunted. It slows or fails from lack of nourishment. Just as our physical bodies need food and exercise, our spiritual selves need food and exercise, as well. That food is God's word, and the exercise is using our faith, using our gifts to serve, and intercessory praying, which strengthens our faith as we see God's answers to prayer. It's studying beyond the basics of repentance and salvation. We already know about the resurrection and eternal judgment. For maturity, we need to move on to effective living in the Spirit, and to discipling, to learning to be real ambassadors for Christ, to sowing and reaping in the kingdom of heaven, and to finishing the race strong, enduring to the end.

How about you guys? Are you maturing in the faith?

Prayer: Lord, teach us the mature things of the faith. As we study your word, move your Holy Spirit to point out those precepts we need to apply to our lives, and incorporate into our walk with you...

Feb 12
Are You Content?

"But godliness with contentment is great gain. For we brought nothing into the world, and we can take nothing out of it. But if we have food and clothing, we will be content with that. People who want to get rich fall into temptation and a trap and into many foolish and harmful desires that plunge men into ruin and destruction. For the love of money is a root of all kinds of evil." I Tim 6:6-10a

When asked how well off financially they are, there's an interesting anomaly. Most people, if they have enough money to pay their bills, and stay ahead financially, even if by just a little, believe they're fairly well off. People who struggle to meet their obligations believe they're poor. Neither of these groups' attitude depends on *how much money they earn*. It isn't much of a factor in their consideration. Some of those who struggle earn far more money than most of those who are in the black with their monthly bills. They just have such a high standard of living that they can hardly make it.

Those who spend their lives trying to become wealthy usually find themselves spinning their wheels. They tend to fall into traps designed to take advantage of those who are greedy. They take foolish risks, and almost always pay the penalty for it.

We're not advocating being financially foolish. You *should* set aside savings for emergencies, and a retirement fund so that you can live adequately when you're no longer able to work. We're assuming you're living according to God's instruction, tithing, and paying your bills.

As believers in Christ, we're taught that if we have our basic necessities, we should be content. Our focus isn't for getting wealth, but to store up treasure in heaven. If we have excess, we can contribute to those in need. Nothing blesses your heart quite like giving to the needs of others. We're not racing to see who has the most toys at the end of life.

We're racing to see what we can accomplish for Christ. To see whom we can bless in the name of Jesus.

With that, we're content.

Prayer: Lord Jesus, you've given us many instructions about money. Help us to follow your precepts, sowing seed for the kingdom financially...

Feb 13
I Have Prepared

"The kingdom of heaven is like a king who prepared a wedding banquet for his son… My oxen and fattened cattle have been butchered, and everything is ready. Come to the wedding banquet." Mt 22:2&4b

In this parable, we get a glimpse of the preparation, work, and effort that went into getting ready for this special event. They decorated the hall, they slaughtered the oxen and cattle, they butchered, and they cooked the meat and many other savory foods, so that when the time came for the wedding feast, everything would be prepared.

Now, we're doing this today, so that you, too, will be prepared for your special event tomorrow. Are you ready? Have you planned your event?

Here's your checklist. Check those that apply.

Did you get a valentine's card that expresses your love and the right sentiment? Check.

Not out loud! It's supposed to be a surprise!

Chocolate candy?

Pick a restaurant?

Will you dress for the occasion (dress up for each other, it'll be fun, because it's just for you two)? Don't forget the right inner wear.

Is there an appropriate movie you can attend (enjoyable without compromising the faith)?

Do you have a candlelit, intimate setting at home for later?

If you're not yet ready for your love feast, start thinking and figure out what you're going to do to celebrate this wonderful love the Lord's blessed you with. Make it as special as you can.

Prayer: Heavenly Father, thank you for the chance to celebrate our love tomorrow as a special occasion. Make our hearts pure and loving as we consider the wonderful spouse you've blessed us with…

Feb 14
"A Time to Love!" Ecc 3:8a

"May you rejoice in the wife of your youth… May her breasts satisfy you always, may you ever be captivated by her love." Pr 5:18b&19b

So what is this Valentine's Day we observe? According to tradition, there were actually three St. Valentines, each supposedly martyred on a 14th of February.

One legend has Valentine as a priest during the reign of Emperor Claudius II (third century) who decided that single men made better soldiers. With that in mind, he forbade young men to marry. The story is that Father Valentine, in defiance of the Emperor's decree, continued to marry young couples in secret, and when found out, was imprisoned and killed.

Another legend has Valentine himself sending the first greeting. It's said that while in prison, he fell in love with a young woman, supposedly the guard's daughter, and just before his death, sent her a letter signed 'from your Valentine', the salutation we use to this day.

Whatever the story, they all have this in common. St. Valentine promoted romantic love. We've celebrated our romantic love in his honor for centuries, dating back into the mid 1700s. Many of us have elevated Valentine's Day to a fine art—lol.

However you've decided to celebrate your love today, remember that God instituted love and marriage. He designed us to enjoy deep, emotional, romantic love, and to express that love in the intimacy that He's created.

Wife, if you took our advice yesterday, you made preparations, and captivated your husband with your love. Husband, if you did what you were supposed to yesterday, you showed your wife a wonderful gift of appreciation today, and you've enjoyed the wife of your youth. Today is our time to love.

Prayer: Lord, thank you for the gift of love, and for the way we can express our love romantically…

Feb 15
Sincerely

"Love must be sincere. Hate what is evil; cling to what is good." Rom 12:9

It's always uncomfortable to be around people when you get the feeling they're just "snowing you" most of the time. When they compliment you, it sounds like "empty praise". Stories they relate don't "ring true". Out in public, or at a party, they seem like nice, social folks, but you get the feeling it's "just for show".

That happens because something in their manner or body language is contradictory. It doesn't have a genuine feel about it. We come away feeling they're hypocritical.

As Christians, we should have an authenticity about us, a transparent openness that is legitimate. We are asked by God to be sincere in our love. Not self-seeking, or shallow, but genuinely looking out for the best interest of those we show His love to.

We should never wink at sin, or condone behavior that the Lord finds abhorrent. Instead, let's focus on maintaining high standards of moral excellence. Rather than skimming by doing as little as we can get away with, we work with excellence, doing the best we can, whatever we turn our hands to. We strive to be absolutely honest in every aspect of our lives. We cling to what is good. We're sincere.

Prayer: God in heaven, help us be genuine in our love relationships, and move us to avoid every evil, clinging to what is good in your sight...

Feb 16
Devoted?

"Be devoted to one another in brotherly love. Honor one another above yourselves." Rom 12:10

What causes an Olympic athlete to spend 9 to 13 hours per day training? What makes them eat only the healthiest foods to sustain them, and give them the energy they need? Why do they abstain from most of the social interaction and relaxation the rest of us enjoy? They do those things because they're dedicated to a goal. They're single-mindedly focused on achieving the best results they can possibly attain.

We're asked to be similarly dedicated to each other in brotherly love. Committed to helping one another, to encouraging, lifting up, and serving each other. Brotherly love is akin to agape love. Agape love is the type that always does what's best for the other person.

To honor is to hold in high esteem, to extol that person's virtues, and/or to lift them up in complimentary fashion. When we honor one another above ourselves, we put them ahead of us. We allow their needs or desires to take precedence over ours. We never seek our own good at the expense of theirs.

These are great traits to practice on each other as husband and wife. When we've practiced, and learned to exhibit these virtues at home, we'll be well equipped to use them in our social circle, and they'll naturally start happening without even thinking about it.

When that happens, we'll know we're becoming devoted to one another in brotherly love.

Prayer: Father, teach us to be devoted to one another, and to honor our spouse above ourselves. We pray this so that we might become that way with those around us, as well...

Feb 17
Never Lack Zeal

"Never be lacking in zeal, but keep your spiritual fervor, serving the Lord." Rom 12:11

Remember when you first got saved? Do you recall the feeling, the excitement, and the impatience to tell others about Christ, and what He'd done for you? That intense desire to spread the word is zeal.

Something seems to happen to most of us as Christians. Along the journey of our spiritual life, we seem to lose that zeal. Those feelings of excitement about Jesus fade away, and we're left wondering why we no longer have that desire to share Christ.

Now, remember when you first fell in love with your husband/wife. Those intense feelings of excitement, the way you couldn't stop thinking about them, and how you lost interest in everything else? Then, the infatuation phase began to pass. You lost the intensity, and the feelings weren't as all consuming anymore. Before long, you began to yawn—lol.

Something happened, though. You made a *decision* to love your husband/wife. Once you did that, your feelings became deeper, more consistent, and you found your love growing stronger again. You began to spend more time and energy on your relationship, and it began to grow, just as it's growing now.

Similarly, that type of situation happens in our spiritual walk with Christ. We *decide* to love Him, to worship Him, to honor Him, to live for Him, and to make Him the *Lord* of *our life*. When we've made that decision, we begin to spend more time in His word. We take abundant time to pray. We worship Him with renewed devotion. Our love for Jesus Christ begins to grow, and strengthen, until, once again, we begin to have that desire to share Christ. We dedicate ourselves to living in obedience, and as we do, our spiritual fervor returns. When that happens, we'll find we never lack zeal for serving the Lord.

Prayer: Gracious Lord, return us to that sense of our first love for you. Give us the *mature* fervor to serve you, so that we'll be consistent in our walk, and in sharing the good news of what Christ has done for us...

Feb 18
Be Consistent

"Be joyful in hope, patient in affliction, faithful in prayer." Rom 12:12

If you notice, these aren't natural inclinations for any of us. If we're honest with ourselves, we have to admit that, given our own leanings, we tend to lose hope when we don't see results fairly quickly, we're extremely impatient when suffering affliction, and a great share of the time rather faithless in our prayer time. Why must the Bible keep telling us to do the things we have to force ourselves to do?

It's like this. You have a car accident; you break your leg, and injure your lower back. You're in the hospital for several weeks waiting for the bone in your leg to mend sufficiently so you can begin walking again. When the time comes, you stand to your feet with the aid of people on both sides of you, only to discover standing sends a stabbing pain through your leg, and you feel like someone just knifed you in your lower back. So you sit right back down. The physical therapist tries to get you up on your feet again, but you refuse. You don't want to suffer any more pain. What are the results if you don't keep trying to get back on your feet? Your muscles begin to atrophy, your back never gets a chance to heal, your legs lose their strength, and given enough time, you'd find you couldn't walk at all. To heal properly, you have to exercise those muscles, loosen up the kinks in your back to take the stiffness out, stretch to regain mobility, and keep pushing past the limits of your pain.

Our Christian walk is like that at times. We have to take control of our minds, renew them in Christ, and make the decision to be joyful. Despite the pain, we always have hope in the Lord, because we have His promise of a better day. We make ourselves be patient as we suffer difficult circumstances, determined not to let those trials steal our joy. We definitely need to be faithful in prayer, because in times of affliction, we need God's strength to carry us through. We need the peace that spending time with Him gives us. Deciding to have these attitudes of joy, patience, and faithfulness will keep us consistent in our walk with Christ.

Prayer: Lord Jesus, so much of walking in obedience requires us to make a decision to follow your instructions. Give us the inner strength to do so, and to be consistent in our faith walk...

Feb 19
Children of the Most High God

"You are all sons (or daughters) of God through faith in Christ Jesus." Gal 3:26

We've often mentioned who we are in Christ. Because Jesus is Lord of our lives, redeemer of our souls, and savior of our eternity, we are adopted children of God. We have the distinction of being coheirs with Jesus. We're brothers and sisters of the King of Kings, and the Lord of Lords.

You're wondering why I bring this up so often. Trust me, it's not to make you proud, or haughty, or arrogant. You have no right, or reason, to be prideful. But sometimes we tend to think less of ourselves than we ought to, also. We need to have an *accurate* perspective. While we shouldn't be proud, we shouldn't go to the other extreme and abase ourselves either. If you do, you may become proud of your humility—lol.

All things in moderation. Think neither too highly, nor too lowly, of yourselves.

When I was growing up on the farm, I was, of course, my father's son. Because of that, I had the privileges that accompanied my position. Dad took care of my needs, and often granted my desires. Because I was my father's son, I also had responsibilities. I was required to work on the farm, and to do so diligently. I mowed and baled, and hauled hay, I plowed and cultivated the fields, I fed the cattle, sheep, and chickens, I worked in the garden, I swathed the grain, I combined grain, I hauled and shoveled that grain, I worked on machinery, and greased it and kept it fueled up.

Our earthly family is a model of our relationship with our Heavenly Dad. We have privileges as His children, we have power in the name of Jesus, and we have responsibilities to do the work He asks of us.

Because we're (Gary & Glenda) His children, we're obedient in His calling, which for us is to share the gospel in music, to help those in need, to counsel and encourage others in their walk, to give money to kingdom work where ever He leads us, to listen to brothers and sisters concerns, to pray with and for people, and the list goes on. Don't misunderstand; we have no reason to pat ourselves on the back. For one thing, we don't always succeed. But we do try to be faithful. We do these tasks because we're God's children, and because we want to please our Heavenly Dad.

Our Heavenly Dad has responsibilities for you to faithfully pursue, too. Let's be about our Father's work.

Prayer: Heavenly Dad, as your children, help us to be faithful in our responsibilities for you. Thank you that we can be called your children…

Feb 20
Useful Scripture

"All Scripture is God-breathed and is useful for teaching, rebuking, correcting and training in righteousness, so that the man of God may be thoroughly equipped for every good work." II Tim 3:16-17

Our children know how to please us. They're aware of our likes and dislikes. They know our moral standards. They have a pretty good idea of what movies we'll watch, the kind we'll turn off or leave, the music we listen to, and that we won't, the food we like, the hobbies we enjoy, the books we read and won't read, the clothing we like, and the clothing we refuse because of color, style, or immodesty. When they set out to do something for us, or find a gift, or plan an outing with us, they're very good at coming up with things that we enjoy, or at the very least, are willing to try. They can accomplish that because they know us inside and out. They know us because they've spent copious amounts of time with us, and learned from our teaching and example.

Our Heavenly Dad wants us to know *Him* that well. We continually encourage you to spend time in God's word every day, because we know that's the main way we learn our Father's heart and mind. You guys should have a good bible reading streak going by now. But if you don't, then today's the day to begin anew. A little time each morning will turn your life dramatically for the better.

We also need to know Jesus. It's not enough to know *about* Jesus, we need to *know* Him. God's word tells us when we know Jesus, we know the Father, too, because Jesus and our Heavenly Dad are one (no, we can't explain that, we just accept it by faith because His Word says so). So spend time with Jesus in prayer and worship.

When we know our Heavenly Dad intimately, we're able to live the way he desires us to, we're able to please Him in our acts of service, and His Holy Spirit makes us the people we should be in Christ. That occurs because as we read a little bit of God's word each day, it teaches us, it rebukes us at times, and corrects our course, and it trains us in righteousness so that we're able to do every good work for Him. Through His word, we've been *equipped*.

Prayer: Dear Lord, help us to spend time in your word, and in prayer, each day, so that we're able to know you, and to hear from you…

Feb 21
Don't Look Twice

"You shall have no other gods before me." Deut 5:7

"Put to death, therefore, whatever belongs to your earthly nature: sexual immorality, impurity, lust, evil desires and greed, which is idolatry." Col 3:5

When we get right down to it, many of us are idol worshipers. It's often pointed out that we might put our job, finances, home, and interests before God, but rarely do we consider the warm, breathing, body in the same office, or workplace, with us, as an idol. He/she is just someone who has piqued our interest. She/he's willing to listen to your gripes, is very understanding, and has problems that need your expert advice… Maybe you could discuss them in depth over coffee: in fact, they could use some help around the house, which their spouse just can't or won't do. Perhaps he/she could use a gift to encourage them. She/he is so appreciative, always alert to your feelings, willing to sympathize with the suddenly important differences you and your spouse are having (here's how she/he would treat you—always in your favor).

A person that you might never ordinarily be attracted to, has slowly converged on your every thought and decision. He/she has become very appealing in his/her own way; always has a smile and admiration, and makes you feel ever so good and desired. Perhaps you married too hastily, you were too young or didn't follow sound advice. Life could be so much more peaceful and fulfilling without the present partner. In fact, his/her children need your loving, Christian influence. You would guide them on a better path, and the home that you make for them would be to their greater benefit.

Oh, how Satan deceives! He'll lead you to rationalize anything. Your enticement has evolved into entrapment. Instead of being a testimony of *God's* love and grace, you are destroying a home (or two). You have disregarded God's words, "I hate divorce". You have placed someone else as a priority in your life, above God.

How did it happen? One look at a time. One compromise at a time. If you continue down this path, you, your family, his/her family, and God's family will suffer terribly. Do *not* be selfish. That's exactly what it is. Do not put your own interests before your family's, but especially, before God's.

Prayer: Dear Lord, please keep my eyes and thoughts centered on you. Help me to remember that it's all about eternity, for myself, and those around me…

Feb 22
Wise About What Is Good

"Watch our for those who cause divisions and put obstacles in your way that are contrary to the teaching you have learned. Keep away from them. For such people are not serving our Lord Christ, but their own appetites. By smooth talk and flattery they deceive the minds of naïve people. Everyone has heard about your obedience, so I am full of joy over you; but I want you to be wise about what is good, and innocent about what is evil." Rom 16:17-19

Have you ever been involved in a church that had folks who always seemed to want to go their own way, and take everyone in the church that direction as well? If not, God has blessed you beyond imagination. If you have, you've been exposed to those whom this passage speaks about. We have, unfortunately, had our share (too many) of such experiences. Often, these folks can communicate their ideas so smoothly, and why it would be good to accept their premise. They let us know how "wise" and "smart" we are to follow them.

We needed this verse many years ago. We might have saved ourselves a lot of anguish about what to do, and how to combat these situations. It's actually simple in principle, though perhaps not in practice. Keep away from them! They'll just drag you down (it's unlikely they'll get glovey—lol). What we *must* remember is that they're not serving Christ, but their own interests. We need to be obedient to God's focus, and His leading. If we steadfastly follow His direction, we'll always stand on solid spiritual ground (the rock, in fact).

Our goal should be to have it said about us that we've been obedient. That brought joy to Paul. It brings joy to God, too. As long as we're wise about what is good, it will be relatively easy to be innocent about what is evil. When we're making Godly decisions based on His word, we won't have time, or the inclination, for dabbling in evil things.

Be wise about what is good.

Prayer: Lord Jesus, lead us to guard against those who aren't following your will. Make us wise in you for what is good. Keep us from what is evil…

Feb 23
Sealed

"Having believed, you were marked in him with a seal, the promised Holy Spirit, who is a deposit guaranteeing our inheritance until the redemption of those who are God's possession—to the praise of his glory." Eph 1:13b-14

When we purchased our truck for traveling and singing, it came with a warranty. It covers everything bumper to bumper. For a little more money, Glenda bought the extended warranty. It's the same guarantee, but for a much longer period of time. The dealership gave us a document detailing the warranty. That document was our guarantee that they would take care of anything that went wrong with the vehicle (excluding accidents, of course).

When we put our faith in Jesus, we received a warranty as well. It doesn't say the body we're driving for the next several years is covered if anything goes wrong, but it says we have something of far more value. We have eternal life in heaven with Christ. So that we know we have the promise, God gave us a *deposit*. That deposit is the Holy Spirit. The Holy Spirit is given for a variety of reasons, but the one we're dealing with today is the fact that He's our guarantee of the promised inheritance. We're *marked*, sealed to God by the Spirit. When we step into eternal life and our glorified body, we're ultimately redeemed. We're redeemed now, but it's completely realized when we get to heaven.

God's promise is as good as done!

To the praise of His glory!

Prayer: Lord, we thank you that we're marked for you with the deposit of your Holy Spirit, so that we *know* we're redeemed...

Feb 24
Think About What?

"Whatever is true, whatever is noble, whatever is right, whatever is pure, whatever is lovely, whatever is admirable—if anything is excellent or praiseworthy—think about such things." Php 4:8

Whenever we read this verse together I stop and tell Glenda that's why I think about her all the time. She's so lovely, so admirable, so excellent, and I find her praiseworthy. I love this verse, because it doesn't tell us what not to think about; instead it tells us what *to* think about. We search out the things that are true, noble, right, pure, lovely, admirable, excellent, and praiseworthy.

In our day and age, we're inundated with things of the world. We'll be better looking, more fit, smarter, healthier, more relaxed, more desirable, more admired, better paid, or more powerful if we buy this, or invest in that. Do you know God's word says that none of that stuff is real? It's going to be burned up in the fire on the final day.

Now, am I saying it's wrong, or bad, to have a nice home, a great job, money, a wonderful family, good looks, or beautiful hair? It depends on your attitude about what you've received from the Lord. Yes, you heard me correctly. You didn't attain *any* of that on your own. God blessed you with any of those things you have, and he's given it into your stewardship for a reason.

Remember, though, that only what's done for His kingdom has eternal value. To store up treasure in heaven, tear your eyes away from the worldly things, and focus on what's true, what's noble, what's right, what's pure, what's lovely, what's admirable, what's excellent, and what's praiseworthy. Those things will take you into His presence with a heart of praise.

Prayer: Holy Spirit, put in our minds those things you want us to think about, and put in our hearts the desire to think about them...

Feb 25
The Liar

"Now the serpent was more crafty than any of the wild animals the Lord God had made." Gen 3:1a

"...the devil...for he is a liar and the father of lies." Jn 8:44c

Let's talk a bit about the temptations laid in our path. The bible tells us Satan is very crafty. This was before he challenged what God told Adam and Eve, and then flat out lied to Eve. Notice how he did that. He told Eve her eyes would be opened, and she could be like God, because she'd know good from evil, just like the Lord. Sadly, from personal experience, Adam and Eve did learn good and evil, to their, and our, detriment. We've been fighting with our sin nature ever since.

The Devil is often portrayed on television and in the movies as an evil looking being that we instinctively abhor. But that's not accurate in light of scripture. Also, they show him as someone who tempts people in a way that any fool outside the movies would never succumb to. But he's not stupid. Satan doesn't work that way. When he tempts us, he goes after our weakness. He makes it look so good. It's very interesting the way he presents it, and he subtly draws us with the picture of how wonderful it will be. Admittedly, when we first begin to sin, it's exciting. It's usually fun, and that's why it's so enticing.

In a court of law, when put on the stand to testify, we're charged to tell the truth, the whole truth, and nothing but the truth. Satan scoffs at the truth. Remember, he's the father of lies, and it's his nature to tell falsehoods. He tells us a portion of truth, withholding "the rest of the story", making the whole thing false.

When he shows us something that looks good, he doesn't tell us what the final result will be. When we see how easy it is to skim a little money or merchandise from work (no one will ever miss it), he doesn't tell us we'll end up fired, disgraced, and in court to answer for theft. When we see how exciting and sexy that gal is, or how wonderful and kind that guy is, he doesn't tell us it's going to ruin our marriage, destroy our children, and leave us outcasts to most of our friends and family. When we go to the casino, and see how grandly we're treated, he doesn't show us the ultimate end of being unable to pay our bills, buy food for our family, and end up in bankruptcy.

When you first meet temptation, turn away from it. The glitz that Satan puts on it isn't real. Don't be mislead, or fooled. Hold to the truth; don't succumb to the liar!

Prayer: Dear Lord, give us discernment to see the true and the false, and the self-control to choose the truth, and reject the lies of Satan…

Feb 26
Everything *Is Permissible?*

"'Everything is permissible'—but not everything is beneficial. 'Everything is permissible;—but not everything is constructive." I Cor 10:23

Once in a while, we'll get a hunger for chocolate. We can put down a fair amount, too, when we set our mind to it. In fact, we could skip a meal completely, and just fill up on candy. Add a coke to it, and we're great!

Well, except for that slight feeling of nausea that comes along a little later. Feeling like we're going to bust isn't so great either.

Eating all that chocolate was permissible. But it wasn't beneficial, either to our health, or our waistlines. It was constructive only in that it constructed extra girth, and taught us it was a bad idea.

Sometimes our Christian life is similar to the chocolate example. It doesn't mean we can sin with impunity. We know from numerous other verses that we're never given a license to sin. Far from it, we're called to *not* sin, and to live holy lives in honor to the Lord.

This speaks more to the fact that it's not always wise to do some normally good things. Discernment is called for. Giving food and financial help to someone who refuses to work is kind, but it's not wise, because it enables that person to be lazy. Providing a place to stay for a friend who needs to be home working on their marriage relationship isn't beneficial for them in the long run, because you're helping them run away from the issue instead of resolving it. These are examples where it's permissible, but it really isn't constructive.

Let's permit ourselves to do only those things that are genuinely helpful.

Prayer: God, give is wisdom and discernment in every situation to do not just what's permissible, but what is beneficial and constructive...

Feb 27

Favor and Honor

"The Lord bestows favor and honor; no good thing does he withhold from those whose walk is blameless." Ps 84:11b

We tend to forget that when we put our faith in Jesus Christ, we become children of God, and people of real privilege. We don't have to go looking for His favor, and we've no reason to seek honor ourselves. God bestows it on us. He doesn't keep any good thing from us when we live obediently in His righteousness. Our Heavenly Dad wants to bless us with His favor, with the good things of life. *No* good thing does He withhold from us. That should make us rejoice, and give God thanks and glory.

When we're obedient to our earthly parents, we walk in their favor. When I was in high school, at times I'd overhear my folks talking about something I'd accomplished. They were honoring me in their conversation. I didn't have to brag about being high scorer in a basketball game, or about being selected to the elite choir. They did that themselves. And when I was doing the chores I was supposed to, and acting in a manner that honored them, they gave me any and every good thing they could. They didn't give me the option of things that weren't good for me, but they allowed me privileges, such as going out with my friends to the movies, or to a concert, or to the ball game. When I behaved, they didn't withhold those things.

When we walk blamelessly before our Heavenly Dad, without our seeking or asking for His favor and honor, He just gives it to us.

What more could we ask than to have the Lord's favor given to us? Thank you Lord!

Prayer: Heavenly Dad, we just give you praise and glory and thanks for your favor, and for the good things you bless us with...

Feb 28
Don't Be Anxious

"Do not be anxious about anything, but in everything, by prayer and petition, with thanksgiving, present your requests to God." Php 4:6

Have you had a time when you were so worried about something negative happening that all you could think of were the disasters about to befall? Have you then had nothing bad happen at all? It hits you that you spent all that time fretting over something that never even occurred.

Over ninety nine percent of what we worry about doesn't happen. Statistically alone, that indicates there's no point in worrying. That doesn't necessarily stop us, though, does it?

We can't tell you how often we've been concerned about something (we can't count that high) only to learn God had it in control all the time.

We're to be in control of our minds. We're instructed here to self discipline ourselves to not be anxious about *anything*. Instead, make your requests to the Lord, thanking Him, because He has it covered. God's still in control, just as He's always been.

Although we often forget, when we turn our attention to Him, we're given a peace and assurance that we can leave our troubles and concerns in His hands, and rest in Him. Just present your requests to God, and turn your attention to other things, because He'll handle our situation much better than we ever could.

Fear knocked. Faith answered. No one was there. So you don't need to be anxious.

Prayer: Lord, give us the comfort of knowing you're caring for us and our situations. Help us to leave our cares with you, and to not take them up again…

(Feb 29)
Reap Holiness and Eternal Life

"But now that you have been set free from sin and have become slaves to God, the benefit you reap leads to holiness, and the result is eternal life." Rom 6:22

As citizens of the United States of America, we're proud of our freedom, and the independence the people and country have stood for since it's inception. But may I tell you, we're slaves. Let me explain.

If you have a habit you can't break, you're a slave to that habit. Now we often talk about alcoholics, and frequently about smoking as well. But what about that addiction to coffee, or rather, the caffeine in it, or in soda pop? Beyond chemical slavery, how about that little sin you can't kick, and don't really want to? Gossiping about coworkers isn't really a habit; it's more a way of life!?! What about that tv show you just can't give up? The cursing that jumps out every time something unexpected happens, or you want to 'emphasize' your point?

These are a short list of things that we're slaves to. The good news is, we can move beyond those habits, free ourselves of our slavery to sinful things, and be slaves of God instead.

God's word says we're set free from sin. We no longer have to engage in those things, because we're reaping a new holiness in our lives every day that we walk with Jesus. That's one of the benefits of faith in Christ. Our faith results in eternal life.

Actively *be* slaves to God. Be obedient to His commands. Live in ways that please Him. Replace bad habits with good ones. Drink pop instead of alcohol, drink water instead of pop, chew gum instead of smoking; take good care of your body, for it's the temple of the Lord. Use your speech to lift up and encourage people, and learn to be articulate without cuss words. Watch only those things on television, or at the movies, that are honorable.

Reap that holiness that has been sown in us, resulting in eternal life with the Lord.

Prayer: Lord we thank you for your gift of eternal life, and that you make us able to walk in holiness with you…

Mar 1
Worship

"Shout for joy to the Lord, all the earth. Worship the Lord with gladness; come before him with joyful songs. Know that the Lord is God. It is he who made us, and we are his; we are his people, the sheep of his pasture.

Enter his gates with thanksgiving and his courts with praise; give thanks to him and praise his name. For the Lord is good and his love endures forever; his faithfulness continues through all generations." Ps 100:1-5

Not only does the hundredth Psalm tell us to worship the Lord, it gives us ideas how to do so. Obviously, God isn't into dour expressions. So if you find yourself rather somber or scowling as you worship, you probably ought to stop. He wants us to shout for *joy* to Him, worshipping with *gladness*. If you're worshipping with joy and gladness, make sure you let your face know.

Part of worship is acknowledging God. Know that He *is* God. He's the creator. He even made us, and that makes us His. Remember that God's creations are good work (reference Genesis one). You're one of His handiworks. Sometimes being the sheep of His pasture could be considered demeaning. We raised sheep, and frankly, they're rather stupid, and willing to follow anyone, or anything, who'll lead. So when we compare ourselves to sheep, if we're honest, we have to admit (sadly) the depiction is pretty accurate. But! We're *His* sheep. And that makes all the difference. I'll be one of His anytime!

Going on, we're to come to Him with thanksgiving. We have so much to be thankful for that there's no way to even begin recounting them. Enter His courts with praise. He's so worthy of our praise. If the only reason we had was our salvation in Christ Jesus, that would be enough to keep praising His name forever and ever. But there's so much more yet.

He's good! We know it. His love endures forever. We feel it. His faithfulness to all generations. He's been faithful to our family back to my parents, grandparents, and my great grandparents.
Worship the Lord!

Prayer: We worship you, dear Lord, for you are worthy of our praise. We come to you with joyful hearts; glad we can enter your presence with thanksgiving...

Mar 2
Backslidden?

"Return, faithless people; I will cure you of backsliding." Jer 3:22

Do you ever find yourself in a strange parallel with the nation of Israel like we do? We've known the Lord for a long time, and He's shown us His favor and love. Yet we often turn away from Him. Sometimes we're brazen in our sin, acting shamelessly. Israel did the same, over and over. In the third chapter of Jeremiah, God compares Israel to an adulteress. He speaks of Himself as a husband. Like us, God showed Israel His favor and love, and yet they continually turned away from Him, following other gods.

Even though the Lord was Israel's God, even though He blessed them abundantly, still they grew complacent and turned away, living 'as a prostitute with many lovers'. Worse, they sinned without remorse; they 'refuse(d) to blush with shame'.

The Lord told how Israel had been divorced by God, because of her adulteries, and her refusal to repent and return. Now Judah is doing the same, and it's even worse. They gave lip service to returning to the Lord, but turned and committed the same adulteries as Israel, even worse, with stone and wood (idols).

It's amazing that, after all this, God calls Israel to 'return, faithless people, for I am your husband'. He still *loves* us, even though we're unfaithful to Him. If we'll repent, he'll forgive us, restore us, and walk in fellowship with us. He'll cure us of backsliding!

Don't pervert your ways. Don't forget the Lord your God. If you have issues in your life that have you walking in areas of disobedience, today is the day to confess your sin to the Lord, and turn away from that sin. He's waiting for you to return. God still *loves* you, and He always will.

Prayer: Lord, we ask you to search out our hearts. Show us any area that isn't pleasing to you, and let us return to you. Forgive us when we sin against you. Restore us, Lord…

Mar 3
Discipline Your Child

"He who spares the rod hates his son, but he who loves him is careful to discipline him." Pr 13:24

    This can really be a sore subject (pun intended) with many parents. We've heard from the world how to raise our children to have a good self-image. We mustn't spank, or say no, or criticize, because it will hurt their self-esteem. Don't raise your voice or hand to discipline. Rubbish!
    Now that I've given my response, let me say I'm not a trained child anything, so this is purely subjective reasoning on my part. But you don't have to be a rocket scientist to look, watch, and see that children today are generally not nearly as well behaved as they were even 25 years ago.
    God's word gives us a pretty good lead on why that's occurred. And I will tell you frankly, that anything and everything the world does in it's humanistic thinking is almost always *wrong*.
    You see children in a store yelling, running, throwing a temper tantrum, and you watch the parent try to talk them down, or bribe them to behave, and it can leave you wanting to paddle the parent instead of the child. The child is doing what works. The parent, for some foolish reason, continues to do what obviously does *not* work. When you see that rare parent swat their child, and see the child respond by behaving, you may want to stand and applaud them.
    God's word tells us that if you're not willing to discipline your children, you hate them. You're unwilling to do what's in their best interest. If you love your children, you discipline them. We do that for *their* good.
    Now, I'm going to use our children as an example, because I'm willing to put their behavior up against any family. We taught our children to be obedient. We did that in a variety of ways, but spanking was definitely part of the curricula. Why did we insist on unquestioning obedience? Because when they're small, you often don't have time to stop and explain. When

we had the time, we explained. But there are times when that obedience is crucial for the good of the child. You don't have time to stop and explain why the child should stop running when, if they continue into the street, they're going to get run over, because a car is coming. We disciplined for *their* good.

Discipline before it's essential, or life threatening.

Look around. You can tell in every crowded place you go to with children in it, which are disciplined, and which are not. Their behavior will tell you. Their parent's calm faces will tell you.

Prayer: Father, give us your wisdom in disciplining our children. Help us to help them through consistent, loving discipline...

Mar 4
Discipline Your Child

"He who spares the rod hates his son, but he who loves him is careful to discipline him." Pr 13:24

No, this isn't a repeat of yesterday. But there are a couple of points that are important to discuss before we move on. We touched briefly on self-esteem.

Children often misbehave because of lack of security. They're wired to push the limits until they know where the boundaries are. When parents don't discipline, when they don't define what is and isn't acceptable, they leave the child continually testing the edges to find out where they are. They're just floating around wondering.

When children are taught what the limits are, and that there are consequences for stepping past those parameters, they actually feel more secure. They're safe in their world, and they know what that world for them is. As they grow, their world expands, and as they responsibly grow in their world, their self-esteem grows as well.

When our children grow up, they must already know that there are consequences, positive and negative, for their actions. The time to teach that to them is when they're children. As adults, when we're continually late for work, are lazy in the tasks we're assigned, or sloppy in the way we accomplish it, there's a negative consequence. We'll probably lose our job. When we arrive on time, ready for work, with a cheerful attitude, and work hard, and neatly, diligently accomplishing our tasks, we'll be rewarded with raises and promotions. When we're honest, and wise with our money, we'll be well off. When we're dishonest, and steal, we'll bear the consequence of fines and jail time.

Positive virtues that bring promotion in our lives as adults are learned as children. Negative habits that bring destruction to us as adults are also learned as children.

When you read statistics about adults, it can generally be traced back to their upbringing. Adults who have low self-esteem, are poor, or who are in trouble with the law, overwhelmingly grew up in families where the teaching was weak, encouragement was lacking, and the discipline was lax. Adults who are confident in themselves, have good jobs, are self disciplined and financially prosperous, and have nice families, overwhelmingly grew up in families where they were encouraged, taught that work was their friend, and were disciplined consistently.

If you want to give your children a huge head start on a great life, you must discipline them, lovingly and consistently.

Prayer: Lord, again we ask that you give us your wisdom. Help us to be consistent in our love and discipline of our children, encouraging them at every opportunity…

Mar 5
Do You Show Love?

"Love is patient, love is kind. It does not envy, it does not boast, it is not proud. It is not rude, it is not self-seeking, it is not easily angered, it keeps no record of wrongs. Love does not delight in evil but rejoices with the truth. It always protects, always trusts, always hopes, always perseveres. Love never fails." I Cor 13:4-8a

This passage tells us what love is, and it gives us a pretty good indication of how to show our love for others, but specifically, let's talk about showing our spouse love.

Husband, are you patient with your wife? When she doesn't understand something, do you act like she's an imbecile, perhaps rolling your eyes, or sighing heavily? Wife, are you patient? When your husband doesn't take out the trash, or help set the table, do you take on a martyred expression and tone, to let him know what a trial he is to angelic, hard working, little ol' you?

Wife, are you kind to your husband? Do you speak harshly, nagging him to death when he displeases you (of course you say, 'no, not to death!')? Husband, do you treat your wife gently and kindly? Do you use soft words, and help her with items too heavy for her?

Husband, are you envious of your wife? Do you criticize her, because in your pride, you want to appear better? Wife, do you boast about your attributes, letting your husband know they're more valuable than his?

Wife, are you rude to your husband? Do you make catty remarks about his girth, or his clumsiness, or the way he does something? Husband, do you treat your wife rudely, or do you honor her? Do you open her doors, walk beside or behind her, and shelter her from the storm?

Husband, does your wife set off your hair trigger temper? Can she spark your anger simply by saying something silly, or bumping you? Wife, do you shriek at your husband when he forgets to pick up the milk, or if he knocks over your vase?

Wife, when you have a 'discussion' with your husband, do you get historical? Husband, do you bring up every failure since you met, and pile it all up for this argument too?

If you see yourselves in any of this, stop it!

Love has to start in our marriage. Protect your mate, show your love by exhibiting these qualities of patience, kindness, consideration, politeness, even temper, forgiveness, and truth, and persevere to a *great* marriage. Love *never* fails.

Prayer: Dear Father, help us to show our spouse our love, by being patient, and kind, and considerate, and polite, and forgiving, and even tempered. Help us to walk in truth, persevering in love. Give us the greatest marriage possible…

Mar 6
Men, Be Strong!

"Be on your guard; stand firm in the faith; be men of courage; be strong. Do everything in love." I Cor 16:13-14

I love the passage in Joshua where God tells Joshua to be strong and courageous, then again to be strong and very courageous.

Men have a role and a responsibility. Men are called to be the spiritual leader of the family. As men, we are instructed to love our wife, and our children.

Men, it is imperative that we stay on guard. We need to guard our hearts and minds in Christ. If we don't, Satan will surely destroy us. He'll tempt us, ensnare us, and crush us if he can. Stay on guard!

It is up to us to stand firm in the faith; to lead our family spiritually. Read God's word every morning, have family devotions each evening. If you will stand firm in the faith, your family will too. If you don't, you will lose the spiritual battle, not only for yourself, but for your family as well. Children who grow up in a home where Dad takes them to church every Sunday, overwhelmingly stay in the faith. It's near 85%. Approximately 30% of children whose' Mom took them to church stay in the faith. Less than 10% stay in the faith when their parents just sent them to church. As *Dad* goes, so goes the family!

Ironic, isn't it, that courage and strength come next? It takes courage to be spiritual leaders when the world is out there mocking us, belittling us as Christian fathers, and doing all they can to intimidate us into being closet Christians. That's why we exert courage. That's why we make the decision to be strong. We will not back down. We will not let our family fail spiritually.

Do everything in love. We don't need to be overbearing, or gruff, or offensive, as we walk in faith. Love covers us, and our family. We have no need of the world's affirmation. In fact, we know that if the world is applauding us, we're most likely doing something very wrong.

So men, be strong!

Prayer: Heavenly Father, give me courage and strength to stay on guard, standing firm, and walking in love...

Mar 7
Rely on the Spirit

"In the same way, the Spirit helps us in our weakness. We do not know what we ought to pray for, but the Spirit himself intercedes for us with groans that words cannot express. And he who searches our hearts knows the mind of the Spirit, because the Spirit intercedes for the saints in accordance with God's will." Rom 8:26-27

Have you had times when you were so troubled in your spirit that you didn't even know what to pray? We all face moments like that. In those situations we can count on the Holy Spirit to intercede for us. We just spend time in quiet prayer, not even saying anything; just being in God's presence, allowing the Spirit to speak for us. His word says the Spirit prays God's will. That's always our intention in prayer. We want to pray *God's* will. That gives us such a sense of peace and comfort.

Sometimes we have relational situations in our marriage that are similar. Our spouse is upset, and we don't know what to do or say, or it may be that there isn't anything *to* do or say. In those times, it's a comfort to just be with them, to spend quiet time with our loved one in empathy. We can minister just by being there.

Always remember that our spouse needs us to partner with them in *all* things. We share in their joy, we commiserate in their trials. What happens to one affects the other. In marriage, the two have become one. Because we're one, we take care of our spouse in every way we can.

In afflictions, we rely on our partner to be there for us, and we must rely on the Spirit to move for us. He can intercede far more effectively than we ever could for ourselves.

Prayer: Father, when we're burdened down with such loads that we can't even pray, remind us to just give it to the Holy Spirit, and spend quiet time with you…

Mar 8
Faithful Commitment

"Don't urge me to leave you or to turn back from you. Where you go I will go, and where you stay I will stay. Your people will be my people and your God My God. Where you die I will die, and there I will be buried. May the Lord deal with me, be it ever so severely, if anything but death separates you and me." Ru 1:16b-17

This comes from Ruth, and her commitment to Naomi, her mother-in-law. She loved Naomi, and decided to stay with her when she returned from Moab to Israel. She refused to leave Naomi, or to be left behind.

Ruth did stay with Naomi, and helped her, took care of her, worked to earn money and food for her and Naomi, and was faithful to her.

Later, Naomi went into matchmaking mode (as mothers are prone to do), and set Ruth on a path that resulted in her being married to Boaz. Boaz and Ruth are ancestors of Jesus Christ.

This is a beautiful picture of God's love, and His inclusiveness, of all people.

We also see in this passage a great example of our marriage commitment, and our vows to each other. As husband and wife, we've decided that we will never leave or turn back from one another. Where we go, we go together (especially true of us, since we sing together). We've decided we will stay together, in covenant marriage. We worship the same God, the Most High God, I Am. When we die, we plan to be buried together. When we live eternally, we shall do so in the same heaven, together praising the same Savior and Lord. Nothing but death will separate us here. As long as we live, our hearts are one.

For your marriage relationship, this is a verse you should post on your wall. What a great reminder and encouragement it is to us.

Prayer: Lord, help us to remain firm in our commitment to each other, and to our lives as one…

Mar 9
Put It in to Practice

"Whatever you have learned or received or heard from me, or seen in me—put it into practice." Php 4:9a

When I was growing up, and learning to play basketball, I'd learn new skills in basketball practice. Coach had been a good basketball player himself, so when he taught us something new, he showed us how to do it, and how to use it most effectively. Coach didn't teach us these new skills just so we'd know them. He didn't instruct us in new techniques so we'd go out and do the same things we did before. He taught us so we'd apply what we learned and become better and better players. When we went out on the court and put those new skills into practice, we had a better chance of winning more games.

Paul is telling the Philippians, "I've set you an example". All those skills they'd seen, all they'd learned, all they'd heard or received from him, all the ideas he'd modeled, all the grace and love he'd exhibited, they were to put into practice. Paul not only taught them what to do, he showed them how to do it, as well. The Philippians were learning from one who was experienced in the faith. He'd played the game. He'd run the race.

Don't just know your faith with head knowledge; ingrain it by living what you've learned in Christ. Run the most effective Christian race you can. As you learn from God's word, apply it to your life. As He reveals each new attitude, or fruit, or godly trait, do it, so it becomes part of your walk. The more new skills you use in your race, the better shot you have of achieving the prize.

Put your new faith skills into practice.

Prayer: God, help us to learn more of you, and of your ways, so that we can become more Godly each day, in every way...

Mar 10
Receive the Fullness of God

"And I pray that you, being rooted and established in love, may have power, together with all the saints, to grasp how wide and long and high and deep is the love of Christ, and to know this love that surpasses knowledge—that you may be filled to the measure of all the fullness of God." Eph 3:17b-18

It's interesting how we're looking at being rooted and established. It takes years for trees to become rooted, and thus established. They have to go through a variety of times. They must go through seasons of plenty of rain, and tough eras of heat and drought. It's during the difficult seasons that they're established. They become strong, and well rooted, not when they have plenty, but when they have to struggle to survive. When they struggle, their roots reach way down deep, finding those underground reservoirs of water that don't run dry.

Once we're rooted and established in His love, we're to have power to grasp how wide and long and high and deep the love of Christ is. Just like the plants, though, to become rooted, and established, so that we're not easily shaken, and cannot be torn out, we have to go through seasons as well. We have to endure tough times. We go through the fire, experiencing drought, and famine, and heat, and hardship. During these trials is when our inner spirit digs down deep, to search out the springs of living water. Once we reach that water, we're established.

It's then that we can grasp the breadth of God's love. His love is beyond knowledge. It must be fathomed in our hearts; understanding is brought to us in the depths of our soul as we struggle through our most difficult tests. And there's a purpose. This occurs so that we'll be filled with the measure of all the fullness of God.

We're praying that you, too, will become so rooted and established in His love, that you receive understanding, and are filled to the measure of all the fullness of God, as you journey together.

Prayer: Heavenly Father, bring us understanding. We do want to be firmly established in you, knowing your love…

Mar 11
Rejection

"Therefore, he who rejects this instruction does not reject man but God." I Th 4:8

Hurts, doesn't it? We feel wounded inside when someone rejects us. That happens even with people we don't even know. The better we know the person, the more important they are to us, the worse we tend to feel when they reject us. Our wife/husband can hurt us more than just about anyone else. Because their good opinion is important to us, we feel the pain of rejection most intensely when it comes from them.

Over time we learn to put things in perspective, though. We realize there are other factors in those rejections that may actually have nothing to do with us. We might want to do something that the other person is just too tired and worn out to attempt. Sometimes they may be okay with doing something, but need to do it another time. And we learn that we don't always get what we want, and that's ok, too.

We also realize how important it is for us to be careful in how we communicate with our husband/wife. In each situation, although we may not want to acquiesce to our spouse's wish, we don't want to cause any pain, let alone undo pain. So think before you speak, and couch your rejection in positives, if possible.

Beyond that though, it's not always us being rejected. When we present something on behalf of someone else, even when we're invested in it, we can understand it's them being rejected. You may do a presentation for your company, and be turned down for the proposed business, learning that they can't do business with your company because of a conflict of interest. There are a whole host of reasons that may have nothing to do with you at all.

This verse tells us that whoever rejects God's instruction rejects Him, not us. We tend to take these things personally, but it's actually not our responsibility to take that rejection in. It's just our responsibility to instruct about Christ and the faith, graciously and lovingly.

Prayer: Dear Lord, help us to be faithful in walking in obedience, sharing your gospel when we have opportunity. Give us a sense of peace so that we're not taking your rejection on ourselves…

Mar 12
Hide Your Charitable Acts

"Be careful not to do your 'acts of righteousness' before men, to be seen by them. If you do, you will have no reward from your Father in heaven." Mt 6:1

Years ago, we did a skit in church called "The Offering". In the skit, it goes through the attitudes of four different people as they're in the midst of the weekly collection, and you get to listen in to what's going through each of their minds. The skit was funny, and it made the point that all four of the attitudes were wrong, even those that at first look seemed correct. One of the people, who was obviously well off, plays a scenario in his head about getting great applause and lots of recognition when his check 'accidentally' falls on the aisle floor, and causes a stir due to the impressive amount. That particular vignette was based on this very scripture.

If we do our so-called 'acts of righteousness' for earthly recognition, we've missed the point entirely, as each of the folks in the skit did, in one way or another. This passage goes on to tell us to make sure that when you do something for someone, or for the Lord, do it in secret, so that any reward you have is from your Heavenly Father.

Now, we don't recognize many opportunities to store up treasures in heaven, and we don't want to wreck the chance by taking our reward here (we may not have that many stored up). It's hard though. We naturally want a little recognition here and there for some of the things we do.

Our Father in heaven prefers we not do that though. It goes back to our purpose as Christians. We, like the Holy Spirit within, are to bring glory to Jesus Christ. After all, if it weren't for Him, we wouldn't have the spirit of love and grace in us that desires to bless others. Since it isn't really us, why should we take credit? See, it all reflects back to Jesus, and what He's done for us. So do your blessing quietly and in secret.

Prayer: Heavenly Father, lead us in how to bless others for you without taking any credit or recognition, because we know that it's for your glory, and we do it out of a heart of thanks to you…

Mar 13
Be Refreshed

"I will refresh the weary and satisfy the faint. At this I awoke and looked around. My sleep had been pleasant to me." Jer 31:25-26

Have you had times, or seasons, when you had to rise very early in the morning and head out to work. You did hard physical labor all day, in the sun and the heat. Perhaps you hauled hay by hand, loading those heavy bales for hours, moved them in and unloaded those same bales, and stacked them. Perhaps you shoveled grain, or laid blocks, or poured concrete, or framed buildings, or maybe you were bent over in the garden pulling weeds all afternoon. You sweated nearly to death, and couldn't drink enough water. At the end of the day, you were so weary you could barely drag yourself back to the house.

But when you got there, oh it was cool. That cool air felt so good. And you got an ice cold drink, and sat down for a while and put your feet up. Then you had a nice, relaxed, wonderful meal. After you'd eaten your fill, you followed it up by having a cleansing shower. How refreshed you felt then!

God's promise is wonderful. Not matter how tired we are, no matter how worn out, no matter how frazzled, no matter how discouraged, no matter how hungry or thirsty, or how faint we grow, he will refresh us. His abilities far outstrip our needs. He never runs out of cool, clear water, or good savory food, to satisfy our bodies and our hearts. When God refreshes us, He gives us an inner peace and comfort as well. And when we awake from our slumber, and look around after God's refreshing, we find our sleep has been pleasant. We feel *rested*. In God we find refreshing. He *satisfies* us when we're faint.

Prayer: Dear Lord, give us your refreshing. We're so weary sometimes, and only you can really give us the care we need to satisfy us…

Mar 14
The Blame Game

"Neither this man nor his parents sinned,' said Jesus, 'but this happened so that the work of God might be displayed in his life." Mt 9:3

When something goes wrong, and something often does, don't we always want to find someone to fix the blame on? For example, I can drive the car for months, and when Glenda drives it and something breaks down, I automatically ask, "What did you *do*?" Since it was working fine when she started, she must have *done* something to cause this! Surely, it didn't just stop, or stall, due to months of wear and tear before she drove it. It has to be someone's fault, and it could hardly be mine.

Here's another one. Glenda's preparing dinner, and has it cooking on the stove. I'm standing in the kitchen, getting a glass of diet coke, and she comes in to find a kettle boiling over. Does she say, "Oh, I shouldn't have left the kitchen?" or "Why didn't I watch that kettle more closely?" No, she says, "Why didn't you turn that down?" Even though, admittedly, I wasn't paying any attention to it, it's my fault, because I was in the kitchen when it boiled over. Just because I had no idea what she was cooking or what was happening, that's no excuse.

We're funny that way. So often, even though we know what's happened isn't anyone's fault, or if it is, it's ours, we instinctively want to shift the blame to someone else.

God's word tells us that, when seemingly bad things happen, they're really to bring honor and glory to God, because He's waiting until just the right time to do a great work in our lives. He has an astonishing blessing waiting for us, and when the time is right, He reveals His miracle for us to see. We forget that our Heavenly Dad has a storehouse of marvelous works that He wants to display in our lives, and so when things go wrong, we focus on the blame game, and try to fix everything ourselves. Obviously, though, we can't do what only God can.

You see, when the car stalled, it wasn't to cause us trouble. It was so that guy in the old pickup truck could stop and help us, even though he didn't know why he was bothering to. We had the chance to plant a seed for Christ, by behaving in a godly way, and giving him our blessing in the name of Jesus. He was blessed in the Lord, and went away thanking God for the chance to help.

We didn't actually need to blame anyone after all.

Prayer: Heavenly Dad, help us to be patient, and remember that when things seemingly go wrong, you want to display your marvelous works in our life. Give us wisdom to look for you in those situations…

Mar 15
Wisdom Is Better than Money

"Wisdom is a shelter as money is a shelter, but the advantage of knowledge is this: that wisdom preserves the life of its possessor." Ecc 7:12

Have you had a time when you had a bit of extra money? If you have, you've felt that sense of comfort and security of abundance in your finances. Now, most people don't keep it long, because there's always more to spend money on than there is money. Unless you're independently wealthy, you don't normally have a lot of extra coin lying around.

Once in a while, we see someone who not only has a little extra, but also uses it wisely. God tells us that wisdom is better than knowledge. One obvious way is that, with wisdom, you can probably accrue more money. But money doesn't buy wisdom. Wisdom comes from God. Wisdom isn't just knowledge, it's knowledge applied with self-discipline and judiciousness.

When your wife is upset, and gives vent to a tirade, the wise man remains silent, thus preserving his life. When your husband hits his head on a low hanging branch, the wise wife commiserates with him, rather than telling him he should have ducked. In our marriage, we need to use wisdom to give life and health to our relationship. When we face difficulties at work, we support one another. When someone slights us, we forgive, and remain loyal to each other, so that we don't descend into anger and bitterness. Wisdom teaches us not to take sides against our spouse. Wisdom teaches us to gently correct each other, lovingly, and without rudeness.

Money can give us sense of security, and it gives us opportunity to bless others, but wisdom is far superior. We can bless others much more with wisdom than we'll ever be able to with money. With wisdom, we can preserve our life, and theirs.

Prayer: Lord, give us wisdom in full measure. Help us to be self-disciplined and judicious in applying the knowledge you give us...

Mar 16
Train Yourself to Be Godly

"Train yourself to be godly. For physical training is of some value, but godliness has value for all things, holding promise for both the present life and the life to come."
I Tim 4:7c-8

To stay in some semblance of good physical condition, we try to eat semi-reasonably (lol), get adequate rest (occasionally happens), and walk and run consistently (we're better at this). We know from the statistical information available that doing these things is good for our overall health, drastically cuts the probability of heart disease, and thus, many other related health issues. We do this to live longer, and keep our quality of life high as long as possible.

Physical training has value in this area. But we know that, aside from an accident unnaturally interfering with our life cycle, we're eventually going to deteriorate and physically die. That's the process of life and death, and we can't change that.

There *is* a training process that has *eternal* value for us. It doesn't begin when we reach heaven. It starts right here, right now. We're to train ourselves to be godly. It has benefits now in this life, and of course, also in our eternal life.

How do we train ourselves to be godly? Once we've put our faith and trust in Christ Jesus, step by step, we grow in Him. We begin by reading and studying the bible (how's your reading streak going?), and by applying what the Spirit shows us to our lives. We fellowship with other believers and learn from them. We spend time with the Lord in worship and prayer. We serve others on behalf of Jesus. We do His work, and bless those around us. We practice self-discipline to bring honor to God. We develop the fruit of the Spirit in our lives.

As you walk in obedience with Jesus Christ, as you listen to that still small voice of the Holy Spirit, and as you join the Heavenly Father where He's at work, you grow in godliness. You can't help but do so. And it provides value for all things, both now and eternally.

Prayer: Father, help us to be mindful to train ourselves to be godly...

Mar 17
Let the Potter Shape You

"So I went down to the potter's house, and I saw him working at the wheel. But the pot he was shaping from the clay was marred in his hands; so the potter formed it into another pot, shaping it as seemed best to him. Then the word of the Lord came… Can I not do with you as this potter does?' declares the Lord. 'Like clay in the hand of the potter, so are you in my hand." Jer 18:3-5a, 6b-d

We're so prone to go our own way, to shape our own lives, to take control of our own destiny, masters of our own fate. We're rugged individualists, able to take care of ourselves in every situation. Well, no, no we're not, are we? In fact, if we're honest with ourselves, we most likely mess it all up when we try to do it in our own strength, and in our own intelligence. Oh, we can *get by* going our own way. But if you want to live life *abundantly*, there's another, far better way.

God can do anything He wants with our lives. He's a gentleman, though. He doesn't normally do that unless we give him permission to do so, and willingly turn ourselves over to him, to shape as He wills. Just as the potter shapes the clay into a useful vessel, God will do the same with us, if we'll allow Him to.

Now, the vessel the potter was shaping was marred, so he formed a different pot with it. We're like that sometimes, aren't we? God was working at shaping us into the vessel He wanted, and then we marred the clay by stumbling, and falling into sin. Just as the potter in these verses, though, God will smush us back down into a lump of clay, and begin anew. He'll stop us from continuing to sin, and when we repent, he'll begin to shape us into a new, useful vessel. He'll take us, and even when we think we're too busted up and broken, He takes the imperfections out of our clay, and He shapes us into a new vessel that's better than the old ever was. He makes us useful again, in ways that we weren't before. That happens, because He's shaped us as He wills.

We're so thankful that He's a God of second chances, but that's not entirely accurate. Far better, we serve the God of new beginnings. Aren't we thankful we're clay in His hands, and that He shapes us as He thinks best?

Prayer: Lord, we know we don't make very good clay, with all our lumps and imperfections, but we give you full authority to shape us, as you want…

Mar 18
Little "White?" Lies

"Therefore each of you must put off falsehood and speak truthfully to his neighbor, for we are all members of one body. Do no let any unwholesome talk come out of your mouths, but only what is helpful for building others up according to their needs, that it may benefit those who listen." Eph 4:25 & 29

Is there such a thing as a little white lie? We view those small falsehoods as those that we tell to avoid hurting someone's feelings, or so that we don't give information we're not supposed to divulge, or to protect someone else, or perhaps their reputation.

Our friend was out doing something she shouldn't have been, so to keep her from getting in trouble, we "cover" for her, and say she was with us, when she wasn't. Our friend tries a new hairstyle, and asks us if we like it, and we tell them we "love it, it looks good," when in reality, we think it's hideous.

Of course, there are other situations that are worse (we categorize sin on a scale, don't we?). There are times when we misdirect people so they won't interfere with what we're hoping to accomplish. We send them off so we can close our business deal before they get a chance. We lie about relationships, telling our wife that woman at work is just someone we work with, when in truth, we're having coffee or lunch with them almost every workday. We don't tell our husband about that man that keeps flirting with us, and asking us to have dinner with him, or bringing us little presents. We pass along tidbits of gossip that may be true, but are harmful to the person we're talking about. We're rude to the people in line at the bank, or the grocery store. The list goes on and on.

We can change this, and avoid white lies or unwholesome talk. First, stop lying! Second, speak in ways that are helpful to those around us. Third, sometimes, we just plain need to *shut up*.

We can bless and encourage people *so much* by saying things that are positive. God tells us to *only* say those things that are helpful for building others up, according to *their* needs, not ours. When you begin finding good things to compliment others about, searching out things that are positive about them, or their accomplishments, and start telling them, you'll be such a blessing they'll want to be around you *all* the time. We all love to be around positive, encouraging, happy people. Rather than being one who speaks "unwholesomely", be the one who lifts up and encourages, benefiting those who listen.

Prayer: Father, give us the heart and mind to speak blessing to others, that we might be a benefit to them, and never a detriment…

Mar 19
Which Fragrance Are You?

"For we are to God the aroma of Christ among those who are being saved and those who are perishing. To the one we are the smell of death; to the other, the fragrance of life."
II Cor 2:15-16a

There's nothing quite like walking into a house where they've just baked fresh bread. The aroma fills the air, and makes your mouth water. You may suddenly find your stomach growling, just from the fragrance. What a wonderful smell that is. That's like the fragrance we are to those who walk with Christ.

The opposite occurs sometimes, too. Have you ever been driving along slowly with the windows down in your car and come by a dead animal carcass? Now that odor is anything but pleasing. It's such a rancid, awful smell; you want to cover your nose and mouth to keep it out. That's the smell we are to those who don't know Jesus personally.

If you've noticed, to those who aren't believers in Christ Jesus, we're very uncomfortable to be around. We just seem to rub them the wrong way. Is it because there's something wrong with us? Are we rude to them? Do we treat them badly? Is there a sign on us that says "We're gonna getcha!"? No, the problem is with them. Darkness flees before the light. The bible speaks of those who don't know Christ as being in darkness. Those who are wicked *like* the darkness, because it hides their deeds. We're a stench to them because of the smell of eternal death that confronts them in their sin. It's not us; it's Christ in us, and the Holy Spirit's convicting presence.

Conversely, the Spirit within us is a wonderful, pleasant fragrance to fellow believers. It blesses them, because it's the pleasing smell of eternal life with Christ. We're like sweet perfume to other Christians.

Remember that, when we're around others, we're an aroma on God's behalf. An aroma of life and death, both.

Prayer: Lord Jesus, help us to be careful to be good representatives of yours, so that your aroma fills the air with life; and to those to whom we're currently the smell of death, let us bring them to life in you...

Mar 20
Dead Faith?

"Faith, by itself, if it is not accompanied by action, is dead... His (Abraham's) faith was made complete by what he did." Jas 2:17b & 22b

If you told your wife how much you loved her, and made continual declarations of your undying devotion, but never did anything to show her that love, do you think she'd feel loved by you? And if you spoke to your husband in adoring words, and verbalized your love in lavish tones, but never did anything to show him love, do you think he'd feel loved by you? No, we know we're loved by the way our spouse helps us, how they meet our needs, how we spend quality time together, and not just by the words we say. It takes the two working in concert to show each other our love.

In the same way, if we worship the Lord, and verbally acknowledge His calling on our lives, but don't do anything, is our faith living? See, we might *know* God has called us into the Gospel Singing ministry, and agree with Him that we've been called. But if we don't write the music, learn the music, record the music, pray through the music, practice the music, and then bring the music in worship concerts to people, our faith is dead. If we schedule churches, if we *do* the music, and have worship concerts, our faith is made complete.

The same holds true for you two. Your faith isn't complete unless you *do* what God asks you to. Without action, and unless you do the work of the Father, your faith is dead. You're no different than the rest of us (hate that, huh?). We're all in the same spiritual boat. Our faith is fulfilled by the *actions* we take, not the declarations we *make*!

Be doers of the Word, and have the living faith.

Prayer: Heavenly Father, help us to take the action you require of us to make our faith complete...

Mar 21
Plant Some Seed

"This is what the kingdom of God is like. A man scatters seed on the ground. Night and day, whether he sleeps or gets up, the seed sprouts and grows, though he does not know how. All by itself the soil produces grain—first the stalk, then the head, then the full kernel in the head. As soon as the grain is ripe, he puts the sickle to it, because the harvest has come." Mk 4:26b-29

Whether we can see it or not, God is always at work. While we're completely unaware, he's nourishing the seeds planted for His kingdom. They're growing, they're maturing, and when they're ripe, and ready to harvest, someone needs to bring them in.

If you've ever gardened, you know the soil is prepared first. Once we've dug up the ground, it's ready for planting, and we put the seed in the ground, or transplant the plants purchased. We water them in, and tamp down the soil. We may put protective mulch around them, to keep them from drying out. Then we go on our way, and attend to other tasks.

One day, we go out to discover rows of plants poking through the surface of the ground. We're excited, but we don't have any produce yet. In time, those plants grow, they become larger and stronger, they flower, and then the flowers fall, and fruit or vegetables take its place. When the beans are mature, or the corn has headed out, or the melons are filled, or the tomatoes turn red, or in some cases (like potatoes), the plant withers, it's time to bring in the food produced.

God's kingdom is similar to this. Someone (perhaps you) prepares the soil of a person's heart. Another plants a seed. Yet another waters, and one fertilizes, and still another pulls out the weeds trying to choke the plant. In between, God's Spirit is working in that heart. When the time is right, the Lord sends someone to harvest, and the seed of God's word is brought to fulfillment. Someone explained the need for repentance, someone else showed God's love, and yet another explained the sacrifice of Jesus Christ. When it all came together, the Holy Spirit drew that soul, and they responded, and put their faith and trust in Jesus (the harvest).

We never know where each person may be in the growing process when we first meet him or her, and we have to be observant to see. But we need to be faithful about planting, about nourishing, and about harvesting in the appropriate season of a person's life.

Prayer: Dear Lord, help us to be good stewards of the planting, growing, and harvesting process. Give us discerning spirits…

Mar 22
Are You Stupid?

"Whoever loves discipline loves knowledge, but he who hates correction is stupid." Pr 12:1

That's rather blunt, isn't it? The writer of proverbs (probably Solomon) doesn't exactly mince words here. Not much wiggle room in this verse. It's to the point, though.

Let us start out by saying we recommend you *not* talk to your spouse this way. That might leave someone's feelings a bit raw. We do need to be gently open and honest with each other. Self-examination in this area will prove to be time well spent, in that it will eliminate any need for your spouse to deal with these issues with you.

There are some (we're not pointing any fingers here), who are not well equipped to handle "constructive criticism". Whatever the reason, some just cannot admit any fault in themselves, and become hurt or angry whenever someone confronts them with even a perceived fault. This is *not* a mature attitude. We often use the phrase "nobody's perfect". That applies to all of us.

In case you think we've never struggled with this ourselves, let us disabuse you of the notion. We have! Sometimes, we still do. We can take on the 'no one understands me, I'm so misunderstood' martyrdom façade as well as anyone. Maybe better. We've had a lot of practice.

Not many of us love discipline. It can be painful. But to love correction is a real mark of maturity. When we're mature, we don't want to continue to do things that are wrong, or lacking in honor to the Lord, or that cause others hurt, or smother their spirit. We want to grow in Christ, and the only way we can do that is to put aside those things that aren't pleasing to our spouse, or the Lord, and replace them with godly habits. Remember to apply knowledge judiciously, so that we gain wisdom.

So don't be stupid! Love discipline!

Prayer: Father, help us to put aside the attitude of pride that won't let us admit when we're wrong, or when we displease you, or each other. Give us the maturity to accept correction, and improve our walk with you...

Mar 23
Yoke Yourself Carefully

"Do not be yoked together with unbelievers. For what do righteousness and wickedness have in common? Or what fellowship can light have with darkness?" II Cor 6:14

How often have we used this verse when discussing the futility of Christians and non-Christians dating and marrying? When the inevitable problems arise, we quickly point out that they should never have married to begin with. The bible speaks to this, too, but that's for another day.

Let us just give this advice to you as Christian parents. Teach your children that it is *not* acceptable to date unbelievers. That should never be an option for Christian kids.

Let's apply this standard to ourselves, though, because we tend to forget this verse when we get involved in business or social events. This command is especially important to remember in the business world. Now, we may not be able to aptly apply it if we work for a company. But when we own our business, it's neither wise, nor acceptable to take on unbelieving partners. We want to overlook this principle when it comes to making money or earning as much profit as possible. But we don't get to pick and choose God's instruction, and if you expect your children to follow this precept, then it's essential that *you* set the example. Let's face it; we know that light and dark cannot coexist. You will have two very different sets of mores if you go into business with someone who isn't a Christian. Areas where you wouldn't consider doing certain things, your business partner won't bat an eye at. And it reflects on you. So if you want to honor God in your business, partner with believers of good character, high intelligence, and solid skills in the areas of expertise you need.

You'll be glad you yoked yourself with a believer.

Prayer: Lord, give us insight into partnering with other believers, whenever and wherever possible, and give us the self-discipline to set the example for our children...

Mar 24
Troubling Message

"God sent the angel Gabriel to Nazareth, a town in Galilee, to a virgin pledged to be married to a man named Joseph, a descendent of David. The virgin's name was Mary." Lk 1:26b-27

"I am the Lord's servant," Mary answered. "May it be to me as you have said." Lk 1:38a-b

Have you been in a situation where someone brought you disturbing news, and you knew hardly anyone would believe you if you told them who it was, and what the message was? Now, add to that by putting yourself in Mary's place. She's a virgin, engaged to be married to a godly man, and she's pregnant. Now Mary knew she was pure, but who would believe that? This was a very conservative community, and these things just don't happen! Consider the gossip that would go around. Consider her reputation, and how the reputation of Joseph, would be impugned. And again, Joseph knew he was innocent, but who could accept that without applying the charge of betrayal, also, to Mary?

Sometimes, we're given news of great importance, and like Mary and Joseph, we just have to discreetly keep it to ourselves. We know that in time, the proof of our integrity will come out, but like Joseph and Mary, we may have to endure slander and social isolation for a time. Maybe a long time, as they did. But they *knew!* They knew in their hearts what was true, and so were able to endure the castigation they had to go through.

We know this was a time of immense blessing for Joseph and Mary. Although they had to endure hardship, ruined reputations, and condescension, they were able to overcome because they were privy to the initial part of God's plan. They knew God's purpose for them.

We're not usually given our messages by an angel. We don't actually need one, because we've been indwelled by the Holy Spirit. But when God tells you something, don't be surprised if the folks around you don't understand how that could happen, or believe you. We've found from experience that those who don't walk intimately with the Lord can't comprehend us when we tell them, "God told me". One word of caution here. When you think God has told you something, test the spirit. Check it against His word, the Bible. He'll never tell you something that contradicts His written word.

When God does speak to you, He'll bless you guys, as well. You'll be able to endure what you have to, because you'll know His plan for you. You'll enjoy a peace within that sustains you through the tough times. Just *remember* His troubling message to *you*.

Take the attitude Mary did. Accept God's specific plan for your lives. May it be to you as He says.

Prayer: Lord, when you speak to us, let us hear clearly, and be obedient. Direct us to the correct scriptures to confirm your message...

Mar 25
Swallowed Up by Life

"For while we are in this tent, we groan and are burdened, because we do not wish to be unclothed but to be clothed with our heavenly dwelling, so that what is mortal may be swallowed up by life." II Cor 5:4

It probably comes as a great shock to most of you that in life you're going to be burdened down with heavy weights that will cause you to groan. You're going to have some days when one thing after another goes wrong. No one responds the way you wish they would. Every machine you touch won't work properly. Even your coffee gets cold too fast.

When we have tough times, we tend to turn to the Lord, don't we? When things are going smoothly, when we don't have a crisis we need help with, we pretty much go our way without turning our attention to God. If you want your days to go more smoothly, try praising Him when things are going well. When you spend time with God, He won't have to allow difficulties to come your way to get your attention. Isn't it better to spend fellowship time with Him when you don't need anything? That's *sweet* time of rest and blessing!

We're not going to just spend eternity with Christ in heaven. Our everlasting life with Him started when we were born again. We've already begun our eternal life. We're still living it in our mortal bodies, and while we're here on earth, we'll have situations to deal with. But God doesn't want us to just groan. He wants us to live in the fullness of His blessing. We do that by communing with Him, all the time. We look forward to a brighter day, but we have wonderfully bright days here when we walk with the Lord, and spend time in His presence.

At the end of our earthly days, we don't have to fear passing on. We're stepping from this life into being swallowed up by life. Life eternal!

Prayer: Holy Spirit, remind us that we need to spend time in God's presence. We don't want to just groan with burdens, we want to live in the fullness of life now…

Mar 26
Enjoy Good Health

"Dear friend, I pray that you may enjoy good health and that all may go well with you, even as your soul is getting along well." III Jn 2

And we pray that for you, dear friends. When speaking of our physical needs, food, clothing, and shelter, God's word tells us if we'll first seek God's kingdom, our Heavenly Father, who knows our needs, will provide them as well. First things first!

As you're spending time together in daily devotions as a couple, as you're each reading God's word every day (how long is your streak now?), your soul is getting along well. That's the Father's desire for you. That your soul gets along well. When your soul is doing well, it eliminates most of the stress, and wear and tear, that comes into our lives on a daily basis. The things that can go wrong don't affect us as much; they don't knock us off kilter. We can continue on without distress, because our soul is well.

John goes on after this verse to tell of hearing how they're walking in the truth, and being faithful to it. Doesn't it give us a great feeling in our heart and spirit to hear that our children are walking faithfully? Our parents feel the same. The same holds true for all of us.

Have you ever taken the time to read the possible side effects of medications that are prescribed? The side effects can be worse than the illness we're taking the medication to cure. When we're walking faithfully, there's an added benefit, because generally, we do enjoy good health. We feel well, and our hearts are light, when we're walking in faith and right relationship with our Heavenly Father. That's a side effect of the lack of stress we have when our soul is getting along well.

But wait, there's more! John's prayer is that *all* may go well with you. Good health is great, but even more wonderful; *all* will go well for us. We want that for you. We pray, too, that you'll live in abundance in Christ, that your every need is met, and that you have strength and self-discipline to walk faithfully. Just follow that precondition. Make sure your soul is doing well.

Prayer: Heavenly Father, give us good health and let everything go well for us, as our hearts are doing well in you...

Mar 27
Money for God

"On the first day of every week, each one of you should set aside a sum of money in keeping with his income, saving it up, so that when I come no collections will have to made." I Cor 16:2

Don't you just hate how the bible keeps talking about money? All we hear, sometimes, is money, money, money. Ironically, we must tell you, if all you're hearing about is money, it's because it's a sensitive subject for you. Most pastors and churches rarely preach on giving. Few scriptures tell you to give, but when they do, they do so as a part of walking in faith, and as part of our spiritual worship. This, too, is a heart issue. If God doesn't have your money, he doesn't have all of your heart. And if you're grudging in your giving, if you're not being faithful in this area, then you're blocking a load of God's blessings for you.

God's word tells us in the New Testament that each of us should decide in our heart what to give, to do so joyfully, and to prepare ahead of time. This is part of our worship. It's not a separate issue. And it's so much easier to give when we've purposed in our hearts what to give, in accordance with our income, and have it prepared. It gives us a sense of peace, because we know we're being faithful in what the Lord led us to do.

When I managed retail stores, or when standing in line to check out, nothing was or is more frustrating than someone who puts all their packages on the counter, watches the cashier ring it all up, and finally, when given the total amount due, begins fumbling in their purse to look for their money. And on top of that, digs in the bottom looking for just the right change. Why waste all that time, making others wait, when you could have had your money ready?

Paul tells us in the verse above, to know what we're giving, and have it prepared in advance. Think ahead, so when it's time for the offering, you're ready. It'll please God! And spare others frustration, lol.

Prayer: Dear Lord, lead us in our hearts to know what *you* want us to give each week for your work. Help us to be faithful and consistent in preparing our offerings ahead of time…

Mar 28
In His Power

"That by his power he may fulfill every good purpose of yours and every act prompted by your faith. We pray this so that the name of our Lord Jesus may be glorified in you, and you in him, according to the grace of our God and the Lord Jesus Christ." II Th 1:11b-12

In 2008, we had the vestiges of a hurricane sweep through our area after hitting the coast of Texas. It was windy! It blew three trees down on our house. The Lord protected us, because they fell on the dormer right where our daughter was sleeping, and didn't even break the window. However, those were big trees. No way could we lift them off of the house by ourselves. Thankfully, there are machines with enough power to move them, and other tools to cut the trees up (lots of firewood). We didn't have to cut them up and move them in our own strength.

God doesn't expect us to accomplish our good purposes for Him in our own strength either. We work in faith to what we feel led to do, but we don't do it in our power. That takes the pressure off, doesn't it? It's by *His* power that He fulfills our good purposes that are prompted by our faith in Him. Not our strength, His. Not our power, His.

There's a godly purpose for this. This is the same purpose in all we do for Christ. The purpose is to glorify the name of the Lord Jesus. The name of Jesus is to be glorified in us, and then, us in Him.

This comes as a result of God's grace. Grace: God's unmerited favor. Even though we don't deserve it, even though we can't earn it, the Lord gives us His favor, and His favor lasts for our lifetime. That's enough to make us rejoice forever. As you go through each day, remind yourself, "I'm walking in the Lord's favor". "I have God's grace." "His power fulfills every good purpose of mine."

So don't be afraid to act in faith when you feel God leading you to do something. You will do it in His power.

Prayer: God, help us to trust in your power to fulfill our purposes prompted by our faith in you…

May 29
Two Are Better than One

"Two are better than one, because they have a good return for their work: If one falls down, his friend can help him up. But pity the man who falls and has no one to help him up! Also, if two lie down together, they will keep warm. But how can one keep warm alone? Though one may be overpowered, two can defend themselves. A cord of three strands is not quickly broken." Ecc 4:9-12

When you got married, you had a beautiful wedding, and a heart full of love and excitement, filled with the joy of starting your new journey together. It was a day filled with family and friends, celebration and promise. You looked forward to love and life together, as a married couple.

Now, as you've lived together, you've found there are more pragmatic considerations than you first had. After the bloom faded from the roses, you realized there were chores to divide, tasks to take care of that your parents always handled before. So you figured out that, if both are working, you may both do the dishes together, or you split the cooking duties, she may wash clothes, while he vacuums the floors, he may wash the car and mow the grass, while she picks up the house and dusts the furniture. But whatever the division of labor has become, you've found that two are better than one. You have a good return when you work together. When one doesn't feel well, the other can help out, and vice versa. Also, you can keep each other warm (Glenda's particularly fond of this one [how *can* her feet be that cold?]). As you've lived together, you've probably found a few other close friends that you can trust and count on, as well. They're blessings from the Lord.

Two of you can defend each other, your relationship, and your marriage and family. In each other, you've found a faithful friend that you can count on, in any and every circumstance.

This concludes with a cord of three strands as one not quickly broken. That third strand in your cord is the Lord, whose strength and power you can always depend on. When your marriage is centered on the Lord, and set on the foundation of Jesus, the rock, it's not easily broken. In fact, if you'll keep Him first, and protect your relationship from those who'd interfere and split you up, standing steadfastly loyal to each other, your marriage *can't* be torn apart.

Just keep walking and working and loving and laughing and living with your friend.

Prayer: Lord, give us a steadfast and loyal heart for each other, that we might always stand firm with our friend…

Mar 30
Do You Have Love Covers?

"Love covers over all wrongs." Pr 10:12b

"Above all, love each other deeply, because love covers over a multitude of sins." I Pet 4:8

Have you ever wished you had a love cover when you did something dumb. Say something stupid, or embarrassing? Oops, slip under the love cover. Buy something you couldn't afford, or should have checked with your spouse about? Pull the love cover over us. Watch the game and blow off taking out the trash, missing the garbage truck? Get under the love cover. Talk on the phone too long, and forget to iron that shirt? Find that love cover.

We all do things we shouldn't sometimes. We say things we regret. We fail to do other things that we should. When those things happen (and they will), we don't hold grudges against each other, we don't keep throwing it back in the other's face. Since we love each other, and we love each other deeply, we forgive it and go on. Remember, you'd better forgive in love, because a time is coming when you're going to need your spouse's love to cover your sin.

Now, don't go out and do things you know are going to cause problems, and count on love to cover it. That's just spitting in your spouse's face. You're not given love to use as a manipulation tool, and we hope you refuse to do so.

Rather, strive to do those things that show you're *not* counting on love to cover a multitude of sins. Be diligent in taking care to show your spouse you love *him/her*.

It's comforting to know that we do have that love, though, because sometimes, we *do* need it. Thank the Lord for the love that sustains us through those situations.

Prayer: Father, we thank you for that forgiving love that you've given us that we can show each other...

Mar 31
Love God

"He who dwells in the shelter of the Most High
will rest in the shadow of the Almighty.
I will say of the Lord, 'He is my refuge and my fortress,
my God, in whom I trust.'
He will cover you with his feathers,
and under his wings you will find refuge;
his faithfulness will be your shied and rampart.
You will not fear the terror of night,
nor the arrow that flies by day,
nor the pestilence that stalks in the darkness,
nor the plague that destroys at midday.
A thousand may fall at your side,
ten thousand at your right hand,
but it will not come near you.
You will only observe with your eyes
and see the punishment of the wicked.
Make the Most High your dwelling—even the Lord,
who is my refuge—then no harm will befall you,
no disaster will come near your tent.
For he will command his angels concerning you
to guard you in all your ways:
they will lift you up in their hands,
so that you will not strike your foot against a stone.
'Because he loves me,' says the Lord,
'I will rescue him;
I will protect him, for he acknowledges my name.
He will call upon me, and I will answer him;
I will be with him in trouble,
I will deliver him and honor him.

With long life will I satisfy him
and show him my salvation.'" Most of Psalm 91
You'll Be Blessed

Prayer: Most High God, we put our trust in you. We love you, and we always want to dwell with you...

Apr 1
Stir It Up

"Fan into flame the gift of God, which is in you… II Tim 1:6b

We have a wood fireplace, and find that as the fire burns down, we lose the flames we love to watch. Embers are still hot and glowing down in the bottom, but to get flames, we have to stir up the coals and wood, and when we do that, the wood bursts into flame again. It's remarkable what poking the wood and stirring it will do.

God has given you gifts and abilities to use for Him. All of us have talents that will fill a need in the body of Christ, the family of believers. Husband, you may be creative in art, or you may have a knack for carpentry. Wife, you may have abilities in music, or mechanical aptitudes. Your gifts may lie in other areas completely. Whatever they are, though, you have them. God's word tells us we have them.

Sometimes, we let the 'fire' of our abilities die down to embers. When that happens, we need to fan into flame those talents. Another translation actually says to 'stir up' the gift within. If you've left your gifts to die down, and lie dormant in the coals, now is the time to dig down in those embers, stir them up, and fan them into flame. Find a place, a way, or an area in the church family you attend to use your abilities to bless the body. If there's no place within your church to use your talents, then find another outlet for them. The Lord will show you where you can be of service, and when you find that place, you'll be a great blessing to others.

When the fire has burned down to embers, it still gives off a lot of heat. But when those coals are fanned into flame, they give more heat, and beauty too. The same holds true for the gifts God has given you.

Stir them up.

Prayer: Dear Lord, help us to stir up those gifts you've given us, and find new ways to use them to serve you, and bless others…

Apr 2
God's Protection

"But the Lord is faithful, and he will strengthen and protect you from the evil one." II Th 3:3

When our kids were young, our son was pretty small. He started school early, and was a bit behind his classmates physically. But blessed with a disarming sense of humor, and quick wits, he managed to avoid problems with other children. Of course, it helped that he always seemed to end up with the biggest boy around as his best friend. That 'large' friend was an intimidating presence in case anyone thought they could pick on him. His friend's strength offered protection when needed.

If we rely on our friends to take care of us, or protect us, we're going to end up being disappointed. There's always somebody bigger, stronger, faster, and smarter out there. On top of that, our friends can't always be there, can they?

We do have one friend we can count on. He'll never leave us, nor will He ever forsake us. There's no one bigger, or stronger, or faster, or smarter than our friend. None can possibly overcome Him. He's the ultimate 'bodyguard'!

Our other friends aren't usually completely faithful, either. They may be better friends with someone else, and forsake us. They may be distracted by love (you're really lost then). They may have to work. Whatever the reason, there are times they won't, or can't, be faithful. Even our husband/wife, our best and most trusted friend, can't always be there.

The Lord, though, oh, He's *faithful*! He's always there with us. No matter where we go, or what we do (you'd better be careful), or who we're with, He's always there. He's always watching, always strengthening, always guarding, always faithful. He *will* protect you from the Devil. The battle's already won. Walk in the assurance of God's protection from the evil one.

Prayer: Lord, we're so thankful that you're faithful, and that you strengthen us, and protect us…

Apr 3
Choose

"I have set before you life and death, blessings and curses. Now choose life, so that you and your children may live and that you may love the Lord your God, listen to his voice, and hold fast to him. For the Lord is your life…" Dt 30:19b-20c

The Lord is my life. The Lord is *your* life if you've chosen to put your faith in Jesus, and the saving grace provided by His sacrifice on the cross. He gives us the options. He lays it all out there for us. Life or death. Blessings or curses.

God never demands we follow Him. We wouldn't really love Him if we had no choice. We'd be puppets, dancing to the puppeteer's whims. Let me give you a couple of examples of why this is so.

When you fell in love with each other, and decided to marry, it had to be a mutual choosing, didn't it? More than likely, you've previously had someone who was in love with you that you just didn't feel the same way about. You didn't have it in you to choose to love that person in return. If we were forced to live together in marriage, we wouldn't necessarily love each other. We might do most of the marriage routines, but we'd do them out of duty, or tradition, rather than desiring to do them because of our love. If we didn't *choose* our spouse, it wouldn't be love, would it?

Way back in the antiquity of time, in the beginning of man and woman, when Adam and Eve were in the garden. Why was the tree of knowledge in the garden? God himself knew that love, to be real, had to be a choice. God wasn't a slave master. He gave Adam and Eve the choice to obey, or to disobey. That was the first place the option was given. Choose life or death. Choose obedience or disobedience. You see, if the tree of knowledge hadn't been there in the garden, then it wouldn't have been real love, or real obedience.

That's why we have to choose. It's up to us. There are blessings or curses, depending upon our decision. Choose the Lord, and receive life and blessing, for you and your children. Choose to leave the Lord, and go your own way, to follow other gods; then the consequences are death and curses, which lead to misery and heartache all along the way of life's journey.

So choose wisely, and hold fast to the Lord.

Prayer: Father, help us to choose wisely; to choose life with you. Grant us life and blessing as we walk with you…

Apr 4
A Gift from God

"I know that there is nothing better for men than to be happy and do good while they live. That everyone may eat and drink, and find satisfaction in all his toil—this is the gift of God." Ecc 3:12-13

If you're able to have contentment in your circumstances, and to enjoy the life you've been given, then God has blessed you.

Just as we have the ability to choose God, or not, we also can decide our attitude. How we view things has little to do with our circumstances. We can have a great attitude, and a heart of thankfulness, in the midst of terrible afflictions. Conversely, we can have bitter attitudes in the midst of health, wealth, and blessings of every kind. It depends on how we choose to think, and what kind of an outlook we decide to have.

You've probably heard the story of the man with two little boys. The one boy was always bright and cheery, never dragged down by anything that happened. The other son was so pessimistic, and always saw the bad in every situation. The man decided for Christmas one year to test them out, to see if he could change their perspectives. He bought the pessimist every gift and toy he could come up with. He lavished every conceivable present possible on him. For the optimistic little boy, he had a big pile of manure hauled in and dumped behind the barn. When Christmas came, the pessimistic child got to open his presents first, and sure enough, no happy face, no expressions of joy or thankfulness. With a downcast face, he said, "all these toys are good now, but soon they'll break, and then what will I do?"

Well, the father took the optimistic child out behind the barn and showed him his present of that big pile of manure. The little boy quickly ran into the barn, grabbed a pitchfork, and came out and began to furiously shovel the manure away. Bewildered, the father asked, "What are you doing?" The little boy replied, "I'm looking! With all that manure, there must be a pony in there somewhere."

There is nothing better for us than to be happy and do good. Find satisfaction in your work. It doesn't matter what your circumstances, and doesn't matter how many failures you've had in the past. You can decide today to have an attitude of thanks and gratitude for God's blessings in your life. You can thank Him today for your job. You can praise Him today for your food. You can find some good thing to do today. You can be happy today. It's a gift from God.

Prayer: Lord Jesus, help us decide to have good, happy attitudes, thankful hearts, and contentment in our lives. We thank you for this gift...

Apr 5
Live Up To...

"Only let us live up to what we have already attained." Php 3:16

When I was younger (that encompasses quite some time), I was a pretty good athlete. I could run, jump, hike, swim, or climb without any trouble whatsoever. Now, it's become more of a struggle. I can no longer run as far, or as fast as I once could. I can't jump as high. I can only hike half as far. I can swim longer, but not faster (fat floats you know). I don't have the strength in my arms to climb like I did when I was much lighter. In the area of physical accomplishments, I can't live up to what I've already attained without some serious work getting back in shape. And even then, I might not be able to reach that peak physical condition I once was in.

You probably have areas like that in your lives too. You might have been a very good trumpet player, or clarinet player, but haven't kept up with it. If you were to go pick up your old instrument now, I daresay you'd find the sound that came out isn't nearly as pleasing to the ear as it once was. Perhaps you were good at sketching, or painting, but haven't done so in a while. You'd find you need to brush up on your skills again.

Thankfully, our Christian walk isn't like that. We're not to let ourselves get rusty. We're not to slide back in areas we've already attained. God calls us to live up to the height we've already achieved. That means we keep working to stay sharp in our walk of obedience. We must hone our vocal skills, continually sharing with those around us. Strengthening our abilities in God's kingdom work is essential.

Are you making sure you're staying sharp, learning more, taking in more knowledge, adding more self-discipline, applying more godly principles to your lives, and staying in touch with the source of our life?

Be sure to live up to what you've already attained.

Prayer: Heavenly Father, help us stay aware of the need to continue in the walk we've already achieved, and continue to grow...

Apr 6
Don't Have Time for Patience or Perseverance?

"Brothers, as an example of patience in the face of suffering, take the prophets... As you know, we consider blessed those who have persevered. You have heard of Job's perseverance and have seen what the Lord finally brought about. The Lord is full of compassion and mercy." Jas 5:10a & 11

The lousy part of patience and perseverance is, they take so long! Time is required for both. And usually quite a bit! We just can't wait for all that stuff. Life is moving too fast to get bogged down with this.

In the beginning of the book of James, we're told perseverance must finish its work so that we'll be mature. Our faith is tested to develop perseverance. Develop. That has an ominous sound. It leads us to believe this isn't going to be a quick process. Develop smacks of taking a long period to do its work.

There's no getting around it. There's a reason we're told to be patient. That's not our natural inclination. We're living in the United States of America. Doesn't God know this is the age of instant gratification? Unfortunately, this age has made it even more difficult to self-discipline ourselves to wait on the Lord to finish His work in us. We have to literally *make* ourselves wait. We have to force ourselves to do so.

God has a prize at the end, though. When we patiently endure the trials we *must* go through to develop perseverance, we become mature in the faith. Just as Job did, we have to hold fast to the Lord. By being steady and loyal, by exercising our faith, we make it to the goal. God wasn't punishing Job; He was proving a point. When you face tests, it may be that God has so much confidence in you He's thumbing His nose at Satan, using you as an example.

I've always felt sorry for Job. But God knew his heart, just as He knows ours. At the end, when we've persevered, God has blessings to pour out on us that will boggle our minds. After all, the Lord is full of compassion and mercy. He'll give us the strength to face any difficulties. All we have to do is stay in sync with Him. He's right here with us as we go through this storm. He'll bless you, too!

Prayer: Lord, give us strength as we face trials of every kind. Help us develop that perseverance we need...

Apr 7
What to Say in Worship

Do you ever have a difficult time finding the words to use when you want to praise the Lord? Well, here are some examples from scripture.

"Holy, holy, holy is the Lord God Almighty, who was, and is, and is to come." Rev 4:8c

"Be exalted, O God, above the heavens; let your glory be over all the earth." Ps 57:5

"To the only wise God be glory forever through Jesus Christ." Rom 16:27

"You are worthy, our Lord and God, to receive glory and honor and power, for you created all things, and by your will they were created and have their being." Rev 4:11

"The Lord gave and the Lord has taken away; may the name of the Lord be praised." Job 1:21b

"Sing to God, sing praise to his name, extol him who rides on the clouds—his name is the Lord—and rejoice before him." Ps 68:4

"Glory to God in the highest, and on earth peace to men on whom his favor rests." Lk 2:14

"Worthy is the Lamb, who was slain, to receive power and wealth and wisdom and strength and honor and glory and praise!" Rev 5:12

"For great is the Lord and most worthy of praise… Splendor and majesty are before him; strength and glory are in his sanctuary." Ps 96:4a & 6

"My soul glorifies the Lord and my spirit rejoices in God my Savior, for he has been mindful of the humble state of his servant." Lk 1:46b-48a

"To him who sits on the throne and to the Lamb be praise and honor and glory and power, for ever and ever!" Rev 5:13b

"Praise the Lord. I will extol the Lord with all my heart… Great are the works of the Lord; they are pondered by all who delight in them. Glorious and majestic are his deeds, and his righteousness endures forever. Ps 111:1a & 2-3

"Hallelujah! Salvation and glory and power belong to our God, for true and just are his judgments." Rev 19: 1b-2a

If you need more ideas of what to say when you worship the Lord, go to the Psalms. You'll find all you need.

Prayer: Lord, let us please you by blessing your name in praise and honor…

Apr 8
Accountability

"As iron sharpens iron, so one man sharpens another." Pr 27:17

Have you ever seen old cogs from a machine, one that's been used until it's worn out? When you look at those old pieces, there are two things you'll notice. One is, they're bright and shiny from rubbing together. The second is, they're sharp! When iron rubs against iron, each piece wears the other smooth.

Men can get to be very isolated. We go to work, we come home, we go to church, we come home, we go to the store, and again we come home. But do we spend time with other men? Men need men. We'll get plenty of empathy from women, and they'll give us comfort, but they won't ask the hard questions. And any married man who's spending time with a woman outside his marriage is headed for disaster. There'll be women who want to spend that time with you. But it always leads to problems, most of which are severe. Don't do it. That's just stupid!

Do spend time with, and develop close friendships with, a few Christian men you can trust. Be willing to find out what they think about things. Spiritual things, financial things, business things, play things, work things, marriage things, and family things. Give two or three or a few very close friends permission to ask the hard questions, and hold you accountable in areas you know are weaknesses for you. And be honest in your answers. If you're struggling with something, say so. They're brothers in Christ who are willing to help you, without being critical or harsh, and who want the very best for you.

Men can wear the rough spots off each other. They can smooth each other out. They can put a shine, a polish, on each other. But without that other iron man to rub against, you've nothing to smooth with. Without iron men friends to rub against, you've no one to sharpen you.

Wives, if you want to really help your husband, encourage him to spend some time with male, Christian friends. He'll be better for it, and consequently, you will be too.

Prayer: Lord, place a couple of good Christian men in our lives that can provide the help we need in this area...

Apr 9
Delight Yourself in the Lord

"Trust in the Lord and do good; dwell in the land and enjoy safe pasture. Delight yourself in the Lord and he will give you the desires of your heart." Ps 37:3-4

When you were a child, didn't you always find that when you were in a good relationship with your parents, and doing the things that pleased them, they'd pretty much provide anything they could for you? You could trust your folks to give you whatever you needed, as long as it was in their power to do so. When you weren't doing as you ought, and were in a tense relational time with them, it was pretty tough to get any benefits from them, if it was like my family.

You also knew your parents well enough to know not to ask for anything that they didn't approve of. You only asked for the things that they thought were alright.

When we spend time with our Heavenly Dad, and study His word, and do those things he asks of us, we can enjoy dwelling safely in His care. We can count on Him to do what's in our best interest. He has no reason to harm us. Quite the opposite, He has plans for our good.

As we delight ourselves in the Lord, as we joyfully spend time in His presence, and take pleasure in finding His will and doing it, He also delights in us. As we please Him, He will give us the desires of our heart. And you know what? Our desires won't conflict with His heart. Our desires will coincide with His purposes, because we're walking in step with Him. Sometimes, He'll bless us with things we don't even need, just because He wants to show us how much He loves us.

So delight yourself in the Lord.

Prayer: Heavenly Dad, we do trust in you, and we're trying to do good for you. Help us to take our delight in you, and we know we can count on you to give us all the good things we need and desire…

Apr 10
She Brings Him Good

"She brings him good, not harm, all the days of her life." Pr 31:12

Remember that verse back in Genesis, the one that said, no suitable helper could be found for the man, so God created woman? You were designed, dear wife, to be your husband's helper, his suitable partner. This speaks of far more than just working for him, or working with him. You were designed to complement (not just compliment) him, and to complete his life (not end it, fulfill it).

In proverbs, the preceding verses start with a wife of noble character. It goes on to talk about her worth. Now, I know wives occasionally get a bad rap. There're some stereotypical slants placed on women that probably aren't true. Wives nag their husbands to distraction. Wives use sex as a punishment/reward system. Wives are bossy and dictatorial. Wives fly off the handle and shriek at their husbands. Wives are vindictive when they're angry, and burn all the food out of spite when they are. The bad stories of the extremes are passed around all the time, while the wonderful wives are rarely mentioned.

This wife of noble character as exemplified here is one who looks out for her husband, who honors him. She brings him good, not just once in a while, but all the days of her life. That speaks of real patience, endurance, and consistency to be sure that her husband is well taken care of. She isn't doing grand things in short spurts. Her acclaim comes from the fact that she doesn't only bring him good, but she sees to it that she doesn't in any way bring him harm. That can be a bit trickier than just bringing good.

So, are you careful to bring your husband good, not harm, all the days of your life?

Husband; show your appreciation for the good she brings you. Compliment her for complementing you.

Prayer: Lord, give us your attitude in the way we treat and care for each other. Help us both to bring the other good, and to be careful that we don't harm, or even allow harm to come to, our spouse...

Apr 11
Don't Agree to Lie

"Ananias, how is it that Satan has so filled your heart that you have lied to the Holy Spirit…"

"Yes,' she (Sapphira) said, 'that is the price." Acts 5:3b & 8b

In case you don't remember this story, Ananias and Sapphira had a piece of land they sold. At that time many were selling their property and giving the money to the church. Ananias and Sapphira sold theirs, too, but wanted to make it look like they were giving the entire amount received, when in fact, they'd agreed to keep some of the money for themselves. Now, the property was theirs, and they could have kept whatever portion of the money or all of it, if they so desired. But they agreed together to lie. Peter confronts Ananias first, and when Ananias continues to lie, Peter tells him he's lying to the Holy Spirit, and the Lord struck him dead. The men who buried him came back just in time to pick up the body of Sapphira after she lied also.

We often talk about how important it is for us as husband and wife to agree together as a couple. We accomplish so much more when we agree together. Our prayers are much more powerful when we're in agreement (more in another devotion). When we work towards one common goal, our work is so much more effective than when we try going different directions.

Just as important as being in agreement, though, is doing so with godly purpose. As believers, we should never enter into plans to do anything *displeasing* to God, let alone sinful. We can expect the Father's discipline when we step out of His will, off of His straight and narrow path, and head off on our own. It may not be as terminal as Ananias and Sapphira, but when the Lord spanks us, you might find yourselves wishing He'd just strike you dead, and get it over with. There are any number of things worse than dying.

Let's agree together to serve the Lord in truth and holiness. Nothing pleases the Father more than walking in obedience with Him, living in a pure and honest way.

Prayer: Father, we want to serve you honestly, living for you in holiness…

Apr 12
Work Matters

'If anyone does not provide for his relatives, and especially for his immediate family, he has denied the faith and is worse than an unbeliever." I Tim 5:8

This is a country whose government seems to be doing its best to take the responsibility for peoples lives out of their hands, and putting it in the hands of the federal government. God's word doesn't view it that way. We're responsible for taking care of our families and by extension; we should also help out our neighbors. Now, we're not against the government providing relief in times of severe need. The problem is, by doing so continually, when there is no real need, we already know we've created a whole class of people with a victim mentality, and a culture of dependency.

Ours is a biblical belief system. We need to provide for those who cannot do so themselves. There are handicapped folks who can't earn a living, many who are too old to work, and those who've gone through natural disasters that have wiped out their means of doing so, as well. But God's word also tells us that those who *will not* work shall not *eat*. Some would say that's cruel. It's not cruel, it's tough love. It's the kind of love that says, "You'll be better off if you work, you'll feel better, and think more of yourself, and because that's true, we're not going to allow you to harm yourself by being lazy."

As a couple, it's so important for us to take care of our families. Sometimes, that means lowering our standard of living (collective gasp). You may be able to create a better family life, and less stress, by not both working fulltime jobs. That improves your family life by allowing you to spend more time with your children, and with each other. It's also essential as parents to teach your children, and set the example, that work is *good* for you, and produces a whole host of benefits and blessings. It's good for the children to have chores they're responsible for. And as they see you doing the important things, as they see you taking care of your family (which may mean helping your parents, or siblings), and as they see you focused on the Lord's direction in life, they'll become that way as well.

Don't be worse than an unbeliever, denying the faith by ignoring taking care of your family. Provide for your family, and enjoy the benefits of doing so.

Prayer: Father, show us what you'd have us do, and the direction you want our family to go, in these work matters…

Apr 13
Stay Calm

"A man of knowledge uses words with restraint, and a man of understanding is even-tempered." Pr 17:27

For the sake of our discussion, where this verse uses man, we take this as the generic term for men and women, or mankind, if you will. The reason we don't want to limit this dialog to men is this. We've read that, on average, women speak about 25,000 words per day. Men, on average, use about 12,000 words per day. This is just the natural phenomenon of one of the differences between the mental and physical make up of men and women.

Note that women use approximately twice as many words per day as men. This, we assume, makes the whole instruction here twice as difficult for women as for men. For that reason, you have our sympathy—lol.

We point these things out so that you have a little better understanding of what you're up against. Two traits are pointed out in this verse.

First is the virtue of restraint, which might be more easily understood as self-discipline. Restraining your speech is stopping when you have more you could, and would like to, say. The one without self-discipline says too much, and divulges information they have no right to, or harms others by being critical and discouraging, and thus wounds their spirit. The person of knowledge, however, thinks ahead to the ramifications of saying too much. That person uses their speech to build up, encourage, and bless others.

Secondly is the virtue of even-temperedness, which could more understandably be translated to patience. Those who quickly become angry, or who panic easily, cause commotion all around them. The one who is patient, and remains calm in the face of alarming situations, can soothe the issues we confront, and provide peace to others. That person understands the big picture. They're not overcome by what is an abnormal occurrence that will soon pass.

Be a man or woman of knowledge and understanding. Use restraint when you speak, and be patient in every situation. Stay calm!

Prayer: Heavenly Father, give us the sense of peace that comes with your presence, and allow us to use that calm to be people of knowledge and understanding...

Apr 14
Have a Full Understanding

"I pray that you may be active in sharing your faith, so that you will have a full understanding of every good thing we have in Christ." Phm 6

Notice how the sharing of your faith comes before the full understanding of every good thing we *have* in Christ. Not *will* have, but that we already have.

This sounds like we activate our understanding when we share our faith. Most of the time we think we have to have the full understanding first, so we'll know how to share our faith. But this tells us just the opposite is true. Rats! There goes that excuse (oops, we mean reason).

One of the quickest ways to learn about something more fully is to teach it. It forces you to study, and it's amazing the insights you receive from those you're teaching. You'll always learn more than the students do.

As a couple, sharing your faith extends to many things. It may be sharing Christ, and if it is, the easiest way is to tell what He's done in your life, for you. It can also extend to many other things. It might be sharing an insight the Lord has given you in your marriage relationship that helped you understand something that was bothering you. You may have been taking personally a habit that wasn't directed at you, or about you at all. It could mean giving an example of a situation God used to point out a truth about handling your children. You might have had a difficult situation where the Lord gave you the answer by showing you something similar.

Whatever it is, be active and open in sharing. We want that full understanding. Don't get the cart before the horse. Understanding every good thing we have in Christ (the cart) comes *after* sharing your faith (the horse). And aren't you just dying to know what all the good things we already have in Christ are?

Prayer: Lord Jesus, give us the boldness and the confidence to share you, and what you're doing in our lives, to those around us…

Apr 15
Renew Your Mind

"Be transformed by the renewing of your mind." Rom 12:2b
"Be made new in the attitude of your minds." Eph 4:23

How? By spending time immersed in the word, and meditating on the things of the Lord, and by choosing to.

When we read the Bible every day (length of your streak?), we automatically are renewed in our minds, because we're planting the seeds of His word in our minds, and He's writing them on our hearts. Our spirit is systematically attuned to how God thinks, and what's important to Him, and those practices and attitudes that are displeasing.

Taking time to pray, and to be still in His presence, teaches us how to *apply* God's word, and it gives Him time to speak to us. God *wants* to talk to us, but too often we don't pay attention to Him.

In the end, we must *decide* to be renewed in our minds. We have to decide to have right attitudes. We can choose to walk in blessing, or spend our time distressing. We can moan and groan about how bad things are, that they'll never get any better, and that the worst is always going to happen. If that's the way we think, we're probably right. If you think you're going to fail, most of the time you're right. Or we can encourage ourselves in the Lord, as David did in the Psalms. We can walk in faith. We can renew our minds with godly thinking. We can have a new attitude every day that says, "In Christ Jesus, we're blessed beyond measure. We're children of the Most High God. His favor lasts our lifetime. God has plans for my good, and not for my harm."

We choose how we think about our husband or wife too. We can be critical, or demanding, or negative all the time. Or we can renew our minds by remembering that our spouse is a gift from God, a good gift, given for our lifelong blessing. You can speak positive words of encouragement, and tell her how beautiful she is to you, or how handsome he is to you, or how thankful you are for her help, or how glad you are he did that task for you. You can show your appreciation for each other when you decide to have new attitudes that focus on *finding* ways to bless your spouse.

Renew your minds in Christ, and give yourselves new attitudes every day. As you journey through life together, you'll be so glad you do.

Prayer: God help us. We need the new attitudes you can give, and we need our minds renewed in you. Today we choose to begin fresh with new attitudes and renewed minds…

Apr 16
What Must Be Taught—Day 1

"You must teach what is in accord with sound doctrine. Teach the older men to be temperate, worthy of respect, self-controlled, and sound in faith, in love and in endurance." Tit 2:1-2

Let's break this down piece by piece to see what we have here.

Sound doctrine would be those beliefs that are grounded in scripture, and take into account the whole of scripture. In other words, sometimes we can take a verse by itself, and without having the context of what is said before and after the verse, it could seem to mean something completely different.

Older men are to be temperate. You've heard the old saying, "All things in moderation." Basically, that's what it means to be temperate. It's saying older men should be moderate in their habits.

To be worthy of respect is to behave in such a way as to earn the respect of others. For instance, no one is going to respect you if you act sulky and pout when you don't get what you want. But when things don't go your way, and you behave graciously, with concern for, and politeness to, others, people will respect you for your godly behavior.

Self-controlled. Hmm, that keeps popping up all over scripture. We don't instinctively act that way. That's why we have to work on it, and work on it all the time. We aren't allowed to just lose our temper, get angry, and do whatever we want to relieve our frustration. Controlling ourselves is another way we gain respect.

Being sound in the faith, in love and in endurance, are all intertwined. To be sound in the faith is to be sound in love. To be sound in the faith is to exhibit endurance in the race of our Christian love. To be sound in love and endurance is inexorably tied to being sound in the faith. They're like the three legs of a stool. The stool won't stand on just two legs. You can't have sound faith without love. Without faith and love, you don't have endurance. Without endurance, you don't have love or faith.

If you're an older man, these are the traits you should be developing. If you're a younger man, look forward to having these traits as you grow older, because you'll need them.

Prayer: Lord, help us to develop sound doctrine, and the attitudes and godly traits you want for us…

Apr 17
What Must Be Taught—Day 2

"Likewise, teach the older women to be reverent in the way they live, not to be slanderers or addicted to much wine, but to teach what is good. Then they can train the younger women…" Tit 2:3-4a

What does Paul mean by "older women"? We're not touching that one with a ten-foot pole. We think we can all agree that *you* know whether you fall into the older or younger category, or perhaps are even in the crossing over stage.

If you're in this "older" woman stage, then it's incumbent upon you to strive to be reverent in the way you live. That means you're godly, treating the Lord with respect and awe, devoted to Him, and to living for Him. You're setting the example for younger women and for children, as they see your life.

The older woman is not to be a slanderer. This addresses those who spend their days being busybodies, gossiping together about every juicy tidbit that comes along. When you tell defaming stories about others, or pass along those stories, you have become a slanderer. Avoid engaging in gossip, and you'll know you're avoiding being a slanderer.

Don't be addicted to wine. Now, this always seems to cause a lot of discussion. Was it real wine, did it have alcohol in it, was it like we have today? The obvious answer is yes, it was real wine with real alcohol, or Paul would have no reason to warn about it. We're not going to get into a discussion about "much wine." Each one has to decide what's right for them in light of scripture, but suffice it to say, you can live without drinking alcohol. If you avoid it, you won't be a stumbling block for those whose conscience is weak.

Teach what is good. We like this one. Have you ever seen someone teach a very small child to do something wrong, just because at that age it's so "cute" and "funny?" That's one of the most foolish things they can do. It's easy to teach what is good unless you first have to make them unlearn something bad. Then the process is extremely convoluted. Only teach what is good. What a blessing you'll be to younger women and children.

Which brings us to the last point. Notice Paul isn't telling Titus to train the younger women. Teach the older women, and have the *older* women train the younger women. Boy, will that save everyone a lot of headaches. And they can do a better job of it anyway.

Which category did you say you fell into?

Prayer: Dear Lord, help us to be reverent in our lives, setting an example of godliness…

Apr 18
What Must Be Taught—Day 3

"Then they can train the younger women to love their husbands and children, to be self-controlled and pure, to be busy at home, to be kind, and to be subject to their husbands, so that no one will malign the word of God." Tit 2:4-5

Does it really seem necessary to train a younger woman how to love their husband and children? Doesn't that just come naturally? If you look around you in our society today, the answer is obviously no, it does not. One of the things glaringly absent from our culture today is the example everyone had when wives were stay at home moms, even in town, and we all worked together on the farm. With the close proximity of living and working together, young women saw up close and personal how older wives loved their husbands, and how they took care of them. Even in Paul's day, though, that didn't automatically mean the young women learned what they should. Paul is saying to them, "Make a conscious effort to train the young women." Remember that love does what's in the best interest of the other. In the family, it means needs are met, affection is shown, and teaching is done.

Again with the self-controlled! It's everywhere. With younger women, it's probably directed at different areas than it is with the older men. Many young women can be easily mislead, easily riled, and when they are, they can fly off in any direction to set matters right, giddy with the anticipation of seeing to it things are taken care of. Self-control is needed. It gives time for thinking to kick in. It's not just self-control; they're to teach them to be pure. That means to be without blemish, or fault, or without muckiness. Fill them with enough good things of the Lord, and it will wash out any dirt, leaving them pure.

Young women are to be busy at home. Where? Yes, at home, taking care of the family. In other words, not off flitting about with friends, gossiping and wasting time.

Kindness is one virtue the whole world could use more of. Being polite and helpful to one another is becoming a lost art (except with us, right?).

Being subject to one's husband is blasphemous in this secular society we live in. "Women are equal to men." "Women have every right a man has." OK, but we don't know why you'd want to lower your standards that way, because in God's kingdom, you have much more honor and privilege than that. Someone has to make the final decisions, and God has given that responsibility to the husband, God bless his soul. By willingly giving him your support, you make sure there's harmony in the home, and you give no one any reason to malign the word of God due to conflict in your family.

Prayer: Dear Lord, help us to be loving, self-controlled, pure, kind, and honoring to each other…

Apr 19
What Must Be Taught—Day 4

"Similarly, encourage the young men to be self-controlled. In everything set them an example by doing what is good. In your teaching show integrity, seriousness and soundness of speech that cannot be condemned, so that those who oppose you may be ashamed because they have nothing bad to say about us." Tit 2:6-8

There's a definite theme running in this passage. Paul is often repeating himself. This is interesting here, though, because he says encourage. Not bust them, not smack them down, not denigrate them, but encourage them to be self-controlled. Unless you want a fight on your hands, or you want young men to rise to a challenge to their strength and autonomy, you don't come with criticism. They don't react well to that, and it would behoove all of us to remember that they'll usually respond better to encouragement.

It's important for all of us, young or old, to set an example to others by doing what is good. Even children can set an example with their behavior. People will learn very little by what you tell them. But they'll learn a lot by what you show them, and they'll apply what they see in you to their own lives.

We cannot be dishonest in any way when we teach others. The old adage, "Do as I say, not as I do", just doesn't hold water. Life does *not* work that way. Your actions have to match your teaching, because what you do has way more impact than what you say. The first song we ever released to radio was called "Walk The Walk." The message is how lots of people can talk the talk, but your walk talks more than you talk talks. Walking the walk shows integrity in your life.

You can't be flippant in your teaching either. If you want to teach something important, you have to be serious, and your speech has to be "sound". That means it must be correct, through and through.

When you teach with integrity, seriousness, and correctness, those who want to oppose you will have nothing of value to say. The mud they throw can't stick, because your life is too clean and slick.

Prayer: Lord, help us to set an example of godly life, that others may see our integrity, and learn to follow an upright, honest path with you…

Apr 20
What Must Be Taught—Day 5

"Teach slaves to be subject to their masters in everything, to try to please them, not to talk back to them, and not to steal from them, but to show that they can be fully trusted, so that in every way they will make the teaching about God our Savior attractive." Tit 2:9-10

We almost ended this series yesterday, but realized that even though this talks about slaves, there's a real application for men and women today. If you work for a company that you don't own, then this verse has applications for you.

First, let's address the slave issue. This acknowledges slavery is a fact of life in that day. We've even heard those who are ignorant of scripture as a whole, argue that the Bible not only allows, indeed it blesses, the practice of slavery. *No*, it does *not*! The Bible is clear that slavery was never, nor will it ever be, God's plan or purpose for anyone. Scripture categorizes slave traders with other gross sins (lumps it in with murderers, adulterers, liars, perverts, etc—see I Tim 1:9-11). It also tells in other places that each should gain their freedom if they can, and then of course, Galatians tells us it's for freedom that we were called.

Now, on to more practical, everyday concerns for us. When we work for someone else, we have a responsibility in the Lord to represent Him in our workplace. We can minister to others, even there, if we don't toss aside our witness for Him.

We can be subject to our supervisor at work. When we went to work for the company, that was our tacit agreement with them as a condition of employment. We should try to please them. We shouldn't argue with them, or gossip behind their back. We ought to do our best to serve them faithfully, so that when they learn we're believers in Christ, it will reflect honorably upon His name.

It should go without saying that we are never to steal from our employer. Unfortunately, we do have to say it. Don't steal from your employer! Theft can occur in more than one area, too. Yes, you can steal money and merchandise from your company. But you can also steal time, and by lack of productivity, you can steal profit they would have made. Work hard, work honestly, and prove you can be fully trusted. Not just trusted, but *fully* trusted, because only that will make the teaching of our Savior attractive.

Prayer: Father, give us a new resolve, and consistent effort, to bless our employer with good, hard, productive work, so that your name will be honored…

Apr 21
Surrounded!

"For surely, O Lord, you bless the righteous; you surround them with your favor as with a shield." Ps 5:12

When I was young, I used to love watching Star Trek. It was so cool the way they had those futuristic inventions. One of those was a force shield. It was a shield of energy that surrounded the spaceship and wouldn't allow anything through, either in or out.

When we put our faith in Jesus Christ, we became righteous. Not because we're so good, or so pure, or so holy. We became righteous because of what Christ did. He purifies us from all unrighteousness, and so the Heavenly Father sees us as righteous, because He looks at us through the filter of Christ's blood.

God has given us a shield that surrounds us. That shield is His favor. He gives it to us freely. It's like when we first began dating our spouse. We looked on them with favor, and because we favored them, we gave special attention and care to him or her. We looked for ways to show them our love, and ways to do special things for them, and to give them unique gifts we knew they'd enjoy.

The Lord blesses us in many distinctive ways as well. He knows what we'll appreciate, and goes out of His way to provide them for us. We gave proof that you're righteous, because God *blesses* the righteous. Because the Lord sees us through that cleansing lens of the blood of Christ, He will bless us, and He has surrounded us with His favor.

No matter where you go, you're surrounded by His favor. At work, you have His favor. At home, you have His favor. In the car, you have His favor. Out hunting, you have His favor. Shopping for your favorite clothes, you have His favor. It's everywhere; you can't step outside of it unless you step into sin. And we're not about to do that.

So go, and enjoy being surrounded by God's favor.

Prayer: Lord, help us to remember your favor, and we thank you so much for it…

Apr 22
Wonderful Love

"Like an apple tree among the trees of the forest is my lover among the young men... His banner over me is love." SS 2:3a & 4b

"How much more pleasing is your love than wine, and the fragrance of your perfume than any spice!" SS 4:10b-c

If you haven't searched through Song of Songs for eloquent phrases to enhance your intimate love life, then it's high time you did. Both of you can learn creative new ways to express your love for each other. Not all of the phrases will fit your spouse, but they'll certainly give you fresh ideas to spark your own creativity. You can adapt some of that poetic prose to fit your situation.

Words are the beginning and completion of romantic love. You began your infatuation with quiet utterances of love, and still today, when you've been intimate, you conclude your special time with assurances of that undying love you still possess for each other. This complimentary articulation of your deepest emotions is the lifeblood of a truly great romance.

You can see the same types of virtues in your husband as the beloved woman does for her lover. And you can see the same beauty and lovely traits in your wife that the lover sees in his beloved. The key is to express those thoughts. They can be in notes, or in gifts that symbolize your feelings, or they can be spoken, but they will require words. The more you use the spoken word, the more they will come into being.

For example, when you tell your spouse you feel such overwhelming love you can't even express it, you'll feel that overwhelming love. When you talk about her beauty, or you compliment how handsome he is, you'll begin to see that attractiveness more and more. Your spoken word will gear you towards what you speak.

Find ways to express your feelings for one another, and make it a habit to do so daily. Search out new ways to compliment each other, and you'll find new feelings arising deep within your hearts.

Prayer: Lord, we know you designed us to enjoy romantic love. Give us the words and expressions to enhance that intimacy...

Apr 23
Whose Precepts Are You Following?

"These people honor me with their lips, but their hearts are far from me. They worship me in vain; their teachings are but rules taught by men.' You have let go of the commands of God and are holding on to the traditions of men." Mk 7:6b-8

This was Jesus talking in this passage of scripture. The Pharisees and teachers of the law had come up with literally hundreds of laws and traditions, on top of the Mosaic Law. They were so caught up in following their own manmade rules that they were neglecting the morals and principles of God's precepts.

We can get caught up in the same situation if we aren't careful. It's so easy to start following a tradition, and we become comfortable with tradition, because we know what to expect, then. We've known people who went to church on Sunday morning, and then went out for lunch with friends afterward. It got to a point where, they might miss the worship service, but they'd sure be there for the lunch. We look at that and think, "Well, that's just ridiculous." Yes it is, but in different areas, and other ways, we can get caught up in the same type of traditions.

The Pharisees and teachers were focused on 'church rules'. We have some of those ourselves. Our church has this routine in the worship service, and heaven help us if we do it a different way one Sunday. If it throws us completely off balance when that happens, it's likely a sign our thinking is following the wrong path.

The Lord is interested in our hearts. He's much less interested in how, and why, and where, and what style, our worship may be. He *is* interested in whether we focus on *Him*, and worship Him in spirit and in truth. He *is* interested in what we do for Him, and even more interested in *why* we do it, and what our attitude is in the process.

Rather than letting go of God's commands, lets leave behind the habits and traditions that interfere with our worship and service to Jesus Christ. When we tune in to pleasing Him, and serving Him, and loving Him with our whole heart, we'll know we're on the right track, following *His* precepts.

Prayer: Father, give us the guidance of your Holy Spirit in our walk, our worship, and our service to you. Make sure we're following you, and not manmade habits…

Apr 24
Be Faithful in the Little Things

"'A man of noble birth went to a distant country to have himself appointed king and then to return.
Well done, my good servant!' his master replied. 'Because you have been trustworthy in a very small matter, take charge of ten cities.'" Lk 19:12 & 17

If you've been in church more than three times (outside of Christmas and Easter), you're familiar with this parable. While the master was away, he gave money to some of his servants to invest and to build a good return while he was gone. The first servant invested his money, and over the course of the time the master was away, he doubled his investment. That prompted the good opinion, and the acclamation of the master.

"When the cat's away, the mice will play." We've all heard this saying. We do have a tendency to get pretty lax in our efforts when the boss is gone. When we don't have a supervisor, or anyone we have to give account to standing over us, we tend to relax and coast, kind of go on a mini vacation while at work.

This servant in the parable didn't do that, though. He went to work and gave good effort to bring a substantial return for his boss. He was trustworthy. He was faithful in the little things. Because he was, he was rewarded with a great area of responsibility.

Do you desire to do more for God, to serve Him in greater capacity? Then be sure you're giving your best where you're serving now. If you're not serving now, then find a place to start, because God's most likely not going to give you a large ministry until you prove yourself.

How are you doing in this area? Are you being trustworthy in the very small matters? Or are you on vacation at work? Do you give it your best, so that when your supervisor returns, you can show him how much has been accomplished?

There are rewards waiting for the one who is faithful in the little things. Do your best for Jesus' sake. Apply it to every area of your life. In your worship, in your godly example, in your giving, in your marriage relationship, in your parenting, in your work, and in your play, be trustworthy. Be faithful in even the smallest things.

Prayer: Dear Lord, give us the good sense and the self-discipline to be faithful in every area, and at every level…

Apr 25
What a Creation

"For since the creation of the world God's invisible qualities—his eternal power and divine nature—have been clearly seen, being understood from what has been made, so that men are without excuse." Rom 1:20

So many people choose to ignore what's before their very eyes. The whole of creation cries out that there has to be God.

Have you marveled at how many people are on a "spiritual journey", seeking God in any and every place they can search—except the Bible? Why is it that men and women everywhere pretend to be spiritually aware, searching, but automatically exclude looking at Jesus? There's a reason, of course. It's because the wisdom of God is foolishness to those who are perishing, and people the world over prove that point day after day.

Glenda and I love to hike. We take any reasonable opportunity to get out and do so. When we're traveling, we schedule hiking into our travels as often as we can, to refresh ourselves and take a break from driving, but also to enjoy the awe-inspiring beauty God has created. It was made for us to enjoy. And it's a time when we get to compliment the Lord on His handiwork. When you get out and look around, it's just flat amazing!

You ought to go and do things together, too. It's not just pleasant, it's therapeutic for your physical health (if you can walk), and it's energizing for your love relationship. When we're out hiking, we talk, and we talk about anything and everything. Nothing is out of bounds. We'll discuss anything from kids, to politics, to concerts, to the economy, to food, to sports, to sex (oh, I already said sports), to global warming, or the lack thereof (it's very cold as I'm writing this).

Hiking may not be your thing, but it's good for you as a couple to make a point of doing things together regularly. Oh, and I have it on good authority that the Lord loves it when you're out enjoying nature and you acknowledge and compliment Him on what a great job He did. You can't help but see the Lord's power and majesty from what He's made.

Prayer: Father, give us open eyes to see your handiwork all around us, and appreciate and enjoy it together…

Apr 26
Let It Die Down

"Without wood a fire goes out; without gossip a quarrel dies down." Pr 26:20

How many times we've seen a war get started, when the dispute could have faded away, we can't even count. Human nature has us enlisting soldiers when we have an argument, busily scurrying about lining folks up on our side of the issue. We don't necessarily want to resolve anything; we just want to make sure we win.

You've heard the old adage, "You can win the battle, but lose the war." Nothing could be more accurate when two sides line up for battle over what is really a meaningless conflict. We go to war, and we can really bloody each other up, but in the end, nothing is resolved, and both parties end up with hurt feelings, wounded emotions, and bitter attitudes. We've won the battle, but we've truly lost the war, because the good relationship that was possible previously, is now beyond our reach, or our ability to mend.

Just as a fire goes out when it's starved of fuel, when the wood isn't replenished, so a quarrel dies out without its fuel as well. The fuel of that conflict is gossip. Running around telling people the awful things the other person did, or said, or didn't do when they ought to have, is the process of enlisting fighters for our side. Gathering together and continually hashing over what happened, getting ourselves all worked up, is the fuel the quarrel thrives on.

To end the process, you have to refuse to participate in the fueling. Don't line up people to battle with you. Don't talk about the issue. Ignore it, and it will fade away. Most things that end up in huge disputes are just silly, insignificant issues anyway.

We've seen this process in churches, in businesses, and in marriages. It's occurred in ours, and it's probably occurred in yours. But the relationship suffers when a small quarrel is blown out of proportion, and not only with each other, but with your mutual friends as well. When you have issues, big or small, gossip will *never* help the situation. Find ways to quietly resolve any dispute between yourselves gently, lovingly, and humbly. Let it die down. You'll benefit tremendously from the good relationship that ensues.

Prayer: Lord Jesus, give us the restraint to gently, quietly resolve our issues without dragging others into the fray…

Apr 27
Do You Recognize Jesus?

"When Elizabeth heard Mary's greeting, the baby leaped in her womb, and Elizabeth was filled with the Holy Spirit." Lk 1:41

We're blessed by the fact that, if we've put our faith in Jesus Christ, He's given us His Holy Spirit. The gift of the fullness of the Spirit is ours for the asking, and it's continuous.

Elizabeth was granted the Holy Spirit, and she immediately recognized in the Spirit that Mary was carrying the Messiah. She blesses Mary because of that, and also the child (Jesus) that Mary was bearing.

When we become believers, Jesus lives within our hearts. That means He resides in the hearts of other believers, as well. When we meet other Christians, as we do all over the country singing, we find an instant fellowship and sense of 'family' with them. We recognize Jesus in them, and our spirits sense that bond we have in Christ.

You too, have that same perception capability. You're able, through the Holy Spirit, to see Jesus in others, and to know you have that 'family of Christ' bond.

The problem we run in to, sometimes, is that we don't turn on our awareness. We can go through our days in a fog, not noticing other believers, because we're not looking.

When you're driving, and it's foggy out, you can still see if you're concentrating, but if you don't pay close attention, you can miss the most important signs. Like, where the shoulder of the road is, or where your corner is to turn, or that there's a deer on the road right in front of you.

Similarly, when going through our busy days, we have to concentrate on seeing other believers. Otherwise, we may not recognize that we've just passed Jesus.

Do you recognize Him?

Prayer: Jesus, give us the awareness to recognize you when you're near in others…

Apr 28
Are You Rich Toward God?

"But God said to him, 'You fool! This very night your life will be demanded from you. Then who will get what you have prepared for yourself?' This is how it will be with anyone who stores up things for himself but is not rich toward God." Lk 12:20-21

In this parable, Jesus tells about a man who was so blessed with prosperity, he was trying to figure out what to do with all his crops and goods. He decided to build big new barns to store it in, and then sit back and enjoy his wealth. We see that the man gives no thought to others, but is focused entirely on himself. He had plenty of money and goods to relax for years and take life easy, eating, drinking, and making merry.

The problem the man didn't know about was that God was taking his life from him that very night. Who was going to get all that wealth then? Someone else would enjoy the benefits of his labor, because he couldn't take it with him.

Jesus gives us a warning here. This is how it will be with those who store up 'stuff' for themselves, without being faithful to God, and to His kingdom work. There's a core principle here. All of life is not about you! The world does not revolve around you, or your wants and desires. Greed is not a virtue we can build our lives upon. It isn't a virtue at all.

Let us discuss a bit more about wealth. Wealth is not bad. Money is just a tool like any other to be used. It can be used for good, or it can be used for bad. If you utilize your money for selfish reasons, it's used for bad. If it's used to provide your needs, fund God's house, and help others, it's being used for good. God will bless those whose priority is faithfulness to His principles, bringing in the whole tithe and offerings. He has to, because His word says He will. He doesn't have to because *we* say so, but because *He's* chosen to, and told us He will. When that happens, God may bless us with even more wealth, so that we in turn can bless others, as well as leaving an inheritance for our children's children.

We as a couple need to remember that we're about the Father's business, and as we're obedient to Him, and to His desires involving money, we can rest assured that we're rich toward God. As Jesus said, "a man's life does not consist in the abundance of his possessions." Lk 12:15b

Our wealth lies in the treasures we store up in Heaven. Be rich toward God.

Prayer: Heavenly Father, lead us into constant faithfulness with our finances, putting you first even in our money…

Apr 29
Stay Alert!

"Be self-controlled and alert. Your enemy the devil prowls around like a roaring lion looking for someone to devour." I Pet 5:8

"For we are not unaware of his schemes." II Cor 2:11b

In your marriage, it's appropriate to keep the attitude that it's *you two against the world.* This is an area where Satan excels. He's so good at drawing husband and wife slowly, but surely, apart, if you give him the chance. That's why we *must* be self-controlled and alert.

A godly marriage is a great picture of the Lord's faithfulness. When we're centered on Him, and living and loving as He instructs us, we're a blessing; we're a blessing to each other, and to those who surround us. In this setting we're able to follow the Lord's instructions for raising godly, Christian children. We have the opportunity to impact our church family and our community for wonderful, positive things.

We have to be aware of the fact that Satan is a schemer. He doesn't normally attack us with an all out frontal assault. He knows that won't work. But he's good at subtlely drawing us away one tiny step at a time. A little compromise with that guy, a tiny step towards that gal, bit by bit he can slowly lead us away from each other. That cup of coffee can be dynamite that eventually explodes in your face. That 'luncheon meeting' to discuss work can be the first step into a slick slide that you find you can't stop.

We have to be careful to never do anything that can detract from our marriage relationship. Don't do things with members of the opposite sex one on one. Never meet them anywhere that's not *very* public, if you absolutely have to meet them for some reason. If you have an attraction for someone, then exert the self-control to immediately remove yourself from that person, and stay away from him/her. It's much easier to do that in the very beginning than it is later on. Don't let the devil devour you, or your marriage, because he *will* if you let him. He'll give you every rationalization why you must do this or that, or that it's ok because of thus. Don't kid yourself, and don't let the devil con you with shallow justifications.

If you'll stay on constant guard against the devil's subtle schemes, you can seal your marriage away from any disaster that he can destroy you with. Outside disasters can be handled together. Inside disasters are extremely difficult to weather. So be alert to the signs that bad weather may head your way. Practice habits that insulate your marriage from devouring schemes of the devil.

Prayer: God, help us to exercise the self-control to do those things that honor my spouse, and help us stay alert, so that we're not taken in by Satan's schemes...

Apr 30
Speak an Apt Word

"A word aptly spoken is like apples of gold in settings of silver." Pr 25:11

Doesn't that make a beautiful picture? Apples of gold in settings of silver. That would really be pretty. Can you see it? Now, think about the value of apples of *gold* in settings of *silver*. They're worth a fortune!

Speaking an apt word means to say just the right thing at the perfect time. If that's happened for you, you're aware of the value of that perfect phrase given in the opportune moment. It blessed you beyond anything you could have imagined.

To our husband or wife, we have many more chances to speak that apt word than we do with others, simply by our proximity to our love. It can also mean we've missed hundreds of opportunities to do so. The importance of finding ways to bless our husband or wife with aptly spoken words can't be overstated. We can influence our spouse's entire day by the things we say. We have the power to help them walk in good humor, or to walk in sadness. We can give them victory, or defeat. Our tongue can be a blessing or a curse to our spouse. Even when we say critical things that aren't true, and our spouse refuses to receive it, it still detracts from their positive outlook, because of our love for each other. When we say uplifting things to each other, we *will* move the other to happier attitudes.

Brighten your husband's day with an encouraging word. Lift your wife's heart by complimenting her in some way. When he's faced a difficult day at work, your assurance of your love and admiration will strengthen him. When she's been troubled with a conflict, you can help her immensely by listening to her, and empathizing with her difficulties by speaking words of affirmation to her. These types of conversation are words aptly spoken. And when you've received that encouragement, you understand the value of those words.

When you receive an apt word from your spouse, be sure you tell him or her, "That was like an apple of gold in a setting of silver."

Prayer: Lord Jesus, have your Holy Spirit gift us with apt words for each other, that we might lift and brighten our spouse's outlook...

May 1
The Lord Will Repay

"Alexander the metalworker did me a great deal of harm. The Lord will repay him for what he has done. You too should be on your guard against him, because he strongly opposed our message." II Tim 4:14-15

Remember those times when someone's done you wrong, said something mean, cheated you, stole from you, lied to you, or harmed you in myriad other ways? We want to find some appropriate way to get even, to show them they can't get away with their wicked behavior. We can be quite creative in our minds, thinking of things that will really get them.

Notice, this doesn't deny that people will oppose us, or do harm to us. Quite the opposite; it shows us that there are people who will interfere, fight against, and harm us if they can. Paul warns us to guard against such wicked people.

We've often talked about the need for us to be forgivers. We do need to be careful not to hold grudges, because it will hurt us more than the person we despise. When you have a real enemy, someone whose desire is to cause you hurt, they'd be happy to hear you can't sleep, are stressed out, and generally a mess due to the commotion they've caused you. Don't let them win even that victory. Your attitude has to be bigger. You have to tell yourself, "I don't have to worry about that problem. It's not going to steal my joy. I'm an overcomer in God's strength. I can do all things through Christ who strengthens me. The Lord is my strength, my defender, in whom I trust."

Finally, the main reason we don't have to fuss or bother about getting even is that, the Lord will repay him or her for the evil they've done to us. If you look back through the Old Testament, you'll find all kinds of examples of the Lord's ability and creativity in finding appropriate punishments. From striking people with leprosy, to banishing them from where they want to be most, to stripping them of power, to taking away their wealth, and ultimately, taking their lives. In the end, it's our responsibility to let God take care of it, and let's face it; He can handle it so much better than we'd ever be able to. Who knows, when we've been gracious about a problem, and not played the tit-for-tat game; then when God gets ahold of that person, they may even turn their life over to Him, and that's what we're all about.

Be on your guard, and let the Lord do the repaying.

Prayer: Gracious Father, give us the correct thinking to let you take care of our enemies, because we know you don't want us worrying and fretting about them. We give these issues to you to deal with...

May 2
We Live by Faith

"The life I live in the body, I live by faith in the Son of God, who loved me and gave himself for me." Gal 2:20b

Does your faith permeate every part of your being and of your life? Does it dominate your mind and your heart throughout your days? Does it affect your decisions? Does it move you to proper actions?

When we interact with coworkers or friends, our conversation should be colored by our faith. We should be keeping in mind to speak only those things that honor the Lord, and which build up others. We ought to avoid participating in rude jokes, and coarse jests.

When we make decisions, again we're to be doing those things that honor Jesus Christ. Make wise decisions about where you go, what you do, what you purchase, how you dress, even the music you listen to (We hear Gary & Glenda cd's are quite good—lol).

Live life in ways that glorify Christ.

Your faith should move you to action too. Because of the sacrifice of Christ, out of thankfulness to Him, we do godly things. When you see a need, and you can help, then take the action to do so. In your family, make it a practice to go to a Bible based church each Sunday where you can be spiritually fed, and where you can serve. Work hard, and do good work at your place of employment. Be on time for appointments, and show respect for the one(s) you're meeting by doing so. Good actions are an outgrowth of your faith.

In your marriage and in your family, both immediate and extended, your faith should be obvious to all. You don't have to wear it on your sleeve, but it should be apparent to all by your speech and your actions that you follow Jesus as Lord. It will be immediately shown by not only what you do, but by those things you don't do. The joy in your life should be a picture to all. Again we say if you're happy, if you have joy in the Lord, be sure you let your face and your voice know.

In the Son of God, we have all of life. It's by faith in Jesus we live in this body, and we enjoy our life with, and in, Him. We live by faith.

Prayer: Lord Jesus, we thank you that we can live by faith in you, for you bless us in every way…

May 3
Filled with Power

"But as for me, I am filled with power, with the Spirit of the Lord." Mic 3:8a

We've been given the Holy Spirit, the Comforter, since we gave our lives to Christ Jesus, and put our faith in Him. The more we make Him lord of our lives, the more we concentrate on walking in obedience, the more He gives us power.

Being filled with power gives us assurance in our faith. It's not power like magic, where we can do anything our minds conceive, supernaturally. It's the power to effect (no, we don't mean affect) God's kingdom results in others, and to effect self-control and faith in our own lives as well. We produce, or cause to happen, things in ours, and others, lives for Jesus as the Holy Spirit leads us.

It works like this for example. You find out someone's in need of a miracle of healing. There's no other hope. The doctors can't do any more, and there's no natural path for them to recover. We begin to pray, and believe God for his touch; the Lord moves, and provides healing for that person. Even the doctors describe it as a miracle.

Here's another example. You learn someone needs a financial miracle. You begin to pray, you speak to others on their behalf, and the Lord touches someone, or several someones, to open their hearts and wallets to provide the needed money to meet that need.

In each instance, you've utilized the power available in the Spirit to bring a miracle into that life. No, you didn't do it yourself, in your own strength, but you accessed the power we've been given in the Lord to bring about kingdom solutions.

As a married couple, we have even more power when we agree together in prayer, and when we work together to compound our effectiveness in our actions. We can do even greater things for Jesus than a person by himself or herself is able to. Work together, and agree together, because you're filled with power, with the Spirit of the Lord.

Prayer: Lord, help us to effect things for you through our prayers and our actions, as we seek your guidance in providing miracles for people, because that brings praise to you...

May 4
Rejoice in Others Salvation

"The man who formerly persecuted us is now preaching the faith he once tried to destroy. And they praised God because of me." Gal 1:23b-24

Have you ever known someone who was an absolute heathen, mean, nasty, dishonest, and obnoxious? Then they got saved, gloriously born again, turned around in Christ, and we found it hard to believe or accept that such a complete reprobate could change. We can have trouble accepting that someone so wicked was born again, and that God changed his or her life.

The early Christians had the same difficulty. Paul, who was the nemesis of Christians, watching over the deaths of so many, actively seeking them out to imprison, stone, or drag back to the Sanhedrin, was now saved and preaching the very gospel he had tried to stamp out.

Isn't that why Jesus came? He came to save sinners. As Jesus said, "it's not the healthy who need a doctor, but the sick." The righteous (self) didn't think they needed salvation, but the sinners *knew* they needed a Savior. I don't know how you felt, but I was very much aware that I was not good enough to get to Heaven, and that I wasn't worth the sacrifice Christ made for me. I still know I'm not worth that sacrifice, but I'm so thankful for His grace to me.

Where are you in your attitude about God's grace? Did you need a lot of forgiveness, or just a little? Were you pretty good, so it wasn't as important? Sometimes, those of us who grew up in Christian homes don't comprehend our need for Christ as much as those who grew up outside the church. They *know* they're sinners. We tend to think we're pretty okay.

Often those who are saved from lives of terrible sin, whether lives of alcohol, or sex, or drugs, or theft, or whatever they were involved in, have such thankful hearts. They're such joyous servants as they minister God's grace to others. They can have such an ability to preach, or evangelize, or serve in other capacities, because they *know* what it means to be completely delivered.

When we see that in someone's life, we should rejoice with them, help and encourage them, and praise God that another sinner has been saved.

Prayer: Dear Lord, help us not to be skeptical when sinners are saved, but accept them as brothers and sisters in Christ, and rejoice with them…

May 5
Is Your Mouth Clean?

"What goes into a man's mouth does not make him 'unclean,' but what comes out of his mouth, that is what makes him 'unclean.'" Mt 15: 11

"But the things that come out of the mouth come from the heart, and these make a man 'unclean.' For out of the heart come evil thoughts, murder, adultery, sexual immorality, theft, false testimony, slander. These are what make a man 'unclean.'" Mt 15:18-20a

My grandparents on my Mom's side lived on the same farmstead as we did when I was growing up. Grandpa used to take a handful of dirt, slap it on his tongue, and stick out his tongue just to show us kids that dirt wouldn't hurt you (he later died of an infection he got from ingesting soil—not really). But it *would* always make an impression on us. I later used the same example with my kids. I *did* learn that putting dirt in my mouth wasn't what made my mouth unclean, or dirty. It really *is* the things that come out of our mouths.

We usually think of how unsanitary some of the things we eat or accidentally swallow are. But those are just bodily functions. Think in terms of our heart, our spirit. This is an area that, what we put into our minds, really makes a difference. When we speak, we let flow what's in our heart.

If our thinking is spent on wicked things, if we watch sinful things, or listen to secular, dehumanizing music, if we read or look at sexually explicit books or magazines, if we figure out how to get away with stealing something, if we lie to others, and tell untrue, negative things about other people, then we'll tend to spew those evil things when we talk.

When we spend our time listening to gospel music or biblical radio programs, when we watch things that are positive with good morals, when we read godly material, or books that are entertaining while avoiding ungodly themes, when we're firm about pursuing honesty in our actions and our speech, when we behave in a manner that honors our spouse and the Lord, then we'll speak good things, because that's what'll be in our heart to draw from.

If your heart is clean, then your mouth will be clean. And you'll be able to tell by what comes out of your mouth.

Prayer: Heavenly Father, fill our hearts with good things that honor you and keep our mouths clean. Let us speak 'clean' things only…

May 6
Rules for Husbands and Wives?

"Wives submit to your husbands, as is fitting in the Lord. Husbands, love your wives and do not be harsh with them." Col 3:18-19

Paul is big into this whole submission thing. And Husband, don't think you're exempt, because elsewhere he says we're to submit to one another, and if you follow the instruction in this verse, then you'll be submitting to God's will.

We don't always think in these terms, but we submit to others most of the time. When we follow the speed limit while driving, we submit to the government's rule (yes, rare we know). When we do what our work supervisor asks us to, we submit to his or her rule. When we go to church and let the usher guide us to a pew, we submit to his decision as to where to seat us. When we count our items to make sure we don't have too many for the express lane at the store, and follow their guidelines, we submit to their request. We could go on and on.

Why is it fitting that we should submit? This tells us it's fitting in the Lord. It keeps peace in our family, and shows a gentle spirit, which is pleasing to our Heavenly Father. There are certain times, not often, thankfully, when someone has to submit, because for some reason our thinking on a subject or issue is intractable. Conflict is kept to a minimum when we submit. That eliminates the wedge that inevitably occurs between the Lord and us, and also between us and the one whom we're in dispute with, and keeps our fellowship sweet with both.

We frequently hear of husbands whose manner with their wives is harsh. There are some who can be overbearing, rude, and brutally frank. Thankfully, they are a small minority, but if you're one of those husbands, then your wife is unfortunate indeed. As husbands, we're to love our wives. Love is not selfish, or rude, or short-tempered, but it's gentle (controlled strength), and patient, and it's kind. A husband's love does what's in the wife's best interest. When you'll do that, kindly and consistently, you'll find it's much easier for your wife to submit when necessary.

These instructions are given to us to keep our home pleasant and comfortable, and to provide a great environment in which to raise our children, and to set an example of Christ centeredness.

Prayer: Lord, help us to remember our responsibility in following your precepts. We know they're given for our good…

May 7
Use Your Tongue

"The tongue has the power of life and death, and those who love it will eat its fruit." Pr 18:21

You have such power in your tongue. With it you can bless, or you can curse. As children of the Most High God, we're called to refrain from using our tongue to curse. We're to bless, for this is what we're called to. In more practical terms, these are some examples of how to use your tongue for life, and for blessing.

Your wife is feeling poorly about her looks, for whatever unknown reason (to us). Husband, you have the power to give her life by telling her she looks great, and she'll always be beautiful to you.

Your husband is concerned that he's not as sharp as he once was (he may never have been, we don't really know). Wife, you have the power to bolster his confidence by telling him how bright you know he is (it'll help if you can give an example).

Your child is struggling with an issue that's causing them to doubt themselves. Parent, you have the power to persuade him or her that there's a solution, and assuring the child that they're smart enough, and able to accomplish anything they set their mind to (this is almost always true).

You have friends who have had a traumatic event, and fear they can't get through it. You guys have the power to give them life by assuring them the Lord loves them and cares about them, and that you do too. You can give them life by encouraging them, and offering any assistance you're able to give.

Coworkers may be floundering at work, and feel they'll fail. You have the power to give that associate life by reorienting them, encouraging them to refocus, and setting them on a new course with the knowledge that they can succeed at their tasks.

We encourage you to continually practice using your tongues for life with each other. You'll reap extraordinary benefits by using your gift of blessing at home. That's fruit you'll enjoy! You can give new and improved life to your relationship by utilizing the gift of your tongues.

Prayer: We pray, God, that your Spirit will give us blessings and encouraging words to pour out from our tongues. Allow us to give life...

May 8
Love = Obey

"Jesus replied, "If anyone loves me, he will obey my teaching. My Father will love him, and we will come to him and make our home with him. He who does not love me will not obey my teaching. These words you hear are not my own; they belong to the Father who sent me." Jn 14:23-24

There is an acid test for whether or not we love the Lord. It's simply obedience. This verse couldn't be any clearer on that point. If we love Jesus, we'll obey His teaching. This message doesn't come from Jesus. He's just passing along the Father's message. Succinct and to the point isn't it?

How can we obey if we don't know the teaching of Jesus? How can we know if we don't read the Bible? How can we read if we don't discipline ourselves to make time? This is such an essential part of walking with Christ that we keep coming back to it. We just can't overstate the importance of spending a little time in God's word each day. If you've lost your momentum, now's the time to start again. If you have a good Bible reading streak going, then congratulations on having made a great start.

Our children are obedient to us because they've spent time with us, and learned from our words and behavior, what we desire for them. They've picked up how we expect them to act, how we want them to speak, how polite we desire them to be, how quick to respond to our requests, how hard they should work, how acceptable various types of play are, and on and on. They learned because we were able to spend time with them teaching.

We can't just glean from the Lord what we need to know, because we can't spend time walking and talking and working and playing with Him. The disciples were able to learn from Him that way, but we've been given the Word in written form, to teach us what we need to know, so that we, too, can be obedient to Christ.

We know from our own children, if we have kids, whether or not they love and respect us, or if they've become self-centered and disrespectful by their obedience level.

Our Heavenly Father judges us the same way. He knows how much we love Him by our level of obedience to Christ's teaching.

Prayer: Lord, help us to stay in your word, and learn your desires, so that we can walk in obedience to you…

May 9
Constant

"Jesus Christ is the same yesterday and today and forever." Heb 13:8

In a world that is so rapidly changing in so many ways, isn't it nice to know that some things will stay the same? We never have to worry about whether God loves us. We know salvation is always available to whosoever will come. We know the Holy Spirit is our continual comfort, and giver of knowledge. And we know Jesus will *never* change.

Keeping up with technology is a full time job in itself. My grandparents went through changes that were phenomenal. They began life in the era of horses and carriages for transportation, the postal service for communication, and medical techniques that were almost as dangerous as the disease or trauma. In their lifetime, they saw the advent of the radio, and eventually the television, then the general expansion of telephone service to everyone. The communication age was born. They went from horse and buggy to automobiles. They went from plowing with horses or oxen to farming with tractors. They saw the explosion of medicine, polio virtually wiped out in the United States, tuberculosis completely gone (although there's been a recent resurgence traced to illegal immigration), measles nearly eliminated; surgery so primitive, to heart surgery so sophisticated, it strains the imagination, and organ transplant techniques that stretch credulity. They died in the eighties. Think of the changes just since then. Personal computers, the Internet, and cell phones that have become unbelievable. Satellites and space travel have become commonplace.

There have been many changes in our culture and society too. Most are for the negative. Over fifty percent of marriages end in divorce. Unmarried pregnancies have skyrocketed. Church attendance has plummeted. Violent crime has increased. Biblical morals as a whole have decreased.

In the midst of all that change, though, people are actually still the same. We still want nice families, good marriages, wholesome kids, good jobs, sound financial footing, and a circle of friends to enjoy. The onslaught of the world's wicked values makes it extremely difficult to attain, though. And we're still all sinners in need of a savior.

Isn't it nice to know that Jesus is the same yesterday and today and forever? He's the *one* who is constant!

Prayer: Jesus, we thank you that you're still the same, that you always will be, and that your blood can cover every sin. Help us to keep you in our hearts, and on our minds as we face the world…

May 10
It's My Love

"Who is this that appears like the dawn, fair as the moon, bright as the sun?" SS 6:10a

Outrageous flattery is never wasted when used on your spouse!

You know your forehead has tripled in size. And you've also noticed your chest has slid down to your stomach area. You may have weakly lost the strength in your arms. The fleetness of your legs may have run off and left.

You know you're not a size five any longer. That statuesque figure may have lost its stature. You've noticed that the firmness you had has softened. Perky has given way to pokey. Silky smooth is turning to parchment like character lines.

Thankfully, we don't actually see each other that way, though. Just as inside, we don't feel the aging process as keenly as it shows on the outside, we don't notice the flaws in each other that have been accruing as the years roll by.

Your husband still sees that young, beautiful, lovely girl he met when he was still growing toward maturity. Anything else is just excess that his mind discards as unnecessary to him. You're his ravishing beauty.

Your wife doesn't see that lack of strength, or missing mane, or any extra pounds that have added to your build. She still sees that handsome, virile young man she fell in love with. You're her knight in shining armor.

After all these years, it still amazes us that when one of us walks into a room where the other is, we're drawn inexorably to each other. My wife is the first person I notice. We instantly connect when we come into the other's presence. Our eyes search each other out and meet. That's because each of us is the most important person to the other, and always will be.

You've probably heard the old saying, "Flattery will get you nowhere." It's not true! Flattery with your spouse will usually get you anywhere. Just make sure you're going somewhere worthwhile. And be sure to use it as liberally as you need to. It's very cost effective to use.

When my Love appears, it's like the breathtaking beauty of the dawn appearing, fair as the moon, as bright as the noonday sun.

Prayer: Dear Lord, we thank you for our spouse, for the wonderful partner they are to us, and for the joy we feel when we come together…

May 11
Bad Is Actually Good?

"But the ship struck a sandbar and ran aground. The bow stuck fast and would not move, and the stern was broken to pieces by the pounding of the surf." Ac 27:41

Bad deal, right? Sometimes, really bad circumstances overtake us. Paul is a prisoner, on his way to Rome on appeal to Caesar, and the ship, which shouldn't have sailed at that time of year, was swept up in a storm. The storm was so violent that all hope was lost. With 276 people on board, they decided to run the ship aground on a beach, having spent 14 days in this terrible storm already. They didn't make the beach, but because they did as Paul asked, all were saved, and made it to land.

Bad deal, right? When they got to land, the islanders came and helped, built a fire to warm them, and while that was going on, a snake crawled out of the heated wood, and bit Paul, fastening itself to his hand. The people thought it meant he was a murderer and deserved to die.

Bad deal, right? Well, not really. God often uses bad circumstances to accomplish good things for His kingdom. The people watched Paul, after he'd shaken the snake off into the fire, and saw that not only did he not die, he didn't even get sick. They thought he must be some kind of god.

Because the ship broke up and sank, they were stuck on the isle of Malta for three months. Publius, the chief official there, entertained them. His father was very sick with fever and dysentery. Paul went in to him, laid hands on him, and he was healed. When that happened, the rest of the sick on the island came to him and were cured.

Because of the shipwreck, because of the snakebite with no ill effect, and then because of God's healing of many, Paul was afforded a three-month opportunity window to preach the good news of Jesus to the islanders of Malta.

This verse is an example of how God sometimes takes bad and works something wonderful out of it. In our lives, we've experienced similar things. What seems like a bad thing turns out for our good, without our ever thinking about it.

We had an ice storm. People were stranded on the interstate, and we went and picked up four of them, brought them home, and kept them overnight, along with another who made it to our house. We were leaving on a tour to North Dakota in three days, and didn't think we had enough money to get to our concert site. Those folks who stayed with us bought five cd's. They left. We headed for North Dakota. When we arrived in Bismarck for the worship concert, between the two of us, we had six dollars left.

God used a bad circumstance for good.

Prayer: God, help us to remember that when bad things happen, they give you a chance to do something great, and we thank you for that…

May 12
We Have What We Ask For

"This is the confidence we have in approaching God: that if we ask anything according to his will, he hears us. And if we know that he hears us—whatever we ask—we know that we have what we asked of him." I Jn 5:14-15

Note that there's a condition on receiving. In this passage, it tells us a number of things. When we're in Christ Jesus, we have confidence in approaching God. We can come boldly to the throne of our Heavenly Dad. There's no fear, no trepidation, no anxiety, no nervousness. He's opened the way, prepared the path, and is waiting for us to come.

Our children don't fear to come to us with a request, particularly one they know we'll grant. Because we love our kids, we don't treat them badly, or verbally abuse them for asking. We just lovingly grant it. No fuss, no muss, no bother.

Here's the trick with our Heavenly Dad. We have to ask according to *His* will. To do that, we first have to know what His will is. But it's great to know that when we ask His will, what He already *wants* us to ask, He hears us. Isn't that simple? He hears us.

Then we have another assurance. We know that if He hears us, we *have* what we asked. Not we *will* have. Not we'll receive it *sometime*. Not *maybe* we'll have it. Not even *no*. We *have* what we asked. In the Lord, even when it isn't instantly revealed, it's as good as done. No, it's even better. It *is* done.

As a couple, together you can more quickly discern what our Heavenly Dad's will is. Between the two of you, as you think about an issue, and talk it out, and verify it agrees with His word, you *can* find His will. He isn't going to it hide from you. He wants to grant those requests you bring to Him that are in accordance with the work He's already doing. You'll be blessed as you seek His will, and as you pray together about it. You've probably got an issue or a situation in mind right now that you need to know our Heavenly Dad's will on. Seek it, and you shall find it. Keep knocking on His door until He reveals it to you. And pray, knowing that you've already received what you've asked. When you pray His will, you have what you ask for.

Prayer: Heavenly Dad, give us the wisdom and insight to know your will for every situation, particularly for…

May 13
Flee from Adultery

"The corrections of discipline are the way to life, keeping you from the immoral woman, from the smooth tongue of the wayward wife. Do not lust in your heart after her beauty or let her captivate you with her eyes...the adulteress preys upon your very life. Can a man scoop fire into his lap without his clothes being burned? Can a man walk on hot coals without his feet being scorched? So is he who sleeps with another man's wife; no one who touches her will go unpunished." Pr 6:23b-29

We're not directing this just to husbands. This has applications for both of you. In these verses, there is a man, and a woman. Each role can also be reversed in real life. But they tell us a lot, and in our society, with television and movies showing us this very scripture, replayed over and over ad infinitum, we need to take some lessons and be on guard.

Wisdom teaches us to commit to a disciplined life. We must be intentional about the way we live. If we don't know where we stand, and what our stand is, we'll almost certainly fall. So decide your standards, line them up with God's design, and live that way.

We see the best looking men imaginable on television and in the movies. The women are chosen for their beauty and sex appeal. Sometimes, we talk about how the looks of actors have diminished over the past several years, but they still know how to catch your eye, and to turn your heads. This tells us not to let that attractiveness captivate your eyes. Don't look twice, and you won't be tempted to follow where your eyes lead.

The immoral woman or man has a smooth tongue. They can flatter you, encourage you, make you feel good about yourself, make you feel attractive, and make you feel desired and wanted. You are desired and wanted, but not for any good purpose. Don't let flattery from one who's not your spouse impress you, and don't stick around to hear any more, because in this case, it's really empty.

Remember, too, the adulteress, or adulterer, preys upon your life. They steal your very life from you, by taking the best you have to offer, using it for their own selfish pleasure, and turning it into something filthy. Don't let someone else be the thief that makes off with your most valuable assets, your romantic love.

It's fitting that this uses the analogy it does. If you sleep with another man's wife, or you sleep with another woman's husband, you're going to get burned. That's a promise you can't possibly evade. When you commit adultery, you're going to be punished, and in many ways.

Faithfulness to your spouse is filled with blessing upon blessing. So follow the corrections of discipline. Flee from adultery!

Prayer: Lord, give us self-discipline in this area, and the wisdom to spot, and get away from, the people who would lead us astray. Bless us with all the good things that faithfulness to each other brings…

May 14
Don't Give Your Pearls to Pigs

"Whoever corrects a mocker invites insult; whoever rebukes a wicked man incurs abuse. Do not rebuke a mocker or he will hate you; rebuke a wise man and he will love you. Instruct a wise man and he will be wiser still; teach a righteous man and he will add to his knowledge." Pr 9:7-9

"Do not give dogs what is sacred; do not throw your pearls to pigs. If you do, they may trample them under their feet, and then turn and tear you to pieces." Mt 7:6

Discernment. That's what's required if we're to follow the instructions contained in these verses. The parallel between the teaching of these Old Testament and New Testament passages is striking.

You've probably seen, or perhaps been involved with, the wasted effort of trying to give wisdom or instruction to someone who's so wicked they just blow it off, and curse you for trying to help. They don't see the value in what you've offered, and hate you for giving it, because they know, deep down inside, that there's a world of difference between you and them. They sense the godliness, and recoil against it, because they're part of those who walk in darkness. When you're that far into the dark, light is revolting to you. Because of their lifestyle, and their sinfulness, they fight back against blessings with insults. Because they're enslaved to the devil, they hate you for your light.

The good news is there are others who are humble, understanding, and accepting of the good things of children of the light. When you correct a wise man, he appreciates it, because he doesn't want to walk in any darkness. He's looking for ways to become wiser. He takes instruction and uses it to add to his knowledge, and will thank you for helping him. The righteous are able to grow through the teaching of others. They'll bless you for it.

What we need is the discernment of the Holy Spirit to be able to ascertain which is which. It's not wise to just toss out sacred thoughts without first insuring that you aren't casting them to the dogs of mockers and wicked men. Learn first who is wicked, and who is righteous, so that you don't inadvertently give your pearls of wisdom to pigs.

Prayer: Holy Spirit, give us your discernment to understand who we're dealing with, whether children of light, or children of darkness…

May 15
Be Joyful Always

"Be joyful always; pray continually; give thanks in all circumstances, for this is God's will for you in Christ Jesus." I Th 5:16-18

There are times when it's good for us to step back, take a breath, and think. Think about all the blessings we have in Christ. He's given us everything.

The body we have, whether good or great, was given to us by Him. No, we didn't use the word bad, because even those who are physically handicapped in some way are living, breathing souls, and every living, human being is an absolute marvel.

The work we have, and the ability to do it, comes from the Lord, too. Likewise, the good things our labor brings us are His gifts.

The family we enjoy is a blessing from God. His word tells us children are our crowns, and whoever gets a wife receives what is good from Him.

The home we live in is by His hand. You may have built it, like we did ours, but the wherewithal to do so comes from the Lord. It's another of his presents to us.

Then there's the ground we walk on, the forest we love to hike in, the flowers that are so beautiful, the breeze that cools us on a hot day, even the very air we breathe; they were all created by God for our use and enjoyment.

Why did the Lord do all of this for us? Two reasons, we think.

First, He's given us every reason, by way of His amazing blessings, to be joyful always. In Him we have everything we need, much of what we want, and beyond that, we have redemption in our living Savior. We can always give thanks, in every circumstance, good or bad, as we talked about a few days ago, because He works all things out for our good.

Secondly, the Lord wants to fellowship with us. That's why we were created, to spend time in communion with Him. He wants to walk with us, and talk with us, as the good friends we are through Christ Jesus, just as He did with Moses.

This is His will for us in Jesus. That alone should move us to be joyful always.

Prayer: Gracious God, we thank you that you have blessed us with every good thing, and we give you praise for the joy you offer us. Help us to walk in that joy continually...

May 16
Finish Strong

"We want each of you to show this same diligence to the very end, in order to make your hope sure. We do not want you to become lazy, but to imitate those who through faith and patience inherit what has been promised." Heb 6:11-12

As we travel life's road, we will have times of smooth sailing, and seasons of difficult terrain. We'll walk in righteousness, and we'll stumble and fall. When we fall, we don't just stay down. We get up again, or the Lord picks us up again. He dusts us off, cleans us up, spit-shines us, and sends us on our way to travel on, and serve on, with Him.

It's important for each of us to continue in our relationship with the Lord, being steadfast in doing the work He's called us to do; making the most of every opportunity He gives us.

The truth is, it's very easy to begin to slack off, to rest a little, and coast a bit when the going gets rough, or we feel tired. The warning is to not let ourselves be lazy. Stay focused. Keep the goal in sight. Keep applying the effort to accomplish our tasks.

Nothing is more disappointing than someone who's served the Lord diligently for years, and then winds down and slides away, losing their devotion and first love for Jesus. That laziness that infiltrates our lives is so *easy*. That's why it happens to so many Christians. Take warning! Don't let that happen to you.

We have a promise of eternal life, and eternal blessings, when we stay faithful and true to the end. We encourage you to stay diligent in your walk, and in doing the good works God has prepared for you to do. Be alert to every chance to bless someone on behalf of Christ. Make your hope sure by being steadfast in Him.

Find others who are strong in the faith, and learn from them. Seek out their heart, find why, where, and how they maintain the joyful service they do. Imitate those attributes that will work for you, and stay connected with the Lord through the reading of His word, prayer, fellowship, and worship.

Keep on keeping on, to the very end. Finish strong!

Prayer: Lord, help us to continue faithfully in our journey with you, doing the tasks you've prepared for us…

May 17
What Are You Sowing?

"A man reaps what he sows. The one who sows to please his sinful nature, from that nature will reap destruction; the one who sows to please the Spirit, from the Spirit will reap eternal life." Gal 6:7b-8

This principle permeates scripture. You harvest what you plant. You're not going to pick apples if you plant beans. You won't get eggs if you raise cattle. You can't drive anywhere in your new television.

No, if you want apples, you have to plant and nurture apple trees. If you want eggs for breakfast, you need to raise chickens. If you want to drive somewhere, you'd have to purchase an automobile.

You're reaping fruit in your marriage right now. What is it? Whatever it is, it's what you've sown. Are you happy with what you're harvesting? Is the fruit sweet, or is it bitter? If you're pleased with what you're receiving, keep planting those same things. If you're not satisfied, then it's time to start planting new seeds.

We recommend you sow seeds of kindness, of generosity, of thoughtfulness, of time, of help, of encouragement, of affection, of politeness, of self-control, of loyalty, and of love. When these are planted in abundance, you'll reap a harvest of enormous proportions, and you'll enjoy fruit more luscious than any you've ever tasted.

We know if we're selfish, self-centered, and careless of the feelings and desires of our spouse, we stand a good chance of destroying our love relationship. Just as in God's kingdom, when we live to please ourselves, destruction is our harvest. When we seek ways to bless our spouse, and show them how much we love, and care for, and cherish him or her each day, we'll reap an overflow of love, and kindness, and gratitude, and affection. Again, as it is in God's realm, when we look for ways of pleasing the Spirit, we then harvest eternal life.

The same holds true in our marriage. We reap death, or we harvest renewing life.

What are you sowing?

Prayer: Father, help us to sow good seeds of godly things, so that we reap eternal life in you, and fresh life in our marriage...

May 18
Behave Worthily

"Whatever happens, conduct yourselves in a manner worthy of the gospel of Christ."
Php 1:27a

When you were kids, how many times did your parents have to tell you to behave? It most likely occurred more than once or twice. How often have you given that instruction to your children? Just once? Well—maybe more than once.

Nothing is more heartwarming than having someone tell you how good your kids are, or how polite they've been, or how well behaved they're being. It honors us as parents, due to it being a reflection of us. Our children, when they conduct themselves well, are using a manner worthy of us, and our family.

When things are going well, it's relatively easy to behave. But look how much more difficult it is when complications arise. Someone treats you rudely, and suddenly it's an exercise in self-control not to respond in kind. Someone calls you a name, or criticizes you, it becomes tough to refrain from self-righteousness, and much more difficult to maintain a polite manner.

What we must keep in mind is, afflictions come. Tough times will hit us occasionally. Complications will enter our lives.

I was at the bank the other day, and complications arose. I had to straighten out a mistake. I had two transactions to do. The second was taking forever. I had an appointment to get to (hate being late). I was feeling impatient. I thought to myself, "be careful, you're a gospel singer, and you never know who's watching. Honor the Lord." The clerk finally finished, came over, and asked me if I was Jackie's dad. Yes, I am. He introduced himself, told me he was a classmate of hers from Ouachita Baptist University, and that he currently worked with her as a youth leader at church. You have no idea the relief that came over me that I had maintained a polite, friendly attitude. That was the Holy Spirit reminding me to conduct myself in a manner worthy of the gospel of Christ.

We all get frustrated at times with the problems that invariably arise. But it's important to maintain the right attitude, and to conduct yourself in a way that honors Jesus Christ. He'll give you the ability to do so. Use it! Behave worthily for Him.

Prayer: Lord Jesus, give us the help we need, the reminders from the Holy Spirit, and the self-control to behave in ways that honor you…

May 19
Do You Have a Good Name?

"A good name is more desirable than great riches; to be esteemed is better than silver or gold." Pr 22:1

Have you decided which name you'd like? Sarah, Brian, Ashley, Joshua, Glenda, Paul, Crystal, Lyam, Brittany, Terrence, Rose, Gary, Hanna, Sean, Xera, Quincy, Cheryl, Adam? What's that? What do you mean, that's not what it's talking about?

What's needed is the roadmap for making the name we already have *be* a good name. We associate names with people we've known, and the character traits they've exhibited. If you've known a Debbie who was mean and selfish when you were a child, you probably still have an instant dislike for the name. You know as an adult that each person has his or her own attributes, but your opinion is automatically colored somewhat by your early life experience. Likewise, if you've known a Steve who was a great guy, friendly, kind, helpful, and gregarious, you instantly feel every Steve you meet is similar, even though in reality, they may be the worst scoundrel you'll ever know.

As folks get to know us, what do they learn? Here's where we get to influence whether we have a good name. If we're honest, and pleasant, and kind, and helpful, and a person of integrity, and prompt, and friendly, then those around us will learn to love us, and we'll have a good name. That means that when someone asks those who know us, they'll give a good, solid, recommendation as to our character. They'll vouch for us.

If you've ever needed a good reference, and didn't have one, you know how valuable a good name is. What do people associate your name with? Do they think you're a reprobate, or a saint? Whichever it is, you can always work to change, or if it's positive, to improve, the good will attached to your name. Only you can do what's necessary to develop your name into a good name.

A good name is more desirable than great riches. Not riches, *great* riches. That good name will open doors that wealth will never be able to. People will give you honor and respect that money can't buy. That's because they'll *trust* you.

Prayer: Heavenly Father, give us the wisdom and the self-control to do what we need to for gaining that good name that you have in mind…

May 20
The Source

"In the beginning God..." Gen 1:1a

You can trace everything back to its source.

For instance, did you know we all have a common ancestor? He was a mariner of sorts, one who built one of the largest vessels ever constructed at the time. He had three sons, and his name was Noah.

Have you heard the story of the scientists who told God they could create life, too? They were pretty smug about it, because this put them on an even keel with the Lord. God told them to go ahead, show Him what they could do. They began by kneeling down and beginning to gather up dust from the ground, at which point God intervened, saying, "Oh no you don't. Create your own dirt."

We have one to whom we should always be thankful. He is the one who is worthy of all of our praise and honor. The one in which we put our trust. The one who gives us life and breathe, and in whom we move and have our being. He is our provider. He is our salvation. He is the author and finisher of our faith.

In short, God is our everything. It all traces back to the Lord. We have life, and it comes from God. We have strength, and it comes from God. We have a spouse, and he or she comes from God. We have food, and it comes from God. We have a home, and it comes from God. We have vegetation around us, and it comes from God. We have wildlife, and domestic animals, and they come from God. We have a world to live on, exactly the right distance from the sun, just the right gravity, with the precise magnetic fields needed, and it comes from God.

The Bible tells us Jesus was in the beginning, and that everything created was done so by Him, our savior, our redeemer, our shepherd and friend.

There's nothing you can think of that doesn't trace its origins back to God. Give Him praise and honor and blessing and worship, for He is the Source.

Prayer: Lord, we're so thankful for all you are, and all you do, and we give you our praise and worship, for you are worthy of our honor...

May 21
Stop Quarrelling

"But avoid foolish controversies and genealogies and arguments and quarrels about the law, because these are unprofitable and useless." Tit 3:9

They say in social circles you should never discuss religion or politics. The reason, as we see it, is because you generally end up frustrated; sorry that your friends don't understand what you do, or believe what you do, and you can go away thinking they're kind of stupid.

In the church, there are those who seem to want to go off on these wide tangents, and it usually seems to be those who don't even have the basics of the faith lined up with their daily life. When you involve yourself with them in a discussion of their pet issue, you tend to find they're always bringing in outside sources who have access to some book, or writing, or more accurate translation of some text, that sheds light and a whole new perspective on this, and surely you must trust them to know where they found these resources is sound and reliable, and there are some mistakes in Bible translations, you know, and on and on. When you search out these people or authors they're referencing, you find that most have no credibility whatsoever, but you cannot persuade them of that. At some point, you have to pray the Spirit will guide them back into truth.

There's a good reason the Bible tells us to avoid these foolish controversies, and the arguments and quarrels that inevitably follow. For one thing, you'll find yourself in a discussion that just goes in circles, exactly like the logic it follows. But most importantly, it's just useless, and it's unprofitable. No one gains anything positive from the exercise.

Stop quarrelling with those who are off in the nether regions. Avoid discussing those topics. Refuse to be drawn in. Turn the conversation to fundamentals, to godliness, to holy living, or even politics if it stops the other foolishness. Just don't participate!

Prayer: Father, give us wisdom to stay out of foolish conversations, and grace to extricate ourselves from them without insulting anyone...

May 22
Abide

"I am the vine; you are the branches. If a man remains in me and I in him, he will bear much fruit; apart from me you can do nothing." Jn 15:5

"God helps those who help themselves." Now there's a godly scripture you can use in your everyday walk, right? Actually, that famous and prolifically used quote is nowhere to be found in the Bible. In fact, it flies in the face of the scripture above.

Now, there are those who will say that God's word teaches us to work, as in, "If a man will not work, he shall not eat." II Th 3:10c And doesn't God instruct us to do the good works prepared in advance for us believers to do?

Yes, those things are taught to us in the New Testament. Here's the rub, though. Scripture does *not* teach us that when you start helping yourself, then the Lord will pitch in and do His part. Quite the contrary, in every situation we can think of, God comes first, the obedient action follows.

Here are some examples.

"It is by grace you are saved, through faith—and this not from yourselves, it is the gift of God—not by works, so that no one can boast." Php 2:8-9 It's nothing that we do. God does it all; it's His gift to us. You see? God first, then we accept.

"For God so loved the world that He gave His only begotten son, that whosoever believes in Him shall not perish, but have eternal life." Jn 3:16 Where did we begin doing something in there? That's right. Nowhere! God did it all before we were even born, or had a chance to give it a thought.

"He saved us, not because of righteous things we had done, but because of his mercy." Tit 3:5a Again, not because of anything we did, or ever started to do.

While we are to walk in obedience, and do the works He's prepared for us, and while we're to be doers of the word, and not just hearers, and while faith without actions is dead, we need to learn this essential truth. Apart from Jesus, we can do *nothing*! That's why it's so important to remain in Christ. We must *abide* in Him. We cannot live without Him. He's the root source of all we are.

So just throw that old saying away. Like many old adages, it isn't true, nor is it very useful. Just do this one thing. Abide!

Prayer: Jesus, help us to remember to seek you first, and to remain in you, so that we *can* do something. Something for you…

May 23
Be Freed from Your Curse

"With the tongue...we curse men." Jas 3:9a &c
"Be transformed by the renewing of your mind." Rom 12:2b

Have you ever thought that your life seems cursed in some way? Have you had a time when you've sat down, and thought back to the reasons you feel the negative things you feel about yourself? Perhaps regarding your looks, or your abilities, or your possibility for success?

Many of us have had, at one time or another (maybe more than one), someone who has said something to us that has defined our thinking in ways that have been detrimental. Because they've said something negative about us, we've accepted that thinking, and it has shaped our lives in ways that have harmed us, and our future.

Some of you may have been told you're homely, or your brother or sister sure got all the looks in your family. You may have overheard someone gossip and tell his or her friend that you'd never amount to anything with your poor upbringing. Maybe you heard that you weren't very bright, and have gone through life thinking you just weren't as smart as most people. Whatever the words that have caused bondage in your mind and heart, it's time to be set free.

We want you to take the time to sit down together, and talk out the hurtful things that you remember that have caused you to think in a self-destructive way. Think about the areas of negativity in your mind, and trace it back to where it began. Once you've identified that, let's join together in prayer, and we're agreeing with you now, that you're going to be freed from that curse, and renewed in your mind by Christ Jesus.

You see, it doesn't matter who said it, or why, or how it was done. What matters is the power of Jesus Christ to set you free from the bondage you've lived under, and the transforming He's doing in you now.

Lord Jesus, we join in prayer for this couple who love you, and walk in your ways. We pray that you break the chains of bondage that have held them enslaved in their hearts and minds, and that you free them completely from this curse. Renew their minds in you, Lord, and give them right thinking that mirrors your heart for them. Give them the assurance of your love, and your care; of your power in their lives, and of their victory. Show them that they are more than conquerors in you, Lord, and that they have your favor, because they call upon your name. Bless them, now, with the sense of this lifted burden, and the complete freedom they have in you. Give them a new joy, now, we ask. In Jesus name we pray. Amen

May 24
"Aim for perfection." II Cor 13:11b

There you go. Title, goal, and verse, all wrapped up in one part of one verse. This is geared, not just specifically towards our Christian walk, but it applies to every area of our lives. Obviously, our faith permeates every part of life for us, but extend your thinking.

I played basketball. I always strived for the perfect game. What does that mean? In basketball, for me, it would mean I hit every shot I took, my defense would keep the guy I was guarding from ever scoring or rebounding, I would get every rebound I went after, I'd never turn the ball over, and I would be successful in every steal attempt I made. Did I ever do that? Nope! I came close a couple of times, but never made it. I tried, though.

In some ways, life is like that. What can be difficult is figuring out what your perfect game is, in work, in parenting, in husband wife relationship, in play, in faith and service, and in worship. We'll never really reach perfection this side of Heaven, but we can sure strive to.

What's your perfect workday? Arrive ahead of time, ready to go? Efficiently perform all tasks without error? Give great customer service with every person? Interact with professionalism, friendliness, and courtesy with every associate, supervisor, and subordinate? Exceed sales or production goals by fifteen percent? You can't come close to hitting the perfect mark if you don't define what that is.

How does your perfect love relationship look? Do you smile and wink at your spouse? Do you speak kindly and lovingly? Do you avoid criticism and focus on total positive reinforcement? Are you affectionate? Do you address issues civilly, finding solutions instead of placing blame? Do you spend quality time with you spouse, doing things you can both enjoy? Do you spend time helping and serving your spouse? Do you worship together? Do you have daily devotions together (you should be scoring well on this one)? Do you pray together, not only regularly, but also when special needs arise? If you calculate what your perfect relationship is, then you can measure whether you're reaching success in it.

The same holds true for parenting, for leisure activities, for your financial plan, and everything else in life. Define the goals.

Finally, saving the best for last, what does your perfect Christian walk encompass? Daily Bible reading? Family devotions? Meals together with believers? Conversation with the Lord, as one visits with a friend? Pure thinking? Awareness of the needs and problems of others? A willingness to help where we're able? Spiritual worship and praise?

In all we do, we are called to be holy, because our God is holy.

Aim for perfection.

Prayer: Lord, give us the wisdom to define correctly what perfection looks like for us, and the ability and focus to strive for that. Thank you for forgiving us when we fail...

May 25
Delayed Obedience Isn't Obedience

"When you make a vow to God, do not delay in fulfilling it. He has no pleasure in fools; fulfill your vow. It is better not to vow than to make a vow and not fulfill it." Ecc 5:4-5

If you have children, you concur with this verse wholeheartedly. All of us have struggled with children who didn't react soon enough when we asked them to do something. Admittedly, that didn't happen terribly often at our house, because there were dire consequences for procrastinating, even a little. We weren't as patient when we were younger as we are now. Now, we'd give them a couple of more seconds to move.

We're thankful that God is more patient than we, but His patience with us in fulfilling our vows to Him apparently isn't that great, either. According to this verse, it's displeasing to Him when we delay in doing what we promised Him we would.

We can empathize with that. We get frustrated when people don't do what they tell us they're going to. We often say, "it would be better if they never told us they'd do that, because then we wouldn't have planned around it." We'd rather have someone not commit to something, than to commit and fail to follow through.

Here's an example. When we built our house, we hired a contractor to hang the sheetrock, and tape and texture it, because we knew we couldn't do it nearly as fast, and we had a schedule to maintain. They told us when they'd be there, and then didn't show up for three weeks. By the time they finished, we could have done it ourselves, and saved the money. More importantly, because they delayed in coming, we had to reschedule the carpet installation, which meant the carpet company sent someone who wasn't as good, which meant the kitchen flooring was layed incorrectly, which meant a mess, because they had to come back and tear it out and redo it. We were moderately frustrated. The point is, there's a domino effect when we, or others, don't follow through on our promises.

When we don't do what we say we're going to, we make liars of ourselves. If you say you're coming Thursday, and don't show up until Saturday, you lied. If you said you'd pay for something, and you 'forgot', you lied. If you said you'd do something, and do so at, or by, a certain time, and you didn't do it by then, you were dishonest, because you didn't fulfill your vow.

It's even worse when that promise is to God. Are you kidding me, you skipped out on your promise to God? Do you know what He can do to you?

Don't delay in keeping your vows. Be prompt in fulfilling your promises.

Prayer: Father God, give us the alertness to be aware of, and to keep, our promises, both to other people, and to you...

May 26
Beguiled, or Eyes Wide Open?

"When the woman saw that the fruit of the tree was good for food and pleasing to the eye, and also desirable for gaining wisdom, she took some and ate. She also gave some to her husband, who was with her, and he ate it." Gen 3:6

There are times in life when we are the victims of an honest mistake. We hear something that appears to be true, nothing at the time shows us it's illegitimate, and we act on the information, trusting it to be accurate. In one sense, that's what happened to Eve. She learned that the tree of knowledge would give her the ability to discern good from evil. That was the only true part of what Satan told her. She was gullible in believing the devil.

In the other sense, though, she should have known better. God had told her the truth. He *cannot* lie. Eve chose to believe the devil, rather than the one who had created her, fellowshipped with her, and always been honest with her.

Adam, on the other hand, was not tricked, or fooled, or swindled at all by this. We often think this happened while he was off somewhere else, tending the garden, and didn't even know what he was eating when Eve gave him the fruit. Nothing could be further from the truth. Adam was there the whole time, watching what happened. Even after seeing Eve be deceived, he just went ahead and joined in anyway, eyes wide open.

Ponder this with us. Doesn't it seem logical to believe that the reason sin is passed down through men is because he sinned intentionally? He saw it, knew it was wrong, was aware of consequences, and with eyes wide open, he dived into sin anyway.

We feel better in some ways when we're beguiled, when we mess up by mistake. Oh, we always look back, feel a bit foolish, see we should have known better, and resolve not to make the same error again. But there are times, just like Adam, when we know better, we know there are negative circumstances coming, and we just go ahead and sin anyway, thinking surely we can dodge the consequences. When we sin with intent, there is much greater fallout than when we do so blindly. Not only is our foolishness shown to everyone, there's a sense of guilt, and of shame, that we bear as a result of our actions. And those who've been hurt by our sin are scarred, and caused much greater pain, than if what had happened had been the result of error.

Don't be beguiled, but more importantly, don't go into sin with your eyes wide open. The results are devastating, and can follow you for years. Resolve to walk with your eyes open, and believing *God*. Never trust the devil. He's the ultimate liar.

Prayer: Father, forgive us when we sin, and help us to be careful to avoid stumbling off your path. Give us the strength to walk the narrow path, and please you by showing in our actions that we believe *you*...

May 27
No Compromise!

"You will be thrown immediately into a blazing furnace. Then what god will be able to rescue you from my hand?"

"If we are thrown into the blazing furnace, the God we serve is able to save us from it, and he will rescue us from your hand, O king. But even if he does not, we want you to know, O king, that we will not serve your gods or worship the image of gold you have set up." Dan 3:15d & 17-18

It's a cool story how God saved Shadrach, Meshach, and Abednego from the fiery furnace, especially considering that King Nebuchadnezzar was so angry for their defiance that he had the fire stoked seven times hotter than normal. The soldiers who forced them into the furnace died in the act. Those three young men not only survived without a scratch or a burn, they didn't even smell like smoke! God shows no matter what the circumstances, He *can* deliver.

God does that sometimes. He's not content to just deliver. He loves to make a point. Like Elijah and the prophets of Baal. Drench the sacrifice, running over and sitting in pools of water, for God to burn up. Then, wham, he burns it all down, sacrifice, water, and the altar it was on. All gone! Proves His point beyond a shadow of a doubt.

The story of the three young Hebrews being saved from the furnace is exciting, and it shows God's power to save. But there's a second side to this story that really impresses me.

When they faced certain death, they stood in faith. They *knew* God could deliver them. They knew they were in His hands. But the firm stand they took for the Lord is stellar. Even if God chose not to deliver them, they would *never* bow to the idol made of gold. They were content to let God do with them as *He* chose. That's a shining example of standing firm in the faith.

There are some things that we can't compromise on, either. The fundamentals of the faith; like the virgin birth, the dual deity and humanity of Jesus, the fact that He is the way the truth and the life, and that no one comes to the Heavenly Father except through Christ; His resurrection and ascension to be seated at the right hand of the Father, and the fact that He makes intercession for the saints. We cannot deny Jesus Christ, and expect Him to stand for us. But oh, when we stand firm for Him, He'll do things in our lives that are beyond imagining.

You can compromise where you're going for dinner, what route you take to the ball game, what clothes to where, and a host of other things, but don't compromise your faith.

Prayer: Lord Jesus, help us to stand as firm for you as the Hebrew men did for our Heavenly Father...

May 28
I Have Nothing to Wear

"Then Jesus said to his disciples: Therefore I tell you, do not worry about your life, what you will eat; or about your body, what you will wear." Lk 12:22

Wives, we know this is extremely trying for you, to be told not to worry about what to wear. We don't know how difficult it is for you to choose what you're going to wear, but in varying degrees, most go through the same basic ritual. Wife looks for an outfit, tries on said outfit, then discards the outfit, and moves on to another outfit, all in a search for the perfect look. This process may be replayed one to a dozen times, depending upon the woman, the occasion, and how many clothes reside in her closet(s). They can't seem to help it. It's instinctive for them. Be generous in your assessment.

Husbands, we know this is extremely trying for you, to be told not to worry about what to eat. We don't know how difficult it is for you to choose what you're going to eat, but in varying degrees, most go through the same basic ritual. Husband eats their meal, relishes said meal, and then asks what we'll be having for the next meal. This occurs in approximately 74% of married households across America (I made that up).

Actually, this isn't talking about choosing what to wear, or what to eat, though. It means not to worry about whether you *have* something to wear, or something to even eat. Don't be concerned about the basic necessities of life, because the Lord already knows what you need, and He'll provide them for you.

We can trust our Heavenly Father to take care of us. We're always intrigued by how much our family life is mirrored in God's kingdom. Of course, it stands to reason that our family life *is* the reflection of His kingdom. That's how He teaches us, and how we're able to understand. Just as we as parents take care of the basic physical needs of our children, so our Heavenly Father cares for the needs of His children, and we *are* His children.

So you needn't worry—even if you have nothing suitable to wear.

Prayer: Heavenly Father, give us the trust in you to know you'll take care of our needs. We thank you for your provision for us…

May 29
If God Says So, Buy a Field

"I knew that this was the word of the Lord; so I bought the field at Anathoth…" Jer 32:8e-9a

"Take these documents, both the sealed and unsealed copies of the deed of purchase, and put them in a clay jar so they will last a long time. For this is what the Lord Almighty, the god of Israel, says: Houses, fields and vineyards will again be bought in this land." Jer 32:14b-15

When prices are rising at an alarming rate, and you're still on the same income as you previously were, we'd caution against going on a spending spree. When the economy fails, and everyone around you is divesting themselves of investments, dumping their property, and running for the hills, it's probably not the best time to buy up those assets. Unless, of course, God tells you to.

Jeremiah was instructed by the Lord to buy his cousin's property, because even though they were being captured and sent off to Babylon, there would come a day when commerce would return to the land of Israel, and the property would again be valuable.

Now, we've never actually had the Lord tell us what specific investments to make, but if He tells you, do it. You'll do just like everyone else, and whine and complain about how poorly your investment is doing, but keep in mind that God doesn't tell us things without reason. Just make sure and test the spirit to be sure it's the Lord instructing you, and not your third cousin Ned.

God sees what's beyond the horizon. He knows what's coming, and when we walk in obedient faith, He rewards us with blessing. So if God tells you to buy land, and seal your deed of purchase somewhere for safekeeping, where nothing can destroy it, you ought to do so. It's a safe bet you're going to be needing that property for something in the future.

Prayer: Holy Spirit, let us clearly hear your voice when you speak, and know that this message is from God…

May 30
You Are the Spice of Life

"You are the salt of the earth." Mt 5:13a

What is salt used for? We usually think of it as a way to spice up the flavor of our food, and normally, in this day and age, that's what we use it for. Most cooked food tastes better if we put a little salt on it. I know, some of you think it tastes better with a *lot* of salt on it. Salt gives food a savory flavor that's missing without it. When salt isn't used in preparing the food, it tastes 'flat'.

When you're working hard, or playing hard, or out in the sun and the heat, you sweat quite a bit, and when you do, you secrete salt in your perspiration. If you don't replenish that salt, you grow weak, your system begins to act abnormally, and given enough time, you'd die. The salt in your system is essential, and has to be replaced. It helps retain the water in your system.

Finally, salt has been used as a preservative for centuries. It keeps food from spoiling, and when meat is salt preserved, it can last extraordinary periods of time. Salt saves the food that would otherwise spoil if it weren't used.

As Christians, we're referred to as the salt of the earth. It has applications in all three of these areas of life too.

We spice up other people's lives with our love, our kindness, our generosity, and our help, or service, to them. Our warmth and caring adds flavor to their lives.

We help folks keep the good things, as well. Just as salt retains much needed water in our body, by fellowshipping, and encouraging others to maintain a decent, holy lifestyle, we help them retain godliness, and pureness, in their walk.

As salt saves and preserves food, when we bring Jesus to the world, we save and preserve the life of each one who receives the 'salt' we offer.

Only *our* 'salt' doesn't keep them for a time, or a season, it keeps them for *eternity*.

So step out confidently, and be savory, with the knowledge that you are the *spice* of *life*.

Prayer: Father, keep us salty for you. Help us to keep sight of you, and not lose our saltiness. Truly make us the spice of life…

Jun 1
Bear with One Another in Love

"I urge you to live a life worthy of the calling you have received. Be completely humble and gentle; be patient, bearing with one another in love." Eph 4:1b-2

Throughout God's word, that theme of living in a worthy manner laces in and out of every topic. It's obviously very important to the Lord that we set an example of holiness when we're in Him. Once you put your faith in Jesus, you begin a growing process that continues the rest of your days. As we grow, we take on the attitudes and temperament of Christ, and people begin to see Him in us.

Those qualities that the Lord desires are listed, here in part, and more expansively in several other scripture verses. The ones listed here are important.

We know from the Old Testament all the way to the end of the New Testament that God is less than impressed with arrogance. Overweening pride is abhorrent to Him, and He tells us that He brings low the proud. It would be much better to just realize, we have nothing to be proud of, and be humble. Humility is much more lovable than pride is, anyway. Note, this doesn't just ask us to be humble, but *completely* humble.

Along with humility comes gentleness. Now we can all be like the proverbial bull in the china cabinet, both physically and conversationally. We all have varying degrees of physical strength. We have a certain amount of power. We can use that strength to hurt, break, and destroy, or we can use it to lift up, heal, and build. Likewise, we have that same power in our tongues. It can be used to criticize, brow beat, demean, and curse. But it could better be used to encourage, affirm, compliment, and inspire. Control your strength, and do positive things with it. We must decide how we're going to use the power we have. For good, or for evil.

They'll know we are Christians by our love, goes the line in a song. Truly, the love we show is the shining light of Jesus Christ to the world. This applies to our outside friends and associates, but it is really highlighted in our marriage relationship. The way we treat each other as husband and wife is the most telling example of our Christian love. We are instructed to bear with one another in love. The fact is you can't do that without being patient. Now, it's quite easy to be impatient, frustrated, abrupt, and brusque. That comes naturally. We have to exert ourselves to be patient. Sometimes, depending on our temperament, it takes Herculean effort to accomplish the patience that's needed. But to honor Christ, to set a godly example, nothing is more important than patience, because without it, you just can't exhibit His love.

So, be completely humble, gentle, and patient, and bear with one another in love.

Prayer: Lord, give us the humility and gentleness we need to show you're in us. Help us to exhibit patience with each other, and with others, to show your love…

Jun 2
The Radiance of God's Glory

"In the past God spoke to our forefathers through the prophets at many times and in various ways, but in these last days he has spoken to us by his Son, whom he appointed heir of all things, and through whom he made the universe. The Son is the radiance of God's glory and the exact representation of his being, sustaining all things by his powerful word." Heb 1:1-3c

Aren't you glad you don't live in the old covenant time, when the Lord only spoke through prophets? No Holy Spirit residing within you, and constantly wondering whether you're meeting all the requirements of the law. What we often forget is that, Jesus came in that time, and lived under those restrictions, having to fulfill every aspect of the law. He's the only person who ever did, being completely sinless.

In these days, we're blessed to have Jesus speaking to us. He's sent the Holy Spirit, and when the Spirit speaks, the Bible tells us he speaks what comes from Christ, and Jesus spoke what he heard from His Heavenly Dad. Now He's our Heavenly Dad, too, and we're able to fellowship with him just as we would with our earthly Dad, or as a friend, who speaks face to face with us.

Jesus is our Lord and Savior. Who is He, exactly? Jesus is the one through whom everything in the universe was made. That's incomprehensible power. Our Heavenly Dad has appointed Him heir of all things. We know that we're joint heirs with Jesus. Because He's our Lord, we share in His inheritance.

Did you know there's no difference between Jesus and our Heavenly Dad? Jesus is exactly like His Dad! They're one. That's why Jesus is the radiance of God's glory. Radiance speaks of Him glowing, shining forth the brilliance of light that flows from the purity and holiness of our Heavenly Dad. When you see Jesus, you see *glory*.

Finally, Jesus sustains everything by His word. When Jesus speaks, he speaks *power*. Whatever Jesus says, happens.

We're thankful that Jesus speaks to us directly, and that we share in His inheritance. As we walk with Jesus, we're privileged to walk in His power, and even better; we get to bask in the glow of the radiance of God's glory.

Prayer: Heavenly Dad, we give you praise for Jesus, and for His power, and for His speaking to us. We thank you that we can sense the radiance of your glory…

Jun 3
Money's the Answer?

"A feast is made for laughter, and wine makes life merry, but money is the answer for everything." Ecc 10:19

We go through all kinds of trials and difficulties in life. Most of the time, it does seem like money would help us resolve many of those problems. Is money really the answer to everything?

The obvious answer is no. When your loved one is afflicted with an incurable, terminal disease, all the money in the world isn't going to keep him or her from dying. If money could cure every disease, there'd be a lot of rich people who never died. But life doesn't work that way.

When your little girl is in the Christmas program, or your little boy is in the school play, money will not make up for not being there to see it. Your little girl or boy wants Mom's and Dad's attention, support, and affirmation. Money can never cover the disappointment of Mom or Dad missing the event.

Face it; we'd often take the easy way out of a lot of situations if we had the money available to do so. Sometimes facing those issues, and working to resolve them, is essential for our good, for our inner strength, for our relationship, and for our integrity. If you have a fight with your wife, and your response is to buy her flowers, or jewelry, but you don't address what you're in conflict about, you diminish her importance, as well as your own worth. No, it doesn't matter how expensive the gift. She's not a prostitute. You don't buy her off. Have the courage to show her the respect and honor due her in the Lord, and face the dispute squarely, and find a solution that helps you grow together.

We're not picking on men, wives, because you're guilty of the same types of things. You may use different methods, but when you sidestep an issue, and head for the bedroom for intimacy instead of facing the problem; when you go out for a nice dinner to avoid it; you've done exactly the same thing we just talked about from the man's perspective. You've just used another tactic. And there are many other ways as well.

The verses preceding and following this verse talk about those who are foolish. They're the ones who take to heart the verse above, but it seems to indicate that this is man's philosophy, not the Lord's.

Money is *not* the answer for everything.

Prayer: Dear Lord, give us the wisdom and the courage to face our disputes head on, and resolve them in a godly way that honors each other, and you…

Jun 4
Did You Forget What You Look Like?

"Do not merely listen to the word, and so deceive yourselves. Do what it says. Anyone who listens to the word but does not do what it says is like a man who looks at his face in a mirror and, after looking at himself, goes away and immediately forgets what he looks like." Jas 1:22-24

    I can honestly say I have a pretty good idea of what I look like. When I see myself in the mirror, I recognize me without any trouble. Sometimes, I wish I didn't remember, but no such luck. Glenda doesn't forget, either, but she looks in the mirror more often than I do. Of course, everyone looks at Glenda more frequently than they do me, but she's so attractive, that only makes good sense.

    We've met people who knew pretty much everything there was to know about a subject. I once had someone tell me he'd studied how to tune a piano. He knew international pitch is A440. He knew what a tuning wrench is, and approximately how to use it. He knew what tuning pins are. He said he knew how to tune pianos. Now, having been a piano tuner for 18 years, I can say with some certainty that he could tune a piano about as well as I could fly an F14 fighter jet. I know from experience that it takes a lot more than reading up on it to know how to do it. It takes practice, for one thing, just to learn how to use the tuning wrench to set the string properly, let alone get it to the perfect pitch. Because I tune pianos, I noticed the muting style missing in his relating of the tuning process. And you can't learn how to set the temperament in a piano by reading. You have to see it, and hear it, over and over to get it right.

    The word isn't meant just for our hearing only. It was given to us so we'd know what the Lord wants us to do. We're to apply it to our daily life. If we don't do what it says, we're fooling ourselves into thinking we're something we really aren't. Mark this down. Knowing *about* Jesus isn't the same as *knowing* Jesus. As Paul often says, that's a trustworthy saying. If we don't do what God instructs us to in His word, we aren't in Christ. To know Jesus is to know and do His work. To know Jesus is to live the way He did.

Don't be like the one who immediately forgets what he or she looks like. Do what the word says.

Prayer: Father, give us the motivation to move, and to do what your word instructs us to...

Jun 5
Have You Exploited Someone?

"Make room for us in your hearts. We have wronged no one, we have corrupted no one, we have exploited no one." II Cor 7:2

Wouldn't it be nice if we could all say that? I know there are many I've wronged, admittedly, some I've corrupted, and a number I've exploited. The more we live and walk in Christ, though, the less we wrong, corrupt, or exploit others. I'm thankful for that.

Even as believers we can be guilty of not taking enough care to avoid doing these things to people. We can still cut people off in traffic, or slip ahead of one who isn't paying close attention at the market, or we take the last cookie. We still sometimes lead others astray by misrepresenting something to them, or cussing where they can hear, or shortchanging someone we do business with. And we're often not beyond using someone for our own ends, or our own profit, when it's unfair to them.

This gives us a goal to attain. We ought to make it our mission to *never* wrong anyone. I often say, "I'd rather be wronged, than wrong someone else." I'm still working on accomplishing that in fact, though, rather than just in philosophy.

We should be so careful about the example we set, because eyes are watching, and we have to live what we believe to avoid corrupting someone weaker who knows we're Christians.

In our dealings with others, we should always seek a win-win, or a they-win, situation. That will keep us from exploiting them.

We'd love for those who know us to make room in their hearts for us. The more honorably, the more fairly, the more generously, the more godly, and the more lovingly we treat others; the more they'll make that room.

Prayer: Lord Jesus, give us your heart, and your attitude, in dealing with others, and in living the example we should for you...

Jun 6
Seek Good

"Seek good, not evil, that you may live. Then the Lord God Almighty will be with you, just as you say he is." Am 5:14

You have two choices. Good or evil, heaven or hell. Which is it going to be?

It's startling how many people call themselves Christians, but live like they've never heard of Christ. Or how many call themselves Christians who rarely look at the Bible, and don't know even the bare rudiments of its teaching. In the United States, people have long identified themselves as Christians, because that's what our 'national' religion is. They've never made a profession of faith, though, or been born again, and consequently can't even make a good attempt at living a godly life.

In one way, they've chosen good. Those folks have chosen to identify themselves with what they perceive is good. They don't know the power, love, and grace of living in Jesus though, because they haven't put their faith in Him. It would seem they've chosen good, but by not accepting Jesus as Lord of their lives, they've actually chosen evil. Many would rather go their own way than take a chance that the Lord God Almighty would actually be with them. They don't understand that to live, you have to genuinely seek good. And as Jesus said, "only God is good".

People seem to think that they're going to lose everything if they accept Christ. They have it in mind that they'll never have any fun, have to give up all their bad habits, which incidentally, they enjoy, and that they'll look weak and foolish. Those of us who've sought the good of being in Christ know that nothing could be further from the truth. The happiest, most fun-loving, peaceful, contented people we know are born again believers. The strongest folks we know are Christians. They have an inner strength, a calm resolve in the face of adversity, that's missing completely in the lives of those who don't yet know Christ.

Yes, we said don't *yet* know Christ. Friends, everyone is going to know Him eventually. The only question is, will they seek Him now, and have life eternal in Heaven, or will they meet Him after they die, and live eternally in Hell. We only have *two* choices!

Seek good, not evil, that you may live. The good, the life, is in Jesus Christ.

Prayer: Jesus, give us the wisdom to seek you, and to walk in life with you…

Jun 7
Don't Get Worked Up Over Nothing

"About that time there arose a great disturbance about the Way. A silversmith named Demetrius, who made silver shrines of Artemis; brought in no little business for the craftsmen...we receive a good income from this business. And you see and hear how this fellow Paul has convinced and led astray large numbers of people here...

Soon the whole city was in an uproar. They all shouted in unison for about two hours: 'Great is Artemis of the Ephesians!'

You ought to be quiet and not do anything rash. You have brought these men here, though they have neither robbed temples nor blasphemed our goddess.

We are in danger of being charged with rioting...we would not be able to account for this commotion, since there is no reason for it." Excerpts from Acts 19:23-40

This is a great illustration of the way the world works. Those who aren't believers in Christ are driven by something completely different than we are. Notice in this passage, they got all worked into a lather about the possibility of losing money. If people started following the Way (early name for Christianity), they'd stop buying the silver shrines these craftsmen made. There aren't too many things that'll get people to riot, but in almost every case, it can be traced to greed or ignorance, or both.

What does getting all worked up accomplish? Oh, it might gain people some ground in one way, but they're just losing ground in another. The problem with rioting, or having a big commotion with lots of shouting and vandalism and violence, is that it creates a whole new set of issues to deal with. For instance, when a verdict goes against a person, and those who identify with that person riot, what happens? They cause a lot of destruction, but they don't change the judicial system. In fact, many of them will experience the judicial system for themselves. And the rest of the country watching on television gets an extremely negative opinion of that group. That makes it more difficult for them to get jobs, have open doors socially, and improve their family situations. The mob mentality is dangerous, because it creates more problems, and solves none, with the exception of working out anger and frustration.

If people were thinking rationally, they'd realize they couldn't solve anything getting all worked up to a frenzy. To actually resolve situations, you have to calmly come up with resolutions that benefit all involved.

Don't just get worked up, think!

Prayer: Lord, help us to stay calm and rational in our reactions to negative circumstances. Don't let us be foolish, and act like the world in ignorance...

Jun 8
How Much Does the World Mean to You?

"May I never boast except in the cross of our Lord Jesus Christ, through which the world has been crucified to me, and I to the world." Gal 6:14

Everyone has to live in this world for a while. As we do, it's important to work hard, be diligent in our service to Christ, try to be as prosperous as we can be, raise our families, make and enjoy good friendships, and fellowship with God and other believers.

When this talks about the world being crucified to us, we need to take on this philosophy. The world, and all it has to offer, is useful to us, but not what's most important. We don't love the things this world has to offer, because 'things' are all it *has* to offer. No matter how much of the world's money and stuff you accumulate, it won't satisfy you in your spirit. They may be enjoyable to have and use, but they're only tools.

Take money, for example. What is money? It's not even real. Its only worth, is that we agree it has a certain value, and agree to use it as such. Our money is just paper. We make all kinds of things out of paper. While we make money of it, we also make disposable plates, napkins, curtains, posters, toilet tissue, and among many other things, fire. The only real value in our money is what we arbitrarily agree it has.

Or how about 'stuff'? A nice car is dependable transportation, and comfortable to drive and ride in, but it's just metal and plastic. Our stove is a useful tool to cook our meals with, but it won't help us solve real problems. The broom is a good tool for helping us clean our floors, but it has no intrinsic value. The cell phone is a great tool to help us communicate with friends and family, but it isn't actually worth much.

We can list thousands of things that help us in life, but they all have one thing in common. They're tools that we use in our *physical* life, and they *won't* fill the void in our spirit that's there if we don't walk with the Lord.

That's why we're dead to the world, and the world to us, because our *life* is in Christ. While the world's goods are useful, we don't need them.

The one thing we have to boast about is Jesus Christ. The world is temporary. Life in Jesus is eternal. Consequently, the world doesn't mean much to us.

Prayer: Lord Jesus, help us to remember that the things of this world aren't important, and to boast in you, and you alone...

Jun 9
Are You Leaving an Inheritance?

"Dishonest money dwindles away, but he who gathers money little by little makes it grow." Pr 13:11

"A good man leaves an inheritance for his children's children." Pr 13:22a

We know that we leave an inheritance of godliness, regardless of what else happens in life. But today, let's talk about a money inheritance.

We talked about how we don't love the things of this world. But lets talk about the importance of having the tools we need. While money isn't the most important thing in life by far, it does play a role, because it's the means by which we provide for the material needs of our families.

If you've never read a book called, "The Richest Man In Babylon", by George S Clason, it's required reading on the subject of work and basic money management, and it isn't like other books on the subject. It's written in story form, and gives you the knowledge you need in this area. The discipline to apply what you learn can only come from you.

Proverbs tells us a couple of key points regarding wealth. If you acquire it dishonestly, or try to get it too fast, it will dwindle away. Money will elude you if you do that. It's the principle of sowing and reaping at work. You can't harvest where you don't plant, and you can't harvest right after you plant.

If you want money to grow for you, you have to acquire it slowly and consistently. You have to protect your seeds, and not eat them, or use them for something they aren't designed for. You have to carefully nurture your seed, and give it the proper environment in which to grow. If you'll do that, it will grow and grow.

God tells us that a good man leaves an inheritance for his children's children. By the time he passes away, his own children have already made a good start on their own financial soundness, and the inheritance ends up being passed on to the grandchildren. If we're wise in our use of the money we earn, that's what will happen.

First, we have to be faithful in God's kingdom, bringing the tithe into His house. He'll bless us, and as we're given the opportunity to earn, we set aside a portion from each paycheck, or each profit, and set the money to working for us. Over time, it will provide a retirement, and be passed on.

Only you can actually manage this process. No one can do it for you. It's like God's word. You can know it, but it does no good if you don't apply it.

Read the book. Both of you. Apply the principles. Leave an inheritance.

Prayer: Lord, help us to do the wise things in our management of money. We want to leave a financial inheritance for our family, along with our godly inheritance…

Jun 10
Great Timing!

"The eyes of all look to you, and you give them their food at the proper time." Ps 147:15

"You see, at just the right time, when we were still powerless, Christ died for the ungodly." Rom 5:6

"For he says, 'in the time of my favor I heard you, and in the day of salvation I helped you.' I tell you, now is the time of God's favor, now is the day of salvation." II Cor 6:2

A few months ago we were at a church in Kentucky, and I was waiting for Glenda to return. I was sitting in the lobby of the church, and there was a crossway of halls, part of which was where I was. I was browsing through a magazine, and out of the corner of my eye, I saw Glenda walk by heading into the hallway straight ahead of her, instead of turning into the lobby. So I whistled at her to get her attention. Just before I whistled, the associate Pastor stepped out of his office, right at the corner of the intersection. Glenda whipped around and looked at him, and the Pastor gasped, "It wasn't me!" He and I couldn't see each other until he stepped into the intersection to proclaim his innocence. We still laugh every time we think about the look on his face, and the panic in his voice. That was one of those situations that happened due to great timing.

There are a number of verses in God's word that tell us His timing is not just great, it's perfect. That's what it means when it says He feeds them at the 'proper' time. He doesn't feed them early, or late. Rather, He does so at the 'proper' time.

Likewise, Jesus was sacrificed for us at just the 'right' time. Having shown Israel that they could never attain righteousness by following the law, having given them centuries of proof, and while all were still in sin, and powerless, Jesus shed His blood to pay the penalty required. He did so at the 'right' time.

I'm thankful that we live in God's time. Because *now* is the time of salvation. *Now* is the time of God's favor. We live in blessing because of His grace, and because of His love for us.

We're living in the perfect time. Great timing!

Prayer: Lord, we thank you for your perfect timing. We thank you that we can trust in your timing, knowing that you'll take care of our needs at the proper time. We thank you that we're privileged to live in the time of your favor…

Jun 11
Don't Miss Them!

"Every good and perfect gift is from above." Jas 1:17a

A few years ago the Washington Post decided to try an experiment to see how people would react to something extraordinary, but in an abnormal setting. They corroborated with Joshua Bell, world famous, singularly talented, virtuoso violinist, who played just days earlier in a setting where the nominal seats cost $100 each to attend his concert. They decided to have Mr. Bell take his $3.5 million, 1713 Stradivari violin, and go play during the morning rush hour in the L'Enfant Plaza Station. They wanted to see how people reacted to this amazing music. Over a thousand people walked by Mr. Bell while he played six of the most complicated, enduring pieces of music ever written for violin. In a time span of about 43 minutes, only a handful of people actually stopped and listened for more than a bare minute (just seven). Most didn't even notice he was there. Mainly, it seemed to be the children who noticed the ethereal, transcendent sound of the music coming from that Stradivari.

How often do you think God watches us walk past something He's presented for our pleasure and enjoyment, and wonders at our lack of appreciation? We're like the people at the train station. We're so busy with our own little concerns, we rush on, not even alert enough to notice, let alone show appreciation, for the equivalent of a world class violinist standing three feet from us, playing some of the most magnificent music ever written.

God's creation is a symphony of sight, sound, and smell, all wrapped up into one exceptional, panoramic display. May I tell you, there are such vibrant, exotic colors in the flower kingdom, that we still can't replicate the color? There are fragrances in nature we also can't duplicate (some we wouldn't want to, of course), an intoxicating aroma of plants that delight the sense of smell. Then there's the sound of birds singing. They're some of the most beautiful notes you'll ever hear.

We have a few roses along the walkway to our house. When they're in bloom, some of those roses waft a scent that's just heavenly as you walk to and from the house. But if you're in too much of a hurry, you can blow right by without noticing, and miss a wonderful sensation.

We're like that with God's garden along our pathway. If we rush too much, if we get too distracted with our own concerns, we miss His blessings of beauty, of any kind, around us. Every good gift comes from God. Don't miss them!

Prayer: Lord, thank you for the beauty of sight, sound, and fragrance that you surround us with. Help us to stay alert, so we can enjoy your blessings…

Jun 12
Don't Ever Be Embarrassed, Rejoice!

"The man who formerly persecuted us is now preaching the faith he once tried to destroy. And they praised God because of me." Gal 1:23b-24

Most of us, if we didn't get saved when very young, can remember the foolish, sinful way we lived. I was saved when I was 12, and I remember many of the things I did wrong. Most of us haven't done quite what Paul did. We didn't hunt people down to have them killed. Some of us have done other things that are horrendous, though. There are those who lived in a drugged stupor, in which they don't recall half of what they did. Some lived in sexual sin, whether in prostitution, homosexuality, adultery, or promiscuity. Others were thieves and swindlers. Some actually were murderers. Whatever your lifestyle, we all have one thing in common. We were sinners in need of a Savior.

We don't bring any of this up except for one reason. To rejoice! When we think of what Christ Jesus saved us from, we marvel at His love, forgiveness, and grace. To think that He'd redeem us, as awful as we once were, is cause for continual, eternal praise to the Lord.

Referring to Paul, they were reporting that the man who persecuted them, who hunted them, chased them down, imprisoned them, and sent them to be stoned to death, was now preaching the good news of Christ that he once despised. If Jesus can save Paul, it's proof that He loves, and can and will save, anyone who's willing to accept His gift.

Sometimes in our marriage we do foolish, perhaps sinful things that hurt our spouse. We're usually gracious to forgive one another when that happens, but it also causes us to remember that we should always be thankful to our husband or wife, too, for their willingness to overlook our trespasses. Forgiveness is a byproduct of our love for each other. If we didn't love, we'd be a lot less likely to overlook the faults of the other. We can praise our spouse, too, for their graciousness in wiping away our faults.

In the Lord, we're not embarrassed about our previous life. It's our biggest reason for rejoicing in Christ, because He forgave us so *much*! And if He can forgive me, there's definitely hope for you.

Prayer: Heavenly Father, we just hope that people will rejoice for how we've changed since you saved us, and praise you because of it...

Jun 13
Praise Each Other

"Let another praise you, and not your own mouth; someone else, and not your own lips." Pr 27:2

How much time do you spend thinking of ways to praise *your* spouse? Now, how often, and how long, do you actually *spend* praising him or her? We don't seem to have any trouble seeing the good in others, but those we're married to, can frequently be overlooked.

The reason that happens in part is, we aren't looking for, or expecting much of anything, from other people. So when we see something positive, we tend to comment on it. Oh, that was nice! Look what he did! Did you see her?

We can sometimes think no one notices any of the good things we do. They don't seem to pay any attention to how we go out of our way to help. We're overlooked in the many ways we sacrifice.

In God's kingdom, it's not up to us to get credit for the good we do. We're not tallying up our glory sheet down here. We store up treasures in Heaven. Besides, we sound prideful or arrogant when we seek praise ourselves, or trumpet our own successes. The real blessing comes when someone else *does* speak praise about, or to, us.

Since we're the 'another' to our husband or wife, we'd better pick up the praise mantle, and go ahead and give our spouse the praise they deserve. And don't tell me *your* husband or wife doesn't deserve any praise. After all, they put up with you. They should be thanked for that alone—lol. The other factor is, if we don't praise them, someone out there will. Don't let someone else gain a foothold where you failed to do what you ought to. Be the one who makes your husband or wife blush from flattery. Tell him how handsome he is. Tell her she's the most beautiful girl ever. Let him know he's the best lover, mechanic, gardener, griller, or whatever. Let her know she's the most fantastic cook, model, driver, mom, florist, lover, or whatever.

See the good qualities, actions, and attributes in each other. Then praise!

Prayer: Lord, bring to our remembrance the responsibility we have in refraining from complimenting ourselves, and help us to praise one another...

Jun 14
Whoa2U

"Woe to you, teachers of the law and Pharisees, you hypocrites! You give a tenth of your spices—mint, dill and cummin. But you have neglected the more important matters of the law—justice, mercy and faithfulness. You should have practiced the latter, without neglecting the former. You blind guides! You strain out a gnat but swallow a camel." Mt 23:23-24

Do you know what a hypocrite actually is? If you remember from Greek theatre, they show two masks. One mask is a frown, the other a smile. Originally, one person would use each mask at the appropriate time, and hide his face behind one of the masks. He was the hypocrite.

We can be like that. Too often we hide behind a façade. We put on some kind of mask to pretend we're someone we aren't. We may go to church every Sunday, put our tithe check in the offering, politely greet and bless our friends there, and then go out and live the rest of the week without giving another thought to Jesus Christ. That's hypocrisy. We act a certain way Sunday, but another way throughout the week.

We're not Pharisees, and most of us aren't teachers, but we can be hypocrites, nonetheless. We can do some of the minor things, and completely neglect the important aspects of our faith. We might usher at church, give our offering, set the thermostats, but forget to be kind to those who're hurting, or help those in need, or be forgiving to someone.

Notice this doesn't say, do the more important, rather than the least important. It says to do the most important without neglecting the other. Do them both. Show everyone that love, joy, peace, patience, kindness, goodness, faithfulness, gentleness, and self-control that you've developed as a result of your walk with Jesus Christ. When we can genuinely practice these traits consistently, then we won't ever have to worry about being hypocrites. We won't be straining out gnats while we eat the whole camel.

If you're doing *some* good things to make people believe something that's more than it is, then *whoa to you*. Stop doing that. Be authentic in your faith.

Prayer: Lord, help us to walk our faith every day, help us to break away from the facades we use, and help us to exhibit genuine, godly attitudes and actions...

Jun 15
Whoa2U2

"Woe to you, teachers of the law and Pharisees, you hypocrites! You clean the outside of the cup and dish, but inside they are full of greed and self-indulgence. Blind Pharisee! First clean the inside of the cup and dish, and then the outside also will be clean."
Mt 23:25-26

We're going to ask you a question, and like in church, don't necessarily raise your hand unless you have something you want to confess. Do you have sin in your life? Are there issues you've refused to deal with thus far, but which need to be resolved? Are you hiding something from your husband or wife that, given the opportunity, they might be able to help you conquer?

If you're harboring sin, then this is the day, this is the hour, and now is the moment to confess that to the Lord, to your spouse, and clean the inside of your cup and dish.

You see, if you have sin in your heart, it doesn't matter how clean you look on the outside. It doesn't matter that you sparkle and shine on the outside. When the inside of you is dirty, you're dirty all over. You may be one who's full of greed, or perhaps you're one whose self-indulgence is a hindrance to your walk with Christ, and/or your relationship with your husband or wife. You may have other hidden sin, but it usually falls into one of those categories. Notice, we aren't enumerating what sins it could be. If you have sin, you know what it is, because the Holy Spirit has already shown you.

Regardless of what it is, it interferes with your relationship with God. He doesn't look at that pretty shell, whether it's shined up to perfection or not. God looks at the heart.

"But the Lord said to Samuel, 'Do not consider his appearance or his height, for I have rejected him. The Lord does not look at the things man looks at. Man looks at the outward appearance, but the Lord looks at the heart.'" I Sam 16:7

The same holds true for us. God sees into our hearts. If you have sin inside, then whoa to you too, my friends. Stop harboring that wickedness. Let the Lord cleanse you from that sin, and once you're clean inside, you'll be clean all over.

Confess, be forgiven, and let God clean you up from the inside out. Then you'll truly be clean, through and through.

Prayer: Dear Lord, cleanse us from every sin that hinders our relationship with you, and with each other...

Jun 16
Continue in Love

"Let no debt remain outstanding, except the continuing debt to love one another." Rom 13:8a-b

Boy, those revolving debts can eat your income alive. Credit cards, mortgage, student loans, automobile loans, furniture loans, jewelry loans, and to top it off, consolidation loans. Whatever they are, they're debt, and debt can cripple us financially. While there are some things we have to buy, like our house, and perhaps a vehicle, most of our debt revolves around items we could well live without. We don't *have* to have a new couch, or new carpet, or a new big screen television, or a new stereo, or new outfits of clothing, or an espresso machine, or jewelry, or a host of other things that we could list all the way to the end of this page. Most things we could purchase outright by saving our money, but we tend to be a bit too impatient to wait six or eight months to get what we can have *right now*, if we just charge it.

We aren't supposed to have outstanding debt, though. Confession time. We do. But we're working steadily to eliminate that debt. For one thing, it really gets in the way of our ministry. Most of our debt was incurred before we began ministering full time, but it's certainly a hindrance to what we're trying to accomplish for God's kingdom. We've resolved not to take on any debt in our ministry, and once we're free of debt in our personal finances, we're not going to incur any more there, either. You can begin the process of doing the same, if you'll agree together to commit to living debt free. We know from our own situation that it takes some sacrifice, but in the end, we also know it will be worth every sacrifice we've made.

We see in our singing ministry up close and personally why the Lord only wants us to have the continuing debt of love. That debt is supposed to revolve forever. He wants our love to go around, and around, and to extend, and to extend even further, to reach everyone, everywhere.

Since we'd like to see the love of Jesus touch every person, we're working to eliminate all the other debts we have that interfere with that process. And if we had no other debt than the debt to love one another, we'd have so many more resources available to facilitate the spread of the good news of Jesus Christ in our music.

So we're only going to have that one debt, the debt of continuing love.

Prayer: Father, give us the plan and the resolve to eliminate every debt, except the debt to love one another...

Jun 17
Let God Deal with Your Enemies

"They who seek my life will be destroyed; they will go down to the depths of the earth. They will be given over to the sword and become food for jackals." Ps 63:9-10

In this life, most of us have enemies at some point or another. A friend of mine who was a school superintendent once told me, "friends come and go, but enemies just keep accumulating." That may be true in your life too, either because of your circle of friends, or due to the line of work you happen to be in.

What this verse tells us is that we needn't try to seek ways to defeat them on our own. We don't have to go looking for ways to eliminate them, or to claim victory over them. We already have our victory in Christ Jesus, and we won't allow anyone else to take that from us. The Bible tells us that we've 'already overcome the world', and that refers to everything and everyone in it. Just stay in faith!

This doesn't mean we shouldn't be on our guard against those who seek to harm us. Paul tells us to be careful with the people who want to destroy us, or our message, and elsewhere we're told to be clever in dealing with those of the world. In other words, don't go around trusting people who have shown themselves to be untrustworthy. While we don't have to actively engage in a dispute with others, we aren't to just allow them to do wrong to us, either. Remove yourself from that possibility if you can.

Beyond that, there's no need to concern yourself, because God's still on His throne, and He's watching over, and protecting us. God is the one who will deal with those who stand against us. He's the one who will destroy those who want to harm us. They will fall to the sword they bring against us.

Our only responsibility is to continue to walk in faith in Jesus, and rest in the shelter of His shed blood, and the mighty power in His name. Praise God! Be encouraged in Christ.

Prayer: God, help us to rest in the confidence of knowing you fight our battles for us, and that our enemies are already defeated in you…

Jun 18
Renew Your Strength in the Lord

"The Lord is the everlasting God, the Creator of the ends of the earth. He will not grow tired or weary, and his understanding no one can fathom. He gives strength to the weary and increases the power of the weak. Even youths grow tired and weary, and young men stumble and fall; but those who hope in the Lord will renew their strength. They will soar on wings like eagles; they will run and not grow weary, they will walk and not be faint." Isa 40:28c-31

We can all empathize with how tired and fatigued we get at times. Sometimes, the responsibilities and busyness of life can make us bone-weary, to the point where we'd like to just lay down and rest. No matter your age, even if you're young, or still have the vigor of the prime of life, you can stumble and fall as your strength wanes.

As we get older, we no longer have the strength we did when we were younger. We used to have a piano business, and we know from experience there are very few people who can pick up a piano. We can't do it as easily as we used to either. But no matter how strong you may be, like everyone else, there's a limit to that strength. We do get tired. We do wear out. We do require rest.

Thankfully, there is one who doesn't get tired, or ever need to stop for rest. There is one who understands like no one else possibly can. He's the one we receive our strength from. He's the one who refreshes us. He's the one who renews our strength. And He doesn't just give us a small measure. When God renews our strength, he gives us such energy we soar like eagles, effortlessly; we run without losing our breath; as we walk we won't grow faint. He gives us such an abundance of power we can go on and on.

We know we're weak. We have no power of our own. All the power and strength and energy we have comes from the Lord. The Energizer bunny has nothing on God. He's the *everlasting* God, the Creator of everything. That's why we hope in Him. He's the source of all of our life. So renew your strength in the Lord.

Prayer: Lord, we put our hope in you. Renew our strength for the journey…

Jun 19
Cause the Ripple in the Pond

"Preach the word." II Tim 4:2a

When we were kids we used to love to go to the pond on our farm (slough really), and on a still day throw stones into the water and watch the ripples spread. It was always interesting, firstly, because it didn't cause just one ripple. It made several in succession and they always kept spreading out to the edges. Secondly, it didn't matter how small the pebble either. A big rock made bigger, and more ripples, but even the smallest pebble brought the same basic result. It caused ripples.

Sometimes we have the chance to cause reactions, too. We don't necessarily know the end results of our actions or words, but we're to keep being a witness for the Lord. When we speak the apt word at a vital time, we can start a process that continues to spread far beyond what it might seem one little, couple of second phrase, could bring about. It works that way in God's kingdom, though.

Many years ago, a preacher named Mordecai Ham had evangelism meetings that lasted for several days. The year was 1934. It wasn't all that productive by most standards, but there *was* a young man who accepted Jesus Christ as his savior in those meetings. You never know what ripples one little pebble can cause. The young man who was saved went on to become a preacher and evangelist himself. In fact, that young man became the most heard evangelist in the history of the world, having preached to audiences over the years that tally over 2 billion people. You've probably guessed by now. The young man converted in Ham's meetings was Billy Graham. And the number of people who've come to know Jesus Christ as Lord and Savior as a result of Dr. Graham's preaching tops 2.5 million. That was quite a *ripple*.

We need to remember to be faithful in tossing our Christian pebbles into the pond of humanity. God will take care of where the ripples go.

You may one day have an opportunity to lead the next Billy Graham to faith in Christ Jesus. Or you may say the word that gets someone thinking, causing them to open their heart and mind to hear another word, causing them to seek more information about Jesus, leading that person to the point of receiving Christ. That's a worthy ripple, caused by one tiny pebble. We never know what our pebble of the word may do. But you can see how those ripples spread.

All you have to do is toss the pebble. Cause the ripples!

Prayer: Father, help us to keep tossing pebbles of your word to those we meet. Bring good results for your kingdom as those ripples travel...

Jun 20
Meditate on the Word

"Do not let this Book of the Law depart from your mouth; meditate on it day and night, so that you may be careful to do everything written in it. Then you will be prosperous and successful." Jos 1:8

If we spoke God's word all the time, we'd find ourselves in a lot less trouble, wouldn't we? Think of how you speak to each other at times. When your husband says he's as strong today as he was twenty years ago, do you retort, "Are we talking smell here?" Or do you say, "You were never *that* strong to begin with?" When your wife asks, "Will you still love me when I'm fat and sassy?" Do you burst out with, "You're not going to get *fat*, too, are you?" Friends, there's a more flattering, articulate answer waiting to be disbursed. One that will be music to your husband's, or wife's, ears. For the husband, a great response will be, "You're always my strong protector, Honey," or the lighter note of, "Hercules is a *weakling* beside you, dear." For the wife, the ethereal, "You're so sweet and lovely, I'll always see you the way you are now," or even a plain, "I'll love you forever no matter *what* life brings," are great ways to enhance your love life.

Do you know what those latter comments are? They're the instructions in God's word put into practical application. We're no longer under the constriction of following Old Testament law, but the New Testament *is* ours to meditate on, apply, and use in our daily life in every way. We use it with our dear spouse, and we use it interacting with people around us.

See, God's word has application in our words and in our actions. The first examples, while they may be funny, will cause hurt and conflict. The latter are examples of encouraging, reassuring, and lifting each other up, as the Bible instructs us.

As we meditate on God's word, we have it written on our hearts and minds by the Holy Spirit, and as we follow it, do it, or apply it, we have a promise, just as Joshua did. We'll be prosperous and successful, in our walk with Jesus, in our family life and relationships, and in our business ventures. His word, and the instruction in it, is given for our good. So meditate on His word. By the way, how's your Bible reading streak coming?

Prayer: Dear Lord, give us understanding as we spend time studying your word. Help us to apply it wisely, giving our actions and words positive purpose, and great results…

Jun 21
Why Must Good People Die Early?

"The righteous perish, and no one ponders it in his heart; devout men are taken away, and no one understands that the righteous are taken away to be spared from evil. Those who walk uprightly enter into peace; they find rest as they lie in death." Isa 57:1-2

Most of us have faced at one time or another the loss of someone close to us to unnatural circumstances, or terminal illness at an early age. It may have been a friend, or a family member, but whichever it was, we always seem to come back to the same question of "why, Lord?" It's a natural question when we don't understand what God's doing. These verses in Isaiah give us insight into the 'why', though.

We need to realize that God stands outside of time. He sees the end simultaneously with the beginning. He's the one who knows the future. Unless we get this concept in our heart and mind, we'll never come to real cognition of the essential core of the message given here.

Think of it this way. If you've ever watched much science fiction, at one time or another, you've seen a scene where someone is given a clear view of both the future and the past at the same time. While they see both, they're also given an opportunity to cross between the two, by some fold in space and time, and affect each of those time spans. Now, for us, that's just fantasy. The difference for the Lord is, He *does* see both, and every time in between.

Now, since God sees the future for each of us, He's able to prevent, or change, what's coming. Sometimes, though, due to other people and other factors, it's more beneficial for the Lord to take someone home to be with Him. That's exactly what this verse explains. Righteous people are occasionally taken from this life to spare them the evil trouble that lies ahead if they were left here. It's not a punishment for them. It's a glorious reward, a homecoming with our Heavenly Dad, and not one of them would wish to leave the presence of the Lord and return here. When they go home, they enter His peace, and eternal rest with Dad.

It's hard for those of us left behind, because we grieve for those who've gone on ahead. We don't grieve as those without hope, though, for we have God's promises, and we know we'll see them again, one day soon. We can trust that our Heavenly Dad wisely decides what's best for all of us. We take our comfort in Him.

Prayer: Heavenly Dad, we thank you that you see what's ahead, and that you spare us when that's best. Help us to be a comfort to others with these verses, too…

Jun 22
Perhaps You Don't Have to Dye

"Gray hair is a crown of splendor; it is attained by a righteous life." Pr 16:31

If you're old enough, you've noticed a certain deterioration in your hair color. If you're male, you've probably noticed a deterioration in your hair thickness, too, but that's beside this particular issue. The point is, we don't actually *have* to dye.

I can't even count how many times people have told me, "You're not going to live forever." I tend to reply, "Why not? I have so far!" We know statistically that in the past, the death rate for everyone born has been virtually one hundred percent. *Not* one hundred percent, though, because Enoch and Elijah were just taken up to Heaven. We're not told if there were others. So you see, there's hope for me.

Of course, we're really talking about dieing here, not dying. I love the book of Proverbs, because it has something to say about just almost anything you can think of. We hate to get old and gray, but the Bible tells us here that gray hair is a crown of splendor. I wonder why none of us want to get gray, then. Why do we fight so hard in this day and age to remain young? Not me, of course, I just don't want to get old prematurely. However, we've lost sight of the fact that, as we live righteously in the Lord, we attain a crown of splendor. It isn't something to fear, or run away from. It should be something we embrace. God has given us gray hair as a sign to the world of His blessing. It's a sign for us as Christians of the fact that we've walked with the Lord through life, and He's enjoyed our company, had a good time with us, and loves us dearly, so He's given us this particular crown.

So go ahead. Let your hair naturally gray. Wear that crown of splendor as God intended for you to. Be proud of what God has blessed you with, and walk with your head held high. Perhaps next year, or possibly the year after...

By the way, did you notice that I had to write this particular devotion by myself? You may not be aware of it, but the word I, keeps popping up, instead of we. I received no helpful input from Glenda whatsoever on this one.

Prayer: Lord, we do thank you that you've given us a sign of your favor when we live righteously before you. Help us to refrain from too much silliness where our hair is concerned...

Jun 23
If You Feed Them, They'll Come

"(About five thousand men were there.) They all ate and were satisfied, and the disciples picked up twelve basketfuls of broken pieces that were left over." Lk 9:14a & 17

"Honey, we've been invited to the Jensen's for a block party Saturday." "Ah, man, you didn't tell them we'd come, did you?" "Yes, dear, I did. It'll be fun." "Oh crud. That's the day we play OSU in football." "Well, all our friends will be there. You'll enjoy it." "I don't want to miss the game." "You've seen every game, it won't kill you to miss one." Silence. Then… "Are they going to have food?" "Yes, Hon, Jon's going to barbeque ribs." "Well—alright then."

How many times has this, and similar conversations, occurred all over the country? What is it about our mentality that we only want to do something if we can eat? We're the same way! If there's food, we're there, buddy. If it's free, all the better, too, right?

We're not the only ones who think this way. It's not particular to our culture or time in history, either. Jesus knew that people would follow if they were fed. He also knew many followed *because* they were fed. But they heard the message!

There was more to it than that, of course. Jesus was teaching the disciples that He has power to take a little, and do something glorious for God's work. He was also teaching that He can, and will, provide for us. The lack of food was no obstacle for Jesus. We look at five loaves and a couple of fish, and we see the lack. Jesus looks at it, and sees the possibilities. He's not deterred by the circumstances, because He sees those circumstances as opportunities for God's miracles in the hands of people of faith.

We use meals and snacks at church to draw people in to hear the message of Jesus Christ. We use food as a way of giving us a chance to visit and get to know new people, and make them feel welcome and loved.

The question is, what do *we* see? Do we see a lack of necessities, or the perfect place for a miracle from the Lord? Are we concentrating on the possibilities, or the problems?

Let's work to provide the right venue for our guests where they get a chance to hear the good news. If you feed them, they'll come.

Prayer: Father, give us the means and the ability to provide food to feed the body, and your word to feed the soul...

Jun 24
Get out of the Boat

"Lord, if it's you,' Peter replied, 'tell me to come to you on the water.' 'Come,' he said." Mt 14:28-29a

It's hard to tell whether Peter was just checking to see if it really was Jesus, or if he was operating in faith. Whichever it was, when Jesus bid Peter come, he got out of the boat, and went. We often focus on how Peter then became fearful of the wind and waves, but let's give credit where credit is due. Peter *did* get out of the boat, and he did walk on the water. He also knew whom to turn to when he began to sink. He called on the Lord!

We can often test to see if it's really the Lord, too. When we discern that it is, are we as obedient as Peter was? Do we step out in faith, and walk where Jesus bids us? When we do step out in faith, do we call on the Lord when we begin to sink, or do we try to go it alone?

The fact is, we'll face many obstacles if we're going to walk where Jesus tells us. When we step out for Jesus, Satan's going to hurl everything in our pathway that he can, and try to scare us out of what we're doing for Christ. He'll tell us we can't possibly succeed, he'll send people to interfere, he'll discourage us and wear us down if he can, and he'll make sure we have disappointments along the way.

We must keep in mind that, we serve the One who's greater than the devil, who's in this world. We have already overcome the world in Christ. We have power in the name of Jesus to fight these spiritual battles and emerge victorious. We can do all things through Christ Jesus our Lord. We're armed with the sword of the Spirit, God's word, the weapon belt of truth, the breastplate of righteousness, and the shield of faith. We can only be defeated if we give up. Otherwise, when we stand firm in the Lord, we have the victory.

So when you know it's Jesus bidding you come, take a lesson from Peter, and realize you can't go to Jesus unless you get out of the boat. Don't let the circumstances cause you to sink in fear. Keep your eyes on Jesus. Depend on Him, be obedient, *get out of the boat*, and walk on the water.

Prayer: Lord Jesus, help us to clearly hear your voice when you bid us come. We'll step out in obedience when we know it's you…

Jun 25
Love Means Never Having to Say You're Sorry

Yeah, try that with your spouse. That's a famous line from a popular movie years ago, but we all know that's a crock of waste. No one who's been in a romantic relationship believes that line. Why? Because no one's perfect. We all make mistakes. We all do or say things that disappoint, bother, or hurt the feelings of our lover. We can't maintain a healthy love relationship by ignoring our spouse's hurt feelings. Denial isn't going to wash away the pain of wounded emotions. A stoic refusal to acknowledge the pain we've caused isn't a strong stance, it's a stupid stance! Since we're stupid too frequently by mistake, let's not go out of our way to be so on purpose.

God's word tells us to keep short accounts with those we're in conflict with.

"Therefore, if you are offering your gift at the altar and there remember that your brother has something against you, leave your gift there in front of the altar. First go and be reconciled to your brother; then come and offer your gift." Mt 5:23-24

That's really essential when you're fighting with your husband or wife. When you're having a dispute with someone, and particularly when it's your spouse, your worship is hindered. God isn't pleased to accept your worship, and along with that, your mind and heart aren't in the proper attitude to do so, anyway. You can't focus on the Lord when something else is nagging at the back (or front) of your mind. To effectively worship, we need a clear heart and mind, free from the encumbrance of a relationship that has issues that have to be resolved.

If you're planning on spending time in worship to the Lord Jesus Christ, then you'd better take the time and opportunity to apologize to your spouse. We don't need that bothering us when we want our attention focused on praising and blessing the Lord. Go to God with a clear heart and conscience. To do that, there's something you have to do first.

Tell him or her you're sorry for the hurt you've caused. Seek your husband's or wife's forgiveness. Resolve that conflict, and restore that love relationship you've enjoyed. Didn't you know? Love means *always* saying you're sorry when you ought to!

Prayer: Lord, give us the words to express our sorrow for causing pain, and allow us the blessing of forgiveness, and restoration, in our relationship when we've sinned against the other…

Jun 26
Gain a More Youthful Looking Face

"Wisdom brightens a man's face and changes its hard appearance." Ecc 8:1b

Ladies, if you're struggling with lines that are beginning to drag down that youthful beauty you had, there's help. Why is it that when women get lines around their eyes, they're called 'crow's feet', but when men get them, they add 'character'? How can it be that when women get lines around their mouth, their mouth looks 'pinched', or 'pursed', but when that happens to men, they look 'rugged'?

Stress or heartache causes us to look haggard. Our face takes on a downcast, tight, hard countenance when we're tired, or overworked, or frazzled, or pressured. We show the afflictions we're dealing with in our eyes, and the set of our mouth. When we face trials, or we're grieving, it takes away our peace, and it's apparent on our face.

Now, we're all looking for the fountain of youth. We'd love to gain a younger visage, as well as that svelte figure we used to have, along with the vigor of our children. Everyone wants to look and feel his or her best. Naturally, none of us desires to feel old and fat and ugly. That's for those other folk out there. We ought to be forever lovely, or forever handsome, as the case may be.

The good news is there *is* help available. It isn't some new face cream. It isn't a new exercise that gives us firm flesh and tight muscles. It isn't even Botox. When we gain *wisdom*, it gives us a brighter countenance. It softens our appearance. When we're at peace within, it shows on the outside.

The only way to really gain wisdom is to seek the Lord. When we're in the Lord, we begin to receive wisdom. His wisdom. When we have that wisdom, we're given His peace, and a very real sense of comfort, resting in Him. When you're at peace within, it drains the stress away, it heals our heartaches, it renews our strength, it refreshes our spirit, and relieves the pressure we feel. Have the circumstances that brought this on changed? Probably not, although the Lord may do that too, but we walk with a light heart that also lights up our face when we travel in God's rest.

So give your cares to Jesus. Gain His wisdom. It'll brighten your face, and soften your appearance.

Prayer: Father, give us your wisdom, and the peace within that comes from trusting in you. We give you our problems, and ask you to take us to your Sabbath rest...

Jun 27
When Should We Retire from God's Service?

"The righteous will flourish like a palm tree, they will grow like a cedar of Lebanon; planted in the house of the Lord, they will flourish in the courts of our God. They will still bear fruit in old age, they will stay fresh and green, proclaiming, 'The Lord is upright; he is my Rock, and there is no wickedness in him.'" Ps 92:12-15

We work all our life, and look to the future, near or far, to the golden years when we can hang up punching a clock, and retire. We have visions of leaning back, putting our feet up, maybe traveling to places we've always been too busy to see, or perhaps spend time golfing and woodworking and quilting and gardening. We can envision the end of our employment days, but about our Christian service, retirement isn't so clear.

It's nice to see that as righteous people, we'll flourish like a palm tree. Palm trees are interesting. They have to endure some of the most brutal winds and storms, but you know they just bend over, get tougher, and when the storm passes, they stand right back up again. As people of faith in Christ Jesus, we're like that. The storms of life come, we get blown around, and bent over, but when the storm is past, because we're rooted in the Rock who is Christ, we just stand back up again.

Not only do we weather those storms, we flourish, because we're in the courts of God. In fact, this verse tells us that even when we grow old, we stay fresh and green. That's an example of how in Jesus we continue to grow, to enjoy fresh new life continuously, always ready and able to produce good fruit.

We have a message to bring no matter what our age. Our Lord is upright. The Lord is our Rock. The Lord is good, and there is no wickedness in Him. He brings refreshing, and is a solid rock, a firm foundation for life. Our God is life and strength, eternally in Jesus. This message never gets old, even when we do. It's still, and always will be, the good news those in the world need to hear. It's the real answer they're seeking.

So we can confidently say we've fixed the time of our retirement from God's service. That time is when we've crossed over to be with the Lord. As long as we're here, we have a witness to give. We will still bear fruit in *old age*. There is no retirement in this temporal life when we're walking in the Kingdom of God.

Prayer: Dear Lord, open our eyes to see the opportunities we have to bear fruit for your kingdom, and keep us fresh in our faith as we bring your message of encouragement…

Jun 28
The Promises

"Now you, brothers, like Isaac, are children of promise." Gal 4:28

God's word gives us many promises from the Lord. When we believe in Jesus, we become children of promise. In the Lord, we have many promises. If we repent, He is faithful and just to forgive us our sins, and cleanse us. Whosoever will may come. God is patient, not wanting any to perish. God loves us so much; He prepared salvation for us, and sacrificed His only Son. We have eternal life with Christ. We have already overcome the world. God will complete the good work in us. The Lord is near. We have the Holy Spirit within. We have His peace. We have his power. We have His favor. We have His grace. We have the mind of Christ.

With the Lord, when He gives us a promise, many of them we have, here and now. We've already begun our eternal life with Christ. He's already forgiven our sins. He loved us before we even knew Him. We already have the Holy Spirit, and on and on.

We make a lot of promises, too. How are we at fulfilling those commitments? Although God is always faithful, and always keeps His word, we often fail. We have to keep renewing our promises. But when we keep a promise, what a blessing it can be.

When we were married, we made a vow, and we made it before the Lord. Our vow is before God, and isn't a legal contract. That's what the state or country we live in has for us. In the Lord, when we make a promise, we have a covenant. If you're not in covenant marriage, then you need to begin now. That means that you take on some godly attitudes. The marriage bed is sacred. Divorce is not an option. It's a word that isn't even in our vocabulary regarding our relationship. We *will* honor our spouse. We love in all the good, and through all the bad. We're one, no matter the situation. We're married until we're separated by death. We're faithful to each other, and we're faithful to God. We live a life of trust, belief, and faith in Jesus Christ. We worship together as a family. We raise our children in Christianity, and we lead them to a personal faith in Christ. We live godly lives that are an example of Christ in us, so that His name is honored and blessed.

These are promises we *must* faithfully keep. When we do, we show the promise we are in God.

Prayer: Lord, remind us in time, to keep our vows, so that you are honored as people see us fulfill our promises...

Jun 29
Fellowship Together

"Every day they continued to meet together in the temple courts. They broke bread in their homes and ate together with glad and sincere hearts, praising God and enjoying the favor of all the people." Act 2:46-47a

There's a curious word in this verse. We often talk about the importance of gathering with other believers. We need that time together. It provides a chance to visit, to encourage one another, to know and love our family in Christ, and to gain a comfort level that allows us to share more intimately.

There are times when we need the help of someone we can trust, someone we can count on to be absolutely discreet. We gain the credibility with each other by spending time together, by being open and nonjudgmental, and by being humble and caring in supporting and praying for the issues we face. We'll have times when we have problems that are really sensitive, and that we don't want to be public knowledge.

That's particularly true in our marriage relationship. When we have issues that trouble us, and they're sensitive to one of us, we cannot discuss these issues with girlfriends or buddies. We have to be *perfectly* discreet to maintain the trust and loyalty needed in our love relationship.

In the early church we have an example of believers spending time in fellowship together. They met every day. They ate together in their homes. We always seem to fellowship best over food, don't we? They gathered together with glad and *sincere* hearts.

There's that curious word. *Sincere*. There was no pretence in their socializing. No trying to impress each other with larger than life tales, or by flashing new jewelry or the latest fashionable clothes. Sincerity speaks of a humble, honest, forthright manner in which they interacted as believers. They saw no social distinctions. They were brothers and sisters in Christ Jesus, and they knew they had nothing to be proud of, and nothing to rejoice in, except the glorious grace of God. That's why they were so open in praising God, and it's also why they enjoyed the favor of *all* the people. They weren't offending people in any way by their actions or attitudes. They loved and accepted anyone, and everyone, who put their faith in Jesus. They were glad, and rejoiced for every new believer.

Do we fellowship together? When we do, are we doing so with glad and *sincere* hearts?

Prayer: Heavenly Father, give us the right attitudes when we fellowship with our brothers and sisters in Christ. Help us to be completely humble, kind and loving…

Jun 30
Worthy Is the Lamb

"Worthy is the Lamb, who was slain, to receive power and wealth and wisdom and strength and honor and glory and praise!" Rev 5:12

That about covers it, doesn't it? But you know, the beginning is the whole message. Worthy is the Lamb. He's the one who gave himself to provide our salvation. By His sacrifice, he redeemed us. He's certainly worthy of our worship.

God desires our worship. He wants to speak to us, to spend time with us, and to commune with us. But He also wants us to worship Him. We need to acknowledge Him, His amazing attributes, and His love, mercy, and grace. When we do, it blesses God, but more than that, it blesses and refreshes *us*.

How can we best do that? That depends somewhat on you, but we encourage you to take some steps out of your current comfort level. First of all, we have to create a block of time if we're going to worship. It can be short or long, but it's best if you find a place of quiet, where you won't be interrupted by phones, or people. Then we have to focus on the Lord, and just lifting up our worship to Him.

Today is a good time to spend a few minutes in worship. Let's turn our attention completely on Him, doing our best to bless God.

Prayer: Lord Jesus, we just lift up your name, for you are certainly worthy of our worship…

Jul 1
Forget the Past

"Forget the former things; do not dwell on the past." Isa 43:18

The past is an anchor, the future a hope.

Nothing is heavier than regrets over failures. They are a weight that burdens us down to the point of having the power to cause continual collapse. We can look back and remember how we've stumbled before, how we've failed, and when we dwell on those times when we floundered, they handicap us from attempting new goals. When our memories of the past are larger than our vision for the future, they will defeat us before we even have a chance to succeed.

God's word tells us to forget the former things. When we're right with Christ, they no longer matter, except as a lesson learned, and not to be repeated. No, we're instructed not to dwell on the past, because when we do, it can cripple us from attaining the level of success God has for us. Success in our relationship with Him, success in our walk of obedience, success in our service, and success in our relationships with our spouse, family, and friends.

After we've stumbled, God has a new plan for us, a new vision of where He wants us, and of what His calling on our life is. He doesn't leave us where we are, wallowing in our misery of defeat and failure. He has a new place for us. He'll take our weakness, and by His power, make it something that reflects His miracle working power, and brings Him glory. He'll take us and do what only He can.

What we have to do is focus on the future, walk in faith, and cut the line that anchors us to the past. God gives us a new vision, and we need to keep our attention fixed on that calling. When we forget the past, we can receive wonderful blessings in the future, as we're obedient to God's plan. We have hope in our future, because that's where the Lord is.

Prayer: Lord, thank you for forgiving us our past sins and failures. Don't let us be crippled by the past, but give us hope and a new future...

Jul 2
Don't Take the Scenic Route

"Enter through the narrow gate. For wide is the gate and broad is the road that leads to destruction, and many enter through it. But small is the gate and narrow the road that leads to life, and only a few find it." Mt 7:13-14

When we were on tour out to Washington and back through Montana last summer, we had a chance to take a couple of days to do some hiking in Glacier National Park. On our way out, even though it was the most direct route, we drove through some of the most beautiful, scenic country, as we traveled along the Columbia River in Oregon. Hiking up in Glacier was some of the most fun, and most magnificent scenery, we've ever seen. It was absolutely breathtaking. We wandered around, followed the trails, hiked three miles up over a glacier to Hidden Lake, and took in as much of that scenic beauty as we could (really—we hiked over 11 miles the second day).

But you know, if we're going to look at this in terms of the Bible, the drive along the Columbia is more like our walk with Jesus. We stayed on the straight and narrow, and still experienced the great beauty of God's handiwork. We enjoyed wonderful, pleasant hours, and didn't have to worry about getting lost, or missing the way. That's like the small gate, and the narrow road that leads to Heaven.

Or we can wander around on our own, following trails that may be gorgeous, providing a lot of lovely viewing, even though they're pretty aimless. We can do all kinds of things along that way, and there are lots of pleasures to enjoy, but those trails don't get us to where we want to go. That's like the wide gate, and the broad road that leads to destruction. It's easy, it may be fun some of the time, it doesn't take any focus, or map following effort on our part, but in the end, we expend a lot of energy and strength, and we miss the goal.

On the journey through life, don't take the scenic route. The devil has all kinds of enticements to distract us, but the genuine blessings, the wholesome fun, the real rest and peace of mind, come from following the straight, narrow, and rather easy path the Lord lays out for us.

Prayer: Father, give us the good sense to follow your straight path, and find that narrow gate that leads to blessed life in you...

Jul 3
On Purpose

"You, however, know all about my teaching, my way of life, my purpose, faith, patience, love, endurance, persecutions, sufferings." II Tim 3:10-11a

Do you sometimes wander through your day aimlessly, not really focused on anything, thereby accomplishing next to nothing? We can do that a lot if we don't decide what our goal for the day is. When we plan what our priorities are, write down in order of importance the list of things we need to do, and schedule time slots for each of those, we're much more likely to attain those goals. In fact, when you purpose to do that, you'll almost always finish every one of those tasks.

Paul is telling Timothy something important here. He's reminding Timothy of his way of life, by pointing out his godly attributes and practices. Paul was disciplined in his work. He set out knowing what he hoped to accomplish, how he needed to teach, how he was going to display his faith, patience, and love. In the process, he proved his endurance as he suffered persecutions and hardships. But he was able to continue in the face of afflictions, because he was focused on a preset goal. He didn't allow circumstances to deter him from his appointed ministry.

Are you diligent in your calling? Have you figured out what your goals in the Lord are? Once that's been established, and you know God's plan for you, then you, too, can determine to attain His goals for you. By seeing the big picture, by having the vision in sight, we can break it down into manageable steps to reach the final end. We can set timetables to see where we are in our process, and manage and adjust our tasks as necessary to fit the timeline we're working in.

To accomplish all this, we have to go ahead with purpose. We have to manage our time and our efforts, rather than allowing our time, our efforts, or circumstances to manage us. By working with purpose, we avoid flying from one crisis to the next.

So decide your priorities for yourself. Lay out your plan for each month. Break down your steps to what tasks must be finished each week, and then knock it down to manageable steps for each day. When you plan out your life, you'll meet the goals you have.

Prayer: Lord Jesus, we want to live a life of purpose and completeness. Help us to know your plans for us, and lay out a roadmap to get us there, step by step…

Jul 4
Walk in Freedom

"It is for freedom that Christ has set us free. Stand firm, then, and do not let yourselves be burdened again by a yoke of slavery." Gal 5:1

We celebrate our independence here in the United States on the 4th of July. We recognize our forefathers who declared that all men are created equal and have God-given freedoms inherent in life. This country was founded by men and women who were willing to sacrifice, fight, and die to secure liberty for their family's future. We have founding documents that recognize those God ordained freedoms, and allowed us to grow as a nation due to the lack of government restrictions that other countries labored under. That freedom gave us the impetus to become the greatest nation this world has ever seen.

We know, also, from history, that most nations collapse from within. Our original founding fathers knew, and wrote about, the necessity of a moral foundation for a free country. They knew, and prophesied, that without that biblical foundation, we'd fail. As we've digressed from the philosophies and the Bible based, self-disciplined, lifestyle and morals that we began with, we see a continual slide in morals, justice, and freedoms in this country. Without reverence for the Lord, and a healthy moral compass that can come only from God, we'll continue to lose the liberty we enjoyed as a nation. The further we get away from God, the more bondage we'll live in.

Bondage or slavery isn't what God intended for us, though. Like godly men and women the world over have known for centuries, we were created to live and walk in liberty. There's a yearning in the human spirit that desires freedom. In Jesus Christ, we've been set free from bondage. We were slaves to sin before we repented and put our faith in Christ. Now we're free from the chains that held us locked in their grip.

It's important for us as believers to walk in that freedom, and not allow ourselves to be yoked again by the burden of sin. It is for freedom that Christ set us free. *Continue* in freedom.

In 1759, Benjamin Franklin is quoted in a book, saying, "Those who would give up *essential liberty* to purchase a little *temporary safety*, deserve neither *liberty* nor *safety*."

He was speaking about those in our country who thought they could trade out freedom for security. Life just doesn't work that way. When we're willing to give up our freedom in Christ for the gratification of temporary pleasure, we don't deserve the liberty we have in Christ Jesus. Thankfully, He's willing to forgive us, and restore our freedom in Him.

Do what's best. Keep walking in freedom.

Prayer: Lord, keep us making right decisions to walk in liberty. You've given us your Spirit of love, power, and self-discipline…

Jul 5
Who's True?

"Let God be true, and every man a liar." Rom 3:4b

We have a tendency to judge things by our own experience. If we go to a restaurant, and we get great service and good food, at a decent price, we think that's a wonderful place to eat. But our friends go, and their service is slow, and the food lukewarm, they think that's a lousy place to eat. Was there even a difference? It was the same place. It may even have been the same wait staff and cooks. The difference was our experience. Ours was good, theirs was bad, and consequently we have very different opinions.

Or take a movie. You go see the newest movie at the theatre and you just love it. It has lots of action, good romantic tension, a mystery you can't unravel, and the good guys win in the end. It's fun and exciting, and you leave feeling happy and positive. Let your kids go see the same movie, and you'll often get the polar opposite reaction. They'll think it was too mushy, or cheesy, or dumb, or whatever adjectives our youth happen to be using these days. Why the difference? It's because we each gauged the movie on our own experiences, which are affected by our mindsets regarding the types of scenes we saw. Our memories of similar situations are quite positive, while our children may have negative connotations associated with those same scenes.

In both cases, neither of us is absolutely right or wrong. We just interpreted our experiences differently. There is a difference when it involves the Lord, though. God's perspective *can't* be wrong. He's *incapable* of falsehood. He *cannot* be mistaken in any way. So when we have an opinion of what God is doing in some area, we may have missed the point, or the application, or His plan, but that means *we're* wrong. When God says something, even when our experience thus far doesn't agree, it doesn't negate God's honesty, or His faithfulness; it's *true*. We usually need more time to ascertain what's happening, and when we reach the end of what seems contradictory to our understanding; we see that, once again, God was faithful and true.

God always proves himself. Not as quickly as we'd like a great share of the time, but one thing you can count on. God is true, and when we contradict Him, *we're* the liars.

Prayer: Heavenly Father, help us to have the understanding that when our circumstances seem to conflict with your word, we can trust you to resolve it correctly, as you always have…

Jul 6
What's That in Your Eye?

"Why do you look at the speck of sawdust in your brother's eye and pay no attention to the plank in your own eye? First, take the plank out of your eye, and then you will see clearly to remove the speck from your brother's eye." Lk 6:41&42c-d

A few months ago I was helping out at Ecclesia College by doing some carpentry work. I'd been doing some sawing, and there was quite a breeze blowing. When I stopped to have lunch, I was sitting talking to this guy, and he asked me if I had something in my eye. I said I didn't think so. He said, "well there's sure something in there. In fact it's quite large. Can't you feel it?" I couldn't, but I wear contact lenses, so I got up and went to the restroom to look. Sure enough, I had the biggest piece of wood stuck to my contact that you could imagine. It was huge! I don't know how it didn't interfere with my vision.

That gave me a new perspective on this Bible verse. It was actually funny, but this talks about a scenario that's even more ludicrous. We try to help others get little specks out of their eyes, while we have a 2 by 8 stuck in our own.

It's always easier to see the faults in others. We seem to have a way of completely overlooking our own shortcomings, while clearly seeing the failures in those around us. Have you noticed that it's so easy to notice someone else cuss, while we blow right by our rudeness in traffic? Isn't it interesting that we can criticize our neighbors work habits while we stuff our face watching the football game? When we try to correct someone else, and they see the ridiculous problems we haven't taken care of in our own life, we have no credibility, and they refuse our advice, even if it's actually sound. Jesus calls that hypocrisy. And it is. He has a solution for us.

Examine yourself! When we take care of our own failures and adjust our lives to line up with God's standards for us, then, and only then, are we in a position to help others with their issues. We have to be walking a life of righteousness before we can effectively lead others into a pure walk. Set an example of godly living, and then you'll be able to see that speck.

Prayer: Dear Lord, make us careful to inspect ourselves, and correct our own issues so that we're walking in a manner that's worthy of you…

Jul 7
Are You Hospitable?

"We ought therefore to show hospitality to such men so that we may work together for the truth." III Jn 8

Sometimes when we're traveling we're amazed at how hospitable people can be towards us. Most places we go folks take good care of us. We don't have high expectations, because we know that as long as we have a bed to sleep in, we're content with that. Once in a while, though, a family goes out of their way and takes extraordinary measures. We sang in Newport, AR, and a family took us to lunch at their country club, and treated us like gold. We were in Chautauqua, KS one time, and the family there gave us their whole downstairs for the night, complete with game room, ping-pong, and a fireplace. In Rugby, ND, a gentleman offered to fill our truck with gas. The list goes on and on. We really appreciate the great hospitality people provide, because we travel a lot in our singing ministry. We also both grew up on farms in the Dakotas, so we don't expect fancy places. Consequently, we appreciate those who exert themselves and are so thoughtful. We've learned how important hospitality is as a result of our concert tours, and try to extend that same kindness to others.

There's another factor at work, here, too. When we share hospitality with those who are working for God's kingdom, we join with them in working for Christ Jesus. If we have a chance to provide some need for them, we've helped them along the way. We've done our part to complete God's work. We've given them the rest they need, or we've renewed their strength with a meal, or we've encouraged them by giving them some financial help. However we have the chance to show that hospitality, we ought to do so. We'll be blessed far beyond what they are.

There are many around us that need that hospitality, too. We have so many families in our churches that need the fellowship that you can provide by having them over for a meal. It blesses them, and even though it's quite a bit of work, it blesses us too. Don't expect a reciprocal invitation. Just share a meal with someone for goodness sake. When you're being hospitable, you can't keep score. That defeats the purpose of blessing others.

Prayer: Lord, give us the energy, and the resolve, to be hospitable to others in any way we can...

Jul 8
I Just Can't See Him

"We live by faith, not by sight." II Cor 5:7

A couple of years ago we were at a concert (not one of ours), and this little girl went up to pray. Glenda went forward and knelt down, and prayed with her. After the concert was over, on our way out the little girl ran up and thanked Glenda. Glenda told her that Jesus loves her very much. She replied, "But I can't see him. I can't see him anywhere." About that time Glenda started praying for wisdom. On an impulse, she bent down and blew on her cheek, and asked her, "Did you feel that?" She said yes, and Glenda explained that, kind of like that, we can feel Jesus in our hearts, but we may not be able to see Him.

Just like the breeze, even when we don't see Him, even if we don't feel Him, Jesus is always right here with us. He promised He would never leave us nor forsake us. That means no matter what the circumstances, no matter what crisis we're facing, no matter how traumatic or dire the situation is; Jesus is beside us, holding our hand as we go through that trial.

Our eyes can play tricks on us. If you want proof of that, go to a show presented by an illusionist. He can do many things that leave us doubting our own faculties, but it's all just a trick. What we see isn't real. Through misdirection, slight of hand, and optical illusions, the 'magician' does miraculous things.

In ways, we don't get to see what God is doing, or where He is, at a particular moment, but that doesn't matter. That's not how we got to know Christ, so we aren't doing anything different than we have before. We know Jesus Christ through our faith in Him and His saving grace, so as we continue our journey with Him, we keep walking by faith. By faith, we met Him. By faith, we received His promised Holy Spirit. By faith, we know the Heavenly Father, and the love He has for us. By faith, we are sure of God's promises to us, because He's proven Himself so many times previously in our life, and so we have a sure hope, by that same faith.

Granted, it would be much easier for us sometimes if we could see what God is doing, but that's not how He works. Jesus told us we would be blessed by believing in Him without seeing (remember the disciple Thomas in the locked house). That's taking Him by faith. And when we do that, He confirms it in our hearts by His Spirit, and by the sense of His presence.

If you want to see clearly, you must continue to walk by faith. If you don't want to be deceived, don't rely on your sight.

Prayer: Father, give us the faith we need not to rely on sight. Then we pray you remind us to stir up our faith when needed...

Jul 9
Don't Be an Enemy of God

"Anyone who chooses to be a friend of the world becomes an enemy of God." Jas 4:4b

We can really let our priorities get skewed if we're not careful. We face a daily onslaught of the world's philosophy everywhere we go. We have marketing that hits us in every place and aspect of life. You can hardly go into a restroom anymore without seeing advertising right in front of you. Bathroom graffiti has been replaced by ads. Billboards, bus sides, television ads, radio, park benches, and street benches all deliver a message. If you've noticed, 99% of these messages are *not* a godly, biblical word for our time. No, they bring us visual images of perfect bodies, perfect automobiles, perfect hobbies, perfect friends, perfect homes, and our wallets filled with perfect money. Not one of those ads tells us that we'll be separated from the Lord if we follow their message. They entice us with the idea that when we use this product, we'll be surrounded by smiling friends, or respectful coworkers, or envious buddies, or beautiful women, or fawning men.

They don't tell us that when we charge that new outfit to our credit card we've just added a link to a chain of bondage. They're not going to inform you that when you buy that fancy new automobile you're adding several more links in that slave chain. They don't let you know that your wife or husband is going to be furious with you for purchasing that beautiful jewelry you can't afford.

But what if you can afford those things? What if you have the money to buy that new Lexus outright, or those clothes, or that jewelry? Doesn't that mean it's okay to have those things? The answer is, maybe. It depends on why you get them, and what your attitude is in owning those things. If you're buying into the world's philosophy that you're only successful if you're good looking, have a great income, loads of money, all the latest new tech gadgets, the sharpest fashions, and the glitzy jewelry, then you've completely missed the Lord's perspective on life.

When we become a friend of the world, we become an enemy of God. The Lord isn't really all that interested in you gaining the world's wealth. God wants your heart. Where your heart is, your treasure is also. When your heart is in attaining more and more of the world's wealth, then that's your treasure. That means the Lord *isn't* your treasure, because you've put your hope in the security that money, power, and influence brings.

The only way stuff is okay, is if the Lord is always first in your life, and in every part of your life. We have to love the Lord with all our heart, mind, soul, and strength. That means that God *alone* has control of how we use the financial resources He grants us. When that's the case, then we haven't bought into loving the world, or becoming God's enemy. We're faithful, instead, to being good stewards of God's blessings.

Prayer: Lord, give us the right heart in making you Lord of every area of our lives. Help us to see through the marketing we're bombarded with every day…

Jul 10
Are You Building Sand Castles?

"But everyone who hears these words of mine and does not put them into practice is like a foolish man who built his house on sand. The rain came down, the streams rose, and the winds blew and beat against that house, and it fell with a great crash." Mt 7:26-27

Have you ever seen, in person, some of the fantastic castles people build at the beach? Some of them are just magnificent. They can be several stories in height, with turrets and towers that stretch up majestically. They're an architectural wonder to behold. They're so vivid that they can inspire daydreams of warrior knights, and beautiful maidens, gracing the halls of the king's court. They bring to mind days of old, when medieval gallantry shown forth in every realm.

We sometimes build castles of sand ourselves, don't we? We have this dream of how things ought to be in our lives, or visions of how we want them to be, and we start right in building our castle. Time is too precious to wait on planning every little detail. We can do that later, as we're in the building process. Our castle begins to rise, to take shape. We start seeing the towers, and soon the spires point up to the sky, as well. We begin to put the finishing touches on our castle, the fine paint, and gold gilding, and everything is looking so beautiful.

Then we make a discovery. Our castle is eroding from the inside, and the edges of the base are crumbling. Soon it becomes apparent that the whole castle is in danger of disintegrating entirely. Of course, like every sand castle, we should expect that. When the storms come, and the tides rise, our castle is washed away. It's just sand, after all. And when we neglect to put into practice God's instruction, we've only built a sand castle.

Our life becomes one of two structures. Our marriage becomes one of two structures. Our family becomes one of two structures. What that structure is depends on what we've built upon. If we build on sand, our structure will wash away in the storms of life. But when we build on the Rock, no matter what storms come, regardless of how the wind roars and blows, however hard the waves crash against that foundation, our house stands solid, impervious to the elements that confront it. When our life is built on our faith in Jesus Christ, when our marriage has the love of God as its foundation, when our family is grounded on the basis of His word, then our structure is indestructible. That happens because we've built on the solid rock, with materials that defy destruction.

Don't build sand castles. Build on the Rock, with Rock!

Prayer: Jesus, give us wisdom to count the cost, and make sure of our foundation, and build on you, the Rock of ages…

Jul 11
In a Rut

"Meaningless! Meaningless!' says the Teacher. 'Utterly meaningless! Everything is meaningless!" Ecc 1:2

Life in the late 20th century was often referred to as the 'rat race'. People were seen as having a drive to get somewhere, and get there fast, while all the time really just going in circles. Husband and wife got up in the morning, got ready for work, drove into the city, worked all day, drove back home at night, had dinner, tucked in the kids, and went to bed, only to get up the next day and repeat the process. Over and over and over again, thereby making a rut where they traveled each day.

Years ago on the farm, when we used the same path continually, we would literally wear ruts in the dirt. Those ruts became deeper and deeper the more we traveled them. When it was dry, we wore the dust away. When it was wet, we splashed out the mud in the track, making them ever deeper. The sides got steeper; the ruts became deeper, until there were places you *couldn't* pull out of the ruts.

If you've gotten into that kind of a rut with your daily routine, it's time you changed up your habits. You need to do something different, travel a different route, so to speak. It's dangerous to be in that kind of a rut, because whether you know it or not, a rut is just a grave that hasn't had the ends filled in yet. When you're at this point, you can feel life is utterly meaningless.

Solomon goes through a whole litany of the pleasures he pursued, the projects he did, the wealth he enjoyed, and the wives and concubines that were his. He found that without God, nothing has any meaning. When you're working to pursue your own interests and pleasures, or when you're doing only the things you 'have to', you're living a pretty meaningless life. We'll never have satisfaction unless we live with real purpose. If you're living life just to get ahead (of what we can't seem to define), you're living a hollow existence.

To leave the rut, to live a life filled with purpose, to find joy and satisfaction in our work and in our rest, we have to live for the Lord. He's the only one who can give us the peace and contentment we seek. He's the only one who provides satisfaction in our toil. He's the only one who gives us real happiness in our wife or husband and our family. That happens because in Christ, we find our purpose.

Sometimes we know Jesus, and still live in a rut. Friends, that's not what He wants for us. He has plans for our joy, peace, and contentment. Don't ignore Him and live in a rut. Find His plan for your lives, for your marriage, and for your family, and you'll leave the rut behind.

Prayer: Lord, help us to keep our attention on you, and show us your plan for us, so that we travel that beautiful journey away from the meaningless rut that we can get into...

Jul 12
Honor Your Bed

"Marriage should be honored by all, and the marriage bed kept pure, for God will judge the adulterer and all the sexually immoral." Heb 13:4

Obviously this doesn't mean we reverence the bed itself that we sleep on. We should be very careful, though, because when this talks about the marriage bed, it does encompass any bed we sleep on, and more particularly, who we're in it with. We *are* supposed to reverence what our bed stands for in our marriage.

The world today will continually tempt us with the sights and sounds of romantic exploits outside the constraining chains of our marriage vows. Images of love and excitement fill the television shows and the movies. Beautiful women and handsome men are just waiting out there for us, and they'll whisk us off to some exotic get-away for fun in the sun. What actually happens is, we only get the idea in our minds, but the reality of affairs is, it never happens that way. We see someone who intrigues us, we begin to converse, to have coffee, and lunch, and we find ways to spend time together, until that moment comes when we cross a boundary. We end up sneaking around, hiding in dives, and losing our self-respect and our integrity, and while it may be exciting at first, the shame that follows is inevitable.

That happens because we've dishonored our spouse, and our marriage relationship. We haven't kept the marriage bed pure. We end up defiling it because of selfish desires. We become adulterers, those who are sexually immoral. When we engage in an affair, we enter into a realm of sin, and the Bible calls that sin idolatry. In more practical terms, we've given up our rights and privileges, and we've stepped off a precipice that destroys our marriage, our family, our relationships, and our standing in the community.

The good news is, we don't have to take those steps. We can turn away from those entanglements. God has given us the power in Him to step aside from temptation before it has a chance to grab us. We just have to be honest with ourselves and realize when a spark of admiration occurs. We have to recognize where we're weak, and guard against that unceasingly.

Only *we* can keep our commitments firmly in mind. And that's where every affair begins. In our minds! When we're unswervingly loyal to our spouse, we diminish the possibility of missteps. When we take great pains to behave as though our husband or wife were always standing right there watching us, we eliminate anything that dishonors him or her. When we reverence the relationship, the spouse, and the covenant marriage God has blessed us with, we stand confidently, knowing we honor our marriage bed, and keeping it pure. And when we keep our marriage bed pure, it allows us a joy, and an excitement, and a contented happiness that can only happen there.

Prayer: Dear Lord, we renew again our promise of fidelity to one another. We commit to being loyal to each other in every way, giving honor and respect, even when we're apart...

Jul 13
The God of Second Chances?

"Repent! Turn away from all your offenses; then sin will not be your downfall. Rid yourselves of all the offenses you have committed, and get a new heart and a new spirit." Eze 18:30c-31b

Yesterday we talked about keeping the marriage bed pure, but we realize that some have already failed in this area. If you're one who's had that failure, and you're still married to the spouse you sinned against, then you know the gratitude you feel for the forgiveness of your husband or wife. You're really thankful, because you know they have the right to leave, and divorce you, for your adulterous act. They've given you a second chance to get it right. In some cases, you may be on your third or fourth second chance. If sexual sin is your weakness, like other weaknesses we have, it sometimes takes more than one transgression to figure out how to combat that particular tendency. As believers in Jesus Christ, we *can* be free from whatever sin we lean towards.

We talk frequently about how we're thankful that when we stumble and fall, God picks us up, dusts us off, and sends us on our way. God does that over and over, and we tell about the second chances He gives us. But we're misunderstanding what the Lord does. He's really *not* the God of second chances. He's the God of *new beginnings*! We understand the verbiage of calling them second chances. Look at this verse, though. When we repent, when we turn away from our sins, God gives us a *new* heart and a *new* spirit. Remember that godly sorrow leads to repentance, and doesn't carry with it guilt and shame.

What does this mean for you, if you've fallen into sexual sin? It means that while we're ashamed of what we've done, we cannot walk in Christ as though we're a second-class citizen. He's given us a new heart. In the end, that sin led to godly sorrow, which led to repentance, and new life in Christ Jesus. God has a new plan for you. He'll take that failure, and turn it into a strength for His kingdom. He may place you in situations to deal with others in that same failing, whereby you can help them through, overcoming and leaving that sin behind, and finding a new beginning themselves. You *will* always have to be on guard against your own weakness. God will not call you to minister to someone of the opposite sex when that's your weakness, too. You may feel empathy and want to help, but you know rationally that would be foolish in the extreme. Don't do that! But you can guide others of your own gender, and teach them the practices and attitudes that are keeping you on the right track in honoring your marriage afresh and anew. That would be God's new plan for you in action. That's what we can do in new beginnings.

Prayer: Heavenly Father, help us to have the self-discipline to protect ourselves from our own weaknesses, and to stay fixed on you, and honoring our spouse…

Jul 14
Still Waters Run Deep

"But when I was silent and still, not even saying anything good, my anguish increased. My heart grew hot within me, and as I meditated, the fire burned; then I spoke with my tongue." Ps 39:2-3

When the river is narrow, and the sides rise up to form a gorge, then the water runs fast and shallow. When the river is wide, it still runs quickly over the rocks, creating rapids that are dangerous. It's odd that, when the river calms down, and seems to slow in its path, when it looks the safest, is when it actually is deeper than anywhere else. When there's that much depth, the water becomes still, and it takes its time, because it has plenty of room.

Sometimes, we can be like the river. We can quickly run across the rocks, cascading over the boulders where the bed is narrow or shallow. We spout off verses, offer quick condolences, give advice right from the top of our head, and we're on our way. That's not really what we're about though. We aren't supposed to be shallow Christians. You normally can't minister effectively, if you try to minister fast.

When the water is still and deep, it may not be as exciting to travel. But even though the depth to drown is enormous, that's the safest place to be traveling. While it goes down a long ways, it doesn't matter, because you're virtually assured that you won't be dumped into the water by the hazards of the river. That's a good analogy in our walk with God, too.

When we take our time, and be silent and still, and let the Holy Spirit speak to us, so He can speak through us, we become that deep water. We need to give God time, and room, and create the space to let our waters run deep. When we allow God to move us, and we meditate on where He's leading, and how, then our fires are stoked. Our heart becomes hot with God's righteousness, and His purpose. Then, when we speak, we convey the very message of God.

Be the deep Christian. Let the Lord work in your heart and mind. Give Him space in your life, time in your presence, and permission to work in you to accomplish His good will and purpose.

Prayer: Dear Lord, help us to take the time to become still and deep in you...

Jul 15
What Are You Producing?

"Land that drinks in the rain often falling on it and that produces a crop useful to those for whom it is farmed receives the blessing of God. But land that produces thorns and thistles is worthless and is in danger of being cursed. In the end it will be burned." Heb 6:7-8

If you've ever worked on a farm, you know what a nuisance thorns and thistles are. They choke out good plants, producing a piece of ground where nothing can be harvested. In addition, they scratch the skin right off of you, should you dare push through them. They have no use (unless you like the flowers when they bloom, but they're a bit spindly), and cause detours on top of it. When we get to autumn, those weeds are cut down, gathered up, and a large and rather impressive bonfire is lit. They aren't good for anything else.

That land that is free of thorns, thistles, and weeds is where the bountiful crops are raised. Wheat that grows thickly, producing heads of grain that are amazing. Corn that grows tall, and gives us great eating, or livestock feed, along with the stalks for ensilage. Barley that gives us bread and certain flours. Durum for the great pastas we enjoy. Oats for cereal, bread, and feed. Sunflowers for cooking oils. Whatever is grown, the land produces a great harvest when it's given the right nutrients and rain.

We're each a field, too. What's in your field? What have you planted? What have you actually nurtured? Is your field filled with the thorns of chasing worldly success, the thistles of striving for more things, or the weeds of time spent in pursuit of your own pleasure? If it is, it's time to reorder your priorities. In the end, those things are in imminent danger of being cursed, and burned up in fire.

Instead, water your field with the rain of generous living, plant the crops of good works, and of helping others, and fill it with the sunshine of kindness, of encouraging one another, and of brotherly love. These will produce a bountiful harvest for the Lord, and for the praise of His glorious name. *They* will receive the blessing of God.

Prayer: Lord Jesus, give us fields filled with useful crops for you. Point out what we should plant, where we should nurture, and when to harvest…

Jul 16
Are You Less Than Pleasant to Live With (a jerk)?

"Better to live in a desert than with a quarrelsome and ill-tempered wife." Pr 21:19

"His name was Nabal and…was surly and mean in his dealings." I Sam 25:3 (excerpt)

Pity the wife who has to live with a man who's surly and mean. He's the kind of guy who treats her rudely, belittles and criticizes her, often both privately and in public, and is harsh with her a great share of the time. He does things just to spite her, finding ways to needle her, and make her miserable at every opportunity. He withholds kindness, and is stingy with his goods. He's the type of man who evokes sympathy from everyone for his wife, and despite towards himself.

Pity the husband who has to live with a woman who's quarrelsome and ill-tempered. She's the kind of gal who castigates him for every perceived failing, squabbles about every action he takes, disputes every statement, and bickers incessantly over every assertion. She does malicious things to him, creating a hostile environment in their home. She treats him offensively, and doesn't hesitate to heap vile predilections on him at every opening. She evokes sympathy from everyone for her husband, and wary contempt towards herself.

We don't intend to startle you, but husband, you can't get your wife to love you more by being surly. She's not going to jump into your arms, and beg for sex, when you've belittled her, been harsh with her, and caused her emotional pain by the things you've said and done. That does not inspire a kind, loving response.

Nor do we mean to alarm you, but wife; you can't get your husband to love you more by being quarrelsome. Arguing with him constantly, nagging him incessantly, or attempting to shame him into being a better husband, isn't going to get you love notes and flowers. If you're treating him worse than the dog (you wouldn't actually kick the dog), you're not going to engender a wash of romantic love, and a generous spirit, in him.

These are reverse examples. These are illustrations of ways we will never enhance our marriage love. No, if you'd like to have a wonderful relationship, you have to do the opposite of these things. You have to be kind, and thoughtful, and generous, and helpful, and encouraging, and supportive, and respectful, and gentle, and affirming, and complimentary, and peaceful, and patient, and agape loving. Do only those things that help your husband or wife *feel* loved. Say only those things that brighten his or her day. Do unto your spouse the very things you'd love for him or her to do unto you.

Prayer: Father, help us to remove any attitudes and behaviors that aren't uplifting, loving, and encouraging to each other…

Jul 17
Who Can You Depend On?

"That we might not rely on ourselves, but on God…" II Cor 1:9b

Some friends of ours had a medical situation, and a brief hospital stay that required us to take care of their 6-month-old baby. As we cared for him, it brought back some poignant memories. Our babies are utterly and completely dependent on us to care for their every need. They cannot do a thing for themselves, aside from the most basic bodily functions, and even those sometimes need help. Without us, they're lost and doomed to die.

Who do you know as adults that you can depend on? Most of us can count on our husband or wife. We may be able to depend on our children, or at least some of them. We usually have at least a few friends we know will help us out. You may be able to count on one hand the family and friends you trust to care for you in a pinch, that you have no doubt will come through for you. That's actually pretty normal. Those types of individuals are tough to come by.

There is one on whom we can rely. He's the only person we know will always be dependable. He never gets sidetracked. He'll never be distracted by other matters. His attention is always focused on us. He'll never leave. He'll never forsake us. We can always depend, with one hundred percent assurance that He'll care for us, and in the way that's best for us.

We often want to take care of things ourselves. We have this body, this brain, this strength, this intelligence, and this will to get us over and through each and every situation, don't we? We like to think so, but none of that would be ours were it not for the grace of God. Even when we think we can go it alone, we get as far as we do because of the body and brains God blessed us with. And when we find we can't do it ourselves, we're frustrated and bothered, and our self-esteem suffers. We can't even depend on ourselves.

If we'll just take everything to the Lord to begin with, then we know that He'll see us through every situation, because we'll be walking in His power, and His wisdom, and according to His plan. We rely on God, because we should. We rely on God, because He leads us and guides us when we let Him.

Rely on God! He's the only one on whom we can really depend.

Prayer: Dear Jesus, we cast our problems, cares, and burdens on you. Lead us in your paths as we wend our way through…

Jul 18
Hot or Cold

"So, because you are lukewarm—neither hot nor cold—I am about to spit you out of my mouth." Rev 3:16

Do you like coffee? I love a nice, hot cup of coffee. The aroma, the taste, and the smooth richness of it, are a tantalizing treat. I also love ice cold Diet Coke. It's refreshing, it's soothing, and it quenches my thirst when I'm hot and sweaty.

Nothing is more disgusting than coffee at room temperature. It really does make me spit it right back into the cup. Conversely, not much is less appealing than Diet Coke when it's been sitting outside while I work, and reaches air temperature. It's not nearly as refreshing then as when it's cold.

This is a great example the Lord used. It's one we can readily identify with. We're the same way. We don't appreciate drinks that are lukewarm, either. They're nearly undrinkable.

In our relationships, we don't want a spouse who can 'take it or leave it'. If our husband or wife was lukewarm, showing a lack of interest, or caring, we'd get the feeling the love they felt wasn't all that ardent. The truth is, we'd be right. When you love someone, you can't be lukewarm. There's a reason we use the terms hot and cold when we talk about relationships. If your love relationship with your spouse is hot, you're doing great. If it's cold, you're in serious trouble. If it's lukewarm, no one cares. Apathy has set in, and that's difficult to overcome.

God is like that with us. He wants our love for Him to be hot, or even cold. He warns us that when we're apathetic about Him, He's about to spit us out of His mouth. Just like we would room temperature coffee. Who can blame Him? He doesn't want a lukewarm response to His love any more than we want a cool, or barely warm, response to ours. The thing is, we're the only ones who can stir up our love to sizzling hot again.

When you do that with your spouse, romantic sparks will fly. When we stir up our love for the Lord, He'll see to it that we accomplish great things for Him.

Prayer: Lord, help us never to become lukewarm in our love for you. Make us hot for your kingdom…

Jul 19
Don't Even Deceive

"You should follow in his steps. He committed no sin, and no deceit was found in his mouth." I Pet 2:21d-22

Think about a time when you didn't want to let someone know what you had been doing. Think about the conversation you had with that person. What you were doing may not have been sin, and not telling that friend or spouse what you did may not have been sin, but were you entirely honest? At times, we're less than forthcoming with all the facts. We don't necessarily have to reveal what we were doing; it may not be any of the other person's business. But when we tell just enough bits and pieces to let the other person draw their own, albeit erroneous, conclusion, while we haven't actually lied, we have deceived.

God sets a higher standard than that. Jesus not only committed no sin, He didn't even deceive people. No deceit was found in His mouth. We are to emulate Christ. That leads us to believe we ought to avoid deceiving people. Our goal is to be open and honest.

When there's something we don't want to tell someone, well, let's talk about that. We want you to have practical solutions to the problems we talk about. Let's say, you have a friend who always wants to know your business. You don't want to let them know about something you did, because your friend will come to conclusions that may not shed the best light on someone else. Rather than tell your friend little bits to throw him or her off track (deceive), it might be better to just say, "I'm sorry, I can't talk about this errand I ran." Or you might say, "I'm sorry, I'm not at liberty to discuss that trip." Either way, it's no reflection on your nosy friend, and it protects the other person involved by leaving them out entirely, as well as offering no clues about the situation. Sometimes we just have to be upfront and let someone know you can't discuss it. What you've just done is tell your friend, "it's none of your business," without actually telling your friend, "It's none of your business."

We deceive our friends and acquaintances other ways, as well. When they ask how we're doing, or how things are going, we often tell them they're much better than they actually are. That's deception.

We need to make a commitment; we refuse to deceive. Let's make it our practice to be open, honest, and forthright. Let no deceit be found in our mouths.

Prayer: Lord Jesus, place in us the virtue of being honest, with no deceit found in our mouths...

Jul 20
Stop Quarrelling

"Don't have anything to do with foolish and stupid arguments, because you know they produce quarrels. And the Lord's servant must not quarrel; instead, he must be kind to everyone, able to teach, not resentful." II Tim 2:23-24

As husband and wife, we have to admit we sometimes argue, don't we? No marriage that we're aware of has ever made it through without some disagreements from time to time. Some suffer that a great share of the time. Is that what God wants for us, though? This verse tells us not to have foolish or stupid arguments. Most of the squabbles we have start with something so insignificant that when we look back, we can't even believe it led to a quarrel.

We've had petty fights that started over one of us getting offended because the other said how hard they worked today, and how tired they were. That was followed by, they worked hard too, and why act like you're the only one who ever does anything. Get the picture? Isn't that stupid?

How about this one? She said she'd take the baby into the bathroom with her so the baby wouldn't be alone. He was sitting right there in the living room. He mentioned since he was there, the baby wouldn't be alone. Followed by, you think I can't watch the baby in the same room with me? That wasn't what she meant, and he was being silly. Boy! That fight ended with Husband at our house, and Glenda having to go over to see Wife. It seems funny now, but that isn't even uncommon. That situation, or one nearly like it, happens every day, all over the country. Our arguments are normally over something so ridiculous that it's laughable. But they cause real pain, because in the middle of our squabbles, we tend to say things that we don't even believe, just to hurt the other person. Friends, those are stupid, foolish arguments.

We're the Lord's servants. We ought not quarrel. In our home is the perfect place to practice the absence of arguments. We need to learn to discuss issues without resorting to verbal violence. Let's talk more about rules for 'discussing' issues tomorrow.

For today, resolve to quit having stupid arguments. Just don't do it!

Prayer: Father, help us to hold our tongues, to think about what we're starting to argue about, and to refrain from quarrelling...

Jul 21
Discuss Civilly (or Rules for Arguing)

"Don't have anything to do with foolish and stupid arguments, because you know they produce quarrels. And the Lord's servant must not quarrel; instead, he must be kind to everyone, able to teach, not resentful." II Tim 2:23-24

Let's concentrate on the last part of the verse today. We already know we're not supposed to quarrel. This also shows us how to avoid doing so. If we'll lock ourselves in to the last part of this verse, it'll give us great rules for 'discussing'.

Before we focus more on that, let's set a few ground rules. Don't use statements from the past. "You always do, you always say, you never," etc. Don't use statements designed to disparage the other. If you have to resort to calling names, or if you start comparing each other to despicable people, things, or body parts, you've shown your argument has no merits of its own. Instead, stick to the current issue. Focus on resolving *this* situation. Here's how.

Be kind. Use statements that don't personally attack or denigrate the other. Gently communicate the problematic issue you face, and how it causes you distress, or pain, or inconvenience, or time. Patiently listen to your spouse as he or she explains his or her side of the issue, and the difficulties inherent from where they are in this.

Teach. This is where we begin to resolve the issue or situation. Explain what you'd like to see, and why you think this is a positive solution. Listen to your spouse for his or her input on what he or she would like to see as a resolution. Find ways to integrate the two, if possible, and if it's wise, and agree on the solution.

Drop resentment. Even when you think your spouse may be 'snowing' you, for the sake of conflict resolution, accept at face value what he or she says. If you feel hurt, for *your* sake, forgive him or her, and don't hold a grudge, or file it away for future ammunition. Refuse to be resentful, and determine to be healed, inside and out. Seek the Lord's healing touch for your emotions if necessary. The devil would like nothing better than to see you wallowing in the misery of spite, hateful feelings, and a grudge. Don't give him the satisfaction. Rise above the conflict, and live from this moment forward in victory. Take satisfaction yourself in knowing that in Christ, you and your spouse have resolved your conflict in a godly, Christian way, and are walking purely as overcomers.

Prayer: Lord, give us the tools we need, and the mindfulness, to be kind in our discussions, to teach our perspective, and to overcome any resentment we might harbor...

Jul 22
Watch Others Carefully

"Satan himself masquerades as an angel of light. It is not surprising, then, if his servants masquerade as servants of righteousness." II Cor 11:14b-15b

    People often present themselves as something they aren't. As believers, we're not immune to being duped by those who are smooth at perpetrating a con. After all, when someone's trying to hoodwink you, they don't come at you showing their wicked intentions. They do their best to persuade you that they're honest, trustworthy, and kind-heartedly trying to help you. That's why it's so important to test the spirits. The incident that really drove this masquerade business home to me was at the shoe store I used to manage. We had a policy of not taking checks without a photo identification card. This older man, about 50 to 55 years old, looked decent, but had no ID, since his wallet had been 'stolen'. Against my better judgment, I let him write a check. As he was leaving, he said "God bless you." In that instant, I knew in my spirit that I'd been conned. Why then, with such a godly statement? Because for some reason, *it didn't ring true*. The verse, test the spirits, came to me in that moment, but at that point, it was too late. I learned my lesson.

    Since Satan himself pretends to be an angel of light, we know that most of those who serve him will do the same. They present themselves in ways that look good that appear on the surface to be honest. They gain our trust by being friendly and helpful, polite and engaging. You see, they've learned something. It's tough to fool someone who doesn't trust you. Skeptics are hard to take in with deception. Of course, skeptics can be awfully hard to reach with the truth, too.

    It's essential for us to learn to see through the mask that covers those who attempt to delude us. When our spirit tells us something isn't quite right, it's most likely accurate. Ask the Holy Spirit whether this is true, or whether we're facing someone false. Don't be mislead by the beauty and grace of the masquerade. Remember the old saying; 'if it looks too good to be true, it is.' Look beyond the surface by watching others carefully, and relying on the Lord's Spirit and His leading.

Prayer: Lord Jesus, give us the insight to look past the shallow surface of those who present themselves falsely…

Jul 23
Be Glad of Heart

"Then I realized that it is good and proper for a man to eat and drink, and to find satisfaction in his toilsome labor under the sun during the few days of life God has given him—for this is his lot. Moreover, when God gives any man wealth and possessions, and enables him to enjoy them, to accept his lot and be happy in his work—this is a gift of God. He seldom reflects on the days of his life, because God keeps him occupied with gladness of heart." Ecc 5:18-20

Life is short when you're feeling blessed and having fun. Life can be very long indeed when you're in misery, stressed out, and afflicted.

This is an interesting passage. We need to keep in mind that it's good and proper to eat and drink, and to find satisfaction in our work. We can do that only when we realize that all this is a gift from God. He wants us to be satisfied with His blessings. If we have an appetite, and thirst, and they can be taken care of, then we're blessed. When we have work to do, and we have the attitude of being grateful to the Lord for our labor, and the ability to do it, understanding this is our lot in life, we can be happy.

Now there are those who will be unhappy no matter how blessed they are. You can have everything you need and want in the world, and still be dissatisfied. Why does that happen? It occurs when we choose the wrong attitude. If you have a nice home, and a good family, with dependable, enjoyable friends, and an income to provide food and clothing, you can have one of two attitudes. You can choose to focus on the things you don't have, and be disgruntled, and strive to continually gain more and more money, more and more property, and more and more possessions. Or you can choose to see God's blessings and provision, and feel happy and blessed. It's not what you have that counts; it's how you view God's blessings, and what frame of mind you choose, that matters.

God blesses some with more than enough. He chooses to give some wealth, and lots of possessions. When God gives you wealth and enables you to enjoy it, that's a great gift. When God enables you to be content with His blessings and your place in life, to love and enjoy your family, and to be happy in your work, that's a great gift from God.

When we step back, and rationally look at all God's blessings in our life, we can't help but realize, we can be happy and contented if we choose to be. God is enabling you to enjoy them right now. Why do you think He sent you this devotion? Choose for yourself which attitude to have. We recommend you choose to be glad of heart.

Prayer: Heavenly Father, give us the wisdom to choose an attitude of contentment and thankfulness, for you have given us an abundance of blessings...

Jul 24
Add-ons for Effectiveness

"Make every effort to add to your faith goodness; and to goodness, knowledge; and to knowledge, self-control; and to self-control, perseverance; and to perseverance, godliness; and to godliness, brotherly kindness; and to brotherly kindness, love. For if you possess these qualities in increasing measure, they will keep you from being ineffective and unproductive in your knowledge of our Lord Jesus Christ." II Pet 1:5b-8

Effort! Visions of working hard, sweating and laboring, and struggling with all your might come to mind. It doesn't have to be that way, though. Just don't ignore the processes you're supposed to go through to become productive in your faith and your walk. We do need to make some effort to acquire these attributes, and to add each successive quality, to improve our effectiveness.

This already assumes you have faith. That should be a safe assumption since you already believe in Jesus Christ, and we know you came by faith; therefore, you have a measure of faith now. Add to that faith, goodness. That means you behave in the right way, and have the quality of doing the right things. That refers to doing the right things in God's eyes.

Now add to your quality of being good, knowledge. That's pretty simple. To add knowledge, you must first be a student of God's word, the Bible (how long is your streak?). As you read the Bible consistently, you add knowledge, and you learn how to apply it. It tells you how to do so. Along with this, find books that delve into particular areas of Christian life you're interested in, and read them. Listen to speakers, or preachers whose teachings and insights are sound. Learn from these authors, teachers, and preachers, and apply what will provide positive values in your life.

Add to your knowledge, self-control. It starts getting a little tougher now. This requires self-discipline. We have to now add that quality which requires more effort than any other. That's true because the effort needed for this attribute is internal effort. This is the one where inside your head and heart, you say, "No matter how upset or angry I am, I will not yell, cuss, kick, or throw anything." This is the one which demands great inner patience.

When you add these qualities on, you begin to improve your effectiveness in your walk with Christ, and in sharing His good news. More tomorrow.

Prayer: Dear Lord, help us to begin now to think about these verses, and these qualities, and to start adding them on to our Christian attributes…

Jul 25
Add-ons for Effectiveness—Part 2

"Make every effort to add to your faith goodness; and to goodness, knowledge; and to knowledge, self-control; and to self-control, perseverance; and to perseverance, godliness; and to godliness, brotherly kindness; and to brotherly kindness, love. For if you possess these qualities in increasing measure, they will keep you from being ineffective and unproductive in your knowledge of our Lord Jesus Christ." II Pet 1:5b-8

We left off yesterday with self-control. Picking up at that point, we should add to self-control, perseverance. This is the attribute of continuing on despite difficulties, opposition, hardship, deprivation, or loss. Enduring will to continue on, and refusing to quit, that's perseverance. These two characteristics go together well. Self-control is stopping when you want to keep going. Perseverance is keeping going when you want to stop.

Now add to perseverance, godliness. That's a quality that's a bit harder to nail down. We all have a vague sense of what godliness is, but putting it into a concise statement is difficult. Look at it this way (and we don't assume this encompasses it all). Godliness is living, walking, talking, working, playing, thinking, worshipping, and behaving in a manner that is holy and pleasing to God. That's a lot, but if you'll do that, you can rest in the assurance you're *being* godly, not just *acting* godly.

Add to perseverance, brotherly kindness. This is the characteristic of being helpful and thoughtful of, and to, those around us. Lending a helping hand where you can, being polite, and looking out for others. That's also the essence of agape love, because we do what's best for others.

Then add to brotherly kindness, love. This is the real deal. Showing others not only affection, but also doing for them anything we can think of to bless them, to encourage them, to lift them up, and to honor them. Again, doing what's in their best interest.

When we've added on these qualities, we can be effective and productive in our knowledge of Jesus Christ. We can make an impact for the Kingdom of God.

Prayer: Lord Jesus, give us these characteristics, and move us to use them to be effective for your kingdom...

Jul 26
Who's Doing What? (or Who's in Charge, Anyway?)

Have you ever noticed that God just doesn't always do the things we'd like Him to? He's all-powerful, so He should be able to fix every problem, provide for every want, and change every person; in short, He could answer every prayer. Yet He obstinately refuses to do so. No matter how worthy our solutions, how honorable our intentions, or how positive our requests, He seems to ignore most of them. Why isn't He doing what we want Him to?

Did we forget who the master is? We're not the ones in charge of the universe. We have little or no say in anything. We're so insignificant, it's a wonder God bothers with us at all. The truth is, when we're not seeing our prayers answered, it's because we're praying incorrectly. God *does* answer every prayer. Often, it just isn't the answer we want. God frequently says 'no'; that's not good for you, or for them, or that's too frivolous, or your reason for asking is wrong, or selfish, or you don't see enough of the big picture.

There is a way to have your prayers answered positively. When you pray according to His will, He answers the way He wants to, accomplishes His purpose in response to your prayer, and you get to enjoy the thrill of seeing God work miracles. To pray His will, you have to spend time with our Heavenly Dad; time in His word, time in His presence, and time listening for His instruction and direction. Ask the Holy Spirit to only let you pray our Heavenly Dad's will, and when you let Him guide you, you can pray confidently, knowing He'll answer positively.

"This is the confidence we have in approaching God: that if we ask anything according to his will, he hears us. And if we know that he hears us—whatever we ask—we know that we have what we asked of him." I Jn 5:14-15

One more thing we need to remember. Unfortunately for our peace of mind, our Heavenly Dad works in His own time. It's perfect timing, in accordance with His plans. But it's hard for us to understand, because again, we don't see enough of the big picture. When it all comes together, we see how God put all the parts in just the right order, in just the right timing for the next portion, until it forms the right picture, like a big puzzle. Then we look at it and marvel how He did everything, and how each person was blessed in order, down to the last person, and most of them didn't even see the other pieces of that big puzzle.

When we keep uppermost in mind that He's in charge, miraculous things will occur. Remember, we're supposed to be doing what God wants *us* to, not the other way around.

Prayer: Heavenly Dad, remind us not to give a litany of things we want. Move us to pray, not for our wants, but according to your will, and let that be done…

Jul 27
Are You a Contender?

"I felt I had to write and urge you to contend for the faith that was once for all entrusted to the saints." Jud 3b

If you've ever watched a boxing match, you've seen the introductions of the fighters. Before they begin, they introduce the contenders in the fight. If you saw a championship bout, then they first introduced the challenger, followed by the impressive rendition of the exploits and accomplishments of the reigning champion. Once that was finished, they had the final instructions, and the fight began. It may have been a 12, up to 15 round, bout. The fight lasted until they reached the preset number of rounds, or one of the contenders knocked the other out.

Friends, when we're in the faith, we have a similar situation. All around us are contenders. They're challenging our faith, and trying to destroy both us, and it. If our challengers can knock us out of the fight, they've won. Our challenge is to keep from getting knocked out. Even when we get knocked down, we're not out of the fight. We have to keep getting up and going on.

So often Christians quit contending for the faith that was entrusted to us. We get bowled over by negative circumstances, and we just stay down. We get waylaid by sin, and instead of climbing to our feet, and getting back into the fight, we just lay there on the mat. We tell ourselves we're disqualified because of our failure. But we're not! We have to remember it's never over unless we give up. Refuse to quit! Don't give in! When you get knocked down, get back up, and start to contend for the faith again. Everyone faces tough challenges in their walk of faith, but we can overcome those. If circumstances are the problem, then bypass those, and continue to strive for the kingdom. If you've stumbled and fallen in sin, then repent, and let the Lord cleanse you again, and jump back into the fray.

There is nothing on earth that can come between the Lord and us unless we allow it. There's no one who can defeat us, unless we give up, because we already have the victory in Christ Jesus. Our responsibility is to contend for the faith that has once and for always been entrusted to us saints. And isn't it nice to be a saint?

Prayer: Lord, help us to keep in mind that we're contending for the faith as we journey through this life...

Jul 28
David's Principle

"But the king replied to Araunah, 'No, I insist on paying you for it. I will not sacrifice to the Lord my God burnt offerings that cost me nothing.'" II Sam 24:24

King David is known as the greatest king of Israel's history. If you want to enjoy success and blessing, it would be a good idea to follow the David principle. David had a reverence for God, and did his best to honor him in every way. King David refused to offer a sacrifice that was given to him by someone else, because he felt it wouldn't be worthy or acceptable if it cost him nothing. He knew that the offering wouldn't really be from him if it were just passed along through his hands from another's.

How careful are we when we bring tithes and offerings to the Lord. Do we bring our offering with a thankful heart? Do we bring the best we have to offer, or do we toss in whatever we have left over? Is our attitude one of reverence, or one of nonchalance? Do we bring to the table the first fruits of our work and our increase, or do we give what's unneeded, or a small portion of what was unused, after we paid our bills and entertained ourselves?

To honor the Lord in our giving, we must give with a pure, reverent heart. When we do our utmost to bless God in our offerings, when we come before Him with the finest our work has produced, when we're diligent and consistent in our sacrifice, and when we give with a joyful heart and a happy attitude, we can rest in the comfort of knowing our gift is acceptable and pleasing to the Lord. When we refuse, as David did, to bring a sacrificial offering to God that cost us nothing, we know we're following the David principle.

God blessed David richly. He wants to bless us, as well, and He can and will if we'll have the same type of heart and mindset that David had.

You don't have to walk in deficit in your life if you'll follow this principle. Notice that David sacrificed an offering. David came with a reverence for the Lord. David paid a price for his gift. David reaped the rewards of his faithfulness.

So bring the first fruits of your labor. Write your tithe check first. Be ready with offerings when God lays opportunities before you, and the desire to give in your spirit. Come with a sense of awe, and joy in your heart, as you give. Follow the David principle, and walk in the blessings that pour out on you that are sure to follow.

Prayer: Dear Lord, give us that spirit of generosity in our tithing and offering that is so pleasing to you. Stir up the joy within that comes from being faithful in this area of our spiritual life…

Jul 29
The Root of Sin

"God cannot be tempted by evil, nor does he tempt anyone; but each one is tempted when, by his own evil desire, he is dragged away and enticed. Then, after desire has conceived, it gives birth to sin; and sin, when it is full-grown, gives birth to death." Jas 1:13b-15

Selfishness is the root of sin! We defy you to come up with a sin that cannot be traced back to selfishness. When we lie, we do so to protect ourselves. When we steal, we do so to provide our own wants. When we criticize, we do so to make ourselves look superior. When we commit adultery or fornication, we do so to satisfy our own desire. When we covet, we do so to have more for ourselves. When we murder, we do so to wreak our own vengeance. When we dishonor our parents, we do so because of our own pride. When we have gods more important than God, we do so out of self-serving convenience. When we skip time to honor God with a day of rest and worship, we do so out of insolence and a desire to do our own thing, and to go our own way. When we deny God's word, we do so out of a desire to be like, or equal to, God.

We can't blame any of this on God. God is holy, and pure, and honest, and faithful. God *cannot* be tempted by evil. There is only good in Him and He does not tempt anyone. No, the devil tempts us, using our own desire. Our innate nature gives us the inclination to follow those things that we find pleasing; pleasing to our eyes, our stomachs, our senses, or our pride. When we dwell on those temptations, when we ruminate on what entices us, we step into sin. And if we continue in sin, hardening our hearts to carelessly take it to its fulfillment, then that sin leads to our death.

Every sin can be easily stopped before it has a chance to start. It's imperative that we recognize our own weaknesses and the signs that impending troubles are around the corner. If your primary weakness is falsehoods, then be prepared to forcibly make yourself tell the truth, regardless of how much easier it is to lie; if sexual sin, then know the signs of early attraction, and be prepared to turn away without another look when faced with that dilemma; if theft, then be prepared to always have a witness, or remove yourself from any chances to steal, and firmly resolve that you will never give in to that temptation; if it's honoring your parents, then plan out ways to be kind, refusing to argue with, or disrespect them, whether they deserve honor or not. If things or hobbies take precedence over God, then remove them from your life, or reduce the time and energy you spend on them. Make God *truly* the Lord of your life. Spend a day of rest and worship, fellowshipping with other believers, and taking your family to church.

Flee from the temptations you face. Don't be selfish!

Prayer: Father, deliver us from the evil that tempts us, and give us the inner strength and wisdom to turn and run away from situations that endanger us…

Jul 30
Whose Will Be Done?

"Your will be done on earth as it is in Heaven." Mt 6:10b

I'd like to have my will be done; done right now, and done just the way I picture it. After all, isn't that the American way? The marketing gurus tell us we can have it all, and have it now. Shouldn't I believe them? It's in the newspapers, the magazines, on the radio, and on television. So surely it must be true.

As the old saying goes, don't believe everything you hear (or read). While the world will tell you what you want to hear, they're very weak on delivering. They'll picture the icing on the cake, the party surrounding the cake, and the happiness we have with the gifts received around the cake. But ironically, they don't provide the cake! Or the icing, or the party, or the gifts. What they deliver is a beautiful picture for us to *buy*. They're in the business of selling products or services. They show you what they think you want, so you'll give them what they want. What they want is *your* money!

As believers, do we really want what Jesus taught us to pray? Do we want God's will to be done, or would we rather He give us our will? Until we come to the place in our spiritual life when we can pray, like Jesus did, "nevertheless, not my will, but your will be done," we'll always struggle in our faith. Faith that seeks our own desires is a shallow faith. If you're ready to leave the candy store faith behind, then you have to come to that point where you can intentionally, meaningfully pray, "your will be done, Lord."

We have to remember that God has a good plan for us. He has blessings in store for us. He has a wonderful place prepared for us. He wants to spend time with us. We can trust Him to do much better for us than we could ever dream of doing for ourselves. You might want a great romance in your marriage, and God wants it better than you can imagine.

You may look forward to children who know Him, and He wants that far more than you do. You have a dream of doing great things for God, and He has a vision and a plan for you that surpasses yours by miles. You have a wish for good health, and He wants you hearty and whole and energetic and happy. You'd like to see your neighbor saved, and God wants him saved even more, and has the steps laid out, just waiting for your prayers, so that you and the angels can rejoice together.

We have to be careful to look for God's will to be done on earth. That's where we currently are. Seek His will, join Him where He wants you to in His work, and see the miracles He's going to show you. Watch God laugh as you marvel at His inexplicable acts.

Prayer: Lord, we pray your will be done, in and around and through us. We give you our goals and desires, and ask you to move the way you want. Let us see what you've done, so we can stand in amazement at how you've worked everything out for good…

Jul 31
After Trials Come Blessings

"We went through fire and water, but you brought us to a place of abundance." Ps 66:12b-d

If you've known people, or perhaps been folks, who've gone through having their homes burned down, or washed away or ruined in a flood, you know the anguish they've faced. When confronted with the devastating loss of possessions that occurs, they remain thankful for the lives preserved. They mourn the loss of photos and documents, of family heirlooms, of antique furniture, of handwritten letters from parents and grandparents, and of other items that hold great sentimental value, because they're irreplaceable. But you see when all the trappings of modern living are stripped away, they look to the essential aspects of life, and they're thankful. They still have health, and strength, and family, and friends, and church support, and the knowledge that they can rebuild their lives from the ashes and mud of tribulations. They see they've been blessed by God's hand of protection. They see His faithfulness, and in talking to those folks years later, you often find that, while they miss the irretrievable mementos, they feel God blessed them. They realize they grew in their faith.

No one wants to go through terrible troubles, and we pray that doesn't happen to you. If God allows it, though, there's a reason, and in the end, He will bring us out of it. He has better things in store for us. His blessings are on the way. Look forward to the Lord fulfilling His promises.

We know from our reading in the New Testament that we *will* face trials and afflictions. We may have to suffer through the flames, as a refining fire purifies precious metals. We may have to face floods that wash away the crud and filth that have bound us. We know, though, that these tests of our faith are only for a season. When that season is finished, when we've learned to endure correctly, when we've persevered, God will bring us out of those adversities and take us to a place of abundance.

Stay strong and walk in faith, for God's promises are true. After you've borne the brunt of those trials, God will bring you blessings you haven't even conceived of.

Prayer: Lord Jesus, help us to weather the storms of difficulties we face, learn the lessons you want us to, and bring us to that abundance you've promised...

Aug 1
Praise the Name of the Lord, He Gives Us Courage

"I...will praise your name for your love and faithfulness, for you have exalted above all things your name, and your word. When I called, you answered me; you made me bold and stouthearted." Ps 138:2b-3

Have you been in a place, a time, a challenge, and a danger that required courage? You may have faced bullies in school, thieves at your business, a dangerous path somewhere, or storms that included tornadoes, hurricanes, or blizzards. In those situations, we need an inner strength we don't possess on our own. Who do we call on then? In dangerous or perilous circumstances, our adrenaline rushes, and we usually feel a certain amount of fear. When that happens we turn to the Lord for His fortitude. He's the one who will answer us. It's He who gives us the boldness we need. It's the Lord who makes us stouthearted in the face of menacing adversity.

God himself has exalted His name above all things. God himself has exalted His word above all things. He has accomplished that through His love towards us. He's the one who has answered our prayers for help. He's proven himself faithful in all His works. When He speaks, things happen. When He moves, nothing impedes Him. He gives us the courage to face what we dread, what frightens us.

Because of your love and faithfulness, we praise you, Lord. We give you worship, and honor, and blessing. All glory and might and power belong to you, Heavenly Father. Yours is the majesty and the holiness and the supremacy over all. We extol, magnify, and laud your name, Lord. We celebrate, exalt, and revere you, Lord Jesus. We give thanks to you, our God, for you alone are worthy of our gratitude and our adoration.

We don't know about you, but we look back and see where we've been granted requests by the Lord over and over. It's actually neat to see the miracles He's performed in our family alone. We rejoice that He's kept us in His care, even when we were unable to understand at the time. We can recount several instances where He's given us the boldness we needed at just the right moment.

As for us, we praise the Lord, because He's given us His courage.

Prayer: Lord, we praise you for your love and faithfulness, and we do exalt your name. Thank you for your answers to our prayers, and for the boldness and stoutheartedness you've given us...

Aug 2
Blessings for Obedience

"All these blessings will come upon you and accompany you if you obey the Lord your God. You will be blessed in the city and blessed in the country. The fruit of your womb will be blessed, and the crops of your land and the young of your livestock—the calves of your herds and the lambs of your flocks. Your basket and your kneading trough will be blessed. You will be blessed when you come in and blessed when you go out." Dt 28:2-6

God has given us a promise. If we obey His commands, we will be richly blessed. If we ignore His precepts, and follow other paths, we will be cursed (that's later in this same chapter).

We are of those who obey the Lord. We are careful to spend time in His word (how long is your Bible reading streak now?), so that we know our Heavenly Dad's ways. We show the love of Christ to those around us. We speak with an encouraging tongue, and we stay away from coarse joking. We give others help whenever we can. We look at others with spiritual eyes, so that we're not judging them by outward appearance. We fellowship with brothers and sisters in the faith, consistently worshipping together in church. We bring our tithes and offerings into God's house and God's work, joyful for the chance to bless others. We also plant seeds for Christ, and look for opportunities to nurture and disciple others in the faith, and for places where we can reap a harvest for God's kingdom, as the Holy Spirit brings them to faith in Jesus. Therefore, we have His favor and His blessings.

Our Heavenly Dad's blessings are numerous. It doesn't matter our location. We're blessed whether we're in urban or rural areas. We'll be blessed in our children, and not only our own children, but our property will have children as well (meaning livestock, of course). Your basket will be blessed and your kneading trough. Now, we understand that not many of you make your own bread and pasta anymore. But this refers to the produce, the food you gather, that will be yours in abundance. When you come in, you're blessed. So you're blessed in your home. When you go out, you're blessed. So wherever you are away from your abode, you're also blessed.

Be obedient to God, and receive and walk in His blessings.

Prayer: Heavenly Dad, we commit to being obedient to your instructions. We commit anew to reading your word, and following your precepts and your ways. Thank you for your promised blessings...

Aug 3
If You Suffer for Christ—

"Dear friends, do not be surprised at the painful trial you are suffering, as though something strange were happening to you. But rejoice that you participate in the sufferings of Christ, so that you may be overjoyed when his glory is revealed. If you are insulted because of the name of Christ, you are blessed, for the Spirit of glory and of God rests on you." I Pet 4:12-14

This passage tells us several things.

First, don't be surprised at your trials. We usually seem puzzled by the painful afflictions we go through. Part of the reason is that so many others have taught us that life with Christ is one big, wonderful party, with clear skies and smooth sailing all the way. We can be guilty of selling the tinsel and the decorations, while overlooking the tree. There *are* glorious blessings in Christ, but we cannot neglect the fact that we'll have trials and sufferings. This isn't strange, it's something normal that Christians face. And think back to Christ's walk on earth. While there were glorious miracles He performed, and wonderful spiritual teaching, He suffered more than any of us. Following His death and resurrection, the Disciples didn't pass on the miracles (the tinsel and decorations) to inspire people to believe; they brought the message of the cross (the tree).

Second, rejoice that you participate in Christ's sufferings. This is a tough concept to wrap our minds around. It helps us, to remember the closing part of the phrase used. The time will come when we're overjoyed. All of our difficulties are for a season, but then God reveals His glory, and we're better off than we were previously. If we bear in mind what's coming soon, it allows us to *rejoice* in participating in those adversities.

Third, insults because of Christ show us we have God's Spirit of glory. If you've ever been insulted for the cause of Christ, you know that in the moment, it's pretty tough to feel blessed. Thankfully, we don't live by our feelings, but by faith; faith in God's word.

There's an old saying. "Forewarned is forearmed!" When we study the Word regularly, we're forewarned of the adversity coming our way. It's all in there. And when we know it's coming, we can prepare to respond, as Jesus wants us to. When we face painful trials, we're no longer surprised by it. When we suffer for the cause of Christ, we rejoice that we've been found worthy to participate. When we're insulted for Jesus' name, we rest in blessing, knowing we have the Spirit of glory.

—You're blessed!

Prayer: Lord, give us an attitude of peace when we face difficult circumstances, knowing we're blessed in you, and we rejoice that we're so filled with your Spirit that we're recognized by the world as yours...

Aug 4
How Is Your Home Built?

"By wisdom a house is built, and through understanding it is established; through knowledge its rooms are filled with rare and beautiful treasures." Pr 24:3-4

Are you building your family on the cornerstone of Jesus Christ? If you'll use Him as your foundation, if you apply wisdom to your construction, you'll have a sturdy home. When you spend time as husband and wife discussing things of the Lord, taking care in your relationship to honor the Lord and each other in holiness, you're wisely raising your spiritual house. When you bring up your children with wisdom, with love, and with an example of faithfulness to God, you give them the foundation they need to succeed personally through the remainder of their lives.

Investing the time to gain understanding of each other, and of your children, brings rewards of its own. That's part of building your home. You have to spend seasons seeking to learn about each member of your family. What do they think? What is their reasoning for that? Why do they see issues that way? How do they view their relationship with the Lord? What do they base it on? What are each family member's goals? Where do they see life going for them? What does each of your children see as essential qualities for their future spouse? Will they settle for less? Why or why not? What are their favorite movies, books, TV shows, clothes, food, color, and hobbies? Who do they look up to? Who do they have little respect for? Why?

As you ask those questions, listen to the answers. Don't formulate responses while they're speaking. Don't feel you need to respond at all. You're gaining knowledge and understanding while you're listening. Spend time with each family member. When you know what each person in your family enjoys, and is interested in, you can create rare and beautiful memory treasures for them by doing what pleases them. You may have to sacrifice somewhat to do that, but that just makes the treasure more valuable to them. You're filling the rooms of each of their lives with rare and beautiful articles.

Build your home in the wisdom of the Lord.

Prayer: Father, give us wisdom, and creativity, to build a home filled with rare treasures as a family...

Aug 5
Have You Prepared?

"Wisdom has built her house; she has hewn out its seven pillars. She has prepared her meat and mixed her wine; she has also set her table." Pr 9:1-2

We know it's the Lord who gives wisdom. See how wisdom has set everything in order ahead of time, so that all is ready for those who will accept the invitation to come and eat of her bounty.

When you plan to have a date with your spouse, do you ready everything in advance? Most of the time we probably just wing it. But there is much to be said for thoughtful preparation. Either of you can do the predate set up. You can take turns! Whatever works for you and enhances your enjoyment of your date night.

We have some recommendations (you *know* we do!). Since the wife is normally the one who prepares for guests, Husband, why don't you go first? Select the activity, whether a movie, miniature golf, a walk in the woods or park, dinner at a pleasant restaurant, a concert (we hear Gary & Glenda concerts are fun and a blessing), or even a ballgame if you both like that. Let her know what time to be dressed and ready. She'll need to know the 'dress code' for the date. Then the 'after the event' activities are planned. Maybe you'll stop for a quiet cup of coffee and pie. If you're having a romantic interlude at home, then have some refreshments available, such as juice or soda, some different cheeses, and flavored crackers are good. Softly playing love music is pleasant. Try making some room to dance together like you did when you were younger. The point is, think about the things you can do to expand your horizons, and stretch into new areas that will raise the level of rapture, bliss, and pleasure in your love.

Don't be afraid to indulge yourselves once in a while. Make your husband or wife feel appreciated and cherished. God has shown us that

He's prepared. He's told us He's preparing a place for us. We want to be like Him. He's shown us His love by planning in advance, by making sacrifice, and doing things for our good and for our pleasure. Let's do the same for each other.

Are you preparing?

Prayer: Father, give us good ideas to make our dates and our love more intimate, and more enjoyable...

Aug 6
Fear for Your Soul

"I tell you, my friends, do not be afraid of those who kill the body and after that can do no more. But I will show you whom you should fear: Fear him who, after the killing of the body, has power to throw you into hell. Yes, I tell you, fear him." Lk 12:4-5

We have no reason, really, to fear people in this world. People can harm us. There's no doubt about that, but the harm they're able to do is limited. Even Satan is limited in what he can do to us. We already know we've been given power in Jesus' name to overcome the devil. We also have power in Jesus' name to battle the people who become our adversaries. People may take away our freedom, they can hurt us physically, they can wreak financial havoc on us, they can slander us, and they can even kill us. But that's the end of what they can do to harm us. Ultimately, *we* have the victory.

It's essential for us to take care of our souls, because there's one who can still devastate it after we've died a physical death. That's a fear we should take care of. We need to be sure that we've repented (told God we're sorry for, and turned away from) our sins. We need to make sure Jesus is Lord of our lives in truth, and not just in words. We must walk in continual obedience to God's word. We have to agape love our neighbors. We spend time in prayer and worship, fellowshipping with the Lord.

We have the assurance of our salvation by the Holy Spirit God's given us. While we know we ought to fear for our souls, and fear the one that has power over it, isn't it fabulous that when we're in Christ, we have no fear? There is no fear in perfect love, and God certainly has bestowed on us His perfect love. This verse tells us that we need to take care of that which is most important. Once we do that, we no longer fear God any more than we would our earthly father. When we do what honors and pleases him, we have his approval. When we do what he forbids us to, we're disciplined. Our Heavenly Dad is the same in that respect. He's just perfect in His assessments. He sees not only the acts, but our heart as well. But we know He *loves* us. He loves us so much He gave His only Son for us. Who can fear someone who loves us that much, especially when we know Him personally?

Remember this; we are a spirit with a body, not just a body with a spirit. We are eternally alive in our spirit. The body will die, but our soul lives on eternally, either with Christ in Heaven, or without Him in Hell.

Prayer: Heavenly Dad, we thank you that we have your love, and that we have no reason to fear you, aside from your discipline. Thank you that we're your children...

Aug 7
Proof Positive

"He said to him, 'if they do not listen to Moses and the Prophets, they will not be convinced even if someone rises from the dead.'" Lk 16:31

We can't tell you how many times we've been frustrated by people who don't believe something, are shown the veracity of what you've told them, but still refuse to accept that proof. Here's a truth you can count on. You can't help people who insist on being stupid. Take this as an example. Let's say, you have a friend (friends are good, usually), and your friend is doing something in their personal life that is destructive to his or her marriage, and they ask you for advice. You give them sound, biblical solutions, and they agree that's a good way to begin to resolve this issue. Then they go their way, and before too long, they're back complaining about the same situation. Why? Because they didn't apply your godly recommendations, and returned to the same activity or attitude that caused the problem in the first place. If you do the same thing over and over and expect a different result, you're deluding yourself with false hope. No, if you want different results, you have to apply new tactics.

Jesus tells us in this story that there are some who refuse to believe, regardless of overwhelming evidence to the contrary. They're people who don't want to be confused with the facts. Just let them go on believing delusions in peace.

We're trusting that you're not that foolish. If you were, you most likely wouldn't be reading this book to begin with. So we have a reasonable foundation for our belief. You're obviously a couple who see the evidence before you, make a rational decision to accept what is obviously true, and apply it to your lives. You have many family members, friends, and acquaintances who've done the same. You're all to be commended for that honest, open acceptance of truth.

Don't assume everyone is as logical and open to the truth as you are, though. When you run into those who are like the rich man in the fire, who have had the right way explained to them multiple times, but have followed a false path instead, don't be frustrated. Accept the fact that there are those who don't *want* the truth. In those cases, you can only present what you know is accurate and correct, and leave the results in their, and God's, hands. Remember, there are those who *will* not believe, even when you give them proof positive.

Prayer: Lord, help us to keep delivering your accurate word, and to keep accepting the truth in our own lives, regardless of what others may do with the message....

Aug 8
Perpetual Active Growth

"But grow in the grace and knowledge of our Lord and Savior Jesus Christ." II Pet 3:18a

This isn't a passive statement. This is instruction. Grow is an active tense verb here. In our life, we must be people of PAG. Our goal is to have perpetual, active, growth.

Perpetual means we never stop. It's a continually ongoing process.

Active means we are doing something to move this process along. We are nurturing the development.

Growth is the learning and improving that occurs in our life journey.

Our first and most important goal of PAG is in our spiritual life. God calls us to PAG in the grace and knowledge of our Lord Jesus Christ. When we're growing, we're acquiring all the tools, information, and abilities we need to be effective in our walk.

We can apply this process to all areas of our life, and they complement what is occurring in our spiritual life, because the two are enmeshed. In every way we implement PAG, it will have positive effects.

When we seek perpetual, active growth in our marriage relationship, we accomplish what God intended for our intimate relationship all along. We find ways of helping, supporting, encouraging, and showing our love for our spouse, and in the process, we become more godly.

In our family interactions, PAG does what's in the best interest of our children. We teach them to be people with an intimate relationship with Jesus Christ. We admonish them to live uprightly, with honesty, integrity, and dependability as their hallmark.

As we seek perpetual, active growth in our workplace, we do what the Lord has instructed us to. We become dependable, trustworthy, hardworking, and pleasant. We treat others respectfully, and give honor to those around us.

Ironically, in our hobbies seems to be the place we're most likely to be most zeroed in on improvement. Whether its golf, tennis, crocheting, painting, writing, riding, or any of a thousand others, we always seem to be focused on acquiring better abilities. There's nothing wrong with growth here, and we recommend it, but it doesn't seem to require the effort of making ourselves do it like we do in other disciplines.

Make it your goal to have perpetual, active growth in every area of your life. Work diligently to produce it in your marriage, your family, your business, and most importantly, in your spiritual relationship with Christ.

Prayer: Lord, move us to have PAG in our lives, that we would refrain from becoming stale, passive, and indolent…

Aug 9
Blessings Awaiting

"Blessed are all who fear the Lord, who walk in his ways. You will eat the fruit of your labor; blessings and prosperity will be yours." Ps 128:1-2

For those of us who reverence the Lord God Almighty, we have a promise from God that we have blessings. Just as in the case of Abraham and Sarah when God said they were going to have a child, in God's mind it was already done. They didn't see it revealed for a period of time, but the Lord had said 'you will', and they did. We sometimes have blessings given to us, but not revealed or brought to fruition as of yet. But when God says it's so, we can count on it being ours.

Just the day before we went on one of our tours, we had a flat tire on Glenda's car. We had needed tires for some time, but didn't think we could afford to spend the money just then. Of course, when we got home, the tires still needed replacing. Because of an ice storm, and having no electricity, we were busy doing other essential duties (like in the 'good old days'), and didn't get to the car for several days. When I had priced tires, I went to take the car in, but I couldn't get into it. There were two brand new tires in the car, one of which was on the drivers seat, waiting to be taken in, mounted and balanced. The Lord had provided for us through his other children. That blessing was waiting for us for a couple of weeks, but we didn't see it until that certain time when I went to the automobile. In my mind's eye, I can see our Heavenly Dad watching for the moment. When I headed toward the car, I just imagine Him calling to Gabriel and Michael, "Hey, you guys, come here and watch Gary's face!" I was nearly shocked.

We have surprises waiting for our loved ones, sometimes, too. So as not to spoil the astonishment, we're patient until they find our gift themselves, and watch with satisfaction to see the curiosity, bewilderment, and amazement cross their face. Just as with the Lord's blessings, they're waiting to be discovered, and may have been prepared for some time.

We're already blessed when we fear God. He has blessings and prosperity waiting for us. He'll give us as much as we can properly handle, because He delights in giving good gifts to His children, much the same as we do.

Prayer: Heavenly Dad, thank you for your many blessings. Give us wisdom to use them, faith to wait on them, and eyes to see and receive them...

Aug 10
Give Glory to He Who Is Able

"To him who is able to keep you from falling and to present you before his glorious presence without fault and with great joy—to the only God our Savior be glory, majesty, power and authority, through Jesus Christ our Lord, before all ages, now and forevermore! Amen." Jude 24-25

Even though we're prone to do foolish things, to stumble in our ways, and to forget to think, act, and speak wisely, God is still able to keep us from falling. When our children are small, we keep a sharp lookout on them, to prevent them from falling down. We can't stop them from stumbling, but we do anticipate that they will, and we're ready to catch them so they don't fall flat. When we pay attention, we're able to do that. Unlike ours, the Lord's attention is never diverted. Consequently, He's always able to keep us from falling.

There's much more, though. Not only does He keep us from falling, He presents us before Himself without fault. That's quite a mouthful. When we look at ourselves, we see plenty of faults, and let's face it; God can see a multitude of faults in us that we don't even recognize. But when we're under the blood of Christ, walking in His grace, we're presented without fault. It's all covered. Our sin is washed away. Jesus forgets our failures and our shortcomings. He gives us a clear conscience and a pure heart because He's paid the penalty, and taken the punishment on Himself that we deserve. Through Christ, we're in right standing with God. No wonder we have great joy when we're in His glorious presence. We no longer carry any sin to feel shame or guilt about. Jesus already took care of that.

When we perceive how God has kept us, and cleansed us, we can't help but offer our Savior all the glory, all the majesty, all the power, all the authority; in short, all the worship we can muster. Our Lord Jesus Christ is eternal, and we praise and honor Him through eternity forward. That's now and forevermore!

Give glory to our Lord and Savior who is able!

Prayer: Lord Jesus, thank you for caring for us, and for keeping us from stumbling. Help us to honor and revere you...

Aug 11
Don't Run Ahead

"Anyone who runs ahead and does not continue in the teaching of Christ does not have God; whoever continues in the teaching has both the Father and the Son." II Jn 9

Have you ever been frustrated trying to teach or tell someone something, because as you showed him or her, or explained, they kept jumping ahead of you, like they already 'got it'? I can say that, to me, it's quite ridiculous, and sorely tries my patience. When that happens, I've learned that certain things are occurring simultaneously. One is, the other person almost *always* gets it wrong. Another is, it breaks my logical train of thought, and takes time to get back on track. Then, in the end, they usually cannot repeat the instruction back to me, proving they weren't listening with their whole mind, and obviously *didn't* 'get it'. Finally, I've learned to softly and politely say, "No, that's incorrect. May I finish?"

The main problem when someone runs ahead, in their thinking or their actions, is they generally don't understand. We're the same way. When we get ahead of our instruction, whether in business, family, or spiritual life, we mess it up.

When we run ahead of the teaching we have in Christ Jesus, we've left behind the sound instruction He's given us, and followed our own, or someone else's, erroneous way. It's then we get in trouble. John tells us when we do that, we've gone away from God. His Holy Spirit cannot guide us in error. He will not, and cannot, bless us when we take a wrong path, following what is false, because He is always true. God's nature is constant.

The good news is, there's another promise in the second half of this verse. When we continue *in* the teaching, we have both the Father and the Son. Our responsibility is to carefully follow the Biblical instruction we've received, and accurately live the abundant life in Christ we're given. As we follow His precepts, as we line our lives up with scriptural principles, we put ourselves in the position God wants us in. We have both the Father and the Son. And when we have the Father and the Son, we have freedom. Freedom from worry, freedom from guilt, freedom from shame, freedom from sin, and freedom to live in joy, as we purposely journey with Christ in a wholesome, holy manner.

Be careful to continue in Christ's teaching. Don't run ahead!

Prayer: Father, move us by your Spirit to walk continually in your teaching, so that we avoid going our own way, and stay hand in hand, in step with you...

Aug 12
Pass It on to Your Children

"One generation will commend your works to another; they will tell of your mighty acts. They will speak of the glorious splendor of your majesty, and I will meditate on your wonderful works. They will tell of the power of your awesome works, and I will proclaim your great deeds. They will celebrate your abundant goodness and joyfully sing of your righteousness." Ps 145:4-6

Sadly, we run across many families in which the parents are solid Christians, walking the faith, but who, for some reason, have failed to pass on to their children the marvelous things God has done for them. They haven't made it a priority to teach their children, to introduce them to Jesus Christ, to get them consistently in the Word, and get them grounded in the faith.

There's a pattern that runs too frequently in families. In the first generation, people are gloriously saved, filled with the Spirit, and faithful in their walk. In the second generation, their children are nominally in the faith, but without the commitment and fervor that their parents had. In the third generation, their children don't even profess the faith their grandparents had as the core of their life. They've slid away from Christ completely. Why does this happen?

In Israel's history, we see the same pattern. They commit, but after years go by, they forget, and walk away into disobedience, and their children forget the Lord altogether. This happens because as parents, we neglect the admonition to teach our children, and our children's children, about the great God Almighty, the Savior of sinners, and all the miraculous things He's done for us in our lives. Every generation has to come to know Jesus Christ for themselves. Our privilege as parents is to tell them of all God has done for us, of the wondrous works He performed in ages past, and presently for us today. As we teach our children of the things of the Lord, we're blessed with the opportunity to introduce them to Jesus personally, so they have the relationship with Him that He desires.

Unless they know about God, they won't put their faith and trust in Him. Unless we teach them, and explain God's goodness, grace, love, and mercy, they won't know about Him. Don't neglect this extremely important task we have as parents. Save yourselves the heartache of seeing your grandchildren walk without Christ. Let's make our generation be one who tells the next generation of the marvelous, glorious splendor of the Lord, and of His awesome works and deeds. Let's introduce the next generation, and the next generation after, to Jesus Christ, and set an example of walking the faith, and of telling of God's miracles in our lives. Pass it on to your children, and to your children's children.

Prayer: Dear Lord, help us to faithfully pass on your amazing deeds in our lives, and teach our kids to put their faith and trust in you...

Aug 13
Are You Cheerful?

"A cheerful heart is good medicine, but a crushed spirit dries up the bones." Pr 17:22

    Circumstances will often come along that can steal our joy if we let them. When we allow the negative things that happen to crush our spirit, it takes away our positive attitude. When our spouse says something critical, it may dull our spirit. When the car has a flat, it can darken our mood. When our day doesn't go as planned because emergencies arose, and we get behind in our work, it can frustrate us. When the kids are sick and we can't go on a planned outing, it can disappoint us. When the food we looked forward to isn't ready, or it's too ready and scorched, it can anger us. A thousand things will come along to crush our spirit and dry up our bones, but we don't have to receive them and let our attitude spin into a downward spiral.

    An interesting phenomenon takes place in sick people who have a cheerful, optimistic outlook regarding their recovery. When they believe they're going to quickly bounce back from their illness, they do so rapidly with little or no complications. For those who only see the worst in their situation, the recovery time is much longer. The reason is, whatever we focus on, or choose to think, generally happens. So when you want to get well, choose to have a positive outlook, and spend your time thinking encouraging, heartening thoughts. A cheerful heart *is* good medicine!

    That principle applies to other areas, as well. When we choose to see the good traits in our spouse, we become good medicine to him or her. When we compliment our wife on the efficient use of her time, we bolster her self-esteem. When we encourage our husband in his wise choice of reading material, or how well his latest project turned out, we lift his spirit and strengthen his confidence. We're able to accomplish much that's positive when we're cheerful with people. We can't count on much good coming out of being negative or critical. Occasionally we may stop someone from doing something detrimental or foolish, but usually we just drag others down, and hinder the good that they intended to do.

Choose today to be cheerful in heart. Tell yourself that you will not let negative situations crush you. You can have a good attitude, focused on all the Lord's blessings, realizing that those bad circumstances are just a blip in your life, not to be bothered by. Let someone else (not your spouse) have the crushed spirit and dried up bones. After all, there really aren't enough to go around, so be generous, and let others have them.

Prayer: Heavenly Father, help us to choose right attitudes and a cheerful outlook, seeing how richly you've blessed us in all things...

Aug 14
Be Faithful in the Little Things

"After a long time the master of those servants returned and settled accounts with them. The man who had received the five talents brought the other five. 'Master,' he said, 'you entrusted me with five talents. See, I have gained five more.' His master replied, 'Well done, good and faithful servant! You have been faithful with a few things; I will put you in charge of many things. Come and share your master's happiness!'" Mt 25:19-21

This is a principle we can readily understand, but are we doing well in executing the task? We can understand it, because we've used it ourselves, in varying degrees, through the course of our life.

When our children reached driving age, we went through a process of teaching them, and giving them small jaunts in the car, before we entrusted them fully with a vehicle. As long as our children were faithful in their use of the automobile, they were given the privilege of using it from time to time. But when they weren't faithful, when they didn't come home by curfew, or we found they didn't go where they said they were going, or took a wide detour, their driving privileges were curtailed.

When we're responsible for a multi-million dollar business, we don't just hand the keys over to anyone. We first train a person, and give him or her small amounts of responsibility, and as we find them trustworthy in those lesser duties, we learn we can count on them to adequately perform with more obligations and tasks.

God has given us 'talents' to use for His work and His kingdom. Are we being faithful in the small things that He's called us to? Are we dependable when working on our own? Do you teach Sunday School? Then do so to the best of your ability, making preparation beforehand. Do you clean the church building? Then do it well, making sure it 'sparkles' when you're finished. Are you in charge of the kitchen? Then be certain it's well stocked, and ready for each event requiring food. Our responsibility is to be diligent in our assignment, making the most of the opportunities we have, because a day is coming, just like in the parable, when we will be called to account for our work. If we have a vision for doing great things for the Lord, then we'd better be able to show ourselves trustworthy in the lesser things He's given us to do. God isn't willing to entrust vast areas of responsibility to us unless we're faithful in the little things. When we've been faithful in the small things, He'll reward us by putting us in charge of many things. The blessings will increase accordingly!

Prayer: Lord, give us the heart and the ambition to be faithful in the things you've assigned us, that we might share in your happiness…

Aug 15
Without Anger

"I want men everywhere to lift up holy hands in prayer, without anger or disputing." I Tim 2:8

Have you noticed that when a child is caught doing something they ought not to, when they're questioned, they have a tendency to hide their hands behind their backs? They don't want to look you in the face, and they don't want you to see their guilty little hands. It's instinctive for them when confronted regarding their actions.

In the Old Testament, when men lifted their hands in worship, it was meant to show they came to the Lord without blood on them. They were proving they came without sin in their lives, and that they were in right standing with God.

Paul gives us this example as something we should do, as well. We can't worship properly when we're not in right relationships. Our hands aren't 'clean' when we have unconfessed sin in our hearts. We don't have a pure heart when we come while angry with someone, or in a dispute with another. Those things interfere with our relationship with God, too, and keep us from giving the Lord our holy worship.

When we recognize these issues within us, we have to take steps to correct them. Our wives can be of great benefit to us here. When they see that closed countenance that accompanies anger, they can gently and lovingly help us to open up and do what's needed to wash away that which hinders our worship. They can encourage us to do the right thing, and repent, or apologize, or face whatever we need to, to resolve the issue that keeps us from the Lord.

As men, we have to have the courage to squarely face these situations. Until we do, whatever hinders our spiritual worship will continue to sit there and fester, and become worse until we cleanse it. We have to clothe ourselves with the attitude that we're going to instantly take care of these things, so that we can put our disputes behind us. We have to move past the discord to get rid of our anger, and when we do, we're on the right path. Once that's done, we can come before the Lord with clear hearts and consciences, and lift holy hands in prayer, bringing God our pure worship.

The Lord wants to meet us when we're in worship. Without anger!

Prayer: Father, let us have the courage to boldly face the issues that cause anger and disputes, so that we're able to lift our hands in holy worship to you…

Aug 16
Who Is Your Enemy?

"But I tell you who hear me: Love your enemies, do good to those who hate you, bless those who curse you, pray for those who mistreat you." Lk 6:27-28

Sometimes we find the worst enemy we have is in our own home. When couples begin to fight, it can escalate to enormous proportions. In the midst of these battles we often say things that are extremely damaging to our relationship, because we find ourselves throwing verbal assaults that cruelly cut our spouses heart and self-esteem to the core. Once those words are spoken, we can't take them back. The damage has already been inflicted.

We saw the movie 'Fireproof' last evening. It brought to mind the sad reality that most, if not all couples, go through similar fights and arguments. So how can we keep our marriage from getting burned to the ground? How can we 'fireproof' our marriage?

Obviously, if you've read this far in the devotional together, you're well on your way to insulating your marriage from outside influences. And even if your most significant enemy is within your home and marriage, this verse helps us with a plan for how to treat that person. It also gives us weapons to help other couples in their marriage difficulties.

First. Love your enemy. That's quite difficult to do, but we have to remember that real love is not an emotion; it's a decision. It's a decision to do what's best for the other person (the enemy).

Second. Do good to those who hate you. It's hard to take having your spouse 'hate' you, but we have to force ourselves to go beyond the hurt feelings, and do good things for our husband or wife regardless of how ugly they treat us.

Third. Bless your spouse, even when he or she curses you. Proverbs tells us that 'a gentle answer turns aside wrath'. It's hard to continue being mean to someone who doesn't respond in kind. So find ways to bless that person, even in the midst of their cursing.

Fourth. Pray for those who mistreat you. It can be arduous to find much to pray about when you pray for someone who's mistreating you. But when you do that, it's encouraging to find that you harbor less resentment, less anger, and less bitterness toward that person.

In the end, you have to start with a willingness to forgive. Then, when you treat your husband or wife the way you'd like to be treated, they normally respond positively. You win a loving, giving, kindhearted, generous, helpful, thankful, and godly spouse. So love your enemy!

Prayer: Precious Lord, give us the internal fortitude to do what's good, kind, loving, and best for our spouse, regardless of how we're being treated. Give us remembrance to pray daily for him or her…

Aug 17
Encouraging Scriptures

"For everything that was written in the past was written to teach us, so that through endurance and the encouragement of the Scriptures we might have hope." Rom 15:4

Isn't that the wonderful thing about Christianity? We have hope! We know there's a brighter future waiting for us. Not only do we have hope, we have the assurance of that hope.

When you're having a terrible week at work, and everything that could go wrong, went wrong, and everyone you work with, and every other customer you have, is unbelievably rude, and acts like evil incarnate, we find our emotional way out with the hope we have for the weekend. We look with hope to those days off that will allow us to rest and recuperate from the disastrous, stress filled, workweek we endured. That's just a faint shadow of the hope we have in Christ, though.

Not only do we have hope, we have the Scriptures. This is interesting, because it tells us that everything written in the past was written to teach us. And when you read through the Bible, you see examples of everything you'll face. You see sin on display in all its sordid wickedness, from murder (Cain and Abel), to drunkenness (Lot), to incest (Lot's daughters), to pride and arrogance (King Saul), to adultery (King David), to coveting, lying, theft and deceit (Laban and Jacob). It also shows us faithfulness in commitments (Ruth), righteousness in maintaining godly standards (Joseph), repentance and God's acceptance of it (King David), answered prayer (King Hezekiah, Elijah, Elisha and a host of others), intercession (Queen Esther), devotion, obedience, and sacrifice (Abraham with Isaac), humility and leadership (Moses), wisdom and romance (Solomon).

When we learn from Scripture the principles we ought to live by, when we endure the trials and afflictions that inevitably come to us on our journey through life, we have encouragement from the Word itself. We see how others have faced similar trials, and how they dealt with them, and how God cared for them, and it gives us the faith to persist in those difficulties with His grace, refusing to succumb to defeat, secure in the knowledge and hope that He will bring us through.

To have the encouragement of the Scriptures, you have to consistently read and study them. How's you Bible reading streak coming? Find your encouragement in God's Word.

Prayer: Holy Spirit, move us to always be faithful in studying your Word, and applying your principles to our lives...

•

Aug 18
The Good Old Days

"Do not say, 'Why were the old days better than these?' For it is not wise to ask such questions." Ecc 7:10

We've had a little experience with 'the good old days'. We grew up when indoor plumbing, electricity, and phones, were just coming to the outer rural areas. We remember when we had to run 100 feet behind our home to the outhouse to go to the bathroom. We recall 'crank and holler' telephones. We know what it's like to have to pump and carry water in buckets from the well every day. We had the privilege of refreshing our memory from an ice storm that came through Arkansas as well, leaving us without power for nearly two weeks. Cutting wood, stoking a fire and carrying water quickly helped us to appreciate the modern conveniences we've become so accustomed to.

We also remember that people were better at keeping their word. There was less sexual sin, and when it occurred, folks were ashamed. Neighbors didn't try to cheat others in business deals. Most people where we lived went to church on Sundays.

As we assess the good old days, we realize that just as today, there were good things, and bad, hard, or difficult things. The crux of this is, we can't live in the past. We accomplish little to nothing dwelling on it. When we wallow in bygone days, we're stuck and unable to reach our future. That's why it's unwise to ask such questions.

Our future is shaped somewhat by our yesterdays, but it isn't bound to it. If our history is good, we can build on it for our future. If our past is bad, or negative, we can learn what to avoid, and seek a new, positive direction for our lives.

God has given us all abilities. In the body, those abilities vary. But the Lord has plans for our good, not to harm us. Our abilities are given to us to enhance our lives, to bless us, and those around us. He doesn't give them to us to hurt others, or to use selfishly for our own pleasures. We build a wonderful future as we use our abilities in a godly manner on our journey through this world.

God has given us His favor to accomplish great things for His kingdom. We may not understand how even the smallest good deed can nurture the spirit in another, and encourage them to pass on something good to others. We just need to stay focused on moving forward in the Kingdom of Christ. We must continue to be obedient when the Spirit moves us to lend a helping hand, or give some money, or encourage someone in the faith. As we leave the past behind, and fix our thoughts on the wonderful future we have in Jesus Christ, both here and in Heaven, we make a wise choice.

The good old days actually weren't that great.

Prayer: Father, help us to learn from our past, and to look to the path ahead as we journey with you…

Aug 19
A House Divided, or United?

"If a house is divided against itself, that house cannot stand." Mk 3:25

There's an old song that says, "United we stand, divided we fall". In our marriage, nothing could be more accurate. *We succeed together, or we fail apart.* Our relationship is too important to take lightly, and as we stand united in heart, in mind, in strength, in love, and in spirit, we can build extraordinary marriages.

When a kingdom is divided against itself, it ultimately results in civil war. When two sides are intractable, and each is set on going it's own way, then fighting is almost inevitable. No kingdom can stand and succeed when it refuses to resolve issues that separate it's citizens. In the United States, it resulted in our civil war, pitting the southern states against the northern states. The consequences for our nation were catastrophic, and took decades to heal.

Each marriage is like that, as well. When we're divided, when we each are set in having our way, and demanding our rights, we allow ourselves to start down a path that, when taken to its conclusion, too often ends in divorce. When two people are unwilling to give, then each one is guilty of selfishness, of pride, of self-righteousness, and of covetousness. We stand apart from each other when that occurs. We're divided in our wants, demands, and desires. And we know what God's word says. That house cannot stand.

The good news is we *can* stand united. We can purpose right now to put aside our differences, put away our selfishness, and lift our husband or wife up by putting their needs first. We can rationally discuss our issues, and agree on solutions that are good for both, or bad for neither. We're well able to commit our ways to the Lord, and allow Him to lead us in paths of righteousness that glorify God. When we treat each other with respect, honor, generosity, affirmation, kindness, gentleness, care, and love, we lay a foundation for our house that gives us the firm footing we need to be of one heart, one mind, and one purpose. We serve the Lord together!

Our house refuses to be divided. Our house stands united.

Prayer: Heavenly Father, help us to stand united in you. We purpose to succeed in our marriage together. Don't allow us to fail apart...

Aug 20
Obsolete

"By calling this covenant 'new,' he has made the first one obsolete; and what is obsolete and aging will soon disappear." Heb 8:13

In this modern age of technology, most of what was cutting edge ten years ago is already obsolete. It has fallen so far behind where computers, or machines, or systems are currently, that they're no longer of effective use. And what is so up to date now will also have fallen into disuse a few scant years from now. It's amazing to think that our phones will do much more today than our personal computers did twenty years ago. Considering the size of those PCs compared to how small our phones are today, it's all the more astonishing. You can't even give those old PCs away anymore.

When Jesus Christ came, he brought us into a new covenant. That was because long ago, God pronounced the old covenant flawed. He told us the time was coming when no longer would we abide by the law, but that His precepts would be written on our hearts. That old law has been fulfilled in Christ. It's no longer of any use, any more than the old PCs are. Its day has passed. No longer are we bound to the shadow of things to come. That shadow, which was the old covenant law, is now obsolete. It has disappeared.

This gives us the freedom to walk in God's love and grace. Because the new covenant is superior to the old in every way, our relationship with the Lord is also superior in every way. No longer do we bring sacrifices of animals for our sins, for Jesus, the perfect lamb, was sacrificed for our sins once and for all time. No longer do we engage in ceremonial washings to be clean, because Christ cleansed us completely from the inside out. No longer do we wonder what we should do, since the Holy Spirit dwells within us and leads us in paths of righteousness. No longer are we restricted from coming into the presence of the Lord, because through

Jesus we have open access to God's throne, and the ability to come boldly to our Heavenly Father.

We're so glad the old law is obsolete. Who could keep track of and follow 627 laws, anyway? More importantly though, is the intimate relationship we can have with our Savior and Lord, Jesus Christ. So love the Lord your God with all your heart, soul, mind and strength. And love your neighbor as yourself. This is the new covenant!

Prayer: Lord, help us not to return to following the obsolete, old laws, but help us to walk in the freedom and grace of the new covenant we have in Christ Jesus…

Aug 21
Don't Praise Yourself

"Let another praise you, and not your own mouth; someone else, and not your own lips." Pr 27:2

There are few places or times when it's appropriate to talk about your own abilities and/or accomplishments. When we go for a job interview, we're required to do the very thing we've been taught from childhood not to do. We have to 'brag' on ourselves. We need to inform the person interviewing us about our work skills, the way we handle difficult situations that arise, what abilities we have that mesh with the position we're applying for, and how we can serve effectively in the position. That goes against what we've been taught, and most of us feel quite uncomfortable doing so. But it is a moment where it may be appropriate, as long as we're straightforward about it, and don't 'embellish' ourselves.

Most of the time, though, we ought to follow the instruction of this verse. We should let others talk us up, recount our abilities, tell about the unusual events, or inform others of an outstanding accomplishment. That really holds true in our marriage relationship. Wife, you can really affirm your husband by telling your friends and family about something he did well. It gives him a sense of confidence, and shows him the respect and honor he covets from the one whose opinion matters far more than anyone else's. Yours! Husband, you can encourage your wife by letting your family and friends know how well an outstanding event was handled by her, and by letting them see how proud you are of her. It gives her a sense of security and self-worth she can't get from anyone else but you.

When we praise ourselves, we look prideful, arrogant, and boisterous. We show a sense of insecurity that can be bolstered by bragging about ourselves. It's a 'hey, look at me, I'm worthwhile because I did all these things, and I'm so smart, or athletic, or good looking' mentality. It's a childish, immature attitude.

There is a proper use for our mouths, a purpose for our lips. We're the ones who should praise another. We're on the other side of this coin. Whether it's your husband or wife, or a friend, or a coworker, you can make a difference in their lives by pointing out to others the good thing they've done. You'll be an encouragement to them, and they'll appreciate your kind words, and be likely to do the same for you when the occasion arises.

Lord: Help us to be humble about ourselves, and the things we do. In the grand scheme of things, they're pretty insignificant. Remind me to brag about my spouse, though, and do it so he or she hears it too…

Aug 22
Pure Joy?

"Consider it pure joy, my brothers, whenever you face trials of many kinds, because you know that the testing of your faith develops perseverance. Perseverance must finish its work so that you may be mature and complete, not lacking anything." Jas 1:2-4

Once again, we're instructed to do that which is completely adverse to our nature. When we face trials of any kind, let alone many kinds, we automatically start to gripe, whine, and complain. We get down in the mouth, our mood turns black, and we may want to yell and throw things.

I have to confess; I'm writing this devotion to myself. I've been facing trials of many kinds, and while I may not be throwing things on the outside, I am on the inside. I'm seriously working on this consider it pure joy thing. Sometimes, it's tough to remember that this testing of my faith is developing perseverance, because even though it seems to me that I'm holding on to God's hand with a steel grip, these afflictions are just overwhelming me. I know that I have to continue on in faith, but when we face serious, what seem to be never-ending difficulties, that's easier said than done. So moment-by-moment, hour-by-hour, day-by-day, we cling in faith to the Lord, because He said, "I will never leave you, nor forsake you." I'm doing my best to face these adversities with fortitude, but it sure would be easier if it weren't so hard. I'm pretty sure this perseverance has finished its work in me (I don't really think I'm persuading the Lord, but I'm trying). Often, we have to cling to God's promises, and His word, because what we experience will cause us to quit and turn back if we don't keep reminding ourselves that God knows what He's doing, He has a plan, and it's for our good. When we get that in our spirit, then we can begin to consider it joy, and maybe even get to the 'pure' joy.

This verse also ends with an encouraging promise. When we have joyfully gone through our trials, when the testing of our faith has developed perseverance, and perseverance has finished its work, then we are assured that we're mature, spiritually complete, and lacking nothing in the faith. We want to be conformed to the image of Christ, and we know He suffered tremendously. In fact, there's a verse that I rather dislike. It's the one that says Christ was made perfect through suffering. But we'll talk about that one another day. The point is, the tribulations we endure in the right way, in faith, and with the correct attitude, bring us to maturity in the faith, and we grow deeper in our understanding of God's will and purpose for us.

So as tough as it is, consider it pure joy when you face trials of many kinds. There *are* positive results coming from it.

Prayer: Holy Spirit, bring to our remembrance, that trials are placed in our lives to test our faith, and that the end result is perseverance, and maturity and spiritual depth. We can think of it with pure joy when we know what's happening and why...

Aug 23
Eschew Self-Righteousness

"To this they replied, 'You were steeped in sin at birth; how dare you lecture us!' And they threw him out" Jn 9:34 Recommended reading—Jn 9:1-34

When we're confronted with something we find hard to accept, and are faced with a story that inspires skepticism, we have a real tendency to resort to self-righteousness. We can puff ourselves up with sanctimonious indignation, and deliver quite the sarcastic, critical put-down, while trying to maintain our own 'purity' and 'holiness.' The problem, of course, is that we don't really fool anyone. Oh, those who agree with us will support us, but of what use is that when we're guilty of arrogance, and uncharitable in our speech? The next time you find a self-righteous retort on your tongue, we recommend you stop, don't speak, and think.

Remember this story from the book of John. This man was born blind. He had to resort to begging, just to eat. Then Jesus came by. His disciples asked him who'd sinned, the man or his parents, that he had received such a punishment. Jesus' answer is startling, at least to the thinking of that day. He said neither had sinned, this happened to show the work of God in the man's life. Jesus spit, made mud, smeared it on the man's eyes, and sent him to the Pool of Siloam to wash. Once the man did that, he could see! Now his neighbors all wondered if this was he, and he told them he was. No one had ever been healed of blindness when blind from birth, yet the evidence was before them. The Pharisees and teachers couldn't accept it. In their eyes, Jesus had no spiritual authority, and He'd broken their law by healing (work) on the Sabbath. They couldn't accept that Jesus was from God. When it was explained, and the Pharisees continued to question the man, he became exasperated, and started preaching to them. No one who's not from God could do these miracles, he said! They were outraged that he should lecture them, hence the verse above.

We ought to take the lesson that we should never speak out of pride. If we have a façade to protect, we need to tear it down, and live authentically. Others may experience things with God that don't fit our preconceived notions, but that doesn't invalidate them. When God's moving, he often does so in ways that we don't expect. Just as in this episode, though, that doesn't mean anything. When God moves, it's real! We have to stay open to where God's working, and accept that He doesn't do the expected. So don't react in self-righteousness. Instead, *be* righteous!

Prayer: Heavenly Father, help us to see when you're working in a situation, and be alert to the fact that you're in the miracle working business, and often don't do what we expect. Keep us humble in our attitudes, and accepting of your moving...

Aug 24
Our Intercessor

"Who is he that condemns? Christ Jesus, who died—more than that, who was raised to life—is at the right hand of God and is also interceding for us." Rom 8:34

It blesses me to think that Jesus intercedes for me. When things are tough, or don't seem to be going well, or something is weighing on my mind, I can go to Jesus knowing He will intercede with the Father on my behalf. We have confidence knowing that He not only died for us, but he also rose from the dead to life. He's the *power* in our lives. He's the one who cares for us, and watches over us.

Have you ever had someone condemn you, tattle on you, or try his or her best to get you in trouble? They were malicious in their attitude, and in their speech, doing everything they could to see to it that you were punished for what you did (whether real or perceived). They accused you of crimes so dastardly they'd have made Satan himself blush. You know the devil does the same thing. He's the accuser. He condemns our actions before the Lord, trying to get us in trouble.

Remember how good it felt when someone stepped in to defend you? When someone took your side, and brought to light the 'real' truth, and you were absolved of any wrongdoing? What a sense of relief we felt when that happened. The good news is we have someone who does that very thing with our Heavenly Dad. When Satan brings accusations against us, we have one who steps in on our behalf, who defends us, and intercedes for us. The verse just before this one asks the question, "who will bring any charge against those whom God has chosen?" The obvious answer is, no one can, because we have an advocate right there, at God's right hand.

We should do our best to be sure Satan has nothing to legitimately accuse us of. But know for certain that when we're in Christ Jesus, even if we slip up, we're covered by the blood of Christ, and our sin is washed away by His atoning sacrifice. Not only has He paid our penalty, He stands right there to prove we're His; consequently, no one can condemn us.

I'm grateful that Jesus is our intercessor!

Prayer: Lord Jesus, we thank you and praise you for our salvation, and for the intercession you continually make on our behalf...

Aug 25
Honor Your Spouse at All Times—Session 1

"You have heard that it was said, 'Do not commit adultery.' But I tell you that anyone who looks at a woman lustfully has already committed adultery with her in his heart. If your right eye causes you to sin, gouge it out and throw it away. It is better for you to lose one part of your body than for your whole body to be thrown into hell." Mt 5:27-29

We know that it's easy to do things that are not honoring to our spouse. Men are especially prone to lust because men are stimulated visually. We see an attractive woman and we can't help but notice. It's instinctive for men to 'see' beautiful women. Women are just as given to dishonor their husband in other ways. Women love to talk, and they have a need to 'share' the 'issues' they have in their relationships, including those they have with their husband. It's intuitive for women to relate to other women the 'less than desirable characteristics' of their husband when they have a disagreement.

The best attitude to keep as the core of our behavior is this; always behave and speak as though your husband or wife were standing right beside you. We can avoid almost every tricky situation if we just keep that in mind. Act with the same honor for your spouse you'd use if he or she were with you. And remember that this behavior, or this conversation, may very well be told to your spouse.

Today, let's talk about men. Tomorrow, we'll address the issue of women.

Men need to be very careful, and very self-disciplined, about the things they look at and the shows they watch. Pornography is such a huge industry because it preys on the natural inclination of men. The number of women who view pornography is a very small percentage as a whole. Women aren't stimulated visually the way men are. Because that's our natural weakness as men, we have to eliminate those situations. Refuse to look at risqué magazines. Stay away from movies with nudity and sexual content. Turn the channel when the show goes into immoral scenes. Keep your speech free from sexual conversation. The truth is, as Christians, there isn't much we can watch on television, at the movie theatre, or see in magazines. It isn't geared toward holiness. When you guard your tongue, or turn the channel, or you turn your head and avert your gaze, you honor your wife, and show her you cherish her above all others.

There's a shocking admonition in this verse. It's better to gouge out your eye than to sin. There's a *consequence* for sin. So don't be in a situation where it's better to lose your eye. Control your natural inclinations, and turn your attention on the Lord. Fix your eyes on Jesus, and keep them focused there, and you won't need to be concerned about these other things, because you won't be doing them. You'll be honoring your wife, and the Lord.

Prayer: Lord, help me to keep my wife in mind, and honor her in everything I do…

Aug 26
Honor Your Spouse at All Times—Session A

"You have heard that it was said, 'Do not commit adultery.' But I tell you that anyone who looks at a woman lustfully has already committed adultery with her in his heart. If your right eye causes you to sin, gouge it out and throw it away. It is better for you to lose one part of your body than for your whole body to be thrown into hell." Mt 5:27-29

If there were a King Gary version of the Bible (and obviously, there's a good reason why there isn't), I believe it should add, 'if your tongue offends you, and causes you to sin, cut it out and throw it away. Better to lose one part of your body than have your whole body cast into the flames.' The principle is the same; only the words have been changed to prick the guilty. In most cases, it's a woman's tongue that gets her in, or causes, trouble. Let's not assume that women don't also look lustfully at men, either. But that's not the central weakness for women, so let's pick up where we left off yesterday.

Women must be careful in their conversation, and in their association. Because women are so relational, they can be easy marks for a guy who knows the way to a woman's heart is through kindness, understanding, and encouragement. A lot of men out there know how to slip their way into your heart through affirmation, consideration, admiration, and showing how they value you. It's important for women to refuse the attentions of men who are too friendly, because they could cause you to dishonor your marital relationship. Also, don't talk about your troubles with your husband to your friends. Talk to your husband. Women have many friends. Men tend to have no intimate men confidants that they can, or will, talk to. Women talk to their friends. Men talk to their friend. Wife, you're that one friend your husband will talk to about intimate things. To honor your husband, you have to respect him, and be loyal to him, by refusing to say critical things of him to your girlfriends. You must stay *more* than arms length from other men. Girlfriends are okay. Guy friends are a death knell to your marital relationship!

Honor your husband by being loyal to him in your conversations, and in your relationships. As we said yesterday, don't say or do things you wouldn't if your husband were right there with you. When you show your husband that kind of respect, you'll have a husband who responds with love and a grateful attitude, because he's honored!

Prayer: Lord, help me to keep in mind all the ways I can honor my husband, and how that honors you, too, Lord…

Aug 27
Who Is Jesus to You?

"But what about you?' he asked. 'Who do you say I am?' Peter answered, 'The Christ of God.'" Lk 9:20

This question is one that is always before us. Who do we say Jesus is? The world has all kinds of answers, some sad, some ignorant, some almost funny. Many will say a prophet, others a great man, a good teacher, a philosopher, spiritual leader for his day, and some will even say a fairy tale. But we need to know a number of things as we walk with Him. We need to have as the core of our faith that Jesus is the Son of God, born of the virgin, Mary, wholly God, and wholly man. He died for our sins, the atoning sacrifice who paid the penalty of death that is required, and whose shed blood cleanses us from sin. He rose again from the dead, and ascended to heaven to sit at the right hand of the Heavenly Father. He is eternal, existing with the Father before creation, and in fact is the creator of all that has been made. He is the way, the truth, and the life, the only means by which we're able to come to the Heavenly Father. He and the Father are one. He sends the Holy Spirit to those who believe in Him, to comfort, to remind us, and to bring us knowledge. He's coming back again, to take His bride, the church, home to heaven.

To be saved, we must be born again. This is the spiritual birth that occurs when we acknowledge our sinfulness, realize we cannot save ourselves, and put our faith and trust in Jesus as our savior. We then begin the process of making Jesus Christ Lord of our life, and submitting to Him, and learn to walk in obedience. This isn't an instant occurrence, but a journey that lasts the entire time we live here on earth.

Now we know that Jesus was, in fact, a prophet. He was a great man, and a good teacher. He gave us the most important philosophy the world has ever known, because it harms no one, and helps everyone. Obviously, He is the most important spiritual leader ever, and always will be. A fairy tale, He is not, though. There is so much more historical documentation for the life of Jesus Christ than there is for Socrates, Aristotle, or Plato combined, that no rational, thinking person can look at the evidence, and dismiss Jesus as a myth. To do so would mean taking the same criteria, and having to throw out more than half of what we consider known fact today.

So, who is Jesus to you? He should be Savior, Lord of your life, brother, master, friend, and much more. If He isn't, you can change that right now.

Prayer: Lord Jesus, plant in our hearts and minds who you are, with an unshakable faith in you...

Aug 28
Pure Sacrifice

"If any of you…presents a gift for a burnt offering to the Lord…you must present a male without defect from the cattle, sheep or goats in order that it may be accepted on your behalf. Do not bring anything with a defect, because it will not be accepted on your behalf." Lev 22:18b-20

Let us be up front here and say that in no way are we encouraging or sanctioning following Old Testament law or customs. But there's a precept in this verse that we should follow. It has to do with bringing our best when we worship the Lord. We know we're to worship in spirit and in truth, and conversely, it infers to do otherwise is really unacceptable in God's eyes.

Let's follow the train of logic that stems from this passage. The Israelites were to offer only males without blemish, with no defects, and without mutilation of any kind. That meant that to be accepted it had to be perfect. They were to bring the very best as an offering to the Lord. This is what it took, and what it takes, to honor the Lord, and to show our reverence for Him. So when we come to worship in spirit and in truth, we must make sure we're doing so with pure hearts, clean hands, and minds free of encumbrances. God deserves our full attention when we offer up our praise and worship.

If we come with a poor attitude, and haven't come to worship with the intention of giving God our best; when we have other things we'd rather be doing, or we're only there out of a sense of obligation, that's probably not acceptable worship to the Lord. If there's sin in our lives, that must be dealt with first. We have to turn from our sin, apologize to God, and ask His forgiveness. He's faithful and just and will forgive our sin when we confess it to Him. We need to be sure we aren't in dispute with anyone, and that we've resolved disagreements. We have encumbered our minds with anger, stress, frustration, and bitterness if we haven't taken care of those arguments. If you know you ought to be giving a certain amount financially, but you're shortchanging what you drop in the offering plate, you're not obediently walking with Christ, and you're not worshipping in spirit and in truth.

God is waiting for us to come to him in praise and worship. How He blesses us with His presence, and His peace, and His love when we bring our best with pure hearts, holy attitudes, and clear minded devotion. How we open the possibilities for uncountable blessings when we bring our full financial offering, because this, too, is part of our spiritual worship. When we come in full obedience, when we come with hearts and minds set apart for Him, it's then that we bring a pure, unblemished sacrifice of acceptable worship to the Lord.

Prayer: Heavenly Father, give us the right attitudes and focus as we come in reverence to worship and praise you...

Aug 29
A Longing Fulfilled

"A longing fulfilled is sweet to the soul" Pr 13:19a

Do you remember when…you couldn't wait to see your girlfriend, the girl who eventually became your wife? Do you remember when…you thought you'd just die if he didn't come to see you soon? Remember the feeling of euphoria you had when you saw each other? Remember the exhilaration you felt when you asked, and agreed, to marry? That gives the sense of what this verse means when it says a longing *fulfilled* is sweet to the soul.

Just having a longing *isn't* so sweet to the soul. In fact, it tends to cause much anxiety, because we're constantly thinking about it, and trying to figure out ways to bring it to fulfillment. It can be downright bitter when our longings aren't fulfilled, or when we face a series of delays.

What are your current longings? Are they dreams you have of a specific work for the Lord? Has He issued a calling that hasn't come to fruition yet? Are you longing for a family? Children (which God's word calls blessings, so remember that when you're frustrated with them) can be a yearning that is almost painful. Perhaps your longing is for a home of your own, or even a better vehicle, or a promotion, or a new job altogether. Whatever it is, give it to the Lord, and let Him bring the fulfillment, instead of doing it on your own. When those longings are fulfilled, they're even sweeter, and much more exciting as we see what God has done for us.

Now plant some new longings in your heart. Think of some neat things you'd like to accomplish together for the Lord. Brainstorm about an exciting, satisfying trip you'd like to take. Be specific! Figure out where you'd like to go, what you'd like to accomplish, and how you'll do it. Plan new romantic outings together (we like these because we normally don't have to wait too long for the fulfillment—lol). Come up with party ideas you can do with a circle of friends. Figure out special events to do for a group at church. Then wait and watch as that sweetness fills your soul, because most of these will be fulfilled, some quite soon.

And remember to thank God each time you have one of these wonderful experiences fulfilled. Trust us, He's having a great deal of fun with you as they are. Where do you think that 'sweet' comes from?

Prayer: Lord God, thank you for giving us that sweet feeling in our souls when our longings are fulfilled…

Aug 30
We're Actually Different!

"When words are many, sin is not absent." Pr 10:19
"Pleasant words are a honeycomb." Pr 16:24
"The words of a gossip are choice morsels." Pr 18:8
"A man of knowledge uses words with restraint." Pr 17:27
"The words of a man's mouth are deep waters." Pr 18:4

We sometimes forget how differently men and women communicate. We mustn't forget that women use 2 & ½ times as many words per day on average as men do (probably why men's ears are more developed). We're very diverse people, yet God created us to complement one another. What is good to keep in mind is the fruit of the Spirit as we're speaking to each other. Words mean things, and we ought to guard our tongues well when using them.

We mentioned this a few days ago, but again, women tend to have many friends they confide in. Because they're so relational, this is how they communicate. They talk. They talk about work, about home, about shopping, about hairstyles, about children, about church, about clothes, about people, about music, about food, and about anything else you can think of. Men should be thankful if their wives have an outlet for most of the words they need to use, so they have a few less to listen to (joke). Men talk, too, but they talk about different things. They talk about work, about the weather, about sports, and that's about it.

When husbands and wives converse, it helps to remember that when women talk, they want for you to empathize with them. They don't necessarily (in fact rarely) want you to take care of a problem, or find a solution; they just want to share, and feel like you understand. Men are analysts. It's difficult in the extreme for us to listen without deciphering the issue and coming up with a fix. Because men tend to think in logical sequence, it takes training to communicate on an emotional level.

Women tend to communicate emotionally, so it exasperates them to be met with a sequential, logical analysis of everything they say. Conversely, when men talk, women want to know how they feel about it, not just what the facts of the story were.

So when you speak, take care to use the knowledge you've been given, and use words with restraint. When angry, speak little, to avoid sinning. Try not to be eager for tidbits of gossip. Use pleasant words as you talk. Think before you speak, and say what's meaningful. And for heaven's sake, *listen* to each other. Spend time ascertaining what's going on in each other's world, so that you can face life together. You'll grow closer as you share what you think, how you feel, what you'd like to see happen, and also what you fear. As the closest friends on earth, you're the main support for each other. Even though you're very different, together you're one!

Prayer: Father, help us to communicate with love, joy, peace, patience, kindness, goodness, and gentleness, and with understanding…

Aug 31
The Welcome Home

"Look,' he said, 'I see heaven open and the Son of Man standing at the right hand of God." Acts 7:56

We as Christians look forward to a big 'welcome home' when our life here is ended, and we cross over to be with the Lord in person. We know that we saints, the church, are the bride of Christ. We know a wedding feast is being prepared for that time when Christ returns, and we're all called home. We know there'll be a great celebration when that time arrives.

Sometimes when we're on tour, we may be gone for weeks. Although we love to travel and sing, and meet and get to know all the fine people we do, it's good to get home at the end of those trips. While our daughter Jackie was there, it was always nice to drive in the yard again, and receive her welcome, with all the hugs, kisses, and smiles that went with it. Then of course, there were the dogs, which were also happy to see us, and they give us an enthusiastic welcome, too. It's such a good feeling to get back again when we've been gone a long time. But that feeling has to pale in comparison to the euphoria when we reach our heavenly home. We've been waiting to get there for so much longer.

We used to sing a song called "Wonderful Time Up There." It tells about the joy and the singing in glory when we get to Heaven. As I introduced that song, I liked to talk about this extraordinary occurrence. You see, in the book of Luke, Jesus told the council of the elders that after this, He would be seated at the right hand of the mighty God. Then in Ephesians we're told that God raised Christ from the dead and seated Him at His right hand. Colossians also tells us that Christ is seated at the right hand of God.

Now in Acts, as Stephen is being stoned to death, he looks up and Heaven is opened to his sight. Stephen proclaims, 'I see heaven open and

Jesus standing at the right hand of God.' I can't help but believe that as Stephen was being martyred for Christ, Jesus *stood* in his honor at the right hand of the throne of the Heavenly Father to welcome him home. I can just imagine the resounding sounds of rejoicing as Stephen entered Heaven that day. What a wonderful homecoming welcome that was!

Prayer: Lord Jesus, help us to be worthy of your great welcome home party when that time comes...

Sep 1
Rules Without Relationship Breed Rebellion

"It is for freedom that Christ has set us free. Stand firm, then, and do not let yourselves be burdened again by a yoke of slavery." Gal 5:1

I can remember the moment when I had a real breakthrough with my daughter. She was complaining about a restriction regarding the kind of party she could attend, and the requirement that parents of the friend be there to oversee it. I had explained this before, but this was the time she 'got it.' Here's the explanation. "I make these restrictions for your good, and for your protection, because I love you. There's no benefit to me to have to argue with you about rules. I receive nothing from it except the peace of mind that it's for your best interest. Can you name one thing I've ever asked of you that wasn't for your good, that I required of you just because I wanted too?" The answer was 'no', she couldn't think of a single time when I made her do something, or kept her from doing something, that wasn't in her best interests.

Because of our open, intimate, lifelong relationship, there was no rebellion. Because of our rapport, the rules were reasonable. When we have a good, *communicative* relationship with our kids, there's much less challenging of the rules we put in place, particularly when we can demonstrate that those limits are for their own good.

You know, the same holds true in our marriage. Neither of us can make rules concerning the other just because we want to, for some spurious reason. That engenders resentment, and causes rebellion in the love relationship. Wives don't happily accept "you can't drive my car 'cause your driving sucks" any better than husbands accept "don't you come in here, I've just cleaned." Hello! From the wife's perspective, what's yours is mine (and what's mine is mine—lol). From the husband's view, I live here too, and I'll go where I want to (I just don't happen to want to go in there right now—lol). No, the restrictions we ask of each other have to make sense, and have to grow out of our love and concern for each other.

Our faith is ultimately the most important area of this precept. We're called to freedom. Not freedom to do whatever we selfishly desire, but freedom from the bondage of sin, and from the laws that govern it. Don't go back into bondage. Refuse to submit to that which moves you into slavery. 'Don't drink, don't smoke, don't go to movies, don't gamble, don't lunch with the opposite sex, don't cuss, don't miss church, don't wear sloppy clothes to church, don't discuss 'real' problems, don't show the pain you feel, and above all, even if you're dieing inside, put on a happy, Christian face. Blarney! If you refrain from those things because you honor the Lord, great! But walk in His grace. Be real! As fellow believers, we're here to support, help, and encourage one another. So dump the bondage of the 'happy face'. Grow in faith and freedom by sharing your problems, and letting the body pray for you and help you. Without that freedom, you'll surely rebel at some point and quit attending, because you didn't get the help you needed. But you didn't get it because you bound yourself to nonsense rules without the relationship you needed with your Christian friends. Walk in Christ's freedom!

Prayer: Dear Lord, keep us from the bondage we often put on ourselves…

Sep 2
When Our Heroes Fail

"Then David sent messengers to get her. She came to him, and he slept with her...put Uriah in the front line where the fighting is fiercest. Then withdraw from him so he will be struck down and die...your servant, Uriah the Hittite is dead...after the time of mourning was over, David had her brought to his house, and she became his wife and bore him a son. But the thing David had done displeased the Lord." II Sam 11:4a,15, 21d,27

I always admired how faithful, how reverent, and how honorable David was, from the time he was young, all the way through becoming king of Israel. Thousands viewed King David as a mighty hero, faithful to the Lord, great in battle, and an extraordinary monarch. The higher the heights to which one ascends, the further the fall when they stumble and sin. King David was no exception. Though God had blessed him, protected him, elevated him, and honored him, still King David forgot his Lord, turned to selfishness, and walked into sin of the most grievous sort.

We hate it when our heroes fail. We have those we look up to in our lives, too. Men or women who have set an example in the faith, shown us great kindness, and displayed God's love to others. But these people are fallible. They're given to the same weaknesses, faults, and frailties that we are. Just as you've made mistakes, gone your own way, and sinned, they're capable of the same types of errors.

It's good to have Christians we can look up to; those we strive to grow to become like, but we need to remember the perfect example. If there are those you admire in the faith, you can count on the fact that they're being conformed to the image of Christ. What you see in them is what the Lord has brought into their character and attitude as they've journeyed through life with Him. We're not called to be conformed to the image of Bob, or

Jean, or Gary, or Glenda, or Steve, or Beth. We're to be conformed to the image of Christ.

So if one of your heroes fails, don't be discouraged in your faith. Realize that we fix our eyes on Jesus, the author and finisher of our faith, "the Son, who has been made perfect forever." Heb 7:28b. We don't cast aside our faith because someone we admire falls into sin. We pray for that person, and seek God's will and grace for their life, because we know that no one is completely immune to sin. We're not, and they're not. So be sure you're following the perfect example, Jesus Christ, and not so closely a friend, or mentor, that we're shaken in our belief in the Lord should they stumble.

Take a lesson from King David. When you forget the Lord, you'll walk away into sin. Walk hand in hand, step-by-step with Christ, keeping your attention on Him, and you'll avoid the heartache of falling in sin, as well as the consequences that surely follow.

Prayer: Heavenly Father, help me to keep my focus on you, and on pleasing you by my words and actions…

Sep 3
On the Step?

"Behold! I stand at the door and knock. If anyone hears my voice and opens the door, I will come in and eat with him, and he with me." Rev 3:20

When folks come to the house, if we've invited them, or if they're friends of ours, we answer the door when they knock. And when we answer the door, we step back and invite them in with a warm welcome. Now if it's someone we don't know, or don't know very well, instead of inviting them in, we may step out onto the porch to talk to them, and see why they've come. We may not be comfortable just having them in. And since we weren't expecting them, we don't normally invite them to dine with us.

Now good friends are another matter. We don't stand too much on ceremony with close friends, and if we're eating, we'll ask them to come in and join us for lunch, or dinner. We want to take the time to visit with them, see how they're doing, what's happening, find out if they have anything on their minds, or events coming up. That's the comfort level we have with dear friends.

The question is, how close is your relationship with Jesus? When He knocks at your door, are you close enough friends that you invite Him in to dine? Do you find out what's on His heart? Question Him as to what He'd like for you to do? Find out any areas of your life He'd like to change? Do you just take time to fellowship with Him, to commune? Or is your relationship more of a casual acquaintance? You know each other, but you don't want to get too close, more of an arm's length friendship? Would you rather step out onto the porch to speak with Him?

See, we get to choose how we respond to Jesus. He's an absolute gentleman. He knocks. He gives you the choice to open the door, or to leave it closed. If you open the door, He'd like to come in so you can dine together. That's communing. Eating, and talking, and sharing what's on your hearts and minds.

Earlier in this passage, it talks about how He wishes we were hot or cold. He hates for us to be lukewarm. That makes Him want to spit! His desire is for us to have communion with one another, to fellowship together. The time we get to spend with Jesus is sweet. So when Jesus knocks, open the door and invite Him in. Don't step out on the porch to talk to Him.

Prayer: Lord Jesus, we give you a standing invitation to come in and eat with us, whenever you'd like to...

Sep 4
No Carping

"Do everything without complaining or arguing," Phi 2:14

Wouldn't you just love it if the next time you asked your husband to take the trash to the garage, he said, "Okay, dear." And just went and cheerfully did it? No grumbling about how there's no earthly reason why you couldn't do it yourself. No arguing about whose responsibility it is, or should be. No complaining about how just when we sit down to relax, she always comes up with something that has to be done, just to make sure we can't rest for a moment.

Wouldn't you just love it if the next time you asked your wife to bring you something, since she's up and standing right beside it anyway, she pleasantly brought it to you? No carping about how lazy you are, can't even get up to feed yourself. No arguing about the fact that she's not your slave, so get it yourself. No martyred complaining about how she does *everything* around here anyway, so she might as well do that too.

The truth of the matter is, when we argue and complain like that, we're just being selfish. We're not looking out for the one we cherish more than anyone else on earth. We're not stepping up to care for the treasure of our heart. We ought to relish the opportunity to show one another how special we feel they are. When we do that, we'll have a lot more peace and harmony in our home.

In fact, we need to do the reverse of complaining and arguing about anything. We'll bless our spouse when we anticipate his or her needs, and take care of it before he or she has a chance to ask. When we think about him or her ahead of time, it shows we love and value and desire the very best for the other.

Dr. Gary Chapman makes a statement in his book "The Five Love Languages". He said 'if vacuuming the floor for his wife fills up her love tank and makes her happy, he'd do it every day.' If you've never lived with a woman or a man whose love tank is full, buddy you've never lived! When your wife is filled up with love, it comes pouring out all over you, man. When your husband is filled up with love, he'll find all kinds of interesting, romantic ways to let it flow back to you.

So do everything without complaining or arguing. You'll be so blessed, and you'll find so many ways to show your love, you'll wonder why you didn't start doing this years ago.

Prayer: Lord, help me to attend to my spouse's needs and desires before he or she even voices them…

We recommend you read "The Five Love Languages", by Dr. Gary Chapman, together.

Sep 5
You Just Can't Hide

"The eyes of the Lord are everywhere, keeping watch on the wicked and the good." Pr 15:3

Have you been tempted to think you're so far from home that you're safe from the gaze of anyone who knows you? The thing is, you might be shopping a thousand miles from where you live and run into someone you know.

We were on tour in Georgia and went out with Glenda's brother and our sister-in-law to an Italian restaurant in Macon for dinner. We got in, and the hostess showed us to our table. As we were getting ready to sit down, I glanced around the restaurant. Not twenty-five feet from me was one of my good friends from Springdale, Arkansas. He was alone, and I went over to greet him, nearly shocking him right out of his chair. We invited him to our table and had a great time. The irony was, we'd been trying for weeks to get together for coffee, and just couldn't make our schedules mesh. The crux of the story is, there are eyes everywhere!

So often we think we can hide. Either by being far from everyone we know, or under cover of darkness. And we often feel like its okay to be a little less disciplined in our habits when we're away. The truth is, that's when we're in the most danger of slipping into sin. We often think we're so strong and independent. Isn't it ironic that without someone to hold us accountable, we lean towards doing things we wouldn't ordinarily do?

It doesn't matter whether you're wicked or good, the Lord sees you. Regardless of what you're doing, He's watching. There's nowhere you can run, no place you can hide. He always knows what's happening. Now, you can use that to your advantage. When you bear in mind that the Lord is with you wherever you are, it makes it easier to do the right thing. His Holy Spirit nudges us in the right direction anyway, but when you turn your attention away from God, it allows you to do things that are wrong.

Keep your focus. Know that the eyes of the Lord are everywhere, keeping watch. Never lose sight of that. It'll help you stay on the straight and narrow road and lead you to do the right things.

Prayer: Father, help us to never forget that you're always watching, and use that to keep us doing what's pleasing to you…

Sep 6
Show Us Your Way

"Let the morning bring me word of your unfailing love, for I have put my trust in you. Show me the way I should go, for to you I lift up my soul. Teach me to do your will, for you are my God; may your good Spirit lead me on level ground." Ps 143:8&10

When we were driving the winding, twisting roads out in Washington last summer, it gave us new insight to the latter part of these verses. After we'd driven up and down thousands of feet, and around so many twisting loops that Glenda had to take Dramamine, we were looking for some straight, level ground to travel.

So many times we have a bad day, and an even worse evening, and it may seem like there's no hope for anything good in sight. But when we've slept, we can awake with a fresh outlook, knowing that the morning brings word of our Heavenly Dad's unfailing love. We've put our trust in Him, and He loves us. He loves us so much! How can we stay in a melancholy mood when the Most High God loves us, and is looking out for us, His children?

When our grandkids are here, it's fun to play with them, and watch them. Just as our children were when they were little, they have absolute faith in us. They know that whether they jump off the porch, or off the roof, or reach to us from someone else's arms, we'll catch them up safely. A couple of years ago, I put our oldest granddaughter up on the porch roof to get a toy down. When she tossed it down, I reached up, and told her to jump. She was about five years old at the time. She looked right into my eyes, and jumped, with complete trust that Grandpa would catch her. And of course, I did. That's the kind of complete faith we can have in our Heavenly Dad. When He tells us to jump, we know to jump, because He'll safely catch us.

Our prayer actually is that the Lord will show us the way we should go. We lift our hearts and souls to Him for refreshing. Sometimes we have to climb high mountains, and in other seasons we go through deep valleys. But as He teaches us His will, we know more and more that we can have faith and trust in Him. When we know God's heart, we can more effectively do His will. As we do His will, His Spirit will lead us on level paths. After all, He is our God!

Prayer: Heavenly Dad, thank you for your unfailing love, and for teaching us your will. Make our ground level...

Sep 7
Value Your Wonderful Wife

"A wife of noble character who can find? She is worth far more than rubies. Her husband has full confidence in her and lacks nothing of value." Pr 31:10-11

I don't know how much you know about the Taj Mahal in India, but it has a fascinating origination. Emperor Shah Jahan built it for his favorite wife, Mumtaz Mahal, after she passed away. It took about twenty-one years to build, and is one of the modern, Seven Wonders of the World. Building began about 1632 and was completed about 1653. The estimated cost was about 32 million Rupees, which in today's currency, runs into the trillions of dollars. He evidently thought highly of his wife, and took steps to show how valued she was to him and how thoroughly he loved her.

How much do you revere and cherish your wife? Is she worth far more than rubies? Is her value to you beyond description? If she is, then the next question is, how do you show your appreciation for her? Do you treat her like gold? Or do you treat her like dirt? The intriguing thing is, the way you treat your wife tells a lot about you! When you're disrespectful, or overbearing, or bullying, or critical, or demeaning to her, you show that you're a man with little self-esteem, a miserly heart, a mean, ugly spirit, and a small sense of honor or chivalry. When you treat your wife like the rarest jewel known to man, with dignity, with kindness, with gentility, with care, and with courtesy, you show the world that she's a woman to be prized, and that you're a man of self-confidence; you're thoughtful, intelligent, humble, disciplined, loving, and godly.

You show you're self-confident, because you don't try to beat your wife down to elevate yourself. You're thoughtful, because you think of ways to honor her, and compliment her real assets and abilities. You're intelligent, because you're smart enough to know that a woman who's publicly cherished responds with love and appreciation in like manner. You're humble, because you realize that you're not the center of the universe, you know your wife is precious, and you show God you're grateful for the blessing He's gifted to you. You're disciplined, because you don't allow your tongue, or your manners, to go astray and curse your wife; rather you keep them in check and use them positively to bless her. You're loving, because you're doing what's best for your wife, and showing her she means the world to you. You're godly, because you're obediently doing what God's word tells you to do as a husband, and as the spiritual leader of your family.

Husband, you have the wife God blessed you with. Thank the Lord, and always show her you highly esteem the gift you've received. You'll be blessed in return.

Prayer: Lord, give me grace to treat my wife with the honor she needs and desires...

Sep 8
Orders from the King

"So the king gave the order, and they brought Daniel and threw him into the lions' den. The king said to Daniel, 'May your God, whom you serve continually, rescue you.'...At the first light of dawn, the king got up and hurried to the lions' den. 'Daniel,...has your God...been able to rescue you from the lions?' Daniel answered,...'they have not hurt me.'
Then King Darius wrote to all...throughout the land: ...I issue a decree that in every part of my kingdom people must fear and reverence the God of Daniel. For he is the living God and he endures forever; his kingdom will not be destroyed, his dominion will never end. He rescues and he saves; he performs signs and wonders in the heavens and on the earth." Dan 6:16,19,20c,21a,22b,25-27b

People with much power can influence many with their recommendations. That's positive when they use that for good things. It's bad news when they use it to lead others astray. Many of our popular sports stars are some of the worst moral examples you'll ever see. Sadly, even though they may be complete reprobates spiritually, a lot of young folks will follow their culture of perversity.

Other sports stars use their fame for positive results, often doing things for, and drawing attention to, very worthy causes, and doing their best to follow high standards of moral excellence in their personal lives. These should be commended for their upright stands.

King Darius was very fond of Daniel, and trusted him and relied on him. But he was deceived into a corner he couldn't get out of by some very devious advisors who felt threatened by Daniel. The king's edict had to be followed, and even though the king tried to think his way out of this situation, he had to accede to the law and cast Daniel into the lions' den. He hoped Daniel's God would save him. Of course, God did save him, and the result was it made a believer out of King Darius, especially when the men who'd falsely accused Daniel were thrown in and the lions tore them to shreds before they even hit the ground. King Darius used his influence to honor God by instructing his subjects to revere the living God.

How do you use your influence? We all have others that respect our thoughts and opinions. Use that seriously to point others to our living Savior. Be sure you set the positive example that shows your love for the Lord, and your obedience to Him.

Prayer: Lord, remind me to set standards of excellence that will glorify you and inspire others to want to meet you, too…

Sep 9
Our Rescuer

"The Lord knows how to rescue godly men from trials." II Pet 2:9b

We know that we'll all have to endure trials of various kinds. Everybody goes through afflictions, whether you're a Christian or not. The difference is we have God, who knows how to rescue us, godly men, from our difficulties.

The passage prior to the verse above talks about Lot, who was distressed by the wickedness around him. Since we live in the modern day equivalent of Sodom and Gomorrah, particularly in certain cities of the United States, we, too, are disturbed by the evil things happening all around us. There's so much crime and moral perversion that we're inundated by it. It's very troubling to us who believe in Jesus Christ, and want to walk in holiness. We can be tormented in our hearts over the sinful things going on around us, whether it's theft, murder, sexual sin, broken relationships, or filthy talk.

This is a day and age when we have to protect ourselves as much as possible from the contamination of the world we live in. Stay away from the seedier areas of towns. Prevent the infiltration that occurs when we watch the wrong shows. Do the things that please God. Listen to gospel music (especially Gary & Glenda—lol), or Christian talk radio, or watch decent movies and television, or read wholesome books that have good morals, or that are good for spiritual growth in your walk with the Lord, and associate with other believers often for your recreation.

We are called to be light in a dark world. You have to interact with the world to be that, but unless you're set apart (sanctified), you can end up losing your value as a witness for Christ by becoming too worldly. To make a difference, we have to *be* different! If we're not holy, then there isn't anything that draws a lost world to Jesus when they're hurting or in serious trouble. We want, and need, them to look to us for answers when the world fails them, and the world *will* fail them.

So live up to the standards the Lord sets for us, and walk in all the light you have. When your friends come to you seeking help, you'll be able to introduce them to the Lord who knows how to rescue.

Prayer: Father, thank you being the one who rescues us from our trials, and shine forth through us so others will come when they're troubled, and meet you…

Sep 10
Teaching Respect

"and the wife must respect her husband." Eph 5:33b

The definition of respect in our dictionary is: to treat with special consideration; to hold high esteem for; courteous or considerate treatment, complimentary. The other day we talked about how the way men treat their wives tells more about them than it does the wife. The reverse is also true. Wife, how you treat your husband says much about your character, your temper, your attitude, and your integrity. It's also what you're teaching other women, and what you're teaching your children, by your actions.

As with so many other instructions in God's word, it doesn't say 'respect your husband if he's worthy of respect.' This is a directive statement to either be obedient to, or not to be obedient to. There's no 'try', there's only *do*, or *do not do*.

If you've bought in to the world's definition of the 'real' woman, you believe that you can be independent, have a successful career, have a wonderful husband (the kind defined by feminists), great, achieving children, and all the toys you want, as well as be happy and contented, and to top it all off, you're rarely tired. Now in the reality within which we all live, that's not only a figment of someone's imagination, it's impossible. It's impossible because God's word tells us what the godly woman is like, and He always shows us what the absolute best for us is, and it doesn't match the world's vision at all. If you'll follow His plan for you as a wife, you'll realize the peace, contentment, joy, and happiness you seek.

You teach your children, and the women friends in your life, what kind of person you are by the way you interact with your husband. When you're rude, demanding, insolent, argumentative, inattentive, critical, and careless of his feelings and needs, you show everyone that you're spiteful, selfish, contentious, and mean-spirited. You also drive a wedge between what you need and desire from your husband, and his willingness and/or ability to meet those needs and fulfill your desires. Ah, but when you're kind, courteous, thoughtful, affirming, considerate, generous, loving, and can peacefully discuss issues, you show that you're gentle, affectionate, uplifting, confident, patient, loving, and happily content. When you treat your husband in these ways, he's 'stoked', and is willing, able, and desiring to be what you need and want him to be.

Glenda is very good at treating me with honor, respect, and affirmation. She's complimentary to and about me, and I never worry about her saying things behind my back, being disrespectful. Sometimes I'd like to meet the man she's talking about, because she sees attributes in me that I've yet to realize, but because she honors and respects me, both in our home, and in public, I strive to become the husband she already thinks I am. I'm not stupid (welllll…). I love hearing those things, even if they're not accurate to my way of thinking, because it builds me up.

How are you teaching respect? By the 'how to' method, or by the 'how not to' method?

Prayer: Dear Lord, help me to be a wife who is respectful of my husband, and who teaches our children and our friends to be respectful, as well…

Sep 11
Get It Inside

"Let the word of Christ dwell in you richly as you teach and admonish one another with all wisdom, and as you sing psalms, hymns and spiritual songs with gratitude in your hearts to God." Col 3:16

We all understand what it means to teach. We communicate and impart knowledge to someone else, regarding facts, processes, or theories. Admonish is an interesting word. We see it often, but it's ambiguous whether we correctly understand its meaning. To admonish is to gently reprove, exhort, or guide another, or others. That's nice. Gently reprove; it almost gives us the feeling that Grandma is telling us something in a kindly manner, so we're not at all offended. We're told to teach and admonish one another with *all* wisdom. Use the applied knowledge and self-discipline we've learned as we instruct others.

And then it goes on to tell us 'as we sing psalms, hymns and spiritual songs'. This must be music that praises and glorifies God; that teaches us and affirms foundational truths as we sing to the Lord. And we're to make this music with thankfulness and gratitude to God.

Now this all revolves around the first phrase. Let the word of Christ dwell in you richly. How does that happen? For the word of Christ to dwell in us at all, we have to read or hear it. Now oft times we'll read the Bible aloud. Faith comes from hearing the message, and the message is heard through the word of God (Rom 10:17). So to stir up our faith, we read it aloud at times. The more we read God's word, the more He writes it on our hearts, and the Holy Spirit brings it to our memory when we need it. As we spend enough time in the word, we begin to get that sense of the word of Christ dwelling in us richly. It's readily at hand, and we have an abundance of His word within. When that starts to happen we'll find ourselves speaking His word more frequently in everyday conversation.

We'll break out singing songs of worship at various times. So! How's your daily Bible reading streak coming?

Read a bit each day, and you'll get it inside!

Prayer: Father, move us to the self-discipline needed to study the word of Christ daily, without breaking our streak...

Sep 12
Inner Power

"I pray that out of his glorious riches he may strengthen you with power through his Spirit in your inner being." Eph 3:16

In the course of life, there are times when we need help. We need an inner strength we don't possess on our own. Thankfully, the Lord gives us power from within through the Holy Spirit, who gives us the fortitude we lack on our own. We've been singing an old song called 'If The Lord Wasn't Walking By My Side.' It starts out saying, 'I don't know, just what I'd do, if the Lord wasn't walkin' by my side'.

Sometimes you hear non-believers say that religion is a crutch for those who are too small-minded to make it in life on their own. Christians need an outside source of help, because they're too mentally and emotionally weak to get by. Okay, that's all right with me. I don't mind admitting that I have no interest whatsoever in going through life without Jesus. His word says when we're weak, He's shown to be strong (my paraphrase). The irony of the situation is, when we're faced with traumatic occurrences in our lives, Christian endure those afflictions with a grace, and an inner strength, that non-believers just don't have. We know that God's still on the throne, and that He has everything in hand, even though we may not understand what He's doing in our trying situation.

The little technicality regarding 'the religion crutch' that makes all the difference though, is this; we're not in religion, we're in *relationship*. We personally know the only son of the Most High God. We interact with God's son, Jesus, everyday. We study His word, we emulate His character and style, and we commune with Him in prayer. Because we're involved with Christ on a daily basis, we have an intimate relationship with Him. We're not following carefully contrived religious rules. We're being obedient to His desire while living in absolute freedom that is completely foreign to those who don't know the Lord.

What we're given isn't just a little sample of what the Spirit has. No, God grants us power through the Holy Spirit out of His *glorious riches*. There's no shortfall, no rationing of what we receive due to poverty, because in His glorious riches, there's *plenty* for all of us. And He freely gives us that inner power.

Prayer: Lord Jesus, grant us that inner power you have for us through your Spirit. Give us an abundance of it, because we need your strength...

Sep 13
Give What You Have

"By faith in the name of Jesus, this man whom you see and know was made strong. It is Jesus' name and the faith that comes through him that has given this complete healing to him, as you can all see." Acts 3:16

We've gotten so used to modern medicine that we forget that for two thousand years, only Jesus has healed people of what, for ages past, has always been permanent disability, or terminal illness. Not only did Jesus heal every malady, He also told us that those who believe in Him would do greater things than He did. I don't purport to know what that means, exactly, but we do have a clear example of something in this verse, and the passage that leads up to it.

Miraculous circumstances occur through faith in Christ Jesus. In some cases it's healing, but in other cases it may be a job coming through unexpectedly, or a financial help at just the right moment, or a relationship restored through a series of situations that could only be from the Lord. When we pray in the name of Jesus, and put our faith in Him, and pray for things that glorify His name, and advance His kingdom, we see amazing things happen.

Now Peter and John came up to this beggar, who had been crippled since birth. He couldn't walk. The beggar was looking for a handout of money. But Peter and John didn't have money. So they gave the beggar what they had available to them, which turned out to be what the beggar really needed. He didn't need money nearly as much as he needed to be able to walk. Peter and John, through faith in Jesus, and by the power of Jesus' name, healed the man, helped him to his feet, and sent him on his way. And he went walking, and jumping, and praising God.

You may not have money, either. You may not have the faith that Peter and John had. What you have to answer for yourselves is; *are you willing to give what you have?* You may have an ability that will bless someone for the sake of Christ. You may have an encouraging word for someone that will uplift him or her at just the time they need it. You may have knowledge that someone needs. You may have faith to pray for and minister to someone who has no one else to turn to.

Put your faith in Jesus to accomplish His will and purpose, and give what you have for Him.

Prayer: Jesus, give us the faith we need to step out and minister to others to bless them for you…

Sep 14
How to Address a Fool

Admit it! Even though it's not the 'Christian' thing to do, you've wanted to challenge many a fool, and address the asinine comments that spew from his or her mouth. You know, the Bible addresses pretty much everything there is to address, and this is no exception. There actually is a Christian manner in which to confront a fool, should you ever chance to be involved in a conversation with one.

> "Do not answer a fool according to his folly,
> or you will be like him yourself.
> Answer a fool according to his folly,
> or he will be wise in his own eyes." Pr 26:4-5

On the face of it, this looks like a contradiction in terms. Don't answer, do answer. Which is it? Well, a little more expansion of the meaning of these verses is necessary.

Verse 4 basically means this: Don't answer a fool in the same manner with which he expresses his folly. If he's blustering, bragging, loudmouthed, and close-minded about something you know to be incorrect, don't answer in a blustering, confrontational, dogmatic, loudmouthed way. If you do, you'll just look like a fool yourself.

Verse 5 basically means this: You must confront the irrational logic of a fool or he'll think his foolish ideas are wise. Deal with these issues humbly, in a calm voice, with a confident manner, politely pointing out the rational, systematic logic of what is accurate. When you answer his error with truth, there's a chance he'll actually understand and gain knowledge.

As is the case with any dispute we have with someone, albeit with a friend, a coworker, your spouse, or your children, we have a pattern of behavior we should always follow. We must always keep in mind whose child we are, and whom we represent, and act in a manner that honors the Lord. We have to be polite, gentle, kind, discreet, loving, and truthful. And we never use 'truth' as a bludgeon to beat the other into submission. Rather, we calmly instruct the other in what we perceive to be true. And then, in most cases, we have to leave it. We have little to no control over the other person's response.

Be careful how you address a fool. Don't be one!

Prayer: Lord, give us wisdom to address others in a respectful, gentle manner that honors and glorifies you...

Sep 15
Be Hospitable

"Share with God's people who are in need. Practice hospitality." Rom 12:13

Here's one of the key elements to growing your church. It doesn't matter what denomination it is, what your style of worship is, or who the pastor is. What counts is how you treat people.

Since we travel all over the country, we see all kinds of churches, and the people who fellowship together in them. One thing that nearly every growing, vibrant, church has in common is this. They practice hospitality! And it's done in a variety of ways.

Here's what we see. In some places, people are polite, but cool, and perfunctory in their greeting of 'strangers'. They'll give the obligatory 'welcome', but anyone who receives their greeting senses they'd rather not be bothered. One almost gets the feeling that "we've come to church, so let's have the worship service so we can head off to what we'd really like to be doing." Visitors leave with the attitude that they were actually a bother to this congregation.

Then we go to fellowships where you *know* they're genuinely glad you've come to visit. They greet you warmly, with a friendly smile. They ask who you are, where you're from, what you do, what kind of family you have; in short, they engage you in conversation and show an interest in finding out about *you*. They often invite you to coffee, or a meal with them, so you can all become better acquainted. Visitors leave with the inclination to come back again, because they've been *loved*.

What kind of folks are you? If you're too busy to be bothered with entertaining visitors, with taking time to get acquainted, and show them you're interested in them, you probably have a 'cool, stale' church. If this is a pervasive attitude in your church, there's only one way to change it, and if you want your church to have a chance to grow, change it you must!

Put your priorities in the correct order. Show people you're grateful they chose to worship with you. Engage them in conversation. Find out about them. Ask questions about them. Follow up with a call later in the week. Invite them to coffee or a meal, whether at home, or to a restaurant, and get to know them better. Practice hospitality!

We're not overlooking the importance of biblical, accurate teaching; that's a given with us, but when several in your church family begin to practice hospitality, you'll see a difference that'll cause a chain reaction that will change the atmosphere in your church, and give it a great opportunity to begin to grow.

Prayer: Father in Heaven, give us the right attitude, the love and interest we need, and the grace to practice hospitality at every opportunity…

Sep 16
You Have the Wife/Husband You Deserve

"He who sows wickedness reaps trouble…a generous man will himself be blessed." Pr 22:8a&9a

Through the course of life, we plant seeds, and we harvest what we plant. This principle is laced throughout God's word. We reap whatever we sow. In the garden, we can't reap corn if we sowed beans. We don't get to pick peas if we plant potatoes. Strawberries don't grow on pumpkin vines. But when we plant beans, we can get loads of beans. When we sow potatoes, we can dig up bushels of potatoes. And when we plant strawberry vines, we get to savor the sweet taste of strawberries.

We do the same thing in our marriage. We sow seeds that produce a harvest after their own kind. Whatever you plant is what you get, and it's also what you deserve. Just as when you plant corn you deserve corn, what you plant in your marriage relationship is what you deserve. Now that can be 'ouch' if you've sowed bad seed, but it's great if you've sowed correctly.

If you've sowed badly, you probably don't have the husband/wife you'd like to have, because when you plant poorly, you reap sour fruit as a natural consequence of the normal responses we all have. When your wife asks you a question, and you respond rudely, she's not going to feel loved. When your husband asks for your help, and you respond as though this is akin to martyrdom, he's not going to feel like you appreciate or respect him. When those types of things happen consistently over a period of time, a negative pattern of behavior sets in that becomes a downward spiral. You end up with a heart hardness to protect your emotions, and a harshness in your responses that continually makes it worse. If you've been treating your wife like a jerk, or you've been treating your husband like you're the definition of shrew, you have the spouse you deserve. Face it; if you're ugly to your husband/wife, you don't deserve any better.

Now if you want the most beautiful, kind, loving, gracious wife there ever was, too bad. I'm already married to her. But for the next best, you can create her for yourself. If you want the most generous, thoughtful, romantic, helpful, chivalrous husband ever, you're too late. He's mine. But you, too, can create the next best. It, too, happens as a natural response to the way we treat each other.

When you treat your wife with politeness, a helping hand, gracious attitudes, and anticipate what you can do to please her, she'll respond with kindness, grace, and love. When you let her know you appreciate all she does for you and the family, and tell her how lovely she is, she'll do even more, and she'll become more beautiful all the time. When you treat your husband with respect, and honor him with affirming words, and give him the affection he desires, he'll respond with good humor, with a serving attitude, and with the love you need. When you let him know that he's still your hero, the knight in shining armor you've always admired, he'll become more chivalrous than ever.

Be generous in your words and actions toward each other, and you'll be blessed yourself! You'll get the husband/wife you deserve!

Prayer: Dear Lord, remind us to sow lovingly, kindly, generously, and graciously...

Sep 17
Live Without Deficit

"Suppose one of you wants to build a tower. Will he not first sit down and estimate the cost to see if he has enough money to complete it?" Lk 14:28

We live in a culture where we're encouraged to buy now, pay later. There's no reason to wait, just get what you want, put it on your credit card, and pay it off over a few months. Want a new car? They have all kinds of attractive financing options, with low interest. Need a house? You can get one with zero down, just pay closing costs and it's yours, with affordable payments. Would you like a new couch? Just borrow the money, and purchase it. Stereo's on the blink, or just outdated? In house payment plans are available so you can take it home now.

The problem? As we've calculated what we pay in interest on these 'must have' items, we find that we usually pay more than double the price of the item, when you take into consideration the thirty year mortgage, the credit cards, the bank loans, and the private financing options you may have used. What could you have done with the extra $400 in interest you paid on the couch? What worthy cause could you have supported with the extra $550 in interest that went to the credit card company for your new flat screen, High Definition, television?

The good news is you don't *have* to pay that interest. You *can* live life without deficit. To accomplish that, you have to think ahead, and plan your way, save the money, and buy your items outright. This requires something we're often in short supply of; it requires patience. You have to make do with what you have, pay off what you already own, then save another few months to accumulate the money to buy the next item. Every time you do that, calculate how much interest you would have paid had you purchased that with a credit card. You'll be amazed at how much money you're saving, and you'll have such a sense of relief that you don't have another payment to keep up with that you'll feel absolutely euphoric.

This doesn't apply to finances only. It applies to life in general. Don't put yourself in debt to someone over something you should've done, but procrastinated and didn't. Keep those obligations up to date, and you'll live without deficit in your relationships, in your spiritual life, and in the physical realm.

You *can* live without deficit. You have to count the cost, come up with your plan, and execute the plan as flawlessly as possible. Complete your non-deficit tower of life.

Live without deficit!

Prayer: Father, give us the wisdom, the patience, and the self-discipline to turn our life into one without deficit. Move us to that place where we owe no one anything but the continuing debt of love…

Sep 18
Delight in Your Weakness

"My grace is sufficient for you, for my power is made perfect in weakness. Therefore I will boast all the more gladly about my weaknesses, so that Christ's power may rest on me. For when I am weak, then I am strong." II Cor 12:9&10c

When I was a kid I was working on moving a machine to hook it up to the tractor. It was setting in an awkward position, and try as I might, I could *not* get that implement into the right position to drop the draw-pin into the slot. I was getting very frustrated. My arms were starting to feel like lead, my back was aching, my legs felt weak, and I was at the point where I wanted to start throwing things, but I was too tired. Finally, I had to admit I couldn't do it myself, and I went and hunted down Dad. Of course, he came over, picked it right up, rolled it into position, and dropped the pin in. The thing is, if I hadn't been too weak to do it myself, he wouldn't have come in his strength, and done it like it was nothing.

In the course of our Christian walk, we often run up against situations and problems that we're not strong enough to take care of. But if we could, we wouldn't learn that God's grace is sufficient for us. His power shows through when we're weak, because He still wants to accomplish His goals and His will, in us and through us. I don't think the Lord ever intended for us to be able to do His work in our own strength, wisdom, or power. Even though we know our abilities and intelligence come from God, when we do things in our own brawn and energy, we don't give Him the glory, and *He* deserves the glory, because we're just servants doing our master's work.

So when you're unable to do something, or overcome a problem, take it to the Lord and let Him move. When He's solved the problem, or resolved the situation in a miraculous way, you get to see Him working, and it's exciting to watch. We stand back and marvel when God does something extraordinary (at least it is to us), and it gives us the opportunity to tell about His wonderful ways. We get the chance to boast about Christ's power as He moves in our lives. We tell about the fact that on our own, we couldn't accomplish what He did, and we'd never have thought to do it that way to begin with. God is awesome, and it's tremendous to see how He performs His will.

So boast about your weakness, and extol God's power! Whatever the problem, He does it like it's nothing, anyway.

Prayer: Gracious Lord, help us to remember that you're the strength and power, and we're too weak to accomplish your tasks on our own. Allow us to boast in our weakness, and in your mighty power...

Sep 19
Faithfulness and the Redeemer—Day 1

Please read the first chapter of Ruth

The book of Ruth is such a rich story of God's faithfulness, provision, and redemption. Let's begin at the beginning.

This takes place during the time of the judges, when Israel had no kings. God was their king, and they needed no other. The foolishness of wanting to have an earthly king came later. During this time, there was a famine, and so Elimelech took his wife Naomi, and his two sons to live in Moab. While there, Elimelech died, and following his death, his sons married Moabite women. Then both sons also died after ten years, leaving Naomi without her husband or her sons.

This is significant. The men took care of the family, and held property in their names, leaving the wives dependent upon them for their provision. Naomi is left without her immediate male relatives, and with two daughters-in-law, and no way to support herself or them. She sends the Moabite women back to their families to be taken care of, and gives them her blessing and prayer.

God had made provision in these cases for the wives left behind. If a man died, the law said that his brother must take the widow as his wife, support her, and procreate to preserve the name and family line of his brother. If there were no brother, then the closest male relative had the right to step in and become the kinsman redeemer. He would marry the widow, take possession of the property and/or land, and any children they had would inherit in the name of the original husband; thus the man's name and line would be preserved. Naomi was now widowed, too old to marry and have children, there were no brothers, and Naomi knew that these women couldn't wait fifteen years for another son, even if she were able to have one. That's why she sent the daughters-in-law back to their father's homes.

An odd thing happened. Ruth refused to leave Naomi. It doesn't say why Ruth was so devoted to Naomi, or what love she had for her, but we know that Ruth obviously held Naomi in high esteem, for she wouldn't return to her father's house. When Naomi realized that Ruth wouldn't leave her, she stopped urging her, and the two traveled back to Israel, to Bethlehem. They arrived in time for the beginning of the barley harvest.

As husband and wife, are we that devoted to each other that we would be absolutely faithful, and *never* leave each other?

Prayer: God, give us the love and devotion to one another, and to our family, that Ruth showed to Naomi…

Sep 20
Faithfulness and the Redeemer—Day 2
Or—Word Gets Around

Please read the second chapter of Ruth

It was the custom of that day that when the harvest was going on, when a few straws of grain would slip from the bundles, the reapers were to leave them lie on the ground for the alien, the widow, and the fatherless to pick up. This was in accordance with God's instruction. Ruth requested of Naomi to let her go and pick up the leftover grain behind the workers. And Naomi gave her permission.

It's interesting that Ruth placed herself in submission to Naomi, and treated her with the honor and respect that one normally reserves for their own parents. She actually asked Naomi's permission to go work in the field, even though she herself was an adult.

As Ruth was gleaning in the field behind the harvesters, the owner of the field came. You can see what kind of man he is by his greeting, and the answer from his workmen. Boaz is the owner's name, and his salutation is 'the Lord be with you'. The reapers call back 'the Lord bless you.' Now Boaz is alert to what's going on, and asks who this young woman is. When he finds out it's the Moabitess who came back with Naomi, he tells her to stay with his servant girls. He's heard of Ruth's kindness and faithfulness to her mother-in-law, and he blesses her, with his request to God that she be richly rewarded by the Lord. Here's an example of a godly man who's going out of his way to protect someone he doesn't know, and give her special consideration for her goodness to Naomi, who is his relative.

Boaz goes a step further. When it's time for their meal, he offers Ruth bread and vinegar and then offers her roasted grain. When Ruth gets up to go, Boaz instructs his harvesters to pull out extra stalks for her to pick up. That means he was willing to give up some of his profits to help someone because he'd heard of her devotion to Naomi. Word gets around when you do something kind, and when you're faithful, and God brings blessings back to that person.

When Ruth came home with about twice as much grain as she should have, Naomi wants to know where she worked, and who's field it was. When Ruth tells her it's Boaz, Naomi asks the Lord to bless him for his kindness. Naomi lets Ruth know that Boaz is one of their kinsman-redeemers. Naomi also tells Ruth it will be safer for her to stay with Boaz' servant girls, rather than take a chance somewhere else.

Because word got around about Ruth's faithfulness and devotion to Naomi, God blessed Ruth by leading her to the fields of Boaz, a kinsman-redeemer, by inclining Boaz' heart to show kindness and generosity to her, and by moving Boaz to protect her and keep her busy gleaning through the end of the harvest.

Prayer: Heavenly Father, we thank you for how you reward those who are faithful and true, and how you bless us in ways that are mystifying to see...

Sep 21
Faithfulness and the Redeemer—Day 3

Please read the third chapter of Ruth

Mothers can be some of the most brilliantly conniving people on the face of the earth. No swindler in the history of the world ever had a better scheme than a mother trying to accomplish something for her child. Now, that may have negative connotations, but that isn't necessarily true, for many mothers are godly women of integrity. They're also sly.

You can see from the beginning of this third chapter that Naomi has set herself to finding Ruth a husband. When you see that matchmaking glint in a mother's, or your wife's, eye, just stand back and get out of the way, so you don't get hurt. Naomi has Ruth bathe, dress up, put on her makeup and perfume, and go to the threshing floor (where only men were supposed to be), and snuggle up to Boaz (that's the short version). When Boaz wakes in the middle of the night to find Ruth warming his feet, he blesses her for her kindness to him. Because she didn't run after the younger men, whether rich or poor, Boaz was honored. He responds with gratitude and takes care of Ruth.

Obviously Ruth being snuggled up to Boaz' feet meant that she was offering more than casual friendship. She was offering an opening communiqué that meant she was open to his romantic attentions, if he so chose. Boaz is more than interested, but he's a godly man of integrity, and knows there's a kinsman-redeemer who's closer than he is. He promises Ruth that if the man doesn't redeem, then he will. He invites her to spend the night at his feet, informing her that all his fellow townsmen know her to be a woman of noble character.

When it was very early morning, so dark no one could see, Ruth gets up and leaves the threshing floor, but not empty-handed. Boaz gives her six measures of barley to take, and his promise.

Naomi is looking out for Ruth, and wants to see that she's cared for throughout the rest of her life. They'd talked about this, and many other life subjects, because they each knew what to do. Naomi knew how to attract Boaz, and Ruth had learned to follow Naomi's advice.

Boaz is a man of integrity. Even though he might have liked to redeem Ruth immediately, knowing there was another redeemer closer, he had the rectitude to first offer her to his kinsman. Boaz feels privileged, because Ruth is younger than he, and he's more generous, because he's been respected and honored by Ruth.

Do we use the wisdom and integrity we ought to? It's important to be faithful, because God blesses that.

Prayer: Lord, help us to show integrity in all that we do, and be faithful to what's honest and true…

Sep 22
Faithfulness and the Redeemer—Day 4

Please read the fourth chapter of Ruth

At the end of the last chapter, Naomi told Ruth that Boaz wouldn't rest until the matter of redeeming her was settled. Isn't that the way it is with dependable people? When they're committed to something, they stay on it until it's resolved one way or the other.

Boaz went up to the town gate and waited for his kinsman. When he arrived, in front of witnesses, Boaz brought up the matter of the property of Elimelech, which Naomi was about to sell, and Boaz told him he was kinsman-redeemer, and asked if he would redeem the property. He said he would. Then Boaz brought up the widow that went with it, at which point, the man declined, not wanting to place his own estate in danger. He tells Boaz, in front of all these witnesses, to redeem it himself, and gives Boaz his sandal. In other words, they agreed in front of witnesses, and shook on the deal.

The crux of this story is, Boaz redeems Elimelech's property, and takes Ruth to be his wife. Ruth becomes pregnant, and has a son, and they named him Obed. Obed became the father of Jesse, who was the father of David, who became king of Israel, the man after God's own heart, from whom Jesus was descended (on his mother's side).

Here we have the resolution of this story. Ruth was faithful. God saw it, and was pleased to bless her, working things out for her favor, placing her in the right places, with the right people, at the right times. God already had in place the process for redemption, which was the picture of how Jesus would redeem us, himself. Boaz is a picture of God's love and favor in redemption; He's generous, kind, and able to save.

Israelite's weren't supposed to marry foreigners. Yet, God shows us that salvation is available to all people, even in the Old Testament. Ruth accepted Naomi's God as her God, and this Moabite woman, a foreigner, becomes an ancestor of Jesus Christ. God's grace has always extended to whosoever is willing to come in faith.

Finally, Naomi, this resourceful, godly woman, gets to take Ruth's child, lay him on her lap, and care for him. Her friends gathered around to praise God, and bless Naomi. God had been faithful, and redeemed her!

Prayer: Dear Lord, we thank you for this picture of faithfulness and redemption. We give you praise that you've redeemed us from sin, and blessed us beyond measure…

Sep 23
The Essentiality in the Middle

"It is better to take refuge in the Lord than to trust in man." Ps 118:8

We're often told that we should do, be, see, believe, and partake of all things in moderation. It's best to take the middle ground. You'll be on sound footing if you're in the center. That may be true at times, but it certainly isn't accurate all, perhaps not even most, of the time.

The world would have us believe that in religious beliefs, one should avoid the fanatical. After all, all roads lead to heaven as long as you're sincere in your belief. How can you say there's only one way? Doesn't that seem extremist? Surely we can trust the God who loves us to encompass all good teaching, and accept us as we come.

This verse, Psalm 118:8, is the very middle verse of the Bible. Its message is clear, and concise. Our rendition of this verse would be a bit more prosaic. You'd be foolish to put your faith in fickle man, so put your trust in the unshakable, unchangeable Lord, and take refuge in Him. The middle of God's word puts in succinctly. Trust God, not man.

If man tells you all roads lead to heaven, rest assured that's wrong. If man says only one way to heaven is absurd, count on the fact that there's only one way. If man declares that fanaticism is fatal to thinking people, the obvious rational answer is we should be zealous in our belief.

If God, who is Jesus says, 'no one comes to the Father except through me', we know we can believe it. When Christ says, 'I and the Father are one', we have the surety that it's true. Since Jesus says, 'I am the way', count on it being accurate. God is trustworthy, and man is not. God loves us enough to accept us as we are, and He loves us too much to leave us as we are.

You may be surely sincere in your beliefs, but you can just as surely be sincerely wrong. No matter how much you sincerely believe you're not subject to the law of gravity, it won't change the fact that you're subject to the law of gravity. Thinking otherwise merely makes you sincerely wrong, and most likely injured.

So we encourage you to be extreme in your belief in Christ Jesus. Follow the essentiality of the verse in the middle. Be foolish enough to trust God's word. Be radical in your thinking, at least by the world's standards. Be a fanatic in your obedience to the Lord, and His instructions. It's far better to take refuge in the one whom you can trust utterly, than to trust in the world's views, when they've proven to be wrong every time.

Follow the essential guidance of the middle verse.

Prayer: Dear Lord, help us to always put our complete faith and trust in you, and take refuge in you…

Sep 24
Follow God's Means

"For where you have envy and selfish ambition, there you find disorder and every evil practice." Jas 3:16

"The ends justify the means." How often have you heard that? We hear all kinds of rationalizations for every wicked practice imaginable. "This isn't really the right thing to do, but it's for a good cause." "If he were in my position, he'd do it too." "If she had to put up with what I do, she'd be doing this and more." "What they don't know won't hurt them." "They'll never know the difference." They go on and on.

Why are those self-justifying statements necessary? Because deep down inside, we know that what we're doing is wrong, and sinful. We rationalize what we do, and we do the wicked things we do, because of selfishness, and because of envy. We can be like crows. When someone has something shiny that we don't have, we try to take it. When someone can do something we're not able to, we try to destroy it. When someone knows something we don't, we try to find something we know, but they don't. When we have a goal, and see a way to get ahead, we don't let anyone get in our way without running them over.

How about this for a different perspective?

"But the wisdom that comes from heaven is first of all pure; then peace-loving, considerate, submissive, full of mercy and good fruit, impartial and sincere." Jas 3:17

When we walk with Christ Jesus, we see things differently than the world does. He gives us a new view, an altered perspective that allows us to see things in the same manner He does. Our motives become pure when we access the wisdom that comes from heaven. We wouldn't consider mowing someone down when they get in our way. Rather, we treat that person with consideration. We don't allow a goal to disturb the peace of our relationship with our friends and coworkers. We treat others with mercy, not as though we're mercenary. As we strive to bear good fruit, we use the wisdom and grace of the Lord. And we're sincere in our interaction with those around us.

As we journey in grace, we never have to use means that aren't pleasing to God. We know He'll always bless us when we do what's pure, honest, upright, and holy. That godly way of doing things *is* God's means. And His means lead to the correct end.

Prayer: Father, remove any vestige of envy or selfish ambition from us. Keep us in your heavenly wisdom…

Sep 25
The Advocate

"My dear children, I write this to you so that you will not sin. But if anybody does sin, we have one who speaks to the Father in our defense—Jesus Christ, the Righteous One." I Jn 2:1

We teach our children the right things to do, say, and think, trusting that when we're apart, they'll continue to follow the good teaching they've received. We teach them the right things in hopes that they'll avoid doing the wrong things. We love our children, and we want the best for them. We know that committing wrong deeds has consequences, and we want to spare our children from those adverse effects of sin.

So it is with the Apostle John. He's writing his teaching, which is really God's teaching, so that we'll behave with holiness. His goal is to instruct us so that we live in purity, and to keep us from sinning. Note that, even though he writes so that we won't sin, he doesn't assume we never will.

As believers, we have a gift of immeasurable value. We have an advocate, one who comes to our defense. Since He loves us, and He's already paid the penalty for our sin, He steps in and speaks on our behalf, and reminds the Father that we are His. Does that mean we can sin with impunity? Of course not! That would show that we despise the sacrifice of Christ, and that we don't truly love Him in return. Those of us who are believers are so thankful for our salvation in Jesus Christ that we honor and glorify Him, and we don't continue sinning. Rather, we turn from our sin, confess it to Christ, and walk in newness of life again.

In our family, we often have these same dynamics occurring. When one of our children messes up, it's not uncommon for one parent or the other to step in, speak on their behalf, and show mercy. When someone attacks our husband or wife, we become his or her advocate. We speak up and defend him/her, because we love our spouse, and we know him/her better than anyone else does. We understand his/her motives, and can explain the offending words or actions because we know how it was meant.

We have an advocate. We're grateful to our Lord Jesus Christ that He is our advocate, because He's perfect. Although we're not perfect, we're the right person to be an earthly advocate, the defender, of our husband or wife because we love and cherish him or her. We're the right ones to be the protectors of our children, too, because we're the ones who model the Christian journey, teach them the essentials of life, and know them and their motives best.

Revere your advocate, and be an advocate.

Prayer: Lord Jesus, thank you for coming to our defense when we need it. Help us to be mindful to sin less and less, and live pure, holy lives for you…

Sep 26
Measure Against the Word

"But there were also false prophets among the people, just as there will be false teachers among you. They will secretly introduce destructive heresies, even denying the sovereign Lord who bought them—bringing swift destruction on themselves. Many will follow their shameful ways and will bring the way of truth into disrepute. In their greed these teachers will exploit you with stories they have made up." II Pet 2:1-3a

If you're reasonably familiar with God's word, you sometimes hear statements in messages that spring out as being 'wrong' somehow. As we listen to preaching, especially if you listen to many who teach on television, you'll find yourself questioning something they said. They may genuinely believe what they're teaching. But that doesn't necessarily make it accurate.

Sometimes we run into people who are so rational sounding, and so persuasive, that we find ourselves going along with what they say. They have charisma and an outgoing, gregarious manner that we like. They tell us wonderful things and events that they've been involved in, and we're impressed. Until we find that something they said doesn't ring true. Suddenly we find ourselves doubting pretty much everything they say.

There are people out there who gather a following just by the force of their charming personality. Even in the realm of Christianity, there are those who gather around them an almost cult-like following. When leaders such as these say something off the mark, their congregations just take it in and accept it, because he said it, and if he said it, it must be true. They're led astray because they haven't built the solid foundation of truth under their beliefs.

There's one sure way to protect yourselves against errant teachings. Most of our pastors have espoused this same rationale. Always measure what you hear against the truth of the Word of God. If you hear something that doesn't square with biblical precepts, don't accept it unless it can be effectively explained in biblical context. If something is taught that goes against your understanding of the word, refuse to accept it unless it's brought to biblical standards. Hank Hanegraaff, on his radio program, *The Bible Answer Man*, always talks about reading the Bible for all its worth. In other words, you have to take its teaching in sum total, meshing it all together, rather than taking a verse or phrase out of the context in which it was written. When you hear something out of context, you can be sure you should take it with suspicion, along with anything else being taught by that particular person.

There are false teachers among us even now. Read your Bible, get God's word written on your heart, and measure all teaching against the truth of God's word. Don't accept the teaching of people who change the word to fit their philosophy, let the word change you to align with God!

Prayer: Lord, by your Spirit, show us when someone teaches what doesn't line up with your word...

Sep 27
Poor Hosea

"When the Lord began to speak through Hosea, the Lord said to him, 'Go, take to yourself an adulterous wife and children of unfaithfulness, because the land is guilty of the vilest adultery in departing from the Lord." Hos 1:2

If all who are called to serve the Lord in ministry were asked to marry an adulterous wife, there wouldn't be many takers, would there? It's tough enough being in ministry without the added heartache and burden of an unfaithful spouse. Also, have you noticed that biblical names are used in abundance, but you rarely hear the name Gomer (the name of Hosea's adulterous wife)? This message in the book of Hosea is important, because it deals with several issues that we can learn from.

Hosea and Gomer are a picture of God and Israel. Just as Gomer loved Hosea and spent time with him, so Israel loved the Lord for a time, and was obedient. Then, just as Israel forgot the Lord, and turned to their own selfish ways, Gomer forgot Hosea, and went off on her own, committing adultery with other men. Israel went off and committed adultery with other gods. Even though Israel was unfaithful, God promises that after the punishment, after their heartache, He would save them, and prosper them once again. Hosea had to go purchase Gomer back again, and take her home to live with him, and love her as God loves the Israelites.

People are fickle. We often go and commit adultery of various kinds. Sometimes it's adultery, as we understand it in its basic sense. We've married, and gone off into intimate relationship with another. Other times, we've committed to a standard of behavior, and broken that promise. As an example, perhaps you've pledged not to drink alcohol, but then went and did so anyway. The point here is; we all fail at times to fulfill our vows and obligations. We act in an adulterous manner in which we're unfaithful to our oaths.

We're also given the example of undeserved love. When we break faith with someone, albeit husband, wife, children, friends, or coworkers, we don't deserve their love. So many times, though, we're blessed with it anyway. They're exhibiting grace towards us, just as God did towards the Israelites.

God gives us the example of forgiveness. Even though we don't deserve it, even though we may not have even asked for it, we're forgiven. That's often the case in adultery, too. While the adulterous partner is off following their own selfish desires, the faithful partner decides to forgive, and chooses to continue to love their spouse.

Only after being forgiven do the unfaithful return in many cases, and not always then. But the allure of loving grace is difficult to turn away from. We ought to be extremely grateful when we're forgiven our adulteries, and given the privilege of returning to our broken relationship in love and restoration.

Hosea is a wonderful picture of God's love, forgiveness, and unmerited favor towards those who don't deserve a bit of it. We still feel sorry for poor Hosea, though!

Prayer: Father, keep us faithful in our commitments, give us love, mercy, and a forgiving heart toward those who break faith with us, and strength to continue in that love...

Sep 28
Blessed

"Blessed are all who fear the Lord, who walk in his ways. You will eat the fruit of your labor; blessings and prosperity will be yours. Your wife will be like a fruitful vine within your house; your sons will be like olive shoots around your table. Thus is the man blessed who fears the Lord." Ps 128:1-4

That's encouraging! Unless you're not walking in His ways. My children were never afraid of me unless they were doing something they knew I didn't approve of. We have the same confidence in our relationship with our Heavenly Dad. When we walk in His ways, and fear Him, and reverence Him, as we ought to, we're blessed. When we don't, we should be afraid, very, very afraid. If you've never been disciplined by our Heavenly Dad, then you don't know the incredible afflictions He can put you through…but that's another devotion.

This is about blessing. This is about the blessings that come from walking in His ways. When we abide in Him, we have several promises.

First, you will eat the fruit of your labor. When we work, whatever our job is, we receive compensation, whether in the form of money, or in produce, as in the case of farmers and ranchers. We have His promise that we will eat the fruit of our labor. Inherent, of course, is that you have to labor, but that's part of walking in His ways.

Secondly, we'll have blessings and prosperity. That shows us that we won't just get by, but that we'll have an abundance. We'll have plenty, so we don't have to be concerned with having enough to share, giving us the opportunity to bless others, as well.

Thirdly, little wife, you'll be like a fruitful vine. We've kind of lost the admonition to go forth and multiply. In our era, we often don't even replace ourselves, but by so doing, we're not raising up generations of believers to carry the message of Christ. God's word calls children a blessing from the Lord. It's also true, I think, that we have kids while we're young because we don't know any better. They're quite tiring to keep up with.

Fourthly, we have the promise our children will be like olive shoots. In case you're wondering, olive shoots come up all over the place, like weeds. They aren't, of course, and neither are our children. Our children are some of the richest blessings, providing the most treasured memories, of our lives. They're also the ones who will carry our teachings to others.

This is how we're blessed when we fear the Lord, and walk in His ways. We're blessed indeed.

Prayer: Heavenly Dad, help us to fear you and walk in your ways. Bless us as you've promised, as we're obedient to your precepts…

Sep 29
Don't Be Puffed Up

"We know that we all possess knowledge. Knowledge puffs up, but love builds up. The man who thinks he knows something does not yet know as he ought to know. But the man who loves God is known by God." I Cor 8:1b-3

There's something about knowing things that others may not that carries an extra passenger, so to speak. Pride always seems to ride along with knowledge that isn't widely disseminated. It's easy to think more highly of ourselves when we know what others may not, or may not even understand, if they do hear it. But pride is a pretty useless attitude.

When we bake pies, we sometimes find that, with certain types of pie, the crust doesn't act the way we need it to. It seems to matter little whether we get everything mixed just right, or if we have the ingredients in the proper amounts. When it's baked, something strange can happen. If the oven is too hot, the crust may rise too fast, and an air bubble is created under the top crust. When that happens, after the pie is removed from the oven, and as the pie cools, the crust sometimes collapses under its own weight, or it may stay puffed up. When it stays puffed up, it's quite deceiving. It can lead you to believe there's a great, overstuffed pie, but when you cut into it, you're disappointed with what's inside.

The same thing happens when we let knowledge puff us up. That knowledge, without love to guide it, is just like the pie. Even though it looks great from the outside, even though it looks as though you can feast, when you pull it apart, you find there's no substance. It's really just hollow words.

This chapter goes on to talk about how we know that food sacrificed to idols doesn't mean anything, because idols are nothing at all, and there is but one God, whom we serve. But that knowledge, without love to guide it, is just a puff. If there are others around who don't understand that idols are nothing, then eating food sacrificed to an idol in front of them can bring them harm, and may cause them to stumble in their faith. Love builds them up by refraining, even though we know it means nothing, so that we don't cause them to be shaken in their faith. By using our freedom with restraint for the sake of others, we build them up. Love gives the substance to our pie of knowledge. And when we use our knowledge linked with love, it's then we know, as we ought to. So don't be puffed up.

Prayer: Lord, give us wisdom to use knowledge wisely, so that we aren't puffing up, but rather we're building others up…

Sep 30
Pretty Up

"Then out came a woman to meet him, dressed like a prostitute...I have covered my bed with colored linens from Egypt. I have perfumed my bed with myrrh, aloes and cinnamon. Come, let's drink deep of love till morning; let's enjoy ourselves with love!
Pr 7: 10&16-18

There's a detrimental philosophy floating around out there regarding our marriage relationship. It has to do with the way we take care of ourselves. Basically it goes like this. We're married, so I don't need to do my makeup and hair every day and dress up. He should love me just the way I am. There's no reason to shave and shower and get dressed, she should love me just the way I am.

Somewhere, we've come up with the idea that when we're married, we can be lazy about our appearance and cleanliness and it won't matter. When we're first married, it's fun to see each other in the morning before we've cleaned up, because we haven't seen it before. It's even comforting to stay that way most of the day once in a while. Oddly, that enthusiasm quickly wanes as we see how disheveled we look, and as we become accustomed to it, it's not charming or cute any more.

If you fixed up like a supermodel when you were dating, why would you stop after you're married, and start looking like a bag lady? If you dressed up slick like a Hollywood leading man, why would you stop after you're married, and start looking like a bum? Isn't that false advertising? We've fallen in love with the person we got to know before we married. If you loved that man or woman enough to go all out for him or her when you dated, you ought to love your spouse enough to continue after the wedding. After all, your husband is worth it. Your wife is worth that small effort of shaving, bathing, and looking your best for her.

The crux of the matter is, you need to keep your husband's eyes on you. It may not be fair, but there are needy women out there who will certainly attract your husband's attention, if they can. She's dressed up, perfumed, looking as sexy as she can get away with. And husband, if you're not attending to your wife, rest assured there are a thousand guys out there looking for any opportune moment to step in.

Protect yourselves from those who would destroy your marriage by being as attentive to each other as you were before you married. In fact, be more caring, because you have much more to lose now. Make every effort to shave and bathe. Look good! Get your hair and makeup on in the morning. Look good! Dress well. You'll feel better about yourself, and you'll honor each other by exerting a little effort for the other. You'll also have a better chance at keeping outsiders from destroying your love and your marriage.

So both of you, pretty up!

Prayer: Father, give us the consistency to look, act, and present ourselves in the best way we can for our spouse, and protect us from those who would step in where they don't belong…

Oct 1
Honesty

"An honest answer is like a kiss on the lips." Pr 24:26

Think back to when you were dating and those particular moments when you first kissed your spouse. Remember the excitement you felt, the elation, and how sweet those kisses tasted? There's a similar sense that comes from giving and receiving honest answers.

Reverse this statement and everything changes. When you're lied to, and given false answers, it leaves a sour taste, and such bitterness in your mouth that it is unacceptable. We don't receive lying well, nor should we. How can we ever trust one who lies to us?

When our children are growing up, building blocks of trust are formed one by one over time. As they're open and honest with us, we give them more responsibility and we offer them more privileges, because we know we can count on them to be truthful about where they'll be and what they'll be doing. When they tell us the truth we don't have to restrict them as much to keep them safe, either from others or from themselves, because we have confidence they're making good choices and being wise. If a moment comes when we find they've lied to us, and done things that aren't permissible for them, we change our course to accommodate the fact that they can't be trusted. We no longer give them the freedom and privilege they had before they betrayed our trust. As good parents, we make wise decisions to teach and protect our kids, even when we have to guard them from their own foolish, dishonest choices.

Sometimes in our marriages, we can get caught up in 'falsifying informational statements'. We may do something our spouse finds objectionable, and even if we don't agree and it isn't a sin, we may lie to avoid the criticism and argument that may come with telling the truth. Oh, we blame it on our spouse. If they didn't react so negatively, we wouldn't have to lie. But that's not the Lord's instruction for us. We're to be honest.

Honesty can become a tough habit to establish if you've been in the habit of telling 'little white lies' to avoid controversy. But it's essential to your faith, your self-esteem, and your marriage relationship that you have the habit of absolute honesty. And we're not talking about the brutal kind of honesty; rather we're talking about kind-hearted honesty that delivers the truth in a gentle, loving way. That's the honest answer that's like a kiss on the lips.

Help each other be honest by probing if there are areas where you've gotten into the habit of dishonesty. Listen without being critical. Don't even purse your lips, or raise your eyebrows. Find ways to accept honest answers without resorting to showing disapproval. You'll insure each other's comfort in being honest. And honesty is a great habit!

Prayer: Heavenly Father, give us the attitude that we'll be gently honest at all times, in every situation...

Oct 2
Uncorrupted

"But Noah found favor in the eyes of the Lord…the Lord said to Noah, 'Go into the ark, you and your whole family, because I have found you righteous in this generation.'" Gen 6:8&7:1

Somehow, when the whole world had gone to wickedness, Noah retained a sense of right and wrong, refused to follow the world's ways, and clung to God's precepts. How did Noah stay uncorrupted, and how can we stay true to God in a world that seems to be heading the same direction as in Noah's day?

The answers are found in Gen 6:9&22. Noah was a righteous man, blameless among the people of his time, and he walked with God. Noah did everything just as God commanded him. That tells us everything. Noah stayed uncorrupted by the world because he walked with God. He was found righteous through that and his obedience to the Lord.

The world has a tough time getting to people whose eyes are fixed on Jesus, and who steadfastly walk with the Lord. When you're in God's presence, the world has no real allure because it pales in significance next to God's glory and His blessings. There's nothing on earth that can give you the contentment, peace, and wholeness of heart found in Jesus Christ. The world cannot offer the joy we have in knowing Him. The excitement generated by the world is nothing compared to the excitement of seeing the Lord move and work in His mystifying ways. The happiness we have in Christ is unsullied by the consequences of the world's style of happiness.

You, too, have found favor in the eyes of the Lord if you've put your faith and trust in Christ Jesus and made Him Lord of your life. He sees you as righteous through the blood of Christ, and you can confidently walk with Him.

The next time the world throws some alluring, too good to be true, temptation at you, file it where it belongs. Put it in the 'not for me' file, because you've found something much better. As we walk with the Lord, we can stay undefiled by the world's wealth without contentment, its shallow form of happiness that brings no peace, its excitement without fulfillment, and its sensuality that never satisfies.

As you journey steadily with God, you'll stay uncorrupted, and in God's favor.

Prayer: Lord, thank you for your strength for the journey, your peace and contentment, and your favor as we walk with you...

Oct 3
Trust Me

How many times have we heard that statement? Too often, it's a leap of faith with no substantive reason to believe we should. Sometimes it works out. Other times, it doesn't come out so well. Even with friends and family we should be able to trust, there are those who just aren't very trustworthy. We find ourselves being skeptical. We wouldn't recommend putting your trust in anyone until they've proven themselves.

There *are* those few that we can rely on. They give godly advice, never contrary to the Word, and seek His wisdom before they speak. They've proven their veracity in being responsible to their vows. I know without a doubt that I can count on my wife. She's loyal, dependable, honest, and trustworthy. She looks out for me, she stands up for me, she supports me, and she even *flatters* me. Some of our children are those we can trust. We even have a couple of friends that I'd trust implicitly.

The thing is, though, there aren't many folks around that I'd suggest you put your faith in. In fact I can only think of four. Most likely, you don't know three of them. But, don't be alarmed. There is one!

"Do not let your hearts be troubled. Trust in God; trust also in me." (Jesus) Jn 14:1

That one little statement by Jesus gives me absolute confidence; confidence that I don't need to worry about what's happening; confidence that there's one I can trust completely, with never a doubt that He won't be found true. In the final analysis, we can place our trust in Jesus. He's given us a host of promises that He's fulfilled, and is fulfilling. There's no reason why I should fret about troubles, or trials, or afflictions, or problems that I can't solve. God has it all under control. He's taking care of us, and He's preparing a place for us in glory.

Since Jesus said, "trust also in me," I will!

Prayer: Lord Jesus, thank you for being *the* one we can really put our complete trust in...

Oct 4
Watch Your Wealth

"Now listen, you rich people, weep and wail because of the misery that is coming upon you. Your wealth has rotted, and moths have eaten your clothes. Your gold and silver are corroded. Their corrosion will testify against you and eat your flesh like fire. You have hoarded wealth in the last days. Look! The wages you failed to pay the workmen who mowed your fields are crying out against you. The cries of the harvesters have reached the ears of the Lord Almighty. You have lived on earth in luxury and self-indulgence. You have fattened yourselves in the day of slaughter. You have condemned and murdered innocent men, who were not opposing you." Jas 5:1-6

Some people are just plain stingy! Have you worked for people (haven't we all) who gave you the impression that if they could pay you less, they would? There are those who are so concerned with the bottom line, they'd use slaves if it were legal!

Now in Jesus' day, at least His days on earth in the flesh, the wealthy were considered blessed of God. Those who were rich were thought to have God's favor, and for many, that was actually true. The Lord did bless quite a few with wealth and long life as a sign of His favor. Look at Abraham, Isaac, and Jacob, David, and Solomon, and more.

Just as today, though, there are several more who are wealthy who do not have God's blessing. They're the ones who are smart, ambitious, shrewd, and in numerous cases, ruthless in their pursuit of money and power. They're the type of rich people the Lord is warning in this passage. Instead of using their wealth to bless others, they hoard it for themselves, even though they'll never be able to use it if they live to be a thousand. Rather than pay a decent wage, and provide a good living for their workers, they pay as little as possible to pad their own, already overfull, bank account. When they could be using wealth in generosity to help those who are needy, they're living in useless, wasteful, dissipating luxury. They could have lived and let live, but in their ruthless pursuit of gain, they ran over innocent people who weren't even in competition with them.

If you're this type of wealthy person, then it's time to repent, and turn from your selfish, inconsiderate, stingy ways. If you don't, God's word says there is misery coming to you that will make you weep and wail. Remember this, the world and all its 'stuff' is going to dissolve in rust, flame, and rot.

The good news; the treasure that cannot be destroyed is the wealth we store up in Heaven. It's products are the immeasurable value of a life lived for Jesus Christ. Be a good steward of your financial resources here on earth, and store up treasure in Heaven.

Prayer: Lord, give us wisdom to evaluate where we are in regard to wealth, and to use it to bless, help, and sustain others who are in need...

Oct 5
Let It Shine

"Let your light shine before???" Mt 5:16b

I know that verse goes on to say men, that the Father may be glorified. However, I want to approach this from an angle that hits a little closer to home. In fact, right *in* your home. Because the real test of whether your light can actually shine forth is how it glows at your house. Is it like the nightlight in the kid's rooms, like the dining light we use for romantic ambience, like the porch light to welcome friends, or is it like the extra bright reading light we use to study by? How your light shines at home determines how well it *can* shine outside to the world.

We're required to use all the gifts, attitudes, and attributes we've learned in our walk in our own family. We *must* exhibit the fruit of the Spirit with those we love most. If you treat your wife rudely or disrespectfully, your light won't shine very brightly to the world. They may not see how you act towards her, but your heart won't have the grace to be a real wellspring of the love of Christ. If you criticize your husband, and slight him just to be ugly, your light can't shine the way it's supposed to. It's tarnished by a bitter edge in your spirit that dampens what the Holy Spirit can accomplish through you.

When you're in a band, you don't go out and do a concert each time you get together. You join each other for practice, so that your music is in tune, in sync, and in rhythm. You have to make sure the instruments are tuned properly, both singly and with each other. You have to make sure you know how many verses and choruses of each song you're going to do, and in what order. You have to be certain you all agree on the correct tempo. Your presentation to the concert attendees would be awful if you didn't rehearse, and rehearse until you had the sound you wanted, to please those who come.

The family is the practice ground for the concert face you present to the world. That's where the real 'you' comes out, due to it being where you let your guard down the most. So when you stumble in your 'glow' at home, apologize and start over. When you ingrain godly habits with your family interaction, you're well on your way to presenting the love of Christ to the world outside your door. You have to be in tune with the Holy Spirit. You have to be in sync with the Father's will. You have to be in rhythm with Jesus. When the fruit of the Spirit is consistently present in your home, and each one is displaying those characteristics, then you can be confident you're ready to be a symphony to the world.

Go let your light shine everywhere you are! Bring glory to the Father.

Prayer: Holy Spirit, prompt us to utilize the fruit of the Spirit in our home, and especially give us grace towards each other…

Oct 6
Touch Jesus

"She came up behind him and touched the edge of his cloak, and immediately her bleeding stopped. 'Who touched me?' Jesus asked…but Jesus said, 'Someone touched me; I know that power has gone out from me." Lk 8:44-45a,46

So often you meet people who have no interest in the Lord. They think they're doing fine on their own, so why should they bother with God? They feel like they don't need Him. They're preoccupied with living life; they're busy figuring out the next deal, closing the sale, playing golf and tennis, going to dinner with friends, and seeing their children's school plays, ballgames, and activities. They don't give a thought to eternity, and see no real reason why they should. Things are going great!

Most people learn their need for the Lord when they're faced with enormous problems. When they have an accident they don't know whether they'll fully recover from, suddenly they have time to think about God. When financial reverses threaten their livelihood and their home and lifestyle, they may turn to Him. When illness hits that is life threatening or debilitating, instinctively they turn to the Lord.

The question is; what kind of God, in their minds, are they turning to? Are they turning to a miracle worker who can repair their accident, give them supernatural financial success, or heal them and prevent their death? Or are they turning to the one who can save them; save them from themselves, from their choices, from their failures, and from their sins? Are they turning to a genie, or the Savior?

In the tough, traumatic afflictions of life, there's only one person to turn to. That's God! But why you turn, and what your attitude is, affects the answers He'll give you. If you want to question why God would let this happen to you, or why He didn't prevent it, the answer likely lies in the realm of not being able to get your attention any other way. It's somewhat like the farmer who bragged about what a good, hard working mule he had. When his friends came over to see this wonderful mule, the mule just stood in the traces not moving, even after the farmer ordered him to pull. The farmer walked around with a short tree limb, and smacked the mule on the head. When the farmer went back to the plow, the mule started right off. His friends said, "I thought you said he's such a good mule." The farmer replied, "He is. But sometimes I have to get his attention first!"

God isn't interested in a one-time encounter with people. He wants a lifelong relationship with them, the same as He has with us. Jesus didn't provide for our salvation so we could ignore Him. He comes so that we can know Him, and so that we can have life, and have it fully. When you really want to have an abundant, wonderful life, you have to slip up and touch Jesus. He has the power, and His power will make you whole, and set you free; free from sin, free from the shallow, empty, fruitless pursuit of living for self, and free to be a blessing. So get in touch with Jesus.

Prayer: Lord Jesus, let us touch you today. Let your power flow forth to meet our needs, and give us the intimate relationship with you that you desire…

Oct 7
Steamy

"Let him kiss me with the kisses of his mouth—for your love is more delightful than wine. Pleasing is the fragrance of your perfumes…let the king bring me into his chambers." SS 1:2-3a&4b

"Your graceful legs are like jewels, the work of a craftsman's hands…may your breasts be like the clusters of the vine, the fragrance of your breath like apples, and your mouth like the best wine." SS 7:1b&8b-9a

"Marriage should be honored by all, and the marriage bed kept pure." Heb 13:4a-b

Every so often, it's good to refresh your memories to take your romantic life with your spouse seriously, so that you can have more fun. The marriage bed is to be kept pure, and the best way to insure that is by keeping it active. Forego the judgment of God that comes from adultery and sexual immorality by staying focused on the romance in your own marriage.

Continue to plan romantic interludes for each other. Your bodies were meant to be of great pleasure to one another. Prepare yourselves. You've heard over and over how the power of life and death is in the tongue. Well your breath has the same power. Never overlook the refreshing of teeth brushing and mouthwash. Shave and shower (yes, both of you, perhaps even together), and use deodorant and perfume. Nothing enhances your libido like cleanliness and fragrance. Dress appropriately. You should be doing your part to keep the lingerie store in business. Have your favorite foods and beverages on hand that you associate with fun times and sex.

Now, look each other over. This is especially important for Mr. Husband. He loves to see you at your best, and he knows what your best is. You can trust him on this. Caress each other for a while. Enjoy all those areas unknown to others. This is important for Mrs. Wife. She warms up more slowly, sir, but she does steadily warm up, and you'll enjoy her heat just as much as she does. This is a mutually endearing exercise; so take care of each other.

The Lord gave us the erotic portion of our love life for our good pleasure, and he meant for it to be that way. Read through Song of Solomon again, and you'll understand that this is the crowning jewel of marriage. So show your appreciation for the Lord's gift. Plan to have a steamy time of it!

Prayer: Lord, thank you for this gift of love, and help us to enjoy it purely with each other…

Oct 8

Restoration Coming

"And the God of all grace, who called you to his eternal glory in Christ, after you have suffered a little while, will himself restore you and make you strong, firm and steadfast." II Pet 5:10

When a woman has a child, she goes through a long process that includes many physiological changes, much discomfort, some illness, and a period of intense suffering. When it comes time to deliver the child, and she goes into labor, her contractions may last for a relatively short time, or it may last for hours. The longer it lasts, the more worn out she is from the struggle and pain, and it may seem like it's never going to end. It does end, though, and the child comes forth, and restoration of her body begins. The Lord has designed us with miraculous recuperative energies that flow within. But it does take time to recover fully from the pregnancy.

When we face suffering and afflictions, it can be like that. The process may seem to go on forever. It may go on for so long that we're worn out from the struggle and stress. And while it may not cause us physical agony, it can bring about emotional anguish. It might seem like there's never going to be an end to what we face. It can bring us to real despair.

But the Lord has a promise for us here in II Peter. He tells us that He Himself will restore us again. He's going to make us strong. He'll make us firm. He'll make us steadfast. We've been called to His eternal glory in Christ Jesus, and He won't forsake us. He is the God of all grace. He hasn't forgotten us. He won't let us down. Don't let yourselves get discouraged about the situation. Don't let yourselves be led into doubt by the circumstances you face. Encourage yourselves in the Lord. Stay in faith, stand on His promise, and know that the end is coming. You'll be standing on the solid Rock once more. Your restoration is on the way!

Prayer: Father, thank you for your promise to us. Help us to stay in faith as we suffer the trials we must face. Use them to make us stronger and more steadfast in our walk...

Oct 9
Real Equality

"Here there is no Greek or Jew, circumcised or uncircumcised, barbarian, Scythian, slave or free, but Christ is all, and is in all." Col 3:11

Have you noticed in the body of Christ, there are no inferiors, and no class of citizens elevated above another? In the entire world, this is the belief system that puts all people, regardless of race or gender, on equal footing. Nowhere are women more highly esteemed and privileged than in Christianity. If you're skeptical, I challenge you to find anywhere it's inaccurate.

Christ Jesus didn't come to save some. His word says, "Whosoever will, may come." It says, "God is patient, willing that none should perish." Note, it does not say, "Whosoever will, may come, except Asians." Or "except women." Or "except Caucasians." Or "except poor." Or "except tall." Or "except skinny." It doesn't say, "God is patient, willing that none should perish, unless you're ugly." Or "unless you're blonde." Or "unless you're highly intelligent." Or "unless you walk funny." There are no disqualifications. The love of God is extended to everyone, no matter what your social standing, financial condition, race, culture, or citizenship.

We look at things differently in our flesh. We see the outward person, and we make 'judgments' based on what we see. We profile. We decide from what we inspect whether that person is a good candidate for Christianity. If he's successful in his business, we'd like to see him in our church. If she's social and friendly, we'd like to see her in our fellowship. We'd like them to join if they're—wealthy—attractive—musical—articulate—talented—funny—or just like us!

When we begin seeing people as God sees them, as individuals, each with a distinct soul, who needs the love and redemption of our Savior, we'll begin to understand the mind of Christ. Inside, we're all alike. We all have the same needs, the same feelings, the same longings, the same misgivings, the same basic desires, and the same sin nature. We all have the same need for our relationship with Jesus.

Here in Christ, we have no need for phony political rhetoric inciting fairness (special treatment) for each, or any, group of people. In Christ, we have true equality. We're all the same in his eyes. We should look at each other the same way, with real equality.

Prayer: Lord Jesus, give us the insight to see as you see, with your attitude...

Oct 10
Be Merciful

"Speak and act as those who are going to be judged by the law that gives freedom, because judgment without mercy will be shown to anyone who has not been merciful. Mercy triumphs over judgment." Jas 2:12-13

It can be quite distressing to watch someone give punishment that follows the 'rules' and deals harshly with 'lawbreakers'. Often we think the sentence doesn't match the severity, or lack of severity, of the crime. It may seem downright mean. If your child is seven minutes late for curfew, and they haven't been late previously, or it's been a long time since they missed it, being grounded for a month seems excessive. Making the child miss the next event, or perhaps even the next weekend, seems more appropriate. Now if the child is continually late, it's probably time to draw the line, and use sterner discipline to change that unacceptable behavior.

Likewise, if the husband says something hurtful without thinking, which, admittedly, can happen, particularly in view of the fact that one day it may be okay, and the next day be a mortal sin; no sex for two weeks seems drastic. (Bear in mind the Bible tells us not to do that.) In the same way, if the wife says something that cuts the husband's spirit, which, admittedly, can happen, particularly in view of the fact that women use more than twice as many words per day as men, not speaking to her for two weeks seems intemperate. (Bear in mind the Bible warns against it, and it's childish.)

No, we don't live like the world, according to our sinful, selfish, natures. We speak and act in freedom, because in Christ, we have that freedom. We're prone to show forgiveness, which is the root of mercy. We show mercy because we ourselves have been shown mercy and forgiveness over and over. And we extend that mercy to those who hurt us, those who do us wrong, those we're in dispute with. We aren't willing to be chained to spite, bitterness, unforgiveness, and grudges. We don't give up our own freedom for the sake of a misspoken word, or a disagreement. We forgive it, forget it, and go on in freedom, showing love, mercy, and forgiveness to that person.

We're not willing to be judged without mercy; therefore we don't act without mercy. Mercy triumphs over judgment, because in judgment lingers anger and resentment, and in mercy we have freedom for ourselves. So be merciful!

Prayer: Gracious Lord, thank you for the forgiveness and mercy you've shown us, and remind us to show mercy to others...

Oct 11
Give Warning

"When I say to a wicked man, 'You will surely die,' and you do not warn him or speak out to dissuade him from his evil ways in order to save his life, that wicked man will die for his sin, and I will hold you accountable for his blood. But if you do warn the wicked man and he does not turn from his wickedness or from his evil ways, he will die for his sin; but you will have saved yourself." Eze 3:18-19

Glenda and I love to hike, and whenever we have the opportunity, we get out and go. We meet people on our hikes all the time, and although we don't know them, either they, or we, give warning if there's a treacherous path ahead of the other. There may be loose footing that could cause someone to slip and fall; there may be a path with no edge beside a cliff that no one would care to plunge off of. But whatever it is, if there's danger ahead, we warn one another so we can all avoid the consequences of a misstep.

As we can see from the verse here, there is a consequence for our missteps with God and His law. If we continue in sin, then the ultimate penalty is death and hell. God does not deal lightly with sin among His people. We should take it seriously, too.

In the Old Testament, Ezekiel was given the task of being a watchman for the house of Israel. Part of his duties was to take the message of God to His people. Ezekiel was charged with the task of confronting sin in the lives of Israelites. God was definitely in an either/or mood. He told Ezekiel, either tell them about their impending judgment, and warn them to turn from their wickedness, or I will hold you, Ezekiel, accountable for their blood. You won't be held accountable if you fulfill your task and warn the person.

I'm thankful we don't live under Old Testament law. Who could possibly keep it? The penalties for failure were tough. We don't have the same threat of punishment like old Israel did, but there's a principle that applies here and now. The person walking in sin faces judgment. We've been called to deliver the good news of Jesus Christ. We ought to be warning the wicked person about their sin, and giving them the opportunity to turn from their evil ways, and seek forgiveness and restoration in Christ. He's waiting to set them free from their sin, enter into a relationship with Him, and walk in His grace.

Don't be guilty of laxity in delivering the message to them; save your own conscience, and give warning!

Prayer: Heavenly Father, give us the boldness, and the love and gentleness, to give warning when we see someone in sin…

Oct 12
Plan Ahead, Work Hard

"Go to the ant, you sluggard; consider its ways and be wise! It has no commander, no overseer or ruler, yet it stores its provisions in summer and gathers its food at harvest. A little sleep, a little slumber, a little folding of the hands to rest—and poverty will come on you like a bandit and scarcity like an armed man." Pr 6:6-8,10-11

We're not accusing you of being sluggards. We are pointing out that there's a healthy principle in this passage for our way of life, for our provision, and for our financial wellbeing.

Growing up on the farm we had a saying. "You have to make hay while the sun shines." When the hay is ready, you have to bale it and haul it in. If you leave it in the field until it rains, you can't bale it, because if it's wet it'll ruin the hay, and also start fires (the pressure and moisture cause heat, which, when it builds to a certain point, causes spontaneous combustion). The same holds true for the garden, or for your grain. When the beans, peas, and corn are ready, you have to pick them. If you don't, they'll over ripen and be ruined. Once they're picked, you have to eat them, or preserve them. Again, if you wait too long, they'll be ruined. When the grain turns white(ish), you have to cut it and combine it, or it'll fall to the ground, and you can't get it to the grain bins. The birds, gophers, and squirrels will eat it, and what's left will rot.

There's a season for everything. A time to plant, a time to fertilize, a time to water, a time to pull weeds, and a time to harvest the fruit produced. We cannot laze around and miss any step, or it reduces or destroys our harvest.

As Christians, we're called to be diligent in everything we do. We ought to be the hardest workers, the most dependable people, and the most honest and trustworthy. If we work for ourselves, we have to do the work to receive the financial or material rewards. When we work for others, we must diligently produce the product or service for which we were hired, to receive our paycheck. No matter what we do for a living, it's what God has given us to provide for our daily needs.

So plan ahead. Work hard in season to produce your harvest. Keep at the work at hand, and you'll avoid the poverty these verses talk about. Take heed not to be lazy, or slough off what needs to be done. Be efficient and productive, so that you'll have plenty to keep you through the winters, the lean times, that may come.

Prayer: Lord, give us the ambition and focus to be hardworking and diligent in our tasks…

Oct 13
Never Be Shaken

"My soul finds rest in God alone; my salvation comes from him. He alone is my rock and my salvation; he is my fortress, I will never be shaken." Ps 62:1-2

Where does your protection and shelter come from? In this country, we put our trust in a lot of things that really are not a shelter. We have Shield of Shelter insurance, but they weren't a shelter when the trees fell on our house. They weren't a shelter when the ice storm broke down huge branches and power lines. Extra money in the bank can be a source of protection, until an emergency wipes those funds out completely. Money is an answer for many things that threaten us, but it has no answer for an incurable disease. Our home shelters us from the elements, until the wind blows the roof off, or fire burns it down. Sometimes we look to our family for protection, and that may be okay if they have the means to protect us, but they can't always be with us, and sooner or later, their strength will fail, too. We might seek protection in a cave, but that won't shelter us from the cold, or the hibernating bear inside. Cities find their protection behind a wall, a fortress of rock and mortar, until someone hits it with a bigger boulder, or bombs that can rip that wall apart.

We find things here that give us some rest. Our families can give us a bit of peace. Our dogs will give us a sense of contentment. Lack of problems can even leave us with tranquility for a time. Having insurance gives us serenity, a feeling of protection against loss. But none of these actually provide real, inner peace. None of these gives us complete rest, the kind of repose that is perfectly sweet and without any fear or concern, because they can all disappear in a moment.

No matter what we look to in the earthly realm for protection, it won't keep us safe. Nothing on earth can keep us from being shaken. Nothing here can save us or protect us. Except! God alone! Only Jesus Christ can provide salvation. Only God can give us the kind of rest we need, the kind of peace that comes only from within when we're in the right relationship with the Lord. He is the Rock upon which we stand, He is the fortress that cannot be broken, and when we're in Him, we will never be shaken.

In God alone will you find rest.

Prayer: God, give us the rest we seek. You are our salvation, and our fortress in our times of trouble. Let us never be shaken in our faith in you...

Oct 14
Lack of Obedience

"Go to the great city of Nineveh and preach against it, because its wickedness has come up before me.' But Jonah ran away from the Lord and headed for Tarshish. He went down to Joppa, where he found a ship bound for that port. After paying the fare, he went aboard and sailed for Tarshish to flee from the Lord." Jnh 1:2-3

Sometimes we don't have a clear understanding of a specific assignment the Lord gives us, and thus fail to do it. That wasn't the case with Jonah. He understood *exactly* what God told him to do, and turned around and headed the opposite direction. In fact, he went so far as to remove himself from the same land. He was fleeing to get as far from the Lord as he could.

We look at that and say, 'well that's ludicrous'. Yes, it is, but how often do we act similarly to Jonah? Jonah didn't corner the market on disobedience. We'd be willing to bet, if we were betting people, that you've ducked out on what the Lord asked you to do at some point, as well. Who among us can say they've done everything God has asked of us, every time we sensed in our spirit that we were supposed to do something? Who among us can even say we did everything our earthly parents asked of us?

We're not inclined to full obedience. We have a tough time rousing ourselves to get off our duff and act. We do sometimes, particularly if it's something we like, or might receive praise and admiration for. But how often do we leap right up and go when it's a task we despise? We tend to be a bit reluctant to move at that point. The Lord has called us, though. He has a calling for me, He has one for Glenda, and He has a calling for both of you. Learn from others. If you're running from God's call, turn and become obedient. Save yourselves a lot of anguish and stress. There are consequences in disobedience to God.

"Then the Lord sent a great wind on the sea, and such a violent storm arose that the ship threatened to break up...then they took Jonah and threw him overboard, and the raging sea grew calm. At this the men greatly feared the Lord, and they offered a sacrifice to the Lord and made vows to him. But the Lord provided a great fish to swallow Jonah, and Jonah was inside the fish three days and three nights." Jnh 1:4,15-17

When you're disobedient, you put yourself, and those around you in jeopardy of God's punishment. Jonah knew he was the cause of this storm because he was running from the Lord. In Jonah's defense, he did the right thing, confessed, and had them throw him overboard so they could be saved. Don't make your family, and possibly your friends, suffer along with you for your disobedience.

Prayer: Lord, give us clear understanding of your call, and help us not to turn from it, but to embrace where you're leading...

Oct 15
Fish Vomit

"From inside the fish Jonah prayed to the Lord his God…and the Lord commanded the fish, and it vomited Jonah onto dry land." Jnh 2:1,10

Just as we do when we're in dire straits, Jonah cried out to the Lord in his distress. While Jonah was on the run, there's no mention of him praying. In point of fact, when we're not behaving as we ought to, we don't spend much time communicating with the Lord either, do we? Even when we know what the relationship can, and should be, we don't turn to God because we already know the first issue He wants to address. And sometimes we're not ready to give up our sinful practice yet.

Yet when we do turn to the Lord, and seek His forgiveness, He's faithful and just and forgives us. He puts us back on the right path again. In the case of Jonah, God rescued him from the fish, and the fish threw up Jonah onto *dry* land. Jonah didn't even have the benefit of coming out of the fish into water so he could wash off the vomit smell. Maybe the Lord had that in mind as a good reminder of the situation that might await should Jonah run again.

"Then the word of the Lord came to Jonah a second time." Jnh 3:1

Never think that when you've turned away from God's call that He's through with you. When we go our own way, He may patiently wait, and continue to pull at the strings of your heart, and cause you unrest, and prevent your peace, until you turn to him in obedience. He may have put you in circumstances that leave a stench in your memory to remind you of the consequence of disobedience. But even when we've messed up God's original call, or missed it so far it's beyond us, He still has a purpose for us. He has a new plan for us. Like Jonah, He may still have the same call on your lives.

As we've traveled around the country, we've come across several pastors who became preachers late in life. Many felt the call as teenagers, but went their own way and forgot about it. Then the word of the Lord came to them again, and they realized they'd missed their calling, but God was giving them a second chance. When the opportunity to serve the Lord came again, they jumped on it, because they knew they'd never have peace in their spirits until they followed in obedience to that call. Now they're pastors and loving it, because it's what they were meant to be.

You may have missed out following God in obedience when you were first called. Now, He's calling again. He may not have called you to be a preacher, or a missionary, or a singer, or a writer, but He called you to serve Him in some capacity. Turn to Him and begin in new obedience now.

Prayer: Dear Lord, give us your grace to fulfill the calling you lay on our lives…

Oct 16
The Angry Preacher

"Jonah obeyed the word of the Lord and went to Ninevah...forty more days and Ninevah will be overturned. The Ninevites believed God. They declared a fast...who knows? God may yet relent and with compassion turn from his fierce anger so that we will not perish. When God saw what they did...he...did not bring upon them the destruction he had threatened. But Jonah was greatly displeased and became angry...the Lord replied, 'Have you any right to be angry? Ninevah has more than a hundred and twenty thousand people...should I not be concerned about that great city?" Jnh 3:3a,5a,9-4:1,4,11

    Not many preachers can claim they saw one hundred twenty thousand people repent and be saved in a three-day revival. None of them would be angry that all those folks turned to the Lord. They would view it as the greatest move of God in their ministry, and be euphorically thankful for it, praising God for His miraculous anointing and response. They would be considered by most of us to be anointed, as well, and wonderfully effective for Christ. We'd praise God for the moving of His Holy Spirit in those services, and worship and glorify Him for saving all those souls.

    Not Jonah! Obviously, the love of God wasn't part of his nature yet, because he got mad. He knew God was gracious. He didn't want to go warn Ninevah because he knew if they turned from their wicked ways, God would relent, and not destroy them. Jonah *wanted* the Ninevites destroyed. He didn't think they were worth saving. That's why he ran away to Tarshish in the first place, so they couldn't be saved. They didn't *deserve* God's mercy. Jonah is the only preacher we've heard of to get angry because he was ultra successful.

    Truly, the Ninevites didn't deserve God's mercy. Neither do we. The Ninevites deserved to be destroyed. So do we. The Ninevites admitted their wickedness. So should we. The Ninevites fasted and prayed. So should we. The Ninevites gave up their evil practices. So should we. The Ninevites *believed* God. So should we.

In the end, Jonah was angry, too, about a vine that grew up and gave him shade, then withered and died, leaving him in the hot sun. Jonah was angry about the vine, and he was angry that Ninevah wasn't destroyed. Jonah was having a bad week! God points out that Jonah was concerned about the fate of the vine, something insignificant at best, so shouldn't He, the Lord, be concerned about all those people. Those people *were* far more important than the vine, but Jonah's priorities were all messed up. Sometimes, ours are, too.

Don't be angry messengers for the Lord. Let's keep God's perspective in view, and realize that people are far more important than anything else on earth, and that doesn't count Fluffy; God is even concerned about the animals. So go give the message and watch the Spirit of God move in miraculous ways.

Prayer: Lord, help us not to be reluctant, or to judge who's worthy to be saved; rather help us to see people your way…

Oct 17
Listen

"Be ever hearing, but never understanding." Isa 6:9b

I find that one of the more difficult things for me to do is to listen. I'm rather fast paced in my work habits, and I'm always concerned about not wasting time, and going on to the next task. Glenda has been coaching me for years to stop and take time to converse, rather than leave people feeling they were unimportant and an inconvenience to me. I don't feel like they are (usually), but I've frequently left them that impression. It's something I'm working on, and I've found that to be really effective in conversation, I have to actively listen.

That's the crux of this verse in Isaiah. God was telling Israel that they'd be ever hearing, but never understanding. That's what happens when we don't actively listen, whether to people, or to the Lord. To actively listen is to engage the senses in your conversation. Look at the person who's speaking to you. Think about what they're telling you, and refrain from formulating your response until you're sure they're finishing speaking. By actively listening, you understand, because you've heard them, sensed their emotion, and thought about what they've told you.

We need to listen when God speaks, as well. We want to understand what He's saying to us, so that we can apply His principles, follow His call, and be obedient to His instructions. We want to avoid the pretense of religion without the substance of the relationship.

Jesus quoted this verse regarding the religious leaders of the Jews in His day. They followed all these manmade rules, but they forgot the heart of God, and neglected the love and kindness they were to show one another. They were so busy doing the regulations they lost the meaning behind the Lord's precepts.

It's not enough to hear. We need to understand. Listen!

Prayer: Father, help us to listen with all our senses, and understand you, and those we seek to converse with and minister to...

Oct 18
Don't Suppress It, Confess It

"Therefore, confess your sins to each other and pray for each other so that you may be healed. The prayer of a righteous man is powerful and effective." Jas 5:16

They say that confession is good for the soul, and that's quite true. It helps us to get things off our chest, because our sins and troubles can really burden us down. While we do need to confess our sins, you already know that, and we're going to focus on other aspects of this verse.

We often, particularly men, suppress our feelings about things so that we don't cause a commotion. We don't want to stir up trouble, so we just bottle it up. Unfortunately, one side effect of stuffing our emotions inside is stress. And stress is the number one cause of heart attacks. How do we alleviate the stress that comes when we suppress?

Exercise is good, it helps us burn off the nervous energy, but it's not a cure. What we need to do to eliminate the anxiety that comes from suppressing our emotions is to confess. That means we ought to talk about it. Go to your spouse, or find a good friend whose discretion you can count on, and talk it out. This does a number of things for you. First, in the process of discussing the situation that troubles you, you get a grasp of how you really think, and the anger, frustration, pain, or anxiety you feel regarding it. Second, you will feel better just being able to vent about the cause of your stress. Something about telling it to someone else lessens the load we carry over what troubles us. Third, when you tell a confidante about it, you can get another perspective that helps you deal with this trial. Fourth, you've enlisted a partner to pray with you, and for you, as you face this. When you take your problems to the Lord, you can rest much easier, knowing He's looking after you.

It's important to pray for each other. It's important to pray immediately together, as well as continuing to pray until the answer is received. When you go to your spouse, or to godly friends who will pray, you have confidence that it's going to be resolved for your benefit. There is power and effectiveness in the prayers of those who are walking righteously with the Lord. Enlist their aid in your trials.

When you have a problem, don't suppress it, confess it!

Prayer: Lord Jesus, help us open up and talk about those issues that bother us, and cause us anxiety…

Oct 19

Your Sanctuary

"A quarrelsome wife is like a constant dripping on a rainy day; restraining her is like restraining the wind or grasping oil with the hand." Pr 27:15-16

"A gentle answer turns away wrath, but a harsh word stirs up anger." Pr 15:1

Ah, a man's house is his castle, his fortress, his sanctuary, unless... Loud noises really echo around in those stone rooms, and they can be ever so cold. Especially when there's constant discord.

We look for our home to be our sanctuary. It's the place we hope to find peace and rest after a hard day's toil. And that's what it should be, and can be, if we'll do the essential things to make it that way.

If you're in a home where one, or both, of you are unhappy, and making your displeasure known consistently, continually, and loudly, then you're not in a sanctuary; you're in a war zone. It ought not be that way. And there are several things you can do to see to it that it isn't.

If you're quarrelsome, and that applies to husband as well as wife, then you have the ability to turn the situation around by simply stopping your tongue. Nothing kills your love life like harsh words. Don't engage in verbal assaults. When you're the recipient of those barbs, don't respond in kind. Use a gentle answer. If you retort in the same manner, you'll just stir up more vitriol. Only the person who's being sharp tongued can stop it. The other can't prevent it any more than he or she can grab a double handful of oil, or stop the wind from blowing, but it doesn't mean you have to enter into the fray.

Discuss your problem issues in a calm, gentle, straightforward, reasonable manner. Issues must be dealt with, but they're not best discussed at the top of your vocal range or volume. Find solutions together that are positive for both of you. Do your best for the other person.

Help each other out whenever, wherever, and however you can. Nothing creates harmony like giving your husband or wife a helping hand out of the kindness of your heart. When you do something nice unexpectedly, it catches your spouse off guard, and blesses them.

Love her in the kitchen, love him in the garage, love her in the bathroom, and love him in the yard. Foreplay begins early in the day, takes place wherever you're working, and lasts right up to playtime.

Be harmonious in your interaction with each other, and you'll find your home is a sanctuary where you'll find the tranquility you both desire.

Prayer: Father, help us to treat each other with gentle tongues, kind words, and loving hands...

Oct 20
Hold Fast

"Let us draw near to God with a sincere heart in full assurance of faith…let us hold unswervingly to the hope we profess, for he who promised is faithful." Heb 10:22a&23

As I write this, the object lesson is at hand. We're on tour, and as I'm writing 'let us hold unswervingly,' Glenda is rocking me back and forth as she swerves in traffic to avoid other vehicles. There are so many circumstances around us that can cause us to swerve in our faith, too, but we have to stay focused on the Lord, and not allow those outside issues to influence our stance for Christ.

We've been given a wonderful opportunity to draw near to God. We can do so with the full assurance of faith as we come to Him with a sincere heart. We can't fool God, we can't mislead Him in any way as to our motives, so we may as well come humbly to Him without guile. He's willing to receive us when we come in faith.

I'm encouraged when I know I can count on someone. My wife has proven that when I depend on her, she'll be faithful to what she has committed to do. I have a couple of friends whom I can depend on in the same way. If they say they'll help, or do something, its as good as done. I don't concern myself with it any longer because I know the one who promised is faithful. There are many others I know that I'll have to double check to see if what they said they'd do, got done. They may forget. They're not as dependable. They may get sidetracked, and go off on some tangent that leads away from their commitment. They're not faithful.

The God who promised us, though, is faithful to the core. He'll never fail us, because He's the one who always keeps His word. Our direction is to hold unswervingly to the hope we profess in Christ Jesus. Stay on the straight path. Refuse to be swayed, or distracted, or drawn off course.

Hold fast to your faith in Jesus Christ. Come with a sincere heart in assured faith.

Prayer: Lord Jesus, thank you that we can come boldly before the throne of God through your blood. Keep is steadfast in our faith...

Oct 21
Who Really Comprehends God?

"Then I saw all that God has done. No one can comprehend what goes on under the sun. Despite all his efforts to search it out, man cannot discover its meaning. Even if a wise man claims he knows, he cannot really comprehend it." Ecc 8:17

Admittedly, there are many things we don't understand. Some things are so far beyond us we have trouble ascertaining the concept in general. Do you understand molecular structure? Do you understand how neutrons and electrons orbit around the nucleus of an atom? Do you understand the precipitation cycle? Do you understand how and why tornadoes form? If you do, why can't you predict when and where they'll form and strike? Can you predict how specific foods will impact your digestive system? Can you figure out why the same food moves different people in a variety of ways? Do you understand the intricacies of the human thought process? Do you comprehend the vastness of space? Do you even understand the relationship between men and women?

If you said yes, everyone knows you're lying—lol.

No matter how knowledgeable we become in any area of study, or how vast our expertise ascends, there will be literally thousands of other studies that we know little or nothing about. If your field is biology, you may know all that's available to date, and yet know little more about the emotional chemistry between lovers than two teenagers. If your expertise lies in the field of nuclear physics, that doesn't mean you know why food cooked on the stove tastes better than that cooked in the microwave.

And all that doesn't even begin to tap into all God has done. Look around you when you step outside. See what God has created. Who would've thought to make trees, so hard we can barely cut them, take their nutrients through tiny canals inside sucked up from deep underground? Who would've thought to create birds to reproduce by laying eggs, and marsupials to have pockets for their young, or elephants to have a gestation period so long it makes us shudder to think about being pregnant for that time span?

Regardless of how wise we become, regardless of what we or any man or woman may claim, we do not, and cannot, really comprehend what God has done. We can only stand back in awe of His mighty works, and give Him praise for the glories He has performed. Look and see! Enjoy the blessings of God's work all around you.

Prayer: Lord God, creator of all, we do praise you for all you've done. Though we cannot comprehend it, we see the delights around us and honor you...

Oct 22
Be Different

"Be imitators of God...and live a life of love. But among you there must not be even a hint of sexual immorality, or of any kind of impurity, or of greed, because these are improper for God's holy people. Nor should there be obscenity, foolish talk or coarse joking, which are out of place, but rather thanksgiving." Eph 5:1a,2a,3-4

At church last evening we were discussing how we as Christians can make an impact in our workplace. The ideas were wide-ranging and interesting. Having had the dubious honor, pleasure, and responsibility of managing a number of retail businesses over the years, I've seen and watched Christians in my workplace, and there are some simple ways in which we can touch others.

To make a difference, you have to *be* different! This is a recurring theme, but one that not many believers take to heart. If we applied the verses in Paul's letter to the Ephesians to our own lives, we'd have the impact for Christ we desire.

Two things in particular I saw, and these are the quickest way to let folks know where your heart is. Don't curse and swear! And be a great worker.

Your speech is the quickest way to make it known whom you serve. If you'll guard your tongue, keeping your speech clean, coworkers will notice. I once chided an employee about cursing in the store, to which they shot back, 'it's not like you don't swear'. It happened two other associates heard, and one jumped in, saying, 'no, he doesn't. In over two years working with him, I've *never* heard him cuss once.' (Don't take that to mean I'm perfect in that area, because I'm not. Growing up with the habit, it was *the* most difficult to break, and I struggled for years to get it under some semblance of control.) Also, don't engage in filthy jokes, or obscene comments about the opposite sex. It should be avoided by us in honor to the holy Lord we serve.

To be a great worker is to set a higher standard. You get paid from the moment your shift begins right through the end. Be on time, ready to work. Work hard all the way through your day. Don't skip work, be honest, be trustworthy, and be loyal to your supervisor. Don't criticize him or her to coworkers. When I was an assistant manager, I had a district manager checking out the store manager, and interviewing some of the employees. When the store manager told me about her session with the DM, regarding my interview, she said the DM told her I was very loyal to her. My supervisor appreciated that, because she knew the DM was digging dirt. I was honored that the DM thought that, because I count loyalty as one of the great virtues, even if it's little used by anyone.

We've only touched on two aspects from the verse, but I urge you to study these verses the next few days, and really get them in your spirit, and apply them to your behavior. When you do, you'll be different, and when coworkers need help, they'll turn to the one they know *must* have the answer. You!

Prayer: Heavenly Father, help us to apply these practical principles and godly attitudes to our lives, so that we can have an impact for you...

Oct 23
Be Different Too

"Be imitators of God…and live a life of love. But among you there must not be even a hint of sexual immorality, or of any kind of impurity, or of greed, because these are improper for God's holy people. Nor should there be obscenity, foolish talk or coarse joking, which are out of place, but rather thanksgiving." Eph 5:1a,2a,3-4

Let's look at these verses today from another angle. Live a life of love. Again, this focuses on holy living, and while we must learn to guard our tongues, we also need to take great care in our actions and behavior. To live a life of love requires some essential aspects of Christian living. We must live without unconfessed sin. To live a life of love, which means imitating God, we have to practice purity in our behavior. God is holy, and we can't imitate God unless we practice holy living, as well. We cannot be greedy, or self-seeking, and expect people to respect us in a way that allows us to minister to their needs.

There must not be even a hint of sexual immorality. Unfaithfulness kills the respect for you that your friends and coworkers have. Even though sexual promiscuity runs rampant in our society, even though a large percentage of the population engages in immoral sexual relationships, they still know what's right and wrong. People still look on a sexually immoral person with disdain, and wouldn't think of taking spiritual advice from one such as this. If we want to be in a position to share the love of Christ, we must keep ourselves pure. Even the world holds Christians to a higher standard of morality, and rightly so, so be careful to live in purity.

You have no chance of living a life of love in your home if you're unfaithful. Regardless of what rationalization you use, no matter what the self-justification, your spouse is not going to feel loved if you're involved with another person. To have a pure love life at home, you have to live a pure love life everywhere. As Christians, it's inappropriate to have relationships that can even be viewed as having a hint of impropriety. So look at your relationships outside your family, and bring them into line with the word of God, so that nothing will hinder your witness to the world.

In the area of sexual morality, purity, and lack of greed, you can be different, too!

Prayer: Father, keep us pure in our attitudes, speech, and behavior, and help us to keep greed and selfishness far from us…

Oct 24
It's Not About Me

"To this John replied, "A man can receive only what is given him from heaven. You yourselves can testify that I said, 'I am not the Christ but am sent ahead of him.' The bride belongs to the bridegroom. The friend who attends the bridegroom waits and listens for him, and is full of joy when he hears the bridegroom's voice. That joy is mine, and it is now complete. He must become greater; I must become less." Jn 3:27-30

When a dispute arose between the disciples of John and other Jews about the people all going to Jesus to be baptized, John gives us the quintessential reply that explains the position of those of us who serve Christ. John understood who he was. He was the messenger, not the sender of the message. He was the one who prepared the way for the one coming who was greater than he. He wasn't in ministry to build a following for himself, but to build a following for his master. He had long been saying that he wasn't the messiah, yet some of his disciples were loyal to him, rather than to the Lord who followed.

John gives a wonderful example of the bride and bridegroom. It's especially poignant, because as believers we're called the bride of Christ. John knows the bride is for the bridegroom, she's not meant for the friend of the groom. His joy is complete because he was directing people to the bridegroom all along. That was his purpose, and he accomplished it, and he's happy for the groom.

Envy is not a virtue. We must always remember whom we serve. We don't touch others by the power of God for ourselves; we bless them for the sake of Jesus Christ. We aren't to receive honor to ourselves for God's working, we're to deflect the praise to the One who did the miracle, or provided the funds, or gave us the insight to say the right word, or moved us to lend the helping hand. Too often, people minister to someone, and want to receive accolades for what they did. Elsewhere, the word tells us we've received all the reward we're going to get when we do that. Give God the glory, and build your rewards for heaven, where it'll actually mean something.

Just as in the life of John, so it is with us. Jesus must show through greater, and we must become less visible. We want Jesus Christ to be honored and glorified everywhere, and in every way. Be true to the one who saved you and called you His own. It *is* about Him, it's not about me!

Prayer: Lord Jesus, help us to remember whom we serve, and to give you all the praise, honor, and glory for what you do…

Oct 25
Find Contentment

"But godliness with contentment is great gain. For we brought nothing into the world, and we can take nothing out of it...for the love of money is a root of all kinds of evil. Some people, eager for money, have wandered from the faith and pierced themselves with many griefs." I Tim 6:6-7,10

Unsettled! That's how we feel when we're trying to attain something that seems to be just beyond our grasp. We try to get something, and we just can't quite seem to manage it, and it drives us crazy. We spend inordinate amounts of time trying to figure out ways to achieve our goal.

To find contentment requires focusing our attention on having what God wants for us. When we become godly we come to the realization that money and 'stuff' isn't that important. Remember, money is a tool. It's one tool for the Christian to use in kingdom work. It is *not* an end in itself. Look at money from God's perspective, and it will cease to have the importance we so often attach to it.

Some folks keep going after more and more money, more and more stuff, and more and more prestige. But no matter how much you accumulate, if wealth is your goal, you'll never have enough. How much is enough? And the warning we're given is to take care not to wander from the faith and pierce ourselves with grief. The pursuit of money becomes a situation where money becomes more important than the Lord.

Let's insert here that money is not evil. Money isn't good. It has no moral character in and of itself. Having plenty of money is neither good nor evil. It's the *love* of money that is a root of all kinds of evil. We can't allow ourselves to love money more than we love the Lord. That becomes idolatry when that occurs.

Regardless of how much money we may have, we get to take exactly none of it with us when we cross over to eternal life. We came into the world without anything, and we leave the world without taking anything along with us. The only way to have money become our treasure in Heaven, we have to use it here to bless people for God's kingdom. When you use money as a way to bless others, and forget accumulating more and more toys, you'll find contentment in the simple, godly life.

Prayer: Lord, put life and stuff in the correct perspective for us. Help us see what's really important, and apply that to our lives...

Oct 26
Advance the Gospel

"Now I want you to know, brothers, that what has happened to me has really served to advance the gospel. As a result, it has become clear throughout the whole palace and to everyone else that I am in chains for Christ. Because of my chains, most of the brothers in the Lord have been encouraged to speak the word of God more courageously and fearlessly." Php 1:12-14

It's tough to accept that when terrible circumstances befall us, it often works best to advance the gospel. Paul has been imprisoned because of his preaching, and he realizes how that has worked out well to advance the gospel of Jesus Christ. Because of his jail time, he's had time to write the letters from prison. Because Paul has been faithful in preaching the gospel even while confined, others have become more courageous in sharing, too.

Obviously, Paul has not stopped proclaiming Jesus Christ. He hasn't allowed negative circumstances to stop him from fulfilling his calling. He hasn't said, "I can't preach anymore. No one will listen to someone who's been thrown into jail." Regardless of where Paul is, he continually brought the message of Christ to whoever was within listening range.

When we're assaulted with trials, we tend to curl up and quit. We deal with the afflictions, rather than staying focused on living for Christ. But that's not God's will for us. He gave us the example of Paul, and many of the other apostles, as well, to show us that even when we think God has forgotten us, or turned His gaze elsewhere, He wants us to continue fulfilling our calling. Whatever the circumstances may be, we can still share the love of Christ Jesus. God will always place people in our path that need to know the good news of Jesus.

When people come against us, and do things that are for our harm, God still has a way of turning it for our good, and for the good of His kingdom. We've often seen that when 'bad' things happen in our lives, it's actually turned out to be very good for us instead. The Lord knows how to advance His message regardless of what happens that seems to interfere. How well does God accomplish this? Paul closes his letter with this.

"All the saints send you greetings, especially those who belong to Caesar's household." Php 4:22

Many in Caesar's own household came to faith in Jesus because Paul was imprisoned there. What a sense of humor God has! And Paul was content, because he saw how God used his situation to effect great things for the Kingdom of Heaven.

Prayer: Heavenly Father, help us to see our negative circumstances in light of your purposes for us…

Oct 27
Use Believers to Judge

"If any of you has a dispute with another, dare he take it before the ungodly for judgment instead of before the saints? Do you not know that the saints will judge the world? I say this to shame you. Is it possible that there is nobody among you wise enough to judge a dispute between believers? The fact that you have lawsuits among you means you have been completely defeated already. Why not rather be wronged? Why not rather be cheated?" I Cor 6:1-2a,5,7

A few years ago this philosophy got into my mind and spirit. The core that became my view is this; it's better to be wronged than to wrong someone. We often forget these verses in the heat of the moment when someone has cheated us, or wronged us in some way, especially in material ways. We quickly jump to our own defense, because it isn't fair that someone would defraud us of our goods, or money, or even opportunities. It's not uncommon at all for Christians to go to court against each other. And we can always rationalize it away. After all, if she were really a Christian, she wouldn't steal my stuff. If he were really a Christian, he wouldn't sneak in and trick me out of my money. So we judge them not to be believers, thereby abrogating ourselves of the responsibility not to take other believers to court.

It's all just a game, though, isn't it? The issue in situations such as described above is this; it puts the cause of Christ in a negative light. We aren't even supposed to be concerned with these disputes we have. We're not to be greedy. We're not to be so selfish, or so in love with goods, that we can't just let them go. If we're so worried about the 'stuff' we may have lost, Paul tells us we've already been completely defeated. Why?

There are a number of things at work in this situation. When we take a dispute to the world, we leave them with the impression we as Christians can't get along. We show them we're no different from the world when we're greedy and selfish. We give them the impression we don't know how to forgive our brothers and sisters. We show them the same lack of love for one another the world displays. When these happen, we cannot be an effective witness for Christ.

It's better to be wronged than to harbor unforgiveness. It's better to be cheated rather than put our own greed on display. It's better to take a dispute to believers with some wisdom, rather than diminish the reputation of faith in Jesus. Above all, it's better to love our brother or sister; to do what's in their best interest. We refuse to allow a wrong to steal our love and joy. We're going to walk in forgiveness, and faith, and in the abundant life of Christ.

Prayer: Lord Jesus, help us to put aside any disputes we may have with others, now or in the future, and keep in mind your attitude in our dealings…

Oct 28
Selfish Pride Displayed

"So the Lord saved Hezekiah and the people of Jerusalem…many brought offerings to Jerusalem for the Lord and valuable gifts for Hezekiah king of Judah. From then on he was highly regarded by all the nations. In those days Hezekiah became ill and was at the point of death. He prayed to the Lord, who answered him and gave him a miraculous sign. But Hezekiah's heart was proud and he did not respond to the kindness shown him…then Hezekiah repented of the pride of his heart…therefore the Lord's wrath did not come upon them during the days of Hezekiah." II Ch 32:22a,23-25a,26

King Hezekiah is an enigma in many ways, and an example for all of us to take to heart and remember. Hezekiah walked closely with the Lord, faithfully following His precepts, but slid into pride and selfish inconsideration. If you don't know, this is Hezekiah's story, in abbreviated form.

When Hezekiah became king, he turned to the Lord. He had the Levites resume fully their priestly duties. He contributed himself, and ordered the Israelites to bring in the tithes and offerings commanded in the law. The Israelites responded faithfully, and after a few months, heaps of goods appeared outside the temple. God had blessed them so completely for their obedience that there was so much brought in they couldn't use it all. Hezekiah had storerooms built at the temple for the excess.

When King Sennacherib of Assyria laid siege to Jerusalem, taunting the Israelites and the God of Israel, Hezekiah went to the Lord in prayer. Because Hezekiah turned to God in prayer, God delivered Israel. One morning, the Assyrian king woke up to find 185,000 of his men dead on the ground without any sign of violence upon them. He packed up and went back to Assyria in fear and defeat.

About that time, Hezekiah became ill, and Isaiah came and told him he was going to die. Hezekiah turned to the wall in prayer (the expanded version is found in Isaiah), and God answered Hezekiah again, and as a sign of the extra fifteen years of life He was giving him, backed the shadows up ten steps on the wall.

Even after all the miracles shown to Hezekiah, he became proud, and showed the Babylonian envoys his great wealth. God judged that pride, and committed Israel to future defeat, but not until after Hezekiah's reign ended. In his selfishness, Hezekiah was relieved that he'd have comfort and peace, neglecting to show any care about his own generations to follow as eunuchs in the Babylonian palaces.

How can one who walked so faithfully fall to such despicable, uncaring, self-serving pride? The same way we can. Unless we are continually diligent in our walk with the Lord, and are careful to stay faithful at all times, we'll slide away from God into our own areas of pride and weakness, too. It doesn't matter how solid your walk is today, you're not immune from falling into sin tomorrow. Stay alert! Never let your guard down. Don't slide into selfish pride.

Prayer: Lord, help us to carefully follow you, never letting our guard down for even a moment...

Oct 29
Hotly Pursued

"Be merciful to me, O God, for men hotly pursue me; all day long they press their attack. When I am afraid, I will trust in you. In God, whose word I praise, in God I trust; I will not be afraid. What can mortal man do to me?" Ps 56:1,3-4

When our daughter was in college, one of her best friends told her she'd found a life verse for herself. It was the first part of this Psalm, 'be merciful, O God, for men hotly pursue me.' It was probably wishful thinking on her part, but you never know; you have to watch out, especially if you're an attractive woman.

These pursuers are enemies. They're not coming after us because they want to make our acquaintance. And at times we *are* the focus of people's malice. We can't help that in a lot of cases, but it does cause us concern when we know people are after us. It can be frustrating when someone is doing their level best to harm us every chance they get, and in any way they can think of.

We have no reason to give in to fear, though. Regardless of what our enemies may say, or think, or do, we have one who is in our corner. We have the Lord, in whom we put our trust, to fight for us. God in His mercy will watch over us, and protect us. We can give our praise to the Lord, without reservation, because He's the one who has the ultimate say in all that happens.

What can mortal man do to us that means anything for eternity? There's no real reason to fear men, because they can only hurt us here, and temporarily. God can doom us forever, so He's the one we ought to fear. Thankfully, we have no reason to fear Him, either, because we've put our faith and trust in Him, and He loves us and promises us eternal life in Heaven.

Now that we know we have nothing to fear on earth, let's turn our attention to this 'hotly pursued' concept. Sir, are you hotly pursuing your wife, and letting her know she still excites you and inspires your passion? Ma'am, are you hotly pursuing your husband, and letting him know you still find him appealing, and that he'll always be your knight protector?

Get moving! You're hotly pursued! (Hey, that could be a new game!)

Prayer: Heavenly Father, help us put aside any fear or worry we may have when others try to harm us. We put our trust in you, and praise you for your strong arm and mighty protection…

Oct 30
No Shrinking

This would be a great title for those who've been losing too much weight. But really! How many of those folks are there? Most of us could stand to take off a pound or three. Often it seems everyone is on a diet, and try as we might, there's no shrinking. There is an area in which we're *not* to shrink back, though.

"So do not throw away your confidence; it will be richly rewarded. You need to persevere so that when you have done the will of God, you will receive what he has promised. He who is coming will come and will not delay. But my righteous will live by faith. And if he shrinks back, I will not be pleased with him. But we are not of those who shrink back and are destroyed, but of those who believe and are saved."
Heb 10:35-39

We're blessed to live a time and place where we face little persecution, comparatively speaking. We're not free of it. It's safe to say we face hostility from the world, and there's more antichristian bigotry in the United States than ever seen before. In the apostle's day, there was a lot of affliction that came with being a follower of the Way. In many areas of the world, there are more people being martyred for the sake of Jesus Christ than at any time in history. The persecution that's happening forces us to face that which is of utmost importance.

We do have confidence in the one who saves us, and sets us free from sin. We have to decide, once and for all, whom we're going to serve and follow. We have to commit ourselves to persevering in the face of trials and troubles, whatever they may be. We have no intention of being one whom God is displeased with for shrinking back.

Our Savior is coming back again. We know neither the day nor the hour, but we know we're going to meet Him, either when He comes again, or when we cross over into glory. For every one of us, it's unlikely that it will be more than seventy-five years before we face the Lord in living color. We intend to face our Lord Jesus Christ with confidence, knowing we have not been one of those who shrink back and are destroyed; rather, we are one of those who make the decision to continue in trust, and stand by it to the end; who believe and are saved.

So hold fast. Don't shrink back. Stay in faith and receive the rich reward God has promised.

Prayer: Dear Savior, give us the fortitude, and inner strength, to be solid to the completion of our lives in faith...

Oct 31

Restored

"Barnabas wanted to take John, also called Mark, with them, but Paul did not think it wise to take him, because he had deserted them in Pamphylia and had not continued with them in the work. They had such a sharp disagreement that they parted company. Barnabas took Mark and sailed for Cypress, but Paul chose Silas and left..." Ac 15:39-40a

Nothing is said about why Mark left Paul and Barnabas in their work, but it's clear Paul didn't have any confidence in Mark's devotion to the faith and the mission in which they were involved. We can understand why Paul had misgivings about Mark, since he'd already proven himself undependable. We know people who've let us down, too, and it's tough to have much faith in someone who has already failed you. It takes time to develop a certain amount of trust in that person again.

Why did Barnabas insist on Mark joining them in the work, then? Again, it doesn't tell us, but in this case I think it's safe to assume Barnabas had spent an adequate amount of time with Mark, and felt that Mark had returned to the convictions he needed, to be faithful to the cause. I don't believe Barnabas would have placed so much loyalty and trust in Mark that he insist he come along unless he was certain that Mark was solid in his walk.

When we've stumbled, and failed in our journey, or in a commitment that betrays the trust of someone close to us, it isn't easy to earn his or her faith in us again. To have that loyalty returned requires us to turn away from our sin and/or failure, and consistently prove ourselves worthy of the trust we've lost. It takes time to show we're on the correct track. That's true whether it's a friend we've failed, a coworker, or our husband or wife, so we have to spend the time and effort necessary to prove ourselves to that person. But in Christ, we have the opportunity to begin anew. We're not chained to our past.

Obviously, Barnabas had spent enough time with Mark to give him his loyalty again, and Barnabas felt it was essential for Mark's continued spiritual growth to show him he was forgiven and had done his part to earn that faith again. What would have happened to Mark's faith if he felt nothing he could do brought forgiveness or trust? It's imperative for *us* to give the one who's failed us, or betrayed us, our trust when they've earned it.

Mark, over the course of the next years, proved to be dependable indeed. We don't know how or when, but somehow during that time, Paul realized Mark had indeed turned around and was responsible and faithful in their mission. They were restored in their relationship. Read what Paul wrote at the end of II Timothy:

"Crescens has gone to Galatia, and Titus to Dalmatia. Only Luke is with me. Get Mark and bring him with you, because he is helpful to me in my ministry." II Tim 4:10c-11

Prayer: Lord, help us to have a forgiving spirit, and to give trust where it's deserved...

Nov 1
Month of the Turkey

"They forbid people to marry and order them to abstain from certain foods, which God created to be received with thanksgiving. For everything God created is good, and nothing is to be rejected if it is received with thanksgiving, because it is consecrated by the word of God and prayer." I Tim 4:3-4

When we enter the month of November, invariably our thoughts turn to the upcoming holiday of Thanksgiving. No one appreciates this day more than Christians, because we know from whom our blessings come. We love the fellowship of friends and family and the fun times together. We enjoy giving God glory for His blessings in our life. In our family, we often go out and play some touch football, waddling around the yard as fast as our overstuffed carcasses can move.

Like Benjamin Franklin, we view the turkey as a noble bird, a useful bird. The turkey is a help to mankind in times of hunger, great or small. Ben Franklin thought the turkey should be our national emblem. He said the eagle was a bird of prey, which attacked the weak to feed itself. But the turkey, there was a bird of good purpose. In our opinion, the eagle is a majestic, noble emblem that we hold in high esteem. You have to admit, though, that the turkey is a more down-to-earth, solid source of sustenance.

While we make grandiose conversation about the wonders of the turkey we have for dinner, the object really isn't the food. It's the day we set aside to focus on the myriad blessings the Lord has rained down on us. As such, it's a great time to recount some of those blessings. It's a wonderful moment to pass on to your children and grandchildren the stories of some of the miraculous works God has done in your life over the years. It's a time when we can share about what your faith has meant to you, how it's sustained you, how it's lifted you up, how it's changed your life for the better.

Begin to think about ways in which you can make this Thanksgiving one of the most memorable and meaningful from the spiritual side of it. We encourage you to set aside a time to call out the blessings you've received from the Lord. And think about at least one story of God's work that you can pass along to your family this year.

Enjoy the month of the turkey.

Prayer: Heavenly Father, we have so much to be thankful for, and we praise you for your blessings in our life. Bring to our mind an important story of blessing to pass on to our kids...

Nov 2
Settling Accounts

"As surely as I live,' says the Lord, 'every knee will bow before me; every tongue will confess to God.' So then, each of us will give an account of himself to God." Rom 14:11-12

When I was a kid, my parents used to trade at the old grocery store in the little town nearest our farm. They'd go in and get food and various other items, and instead of paying each time, they'd tell the grocer "put it on my account." The clerk would just write it down, and charge it to my folk's account, and every so often, when they sold some grain or cattle, they'd go in and pay it off, or even put some ahead for the next series of purchases. That was the time when they settled the account. There probably isn't anywhere around where you can do that anymore. Times have changed, people have changed, and the grocer had too many people who never settled their account.

Life is like that, too. Everything we do goes onto a tally sheet. We do something good, and it's marked on the page; we do something bad, and it's put on the sheet, too. Over the course of our life, all those things go onto our account page. It keeps getting longer and longer and longer and longer. Regardless of how much we'd like to put it out of our minds, and push it off to worry about some other time, there will come a moment when we have to settle our account.

The good news is, for those of us who've put our faith in Christ Jesus, there's nothing on the expenditure side to pay. All those charges of sin billed to us have been erased. When we meet the Lord, our statement will already have stamped on it, 'paid in full'. Your kingdom investment account is favorable; enter into your heavenly reward.

The bad news is, for the one who does *not* know Jesus as Lord and Savior of his or her life, there *is* an account to be paid, and no longer any way to pay the debt. In the case of the unrepentant sinner who didn't face the need for a Savior, and trust in Christ, the penalty is eternal destruction. Only in this life do we get to make the right choice. When it's time to give an accounting, it's too late.

For your unsaved friends and family, it's urgent that they come to the Lord today, while He may still be found. We don't want them to come face to face with God without the debt paid in full through Jesus.

Prayer: Lord, give us wisdom, grace, and the correct words to lead our unsaved family and friends to you. Have your Spirit move on their hearts to put their faith in you...

Nov 3
Come and Worship

"Come let us sing for joy to the Lord; let us shout aloud to the Rock of our salvation. Let us come before him with thanksgiving and extol him with music and song. For the Lord is the great God, the great King above all gods." Ps 95:1-3

Now is the time to enter in, and worship the Lord, for He is our savior, our provider, our protector, and our foundation.

"Sing to the Lord a new song; sing to the Lord, all the earth. Sing to the Lord, praise his name; proclaim his salvation day after day." Ps 96:1-2

We will sing to you, Lord, for you alone are our song in the night, our chorus by day. May our songs of worship and praise be sweet music to your ears.

"Declare his glory among the nations, his marvelous deeds among all peoples. For great is the Lord and most worthy of praise; he is to be feared above all gods. For all the gods of the nations are idols, but the Lord made the heavens." Ps 96 3-5

Let us tell all those around us of the wonderful works you've performed for us. Your miracles make us want to praise you, and because of who you are, you're worthy of our praise. We have no fear of idols, for they are nothing at all; rather we revere you, for you are God almighty, creator of heaven and earth.

"Splendor and majesty are before him; strength and glory are in his sanctuary. Ascribe to the Lord the glory due his name; bring an offering and come into his courts. Worship the Lord in the splendor of his holiness; tremble before him, all the earth." Ps 96:6,8-9

Our offerings we bring to you, Lord. Gratefully we give back part of your blessing to bless others. We worship you for you are the ultimate in holiness, splendor, majesty, and glory. We revere you, Lord God, and we praise and honor and worship you.

Prayer: God, let our worship be pleasing in your sight. We come humbly before you to bring you praise…

Nov 4
Marry, Don't Burn

"It is good for a man not to marry. But since there is so much immorality, each man should have his own wife, and each woman her own husband...for it is better to marry than to burn with passion." I Cor 7:1b-2,9b

Paul obviously had a gift for celibacy that most of us lack. He understands that, and talks about it in the intervening verses, realizing that most people cannot, and aren't willing to, discipline themselves to refrain from sexual relations. He concedes that to stay unmarried is likely to lead to rampant immorality, even in the church.

Sometimes we come to the erroneous conclusion that as Christians we're not subject to the same physical sexual desires as unbelievers. We don't assume that because we have faith in Jesus we don't get hungry and need to eat. We don't assume that because we're believers in Christ that we don't get thirsty and have to drink. We don't assume that since we've put our trust in the Lord we don't get cold and need a jacket or blankets. We don't assume that as believers we don't get tired and need to rest. So why do we assume that belief in Christ Jesus means we won't feel the same passions and desires as everyone else?

We live in a society where sexual immorality runs amok. There seem to be no social rules that make fornication, adultery, or other sexual immorality unacceptable, nor do we seem to ostracize those who engage in it. In fact, in the world's eyes, those who are active are applauded as enlightened, or free thinking, or uninhibited, instead of something they ought to be ashamed of. Ironically, even those in the world lauded as 'open' face the same negative consequences of their behavior as those who have a moral compass that tells them they shouldn't engage in that practice.

There is a cure for that behavior. God didn't create sexual activity to be shunned; rather He made an extraordinary, perfect, safe place for that behavior to be freely, purely, wholesomely, thoroughly enjoyed. Since most of us aren't gifted with celibacy, it's better for us to marry and have our own husband or wife. We remain holy when we engage in intimate love within the blessed sacrament of marriage. We may still burn with passion at times, but God, in His wisdom, has given us the perfect outlet to release that passion in the kind of love for which He meant it to be used. And that place is in covenant marriage!

Encourage those you know to enter into the covenant of marriage, rather than live in sinful, passionate lust like the world around us. There, they'll enjoy the freedom to love intimately in the fullness and abundance which God intended.

Prayer: Heavenly Father, thank you for marriage and the intimate love we're able to share in it. Keep us pure, so that our worship and relationship with you are unhindered...

Nov 5
Keeping a Trust

"Jesus gave them orders not to tell anyone what they had seen until the Son of Man had risen from the dead. They kept the matter to themselves, discussing what 'rising from the dead' meant." Mk 9:9b-10

From the standpoint of looking back after the events have already occurred, we sometimes laugh at how obtuse the disciples could be. It amazes us how they missed the real point of so many conversations they had with Jesus. Of course, we still make the same types of errors ourselves.

Put yourselves in Peter, James, and John's place, and think about the difficulty of keeping secret the transfiguration. Jesus was transformed before their very eyes, shining forth with His heavenly glory. Not only that, they see Moses and Elijah in their glorified bodies, discussing with Jesus His upcoming departure, and they can't tell anyone about it. Even if you're not given to gossip, it would be extremely tough to keep an event of that magnitude to yourself.

We tend to be more like the three friends who went fishing together and decided to open up and share with one another their individual weaknesses to inspire more trust in one another. The first confessed that his weakness was money, and he would sometimes skim from the church offering extra cash for himself. The second confessed his weakness as one of passion, and he couldn't seem to keep control of his desire for some of the women in his church. The third friend started rowing for shore as fast and furiously as he could. The first two friends asked him what he was doing, to which the third friend confessed, "I'm a terrible gossip, and I just *have* to get back to town."

We all like to let others know information that we alone have been privy to, but the disciples didn't seem to be challenged in this area. In fact, where we would have struggled, they focused on something else entirely.

What does 'rising from the dead' mean? We look back and see it as obvious. Hadn't Jesus already raised three others from the dead? But that's not really the point.

We sometimes are called upon to walk in discretion. When we're given knowledge of something meant to be kept private, we're under an obligation that depends on our integrity. When we're called on to keep that faith, perhaps we should take the disciples example, and think and talk about something else entirely! Keep that trust.

Prayer: Lord, help us to control our tongues and be perfectly discrete...

Nov 6
Don't Look down on the Short

"Zacchaeus...I must stay at your house today.' All the people saw this and began to mutter, 'He has gone to be the guest of a 'sinner.'...Jesus said to him, 'Today salvation has come to this house, because this man, too, is a son of Abraham. For the Son of Man came to seek and save what was lost." Lk 19:5b,7,9

Most of us know the story of Zacchaeus, who wanted to see Jesus, but since he was so short climbed the tree to get a view. When Jesus arrived under the tree, He stopped and invited Himself to dine at Zacchaeus' house. All the church folk started their tongues to waggin' about how awful it was that a 'righteous' man like Jesus, the teacher of Jews, would go to the house of a lousy, God forsaken sinner like that tax collector (read: cheating thief), Zacchaeus. Why, didn't Jesus know what a reprobate he was?

While we have no choice but to look down on those who are shorter than we are, we ought not look down on those who don't know the Lord, or who aren't as far along on their journey in the faith as we may be. The sad part of this story is, too often when folks are looking down on others, it isn't because they're deeper in their walk, it's because they're deeper in their self-righteousness. They esteem themselves more highly than is an accurate portrayal of their faith.

Another aspect at play in this example from Christ's life is this. It's difficult to reach those who think they're righteous when they're only self-righteous. How do you teach someone who thinks they already know all about the faith, and is unwilling to accept someone else's wisdom to expand their understanding of scripture and it's application to their life?

The people who are reachable in the faith are those who are humble enough to know they don't have all the answers; they have much to learn about the faith, have a long way to go on their journey with Christ, and subsequently have a teachable spirit. Those with that attitude are the ones who continue to grow in their spiritual walk, and who soak in all that's offered, and are willing and committed to making things right in their lives. Because of their humble, contrite spirit, they're sought out and saved.

We need to have the mind of Christ in this matter. We have no right or reason to look down on others in self-righteous indignation. We're only sinners saved by grace ourselves. We can't be saved if we don't realize we're lost.

Prayer: Lord Jesus, help us to have the wisdom to apply humility and grace to our opinions and our outlook towards others...

Nov 7
Good Fruit?

"Watch out for false prophets. They come to you in sheep's clothing, but inwardly they are ferocious wolves. By their fruit you will recognize them." Mt 7:15-16a

A few days ago Glenda was hungry for an apple. In the refrigerator we had beautiful, shiny, delicious looking ones. They looked like the poster child of the apple-marketing cooperative of the world. They smelled good, and had her looking forward to the juicy, sweet taste. As she cut into one, she noticed on the inside it didn't look like the outside. As she sliced it again, it became quickly apparent that the whole inner core of the apple was bad. She took another one, and cut it up, and it, too, was rotten all the way through. At the heart of that batch of apples, they were all eaten away with decay.

This verse is using fruit as an example of how to recognize your prophets, or your proclaimers, or your preachers, for what they are. Just as we know whether fruit is good all the way through by cutting to the inside, that's how we know whether our teachers are good deep in the heart. We can't just observe how good they look, act, sound, or smell. We have to delve into the core of their beliefs, and line it up against the word of God to see if they match that standard; to see if they're really good fruit. Just because someone gets up to teach doesn't mean they teach what's accurate. Just because they stand in a pulpit doesn't mean their preaching isn't off on some distorted theology.

Fortunately, we had another batch of apples, and even though they weren't as pretty as the others, nor did they look as tasty, when Glenda cut into them, they were good fruit all the way through. She was able to enjoy the savory sweetness and fragrance of good apples.

In the same way, there are mostly good, accurate, led by the Holy Spirit, men of God in the majority of our churches. They seek His direction, they study diligently to have an accurate, timely message, and they're careful not to stray from the teaching of scripture. They're vigilant about not taking verses out of context, and keeping the central meaning of the text foremost in their preaching. Those godly teachers are the ones whose teaching we want to soak up and apply to daily living.

Just as we go search out a good apple when the one we have is rotten at the core, we ought to search out a good pastor if the one we have is distorted on the inside. We're warned to protect ourselves, and not accept false teaching, so if your apple is bad, go somewhere else and find one that's pure. Be sure you find the good fruit.

Prayer: Father, help us to accurately identify whether our teachers are pure and true to your word…

Nov 8
The Ability to Choose

"But if serving the Lord seems undesirable to you, then choose for yourselves this day whom you will serve." Jos 24:15a

"Accept him whose faith is weak, without passing judgment on disputable matters." Rom 14:1

Why is this verse from Romans tucked in with the topic of choice? Because when you read that passage in Romans, it shows us that we have the ability to reason things out, and to make choices that are right or wrong, good or bad, helpful or hindering. The Lord has given us a great gift. He's given us the privilege of deciding for ourselves what we're willing to do, and whom we're willing to serve.

The Bible is full of texts and verses that tell us that God chose us. And there are those that take those verses and forget the others, telling us that those of us who are saved were chosen by God, and had no choice of our own, but were compelled to respond. To use a semi-Greek term—poppycock! If we were compelled to respond to God's invitation to believe in Him, and had no other choice, then we would be nothing more than slaves, without any will of our own. But those that take the view of God choosing whom He saves, and discarding the rest, miss out on the whole context of God's word. If God chooses only some to be saved, then the verses that say He died so that whosoever will, may come, are false. The verse that says He's patient, willing that none should perish, is false.

Yes, God chose us in Christ Jesus. No, He does not force us to believe in Him. From the very beginning, the Lord has always given mankind the ability to choose for ourselves, to decide whether to believe Him, or not. In the best of circumstances, in the Garden of Eden, there was a choice to be made. Don't eat from the tree of knowledge in obedience to God's command, or choose to disobey and eat. Noah had the choice to believe

God, and obediently build the Ark, or perish with the rest of mankind. Abraham had the choice to believe the Lord's promise of a son, and continue to have intimate relations with Sarah, or not to believe, and stop his activity in his old age. Throughout the history of the Old Testament, we see choices laid before men to decide for themselves how they would respond.

The Bible doesn't say, "I am a triune God, consisting of Father, Son, and Holy Spirit, three distinct persons, but one God, united completely." No, we're given all the facts and knowledge from the Bible to put it together. The same principle holds true for the subject of choice. We understand from the word that there is a simultaneous dichotomy and unity in the fact that God chooses us, and we choose Him because of our own reasoning and understanding of our need for Him as Savior, and obediently accepting His call.

He's given us the gift of the ability to choose.

Prayer: Lord, thank you for your grace in allowing us to choose you, and serve you, and for choosing to love us…

Nov 9
The Ability to Stand

"He (Jesus) will keep you strong to the end, so that you will be blameless on the day of our Lord Jesus Christ." I Cor 1:8

"Who are you to judge someone else's servant? To his own master he stands or falls. And he will stand, for the Lord is able to make him stand." Rom 14:4

"He who began a good work in you will carry it on to completion until the day of Christ Jesus." Php 1:6b

"Therefore, put on the full armor of God, so that when the day of evil comes, you may be able to stand your ground, and after you have done everything, to stand." Eph 6:13

The Lord has given us the ability to stand, and not just stand, but to stand firm in the faith. That's important to remember, because in this journey of life, there will be plenty of people, things, and circumstances that will test you, and try to knock you down. When a coworker tries to steal your idea, displace you in your position, or take credit for your achievements, remember, you have the ability to stand. When a storm comes and blows trees down on your house, or someone hits and totals your car, or illness strikes you, remember Christ and stand in your faith. Sometimes things may be so bad you may not be able to stand on the outside, but you can always stand on the inside, because you stand in Christ, and He is well able to make us stand.

Never confuse the ability to stand with putting on a happy, false façade for others to see. That's not what standing is. Be honest. Smiling on the outside while crying on the inside may be great acting, but it isn't real. When you struggle, encourage yourself in the faith, and remember the one in whom you trust. He will keep us strong to the end when we cling to His hand through every storm.

We can confidently walk in our faith knowing we have the ability to stand. We can see how far we've come in our faith journey, and we know that Jesus Christ is going to complete the good work He's already begun in us. We have the peace and joy of knowing that Christ is bringing us through every circumstance, keeping us strong to the end, standing firm in the full armor of God.

Prayer: Dear Lord, thank you for making us stand, and giving us the armor of God to stand in, while bringing to completion all the good works you're performing in us…

Nov 10
The Ability to Be Grateful

"He who regards one day as special, does so to the Lord. He who eats meat, eats to the Lord, for he gives thanks to God; and he who abstains, does so to the Lord and gives thanks to God." Rom 14:6

"Sing and make music in your heart to the Lord, always giving thanks to God the Father for everything, in the name of our Lord Jesus Christ." Eph 5:19b-20

I'm thankful that I can be thankful. I'm grateful that I can be grateful. You can't be happy if you're not grateful. Without a thankful heart, there is no joy. Without the ability to appreciate your blessings, you have no peace or contentment.

We usually find ourselves expressing gratitude when we receive something we like unexpectedly. Someone may sacrifice of their own time and money to find and purchase a gift for us because they know it's something we've been admiring or wanting. When it's something we don't believe we can get, it makes us especially thankful to the one who provided it, because we know it cost them significantly.

People who are always negative, who continually whine and complain about anything they can think of, are folks who don't recognize their blessings. They're like the farmer who always complained, no matter what happened. It's too dry, it's too wet, it's too hot, it's too cold, the price of grain is too low, and the price of farm machinery is too high. Then one year, everything goes perfectly. The rain came when needed, the sunshine and warmth made everything grow splendidly, the price of grain was at an all-time high, the harvest went beautifully, and it was a record yield. When someone said to the disgruntled farmer that he must love the bumper crop and these wonderful grain prices, all he could say was, "Yea, but it sure takes all the nutrients out of the soil." We have to resign ourselves to the fact that some people refuse to see the blessings that surround them. Those poor people will never be happy.

Because we can see the Lord's blessings all around us, and because we see God moving in miraculous ways all around us, we're grateful to Him for how He helps us. Because we have an intimate relationship with Him, we're thankful. Because Christ gave us the ability to recognize the blessings he bestows, we have the ability to be grateful. Because we're grateful, we're happy.

Prayer: Lord Jesus, we actively look for your blessings in our lives, and we give you thanks for your gracious gifts to us...

Nov 11

The Ability to Have Purpose

"For none of us lives to himself alone and none of us dies to himself alone. If we live, we live to the Lord; and if we die, we die to the Lord. So whether we live or die, we belong to the Lord." Rom 14:7-8

"Therefore, since through God's mercy we have this ministry, we do not lose heart. Rather, we have renounced secret and shameful ways; we do not use deception, nor do we distort the word of God. On the contrary, by setting forth the truth plainly we commend ourselves to every man's conscience in the sight of God. And even if our gospel is veiled, it is veiled to those who are perishing. For we do not preach ourselves, but Jesus Christ as Lord, and ourselves as your servants for Jesus' sake." II Cor 4:1-3,5

As believers, we have a calling. We all have a general calling, which all Christians share, and we all have a specific calling, as well. Our general calling is the core purpose of our Christian life. We are to love the Lord with all of our heart, soul, mind and strength, live in obedience, stay away from sin, live in holiness, love others as ourselves, teach and exhort one another about the Lord, and share the good news of salvation in Jesus Christ.

We all have a purpose in Christ. We are all ministers of the gospel. How we minister to others is different, how we deliver the message of His love and grace are different, but we can all deliver the love of Christ plainly. The world is floundering around looking for answers, and just once, they'd like someone to give them a straight answer.

None of us as believers lives to himself alone. What you do has profound effects on your family, for instance. Husband, if you decide to go to work in another city, you affect your wife and children. If you move, they're uprooted and required to move, as well. They also have to find new friends, grieve for the loss of companionship of old friends, become familiar with a new town, new school, new church, new stores, and new neighbors. What you do also has effects on your church. Perhaps you were in a key position(s) in the fellowship you attended. They have to replace you. They have to go through the loss of fellowship with you, too.

Regardless of what we do in life, we live to the Lord. If we die, we die to the Lord. We cannot separate ourselves from our walk with Christ, or the responsibility we have in connecting others to God. Jesus Christ is Lord! We belong to Him, and He is our purpose in life. In Him we live, and move, and have our being! Fulfill your purpose.

Prayer: Father in Heaven, thank you for the purpose in life you've given us...

Nov 12
Avoid Disgrace

"When pride comes, then comes disgrace, but with humility comes wisdom." Pr 11:2

Boy, that verse applies to so many areas of life we can't even begin to cover them all. Some examples and applications will have to do.

Pride is *the* biggest stumbling block ever devised by Satan. When we're proud, we don't seek advice. When we're proud, we don't listen to the cautions of those around us. When we're proud, we refuse to even look at what's evident to all.

When we're humble, we understand that we have limited perception, limited knowledge, and limited abilities. Because we realize we don't have all the answers, we're willing to seek advice, ask for direction, and search for knowledge. When we're humble, we're able to apply what we learn in godliness, and gain wisdom.

When we're proud, someone offers us the chance to buy a new gadget that will streamline production for our customers. We refuse it, because we know we've built this company through our own brains and savvy, and we know how everything works. It's always been done this way. Just because there's some new technology doesn't mean it'll affect us. Our customers are loyal to us, and we can schmooze them to keep doing business with us, regardless of what new gizmos are coming along. Then our customers find out the new gizmo will save them tens of thousands of dollars a year, starts buying from our competitor, and our business is bankrupt, because we were too proud to see what was right in front of us.

When we're humble, our friend comes to us and says he or she is concerned about the amount of time we're spending with an associate at work. For the sake of our family, we might want to consider backing off. We look at the situation through that person's eyes, realize that there really are dangers on the near horizon, and follow his or her advice, and end the relationship before it leads to unfaithfulness, disgrace, and pain and suffering for all involved.

When we're proud, we don't heed our spouse telling us to slow down, so we don't get picked up for speeding. Rather, we get picked up for speeding, and have to live with "I told you so" for months, or years.

When we're humble, we stop and ask for directions, thereby saving ourselves hours of wasted time.

Cast aside your pride. Be humble in your attitude. You'll avoid disgrace.

Prayer: God, give us a humble spirit, and wipe away our pride. Let us walk in wisdom and keep us from disgrace…

Nov 13
Be Kind

"A kindhearted woman gains respect, but ruthless men gain only wealth. A kind man benefits himself, but a cruel man brings trouble on himself." Pr 11:16-17

Which would you rather have, respect or wealth? It's possible to have both, but not if you're ruthless. And it's interesting to note that the inference here is that it's far better to have respect. Proverbs are interesting, because they start with a positive statement, and then contrast that with a negative one, or vice versa. Obviously, respect is to be sought after, while the deduction is that if you only have wealth, you're actually a poor man indeed.

Wealth. What is it that's actually most valuable? Is it money, houses, cars, furniture, and jewelry? Or is it good friends, a loving family, the warm esteem of acquaintances, and the respect of the community around you? I would argue that the latter is the real treasure. The heart-warming companionship of people who love and respect you is far more pleasant that the cold surroundings of things that provide comfort but lack any friendship.

And then there's the next verse, that continues in the same vein. Put the two together and we find this: a kindhearted woman, and a kind man both gain benefits for themselves that are missing in the life of the ruthless, cruel man. While the cruel man gains monetary wealth, in the process he brings trouble on himself. He'll never have the support of friends; rather, he will find himself deserted in his time of need. Help will be far from him because he has no friends to come to his aid, and acquaintances will fear betrayal if they offer assistance.

The kind person is surrounded by friends and well-wishers. Because everyone knows they can count on the thoughtful person to return their help with favor and blessing, they're willing to aid them when needed.

The accommodating person benefits from the old adage, 'what goes around comes around.' When we sow seeds of benevolence, we reap a harvest of affection. So be kind!

Prayer: Dear Lord, give us the heart and mind to be caring and kind…

Nov 14
Put Aside Anger

"In your anger do not sin: do not let the sun go down while you are still angry, and do not give the devil a foothold." Eph 4:26-27

So if you want to stay angry for a while, wait to get mad until just after sundown, and then you'll have nearly twenty-four hours to stay that way. Just looking at all the angles here. While that might conform to the letter of the law, it doesn't exactly mesh with the intent of the instruction.

Let's look at the authentic aspects of this, though. Apparently, it's possible to be angry and not sin. Anger is an emotion that we feel. Emotions move us to actions. Self-discipline can harness our behavior to be good, rather than wicked. We can easily lose our composure and our control when our emotions are at a peak. Paul recognizes that and cautions us not to allow ourselves to sin when the emotion of anger is running high. Don't let your emotions overcome your sense of self-control.

The next portion, do not let the sun go down while you are still angry, is tough for many of us. There are those who quickly get angry, but when the issue is resolved, that intense emotion abruptly fades, and they're over it. For those of us who don't have that attribute, this is a difficult principle to follow. When some of us get angry, it takes a much longer period of time for that emotion to subside. And it isn't that we *want* to stay mad, it just takes a certain amount of time for the adrenaline rush to decline. This verse gives us a good precept, to curb our anger for a relatively short period of time, so that it doesn't simmer and cause us to become bitter, which leads to spite and hatred, which can lead to a long-standing grudge. So we need to be rational, and think our way clearly to a solution that keeps us in righteous actions, even when our emotions are flowing.

The reason for us to follow the first two phrases is given in the last one. If we're not careful to control our anger, and limit its duration, we can give the devil a foothold to work on our minds and hearts. He likes nothing better than to stir up disputes, and cause us to say and do things that destroy our testimony, and our confidence in our right standing with the Lord. When we behave inappropriately, we tend to question our spiritual life.

But we're not giving the devil a foothold in our lives. We're not sinning in our anger because we exercise self-control. We limit our anger, and refuse to stay mad. In Christ, and by the power of His Holy Spirit, we intentionally put aside our anger.

Prayer: Holy Spirit, we ask you to tell us when and how to restrain our emotions when they're running high, so that we don't sin...

Nov 15
Flee Religious Rules

"Since you died with Christ to the basic principles of this world, why, as though you still belonged to it, do you submit to its rules: "Do not handle! Do not taste! Do not touch!"? These are all destined to perish with use, because they are based on human commands and teachings. Such regulations indeed have an appearance of wisdom, with their self-imposed worship, their false humility and their harsh treatment of the body, but they lack any value in restraining sensual indulgence." Col 2:20-23

If you grew up in a Christian family attending church regularly, you can think of all kinds of rules that you learned that Christians don't do. There was a time when it was considered evil not only to drink, but also to dance or go to movies. The problem with those commands is they focus on the rules, rather than on the relationship with Jesus Christ. Man-made regulations may be based on solid Biblical teaching, but they seem to take on a life of their own. We can end up so busy following all the laws imposed by the church leaders that we forget the reason we fellowship with other believers. We can become slaves to the new law. We lose our focus on worship, and the encouragement of meeting together.

Remember! We died with Christ to the basic principles of this world. We're freed from the rules. When we live in Christ, our purpose in loving Him, and those around us, takes us beyond shallow regulations. When we live in purity before Jesus, we automatically fulfill the desire for holy living God has for us. He lays on our hearts those activities He wants us to avoid. He directs us to wholesome things that are good, enjoyable, and exciting for us, and those things honor the Lord. When we fix our eyes on Jesus, and seek to live for Him, we're free to live life fully, abundantly.

Notice the way Paul describes those human regulations. They may have an appearance of wisdom, but they're really false. They have no value in moving us to purity. They cannot restrain sensual indulgence. Those rules have no power

Look at it this way. We want to get to a place called 'Purity and Holiness'. Purity and Holiness is three thousand miles away. Since I'm going by Jesus way of travel, I'm going in a full size, comfortable, luxurious automobile that travels seventy miles per hour on smooth paved highways. But you've decided to go man's way, so you're traveling on a bicycle along dirt paths. The fact is you can't get there from here that way. You'll be exhausted long before you ever reach the land of Purity and Holiness.

When we live in Christ Jesus, adhering to His principles, we move in power. When we live according to human rules and regulations, there is no power, and we're bound up to the point of being in stasis. So flee those religious rules. They're of no value anyway.

Prayer: Father, help us to see through the things we do that have no value for your kingdom, nor for our relationship with you…

Nov 16
Hidden with Christ

"Since, then, you have been raised with Christ, set your hearts on things above, where Christ is seated at the right hand of God. Set your minds on things above, not on earthly things. For you died, and your life is now hidden with Christ in God." Col 3:1-3

Yesterday we talked about how we've died with Christ to the principles of the world. Today, we move on to the glorious part of being raised with Christ. New life is ours in Him, we're no longer shackled by the weight of human regulation, and we have the freedom to walk in completeness of faith.

Many times when we're feeling low, and our gaze seems to constantly be on the troubles we face, and the afflictions that surround us, we feel the earthly burdens we carry. We get caught looking down at the mud of circumstances that mire us, and we see only the fog of the predicaments all around. Just like being in a thick, foggy night, we can't see anything at all except the gloom that surrounds us. But then we look up, and are astonished to see the fog is only a few feet high, and we can see clear sky and brilliant stars above us. That's an example of what we need to do in our daily lives.

We've already been raised with Christ, so we need to set our hearts on things above. We ought to look up to Jesus, and see the stars of blessing we have in Him. Our Lord Jesus Christ is at the right hand of our Heavenly Dad, so what reasons do we have to be anxious or concerned about mundane things here that He'll take care of anyway? We're already hidden with Christ in God, so we don't fret about what's obviously of little importance.

No, we set our minds on things above. The earthly things will pass away, and while we do live here for a while, it's the heavenly things that are of the most value. Stop and think about this. We look around us and think we see, hear, taste, smell, touch, and feel that which is real. But all that surrounds us will one day pass away. Our spirits, on the other hand, will live forever, along with the Eternal God. It's the spiritual world that's actually real. So while we're here and we journey in this earthly realm, it's only temporary. With that in mind, our focus should be on the things that will store up treasure for the real life, the eternal life that began when we became saints of God, which will continue forever.

So live hidden in Christ, and keep your focus on the things above.

Prayer: Lord Jesus, move us into fixing our gaze on you, and on things above…

Nov 17
What Price for Your Spouse?

"Rachel was lovely in form, and beautiful. Jacob was in love with Rachel and said, 'I'll work for you seven years in return for your younger daughter Rachel." Gen 29:17b-18

It's safe to say in our age of instant gratification that there wouldn't be many marriages if we had to work seven years before we got married. We want what we want now, if not yesterday, and no matter how hot the guy or gal is, we have to consummate this relationship right away.

Jacob must have been overwhelmingly smitten. The Bible tells us that Rachel was lovely in form, and beautiful. Apparently that's the biblical way of saying she had an amazing, sexy figure, and was drop-dead gorgeous. To be willing to work for seven years, which would have been about a third of his current life, for the privilege of having Rachel for his wife is some kind of commitment. That's impressive!

What sacrifice and commitment are *you* willing to enter into for your wife or husband? Many young men and women relinquish wealth and privilege, honor, social status, or even education to enter into the covenant of marriage. Their love and dedication to each other is deep, and it's sweet to see. Since you've already married, the question now is, what are you willing to surrender, renounce, abnegate, or forfeit to *keep* your wife or your husband? What are you willing to do, try, utilize, or commit to, to *keep* your wife or your husband?

Are you willing to work as hard to keep your relationship exciting as you did when you dated? Are you willing to give up your job for a lesser one if needed? Are you willing to give up friends that are detrimental to your relationship? Are you willing to pursue your spouse with the same ardor you once did? Are you willing to give up hobbies that interfere with your love life? Are you willing to spend the quality time necessary to fulfill the desires of your spouse? Are you willing to grow in your love together?

Are you willing to try creative new ventures that you can both enjoy? Are you willing to put aside apathy so you can begin to do what's needed?

One thing is sure; if you spent seven years working for the spouse you ardently desired, you wouldn't take him or her for granted. You'd cherish that love, and relish it every moment of every day. Contemplate how much your husband/wife means to you, and how you treasure him or her as the prize he/she is.

Prayer: Lord, never let us forget how much our spouse means, and how privileged we are to be married. Thank you for blessing me with my wife/husband...

Nov 18
Don't Lose Heart

"David said to Saul, "Let no one lose heart on account of this Philistine; your servant will go and fight him. Your servant has killed both the lion and the bear; this uncircumcised Philistine will be like one of them, because he has defied the armies of the living God." David said to the Philistine, "You come against me with sword and spear and javelin, but I come against you in the name of the Lord Almighty, the God of the armies of Israel, whom you have defied." So David triumphed over the Philistine with a sling and a stone; without a sword in his hand he struck down the Philistine and killed him." I Sam 17:32,36,45,50

When you face a seemingly unbeatable foe, an enemy of overwhelming might, an adversary of unmatched fighting prowess, you might be tempted to turn and flee from your wife—lol. Just kidding! We know you're a loving couple who rarely disagrees, and who never actually fight about anything. But we do sometimes face people or circumstances in which it might seem we have almost no chance of victory whatsoever. Whether we're able to face that challenge depends entirely on whom our confidence rests.

None of the Israelite army was willing to go face the giant Goliath because they were looking at doing so from their own puny strength in the face of an overwhelming opponent. They knew they could never overcome him, because they couldn't even reach him with their sword or spear. They were too short compared to Goliath's reach and the length of his weapons. Because they were operating in their own small strength, they instinctively knew they were too weak to succeed.

David's confidence was in the Almighty, living God of Israel. David didn't have battle experience, so he wasn't dissuaded from previous fear of failure from seeing men dying in fighting around him. He had faith in his ability to conquer from his experiences in which God protected and helped him when he faced a lion and a bear in the course of shepherding his father's flocks of sheep. He realized he didn't have the power on his own to kill the lion or the bear. He knew the Lord had helped him. He also knew he wasn't going to get any closer to Goliath than he had to the bear. Since his confidence was in God, and in the way in which he was to fight, David knew he could overcome the giant Philistine who was frightening the entire army of Israel.

When we place our confidence in the one who fights our battles for us, and are obedient to His instruction as we face our challenges, we'll overcome them. Not because of our might, but because of the Almighty Lord who goes before us. So don't lose heart, put your confidence in the living God we serve.

Prayer: Almighty God, we put our faith, trust and confidence in you to take us through the adversities and foes we face...

Nov 19
Please Her, Please Him

"But a married man is concerned about the affairs of this world—how he can please his wife...But a married woman is concerned about the affairs of this world—how she can please her husband." I Cor 7:33,34c

Granted, without the encumbrance of a family, we would be able to devote ourselves completely to the work of the Lord. Paul was single and thought it best for all to be that way if they could. Of course, it's hard to accept that God meant for all of us to be so, since He made us male and female, and commanded us to be fruitful and multiply and fill the earth. We can't raise godly children to carry on the gospel if we don't have any. And even the other Apostles took their wives with them in their work of evangelizing.

I frequently tell Glenda, "I live only to make you happy." I tell her that so often because I want to affirm my commitment to her to please her in every way that I can. Yes, as married men, we are concerned about the affairs of this world, because it affects our wives and families. We're interested in taking good care of our loved ones, and making the best, most comfortable home we can provide for them. Our desire is to give them the necessities of life, and bless them with abundance.

The married woman has the same intentions as the husband. She devotes herself to pleasing her husband. She's instructed to do so while she also lives for the Lord. This is commanded as an example of godly living, and shows how the family is designed by the Lord to function. God is honored when husband, wife, and children all live in holiness, and worship Him together to show the lost world the blessing of following His perfect plan for the family.

The husband pleases his wife when he honors, respects, and helps her as the weaker partner. The husband makes his wife feel appreciated and cherished when he treats her with love, gentleness, and kindness. The husband pleases his wife when he actively leads the family spiritually, and plans family worship and devotions. The Christian wife is esteemed and valued more highly than in any other society in the world.

The wife pleases her husband when she affirms, respects, and honors him as her most desirable of partners. When she looks after him, and looks out for him, and supports him, she makes him feel like the man of God he's striving to be.

Seek to please one another, and please God in the process!

Prayer: Heavenly Father, thank you for our partner, and give us grace to please him/her in every way possible...

Nov 20
Ascertaining Noble Character

"Now the Bereans were of more noble character than the Thessalonians, for they received the message with great eagerness and examined the Scriptures every day to see if what Paul said was true. Many of the Jews believed, as did also a number of prominent Greek women and many Greek men." Ac 17:11-12

There you have it. The Bereans were more noble of character than the Thessalonians simply because of their openness to, and acceptance of, the truth. Yes, the truth. Not some concocted, whimsical fairytale, but the truth. And notice they didn't just take Paul's word for it. They searched, studied, and examined the Scriptures to verify that what Paul was telling them was accurate. And when they found his teaching to be true, they believed.

It all seems so simple. Except that most people don't seem to have the noble character of the Bereans. Remember that Jesus is the way, the *truth*, and the life. People follow false gods, false ideas, and false paths all the time, yet they won't accept the truth. Even those who claim they're on a spiritual journey, searching for the truth, always seem to be willing to search every other religion while automatically excluding Christ, refusing to even look at the Bible, and see if it's true. The resistance to truth is evident everywhere. If you don't believe it, just try telling someone what he or she thinks is inaccurate. You'll have an argument on your hands instantly. And sadly, those type of people have no interest whatsoever in being confused with the facts.

This is educational for me. Although I've read this verse a hundred times, I never noticed before that it gives us a test to use. And isn't it interesting that Paul equates acceptance of the truth of the gospel with noble character? So when you're going about your daily agenda and you meet people who are believers, I guess you can assume they have a more noble character than the non-believers you meet.

The crux of life really is whether people have faced the question of Jesus and settled it in their own minds. Those who *have* settled the issue, and put their faith in Christ Jesus are those who accept the truth. It's foolish to do otherwise. And you can ascertain a person's character by their choice.

Prayer: Lord, help us to gently introduce people to the truth, in a way in which they'll accept it, and come to know you...

Nov 21
Favor from the Lord

"He who finds a wife finds what is good and receives favor from the Lord." Pr 18:22

"Houses and wealth are inherited from parents, but a prudent wife is from the Lord." Pr 19:14

A wife could get to be proud as a peacock when you read some of these proverbs. After all, you're what is good, and you're a favor from the Lord to your husband. Of course, left unsaid is, if you're not a prudent wife, who are you from?

We husbands already know that you wives are a wonderful blessing from God to us. We also have learned that at times, and in some marriages as a whole, that blessing can turn into what feels like the worst curse. Don't misunderstand; we husbands are rooting for you wives. We want you to be what is good in our lives. We want that favor from the Lord embodied in you. We love having a prudent wife, and we know that's God's gift to us. We know because we see many wives out there that aren't! And we have no desire to be in the position of that particular husband.

So wife, how are you fulfilling your obligation to be what God designed for you to be? Are you intentionally making efforts to be what is good? What are you doing to be good? How are you going about it? What manner are you using to be good? How are you insuring that you're a favor from the Lord? What does it take to be that favor? Are you a prudent wife? Do you use wisdom in your purchasing? Do you think through your tasks? Do you analyze your budget? Are you being a good steward of your resources (given by God)? Do you use your tongue prudently? Are your actions with friends and acquaintances circumspect? Is your service to the Lord appropriate? Do you love your husband as you ought to?

Most of us have great, godly wives. We can all use some tweaking to improve ourselves in various areas at times. When you think of things that you can do, or say, or perhaps get an idea of better ways to act, apply those ideas so that you grow in that particular attribute.

We encourage you to do all that you can to be the good thing God intended. Be the favor from the Lord. Be the prudent wife. You are the best blessing we've received.

Prayer: Dear Lord, we want you to help us be exactly what you designed us to be. Make sure we're growing into your purpose...

Thanksgiving (keep for the day)
What's Your Blessing Quotient?

"Then celebrate the Feast of Weeks to the Lord your God by giving a freewill offering in proportion to the blessings the Lord your God has given you. And rejoice before the Lord your God..." Dt 16:10-11a

Did you know that only blessings can be translated to happiness? First of all, every good and perfect gift comes from our Heavenly Father. We know that, but we have to think about it for it to help our attitude. Every blessing is something we have to be thankful for. When we think about and count our blessings, we see so much of what God has done in us, through us, and for us. Ruminating on His blessings encourages us, because it lifts our spirits when we think of how well off we are in Christ Jesus.

Some people seem to be happiest when they're miserable. Have you been around people who continually complain, always see the worst in every situation or person, never have enough? It's always a crisis and they seem to thrive on disaster and trauma in their lives. People like that are very difficult to be around. They can crush your spirit.

Now think about those you know who are happy, positive, encouraging folks who look for the best in people, and see the good in each situation. Aren't they wonderful to be around and visit with? You feel better just being in their presence. They lift your spirits.

Which person are you? On a scale of 1 to 10, how blessed are you? If you're blessed, does your attitude and temperament show it?

Do you know Jesus? Do you have a nice family? Do you have good health, a job, income, a home to live in, friends, and a church? Do you have love?

If you have some or all of these, you have every reason to decide to live with a happy, positive outlook on your life. How high is your blessing quotient?

Prayer: Heavenly Father, thank you for your love and blessings to us. Move me to keep the correct perspective and attitude in my daily walk…

Nov 23
A Righteous Husband

"Many a man claims to have unfailing love, but a faithful man who can find? The righteous man leads a blameless life; blessed are his children after him." Pr 20:6-7

"After all, no one ever hated his own body, but he feeds and cares for it, just as Christ does the church…each one of you also must love his wife as he loves himself." Eph 5:29,33a

Well, ma'am, we hope you've found a faithful man, because a righteous husband is an extraordinary blessing to his wife. Conversely, an unfaithful man causes heartache, anxiety, and sorrow for his wife. And have you noticed all the verses proclaiming the wife as a blessing from the Lord, while there don't seem to be any about the husband being a favor from God? Perhaps it's because everybody just knows that, already. Yea, that's it!

In the flesh, there's a sad system in place. A man will claim undying love to get sex. A woman will give sex to get undying love. Unfortunately, both paths are false and lead to negative consequences. Deep down inside, the man knows he's a liar, and selfishly used the woman to engage in sinful relations. Deep down inside, the woman knows she's engaged in sinful relations, and selfishly believed what she suspected to be false to receive emotional support. But genuine love comes from the commitment and honor that occurs only in marriage.

The righteous man is evident by his actions and his speech. To be righteous means to be in right standing with God. But it's also important for the Christian husband to be in right standing with his wife. So husband, are you righteous before your wife? If you are, the evidence is there to prove it. If you're righteous, you speak truth, and only truth to your wife. You're the spiritual leader of your home. You enter into only those activities that honor the Lord and your wife. You treat your wife kindly, lovingly, and affirm her. You encourage her, you bless her, and you serve her as your partner in the journey of life. You care for her as your most cherished blessing from the Lord. You lead a blameless life, walking in purity at all times and in all places. You don't *claim* unfailing love, you *give* unfailing love, and you're faithful to your wife.

We mentioned that we all have areas in which we could, and should, improve. Apply anything that's lit up ideas in your mind, and grow in that grace, doing what blesses your wife. When you do those things listed above, you *are* a righteous husband, and your wife is blessed, and so are your children.

Prayer: Father, give us wisdom and self-discipline to grow in the areas we need to, so we become what you want us to...

Nov 24
Examine Yourselves

"A man ought to examine himself before he eats of the bread and drinks of the cup. For anyone who eats and drinks without recognizing the body of the Lord eats and drinks judgment on himself. But if we judged ourselves, we would not come under judgment. When we are judged by the Lord, we are being disciplined so that we will not be condemned with the world." I Cor 11:28-29,31

There's a principle regarding taking the Lord's Supper that is vitally important for us as believers. It's incumbent upon us to be sure we're recognizing the reason we take Communion, the worship involved in this act of obedience, and the clear heart and attitude with which we should approach this sacrament. Since Jesus gave His life for us, enduring the beatings, humiliation, and pain of the cross, we should be very careful not to dishonor His sacrifice for us by coming to the table of remembrance lightly, or with a flippant, irreverent attitude.

To be sure, we ought to come to His table with thankful hearts for the gift of salvation, and for the sacrifice Christ made for us. We should be sure we've confessed, and turned away from, any sin that we've been practicing. We should come with reverence and worship to the Lord in this sacred act of entering into Christ together with other believers. It's essential to examine ourselves to be sure we're right with God before we join in the Lord's Supper. When we do, we're blessed in this event.

While the practice of examining ourselves is specific to the subject within this text, it also applies to other aspects of our lives. If we judge ourselves, we won't come under judgment! This practice applies to work, to relationships, to hobbies, to our social life, to our families, and to anything else we engage in. When we look at our work, and realize we're doing something we shouldn't, and correct it immediately, we don't have to face the unpleasant confrontation from a supervisor that's likely to come if they have to judge us themselves. If we're engrossed in a hobby, and see that it's not honoring to the Lord, or our spouse, then we can take steps to eliminate it, change it, or do something else before it causes damage to our relationships. And if you're in a relationship that you don't want your husband or wife to know about, then break it off quickly and cleanly now, before the Lord disciplines you. If habits within our own family are harsh, critical, unkind, or rude, then figure out what needs to change, and do so before it causes irreparable harm.

Having been disciplined by the Lord, trust me when I say you don't want that to happen to you. So I encourage you to judge yourself in every area of life, and when you find something that shouldn't be there, resolve it yourself and avoid the judgment and discipline that are sure to follow if you don't. Live free! Examine yourself!

Prayer: Lord God, help us to see what we need to change or improve in our lives...

Nov 25
A Pure Walk

"I will sing of your love and justice;
to you, O Lord, I will sing praise.
I will be careful to lead a blameless life—
when will you come to me?
I will walk in my house with a blameless heart.
I will set before my eyes
no vile thing.
The deeds of faithless men I hate;
they will not cling to me.
Men of perverse heart shall be far from me;
I will have nothing to do with evil.
Whoever slanders his neighbor in secret,
him will I put to silence;
whoever has haughty eyes and a proud heart,
him I will not endure.
My eyes will be on the faithful in the land,
that they may dwell with me;
he whose walk is blameless
will minister to me.
No one who practices deceit
will dwell in my house;
no one who speaks falsely
will stand in my presence.
Every morning I will put to silence
all the wicked in the land;
I will cut off every evildoer
from the city of the Lord." Ps 101

Prayer: Lord, move us to worship you in song. Let our lives be blameless, free of pornography, betrayal, gossip, slander, pride, or deception. Let our lives be a praise to you as we live in holiness, able to minister to those who need help…

Nov 26
He Knows

"Deal with each man according to all he does, since you know his heart (for you alone know the hearts of all men)." I Ki 8:39c

"But I know where you stay and when you come and go and how you rage against me."

II Ki 19:27

"But Jesus said, "Someone touched me; I know that power has gone out from me."

Lk 8:46

"I know him because I am from him and he sent me." Jn 7:29

"I know where I come from and where I am going." Jn 8:14b

"For I know the plans I have for you," declares the Lord, "plans to prosper you and not to harm you, plans to give you hope and a future." Jer 29:11

You can run, but you can't hide. No matter where you go, regardless of what you do, notwithstanding anything you think, God knows. God the Father, God the Son (Jesus), and God the Holy Spirit know. We can forget, or put out of our minds that the Lord is always aware of everything happening in our lives, both outside our body and within, but that doesn't negate the fact that He knows.

And God knows everything else. We use a word for one of God's attributes. It's omniscient. It means all knowing. There isn't anything that He doesn't comprehend, or that passes Him unnoticed.

Take heart! God knows where we live. He knows when we come and when we go. He knows what our attitude toward Him is, whether we rage against Him, or languish in joy in His presence. The Lord knows our heart.

Christ Jesus knows when His power flows, whether it flows to us, or through us to others. He knows when someone has touched Him. And

He knows we all need to touch Him. Jesus knows He loves us, and He knows we love Him in return. He knows whom He came from, and who sent Him. He knows why He came, where He came from, and why He returned to the Father, and that He's coming again.

God knows the plans He has for each of us. His plans aren't for our harm, but for our good. His plans aren't to bring us pain and misery, but to give us hope and a future. His plans are not to our detriment; rather our Heavenly Father's plans are to prosper us, and to give us eternal life.

We don't wonder if things are ever going to get better. We don't think that we're stuck in negative circumstances forever. While we don't know the way in which many of these situations in our lives are going to resolve, we know that we have God's favor, and He sees how they're working together for our good. We have great confidence in our Lord, and we know we can trust Him, because He knows!

Prayer: Heavenly Father, we thank you that you know all about us, and all we face, and we trust you to bring us through every circumstance in a wonderful way...

Nov 27
Keep at It

"The God of heaven will give us success. We his servants will start rebuilding." Ne 2:20a-b

"When Sanballat heard that we were rebuilding the wall, he became angry and was greatly incensed. He ridiculed the Jews…so we rebuilt the wall till all of it reached half its height, for the people worked with all their heart." Ne 4:1,6

"When our enemies heard that we were aware of their plot and that God had frustrated it, we all returned to the wall, each to his own work." Ne 4:15

"Sanballat sent me this message, 'come, let us meet together in one of the villages…but they were scheming to harm me so I sent…this reply: 'I am carrying on a great project and cannot go down. Why should the work stop while I leave it?" Ne 6:2-3

"So the wall was completed on the twenty-fifth of Elul, in fifty-two days." Ne 6:15

Perhaps there's been a time when you had a large project that you were working on; you may have been building a house or a garage, or painting a mural, or learning a part and rehearsing for a play, or even writing a book. If you have, you know how easy it is to be distracted. People and other tasks of immediate concern always seem to crop up and steal our time and attention. It sometimes requires immense self-discipline and focus to stay on track in the main project you're working on. And that's even without having enemies around that hate you and want to attack and kill you.

You have to hand it to Nehemiah, though. He was wily and shrewd, and pretty clever at seeing past all the plots and machinations of his enemies. When they planned an attack, he found out and got ready to meet it. When his life was threatened, he refused to run and hide, willing to boldly face his antagonist. When they tried to deceive him and lure him out where they could betray his trust, he saw their duplicity for what it was and taunted them in his return message with all the work he had to do on the rebuilding they were so frantic to stop.

While we probably won't face the kinds of interference Nehemiah dealt with, we can take a page from the example he set. When we're doing a good work, stay focused. Refuse to allow phone calls, or housework, or yard work, or breakdowns, or crises to get you off track. There are things that may need to be attended to, but we have to stay zoned in on completing the work we've begun. Especially when it's a project that will be a blessing and an encouragement to others.

Because Nehemiah wouldn't allow himself to be dissuaded from keeping on task and completing the project, and even with the encumbrance of having to work with a weapon in one hand, the wall of Jerusalem was rebuilt in only fifty-two days. So whatever your goal, keep at it!

Prayer: Lord, help us not to be led astray from what you've led us to do, and help us accomplish what you've set before us...

Nov 28
Don't Give Me That Attitude

"Your attitude should be the same as that of Christ Jesus." Php 2:5

Do you have brothers and sisters? Did you have one who always seemed to be the perfect child; while you were always doing something that got you in trouble? That can be very disconcerting for someone as sensitive as I am, leaving a person feeling inferior most of the time. And that may have led to my not having as good an attitude as I should have.

Of course, then there are our own children, and their attitudes to deal with as well. And that's a whole trip of it's own. We can see from watching our kids why the Lord gave us the instruction about whose attitude we should emulate.

What does that attitude entail? We know from reading Scripture that there are several attributes that Jesus displayed in His attitude. Let's go through some of them so that we can work on applying them to ourselves.

Jesus has an attitude of compassion. He looked at people, and saw not just their faults, of which we have many, but He saw their needs. He had empathy for the struggles of people.

Jesus has an attitude of helping. When He met folks who were in need, whether physical, emotional, or spiritual (there's always spiritual), He fulfilled that need. He healed people, raised some from the dead (for the sake of the living), fed many, and helped them resolve their 'issues'.

Jesus has a humble attitude. Even though He's God, he didn't grasp that; rather He took on human flesh, and sacrificed Himself as the lowliest of people. He was willing to forsake His glory to live in comparative poverty. There is no pride evident in Him at all.

Jesus has a servant's attitude. He washed His disciple's feet to set an example of how they should treat one another, and those they would go out and minister to. He showed there is no task beneath our dignity, and that there's dignity in every task.

Jesus has an attitude of obedience. He placed Himself in a position where He became obedient to His Heavenly Father. He always walked in obedience, and always followed the Father's will instead of His own desire.

Jesus has an attitude of faithfulness. He faithfully completed every mission He came to perform. Though it caused Him great pain and trauma, He held fast to the tasks He was sent to do.

Jesus has an attitude of love. He showed His love for all in His caring for them, teaching them, fellowshipping with them, and sacrificing for them. He did that which was best for us.

Prayer: Jesus, give us the mind to have your attitude in every area…

Nov 29
Are You Fully Persuaded?

"Yet he did not waver through unbelief regarding the promise of God, but was strengthened in his faith and gave glory to God, being fully persuaded that God had power to do what he had promised." Rom 4:20-21

Are you fully persuaded that God has the power to do what He's promised, and not only that, but that He *will* do what He's promised? The more fully persuaded you are of that, the greater your faith will be. The greater your faith, the more solid your walk in Christ will be, and the more effective your service for Him.

When we first began to date, and perhaps even after we'd been going together for a while, we sometimes feel shaky in our relationship. We question whether he or she loves us as ardently as we love him or her. We know that there's always the possibility that our love isn't returned as fully, or that something might happen to change the other's mind about us, and sever our romance. We're not completely convinced about the permanence of our relationship until we marry. Once we've 'tied the knot', we're fully persuaded that our love and union is sealed forever. We walk in complete confidence regarding our love, because we now have the assurance that allows us to move forward boldly to start and build our family, and look to our future together with certainty.

We have to be fully persuaded in our faith in the Lord. For us to grow in His grace, and walk in that grace and in His love and power, we must know, and we have to know that we know that we know that we know, that God will do what He's promised to do. It's not enough to fully believe that He *can* do what He's promised. All of us understand that God has the power to do whatever He chooses to. To walk in complete assurance, we have to have unwavering faith that He *will* do what He promised us He would. There's a world of difference between the two.

All of us have seen God work in our lives, and provide for us, and help us, in many situations. To bolster our faith, it helps us to remember what God has done, talk about it, give Him glory and praise, and encourage ourselves that He will continue to work in our lives. The more we think about the ways He's moved on our behalf, the easier it is to cling to the promises we have, and know that when the time is just right, He'll work in a miraculous way for us again.

So think about the Lord's mighty works in your past, and you'll be fully persuaded about all He'll do in your future.

Prayer: Dear Lord, give us good memories, so that we can ruminate on all you've done for us, and have full confidence in you for the future…

Nov 30
Rooted and Overflowing

Are you growing? Are you overflowing? As we continue to walk with the Lord on our journey through life, we should also be growing. To grow, we have to be rooted. But it isn't enough to just be rooted in any old thing; we have to be rooted in Jesus Christ. We derive our nutrients, our sustenance, from what we're rooted in.

Plants can be rooted in various types of soil, and they'll grow. How they grow depends on whether they're rooted in the premier type of dirt. If it's a plant that grows best in acidic soil, but it's planted in a clay base, it's not going to do well. It may survive, but it won't thrive. If it's living in acidic soil, and receives appropriate amounts of water and sunlight, then it'll grow well and produce a bounty of flowers, or seeds, or fruit, or gourds, or vegetables according to its kind.

We need to be rooted in the right soil, too. When we're deriving our nutrients from the vine, which is Christ, we can be a branch that grows fully, and as we're pruned, produce copious amounts of fruit. It's then we're built up and strengthened in our faith. And that comes from what we're taught.

"So then, just as you received Christ Jesus as Lord, continue to live in him, rooted and built up in him, strengthened in the faith as you were taught, and overflowing with thankfulness." Col 2:6-7

We have so much to be thankful for. The longer we walk with Jesus Christ, the more fully we understand all that we have to be grateful for. As we talked about yesterday, being fully persuaded that God is faithful allows us to work confidently in His love and grace. As we see Him move, He gives us more and more reasons to bless Him, and give Him praise, honor, glory, and thanksgiving. The more we dwell on His blessings to us, and to His mighty works, the more we overflow with thanksgiving to Christ Jesus.

We are rooted in Him, and overflowing with thankfulness. And we're not willing to just survive, no, we want to grow and thrive.

Prayer: Lord Jesus, we thank you that we *are* grafted into you. Teach us, feed us, prune us, and help us grow and be fruitful, and we'll give you thanks all the while…

Dec 1
Merry Christmas

"I want to know Christ and the power of his resurrection and the fellowship of sharing in his sufferings, becoming like him in his death, and so, somehow, to attain to the resurrection from the dead." Col 3:10-11

I know; this isn't the normal Scripture verse used in Christmas messages. But bear with me; there is point that will make sense here.

For those of us who truly celebrate Christmas, the core of our faith is Christ Jesus. To really understand the coming of Christ in the flesh, it helps to look at His coming in light of His destination on the cross, and the power and salvation of His resurrection. When we know Christ Jesus, we fellowship with Him, and the trials and afflictions we endure take on a new meaning, and we have a clearer understanding of the purpose of our adversity and suffering. Unlike the world, our hardships lead us to hope, a bright future, and completeness of our faith. And when we understand that deep in our spirit, we celebrate the season of Christmas because of the glorious hope it elicits.

Over the last several years, there's been a huge push by the collective, socialist, fascist, political correctness crowd to do away with Merry Christmas and replace it with Happy Holidays. That way we include all of the holidays around this time of year, and we don't exclude anyone's celebration, or offend anyone. Except Christians! This is the enemies' way of silencing believers, and the message of hope that Christmas brings. I, for one, am tired of the nonsensical thinking entailed in desperately wanting the business revenue that Christmas provides from Christians, while simultaneously insulting them, trying to intimidate them, and shut them up. Consequently, I refuse to use the greeting Happy Holidays, and insist on using Merry Christmas, because I am a Christian who celebrates Christ's birth! And I also refrain from doing business with those stores who engage in that silliness.

Why would businesses be willing to chance Christians shopping elsewhere by using a generic greeting that eliminates Christmas? Because they think there's nowhere to go where it's different, they believe from past experience that Christians won't take a stand against them, and they know Christians tend to be pretty apathetic as whole. Some of us *are* taking a stand, however, and the more believers that put aside their own selfish desires, and also exercise the courage to take a stand for Jesus Christ, the more impact it will have on businesses, changing their attitude regarding Christ, and Christians.

The bottom line is this. In the United States we've enjoyed the greatest financial prosperity of any nation in the history of the world. This is the only country I'm aware of that was founded on Christian principles, and the only one that has celebrated Christmas to the extent we have. Maybe that's why we've enjoyed God's financial blessings so greatly. So keep Christ as the foundation of your celebration. And Merry Christmas!

Prayer: Lord, help us to take the little stands for Christ Jesus that can lead to large results for the honor and praise of His name...

Dec 2
What Lens Are You Using?

"The Law is only a shadow of the good things that are coming—not the realities themselves." Heb 10:1a

"Now we see but a poor reflection as in a mirror." I Cor 13:12a

"You will be ever seeing but never perceiving...they have closed their eyes. Otherwise they might see with their eyes." Ac 28:26c,27c

His brain is in a fog! When we hear that said about someone, it means they aren't thinking clearly, they're befuddled and confused, and not following the logic or recognizing the solution. The information is right there and the conclusion is obvious to everyone around, but it's just not clicking into place for the one who's in a fog.

Part of the reason behind what we talked about yesterday regarding the move away from celebrating Christmas is the way unbelievers see things. Even though they can see from what's been created that there is a God, they refuse to acknowledge what's obvious. They have closed their eyes to the truth.

The world sees through the lens of unbelief. Because they don't know Jesus, they cannot understand the things of the Lord, because those things are spiritually discerned, and they cannot comprehend what believers see as obvious. The world has its religions. One need only look at the way in which much of the world believes in the theory of evolution, clinging faithfully to it as the way to explain the origins of life and the universe. The fact that all the research points to the error of the theory is irrelevant to them. Just because it defies every basic scientific law means nothing. Logic does not matter, because it's a way to deny a creator. That theory becomes their religion, because regardless of all evidence to the contrary, they have unshakable, dogmatic faith, in evolution.

What lens are you looking through? We have the advantage of seeing clearly through the Spirit of Christ Jesus. We see honestly because we have no pet theories to protect, no ulterior motive to have facts fit our thesis. We look at the truth, Jesus Christ, and since we know God's word, we see the world more clearly. We see it through the lens of truth. We look at the theory of evolution and see it for what it is, a theory, with very little to support it, and a mountain of evidence to crush it. We look at the lives of nonbelievers, and we see clearly that with all they face, the pain, the heartbreak, the frustration, the emptiness, and all the chasing after fulfillment, they need Christ. They desperately need the good news that God came in the flesh as a baby; to grow up, to face what we face, to overcome it, to teach us about the Father, to provide salvation for us, and to rise in victory over death, so we can have life, too.

We see clearly, and understand the needs of the world, and have compassion on them, because all that we see is filtered through Jesus Christ.

Prayer: Lord Jesus, help us to see everything around us clearly indeed, by the power of your Holy Spirit…

Dec 3
In the Beginning

"In the beginning was the Word, and the Word was with God, and the Word was God. He was with God in the beginning.

Through him all things were made; without him nothing was made that has been made.

The Word became flesh and made his dwelling among us. We have seen his glory, the glory of the Only Begotten, who came from the Father, full of grace and truth." Jn 1:1-3,14

Putting a little different twist on the Christmas season, and having a memorial Birthday party, read the above again, but substitute 'Jesus' for 'the Word.' You see, Jesus *is* the Word. Jesus was in the beginning, He was with God; in fact, He is God. Jesus made everything there is. There's nothing that He didn't make. He created it all.

Now for the Birthday party. Jesus became flesh. He wasn't always flesh apparently, but He became flesh. We'll get to the Christmas story closer to the actual day we celebrate it, but remember this same Jesus, who was in the beginning, with God, and who actually is God, came in the flesh. He actually dwelt among us men for a little while.

There's a claim in one religion that Jesus and Satan are created, and that they're brothers. According to the Bible, this is nonsense. First, Jesus wasn't created, since He was in the beginning. Secondly, Satan was created, since He's a fallen angel. Thirdly, since Jesus was the creator, He created Satan. Fourthly, they cannot be brothers since Jesus is the only begotten son of the Father. That means He's the one and only son of the Father, and even that only applies to His human form.

I don't pretend to completely understand the dual nature of Jesus. I comprehend in part, but it's difficult to follow, since our experience is so finite. Jesus is fully God while simultaneously fully man. That's a tough one, but we see in the Gospels the Son of Man living as any other human

man would for the most part. And even though Jesus veiled His divine nature while living the life of a man, we see glimpses of what appear to be His deity coming through in His miracles. His authority over demons, diseases, disabilities, and physical laws of nature show the power of God in Him.

We'll never know completely this side of Heaven how this all works. We'll understand when we get there. For me, it's enough to know that Jesus is God, he came in the flesh and is a man, and we've seen His glory, and experienced His grace and truth. That's a great beginning!

Prayer: God, we thank you for helping us understand what we do about Jesus. Give us more grace and we'll continue to give you the glory, honor, and praise you deserve...

Dec 4
Paddle or Ride

"But when he asks, he must believe and not doubt, because he who doubts is like a wave of the sea, blown and tossed by the wind. That man should not think he will receive anything from the Lord; he is a double-minded man, unstable in all he does." Jas 1:6-8

This starts out talking about asking for wisdom. We know from other Scripture that when we pray, and believe what we've asked for, we have it. There are many verses that lead us to the conclusion that we when we pray in our Father's will, we can rest assured that He will answer.

I could have great faith if only circumstances didn't keep cropping up that seem to point to the opposite thing happening as what I've prayed for. Too often, we give up before the answer comes. It usually takes patience and perseverance to see the Lord work everything out in ways that, firstly astonish us, and secondly, often work to the benefit of much, and many, more than we even prayed for.

We like to go canoeing sometimes. It's usually a pleasant, albeit somewhat strenuous, way to spend an afternoon. The weather is beautiful with bright sunshine, it's warm to hot, and the breeze is lightly blowing. The scenery is very pretty, because Glenda's always in my canoe, and the landscape (waterscape?) is nice, too. We've noticed something while canoeing, though. To get where you want to go, you have to paddle. You control the direction of your boat and move where you want to go when you paddle. Granted, sometimes when you're on a lake, it's pleasant to just float for a while. The thing is, when you just float, you go wherever the wind and current decide to take you, and if you're canoeing in a creek or river, it always takes you down. But to go up, you have to paddle!

Praying in belief is paddling your spiritual boat. Applying God's Biblical principles to your walk is paddling your spiritual canoe. When you coast along, and don't move intentionally in your spiritual life, you're going to float down with the world and it's values.

Verse five tells us that God gives generously to anyone who asks. Stand on God's promise. Ask and believe, applying all the godly precepts you comprehend to your walk with Him. You make the choice; ride wherever the worldly current takes you, or paddle up the spiritual stream to glorious blessings in Christ.

Prayer: Father, help us to purposefully apply your word to our lives. Keep us from being tossed about by worldly currents…

Dec 5
Have a Continual Feast

"All the days of the oppressed are wretched, but the cheerful heart has a continual feast." Pr 15:15

This seems to infer more than meets the eye at first glance. Since all of us face oppressing circumstances from time to time, sometimes more, sometimes less, we all have reasons to feel like our days are wretched. Some of what we face is painful, either physically or emotionally, some of it's discouraging, some of it is stressful, and all of it can cause us misery. When we accept that melancholy feeling, and allow ourselves to be depressed by the afflictions we face, our days really are wretched.

Have you noticed, though, that two different families can go through the same type of hardship, grief, or predicament, and react and come through the difficulty in opposite fashion? One family is crushed by the ordeal, and ends up beaten, down, and pulled apart, while the other endures it with grace, and an inner strength, and comes through more closely knit as a family, with a cheerful heart, and a positive outlook, thankful in the end for what the Lord did for them.

The difference seems to be in the attitude they face their trials with. One family sees the entire negative in the situation, and feels the pain, misery and strife of being a victim of circumstances. The other family faces it with a positive attitude. They don't enjoy going through the suffering, and they do suffer, just like the first family. But they see it as a problem that is temporary, and as one that God will get them through. They walk it in faith, and learn from the experience, and grow through the challenges in their spiritual life. They're the family with a cheerful heart.

When you can see your plight or crisis as a tool to find new wisdom in the Lord, and look at it as a way to grow in your faith, patiently waiting and persevering while God works, you can face it with a cheerful heart. As you watch how the Heavenly Father moves, you're excited to see things working together for your good. Seeing the miracles God performs is like having a continual feast of spiritual meat and fruit. It's a culinary delight for the soul.

How are you facing, or going to face, your troubles? Will you allow them to defeat you and destroy your faith, or will you walk with a cheerful heart, knowing the Lord has everything in hand, and growing as a result?

Decide on the cheerful heart method. Have a continual feast.

Prayer: Lord, give us your grace to have a cheerful heart regardless of what we face...

Dec 6
The Father

"There was a man who had two sons. The younger one said to his father, 'Father, give me my share of the estate.' So he divided his property between them...but while he was still a long way off, his father saw him and was filled with compassion for him; he ran to his son, threw his arms around him and kissed him." Lk 15:11-12,20

These are excerpts from the parable of the prodigal son, contained in Luke 15:11-32. If you're not familiar with it, or need to refresh your memory, now is a good time to read the whole parable. We often focus on the son, or sometimes sons, in this story, but the father is truly the interesting one.

This father had two sons. Call them Israel and Gentile. Now Gentile was a wayward son, and insulted his father by asking for his share of the estate before his father had even bothered to die. Israel stayed and worked with his father, but despised his brother, Gentile.

The father, brokenhearted as he had to have been, nevertheless gave Gentile his share of his blessings. He did not keep it from Gentile, as was his right, thereby giving his son no cause to resent him or hate him. In giving Gentile his wealth, he gave him the means to live in hedonistic, sinful pleasure for a time. The father knew he could not force Gentile to love him or live in a manner worthy of his heritage. But the father could keep the door open for his son's hoped for return by refusing to allow any wedge between them.

The father could have barred the way. He could have withdrawn his love; he certainly had good reason after the way his son despised him and insulted him. But the father's love for his sons never wavers. His hand of welcome stayed extended.

When the prodigal son finally squandered his wealth, he was forced into poverty and came to his senses. He headed for home, with his apology already written and ready. The father saw his son from a long way off, and didn't wait for his son to get there. He ran to his son to welcome him home. He brushed aside the apology, and the inferior status his son offered as a servant, and brought him into the house as an heir again, with the privilege that accompanies that position.

Israel was angry with his father. His brother, Gentile, didn't deserve to be returned to his father's house as a joint heir with him. And that's true, Gentile didn't deserve it.

The father is our Heavenly Dad. He loves us so much He's always waiting for us to come, or to return, to Him. As children of His, we ought to rejoice with our Dad when one of His wayward children comes home. We don't deserve to be here, either. But our Heavenly Dad loves us, and accepts us with all of our faults and failures, too, and we can do no less for those who come home. Rejoice with, and for, your Father. He loves us!

Prayer: Heavenly Dad, thank you for your unending love and forgiveness extended to us…

Dec 7

Sunshine on Stained Glass

"For in the gospel a righteousness from God is revealed, a righteousness that is by faith from first to last, just as it is written: 'The righteous will live by faith." Rom 1:17

"Now faith is being sure of what we hope for and certain of what we do not see." Heb 11:1

We've had the privilege of seeing some amazing stained glass windows in churches around the country, and we've seen a wide variety of Scriptural stories depicted in those windows. Have you seen stained glass without a light behind it? If you have, you've noticed how dull, colorless, and lifeless it appears in the shade. But oh my, when the sun shines in through it, it just comes to life. The colors are so vibrant and beautiful whatever scene is depicted is phenomenal.

In our walk with the Lord, we're bestowed a righteousness from God. This righteousness we have is by faith. It's not by any task we do, and it doesn't come as the result of any work we do. If it were given as payment for a task, it wouldn't be by grace, through faith. From beginning to end, our spiritual journey with Christ is undertaken in faith. If we don't use that faith, though, our spiritual life is dull and colorless.

The book of Hebrews informs us that faith is being *sure* of what we hope for and *certain* of what we don't currently see. That means we have unwavering belief that what we hope for will come to pass. When we're certain of something, we have no doubt. Just as we know the sun will rise in the morning, we know Christ has saved us. The proof in the morning happens at sunrise. The proof in our salvation will come when we step into Heaven. But we've been given a deposit. It's the Holy Spirit within, and He guarantees the promise of eternal life. So we can know we have the righteousness given by God, because that faith wells up inside us, and shines forth in a life lived for Jesus.

Sometimes we have to exercise our faith consciously. Jesus told us to have faith, He asked the disciples at times where their faith was, insinuating they had some they weren't using, and we're instructed to stir up the faith we've been given.

So remember this. Faith brings our righteousness alive in the same way sunshine brings stained glass windows alive. So shine brightly!

Prayer: Lord Jesus, give us an extra measure of faith, and help us to use our faith consciously to shine forth a beautiful picture of you in us…

Dec 8
Getting to the Right Place at the Right Time

"In those days Caesar Augustus issued a decree that a census should be taken of the entire Roman world. (This was the first census that took place while Quirinius was governor of Syria.) And everyone went to his own town to register.

So Joseph also went up from the town of Nazareth in Galilee to Judea, to Bethlehem the town of David, because he belonged to the house and line of David. He went there to register with Mary, who was pledged to be married to him and was expecting a child." Lk 2:1-5

Ever wonder how God moves all the pieces into place to accomplish His will? Well, one of the things He does is have the emperor of a country call for a census at just the right time, forcing people to go various places, specifically in this case, to send Joseph to Bethlehem, taking along his fiancé Mary, so that she'd be in Bethlehem at the right time in her pregnancy to have her baby there, since that's where Jesus was supposed to be born. It seems convoluted, and like me, you may be thinking, why didn't He just tell Mary and Joseph to go there without dragging all those other people through the mill? I think it's because they didn't have ball games. Since there was no football game, and therefore, no football fans, to fill up all the hotels and motels so that Mary and Joseph would have to sleep in someone's barn, God used a census to fill all the Inns.

You've heard the phrase, 'timing is everything'. How long prior to the birth of Christ did Caesar have to call for the census before the word got out to all the outlying districts, and giving people the proper amount of time to get where they had to go to register? I've heard people say God's timing is perfect. Admittedly, I sometimes think His timing is off because of something that's happening with me, but I don't really have the best perspective in those cases. Glenda and I have seen enough situations where His timing has been astonishing to realize it's perfect. We just can't see it all. We don't always (hardly ever, in fact) see the big picture.

The crux is, just as God knew how to get Mary to the right place at the right time, He knows how to move us into the correct position at just the perfect moment, too. Open your spiritual eyes to see how God is moving and you'll see some marvelous moments in which He put you in the right place at the right time.

Prayer: Lord, help us to remember to trust in you to work out your perfect timing for us...

Dec 9

In the Midst of Lament

"Yet this I call to mind and therefore I have hope: Because of the Lord's great love we are not consumed, for his compassions never fail. They are new every morning; great is your faithfulness. I say to myself, "The Lord is my portion; therefore I will wait for him. The Lord is good to those whose hope is in him, to the one who seeks him; it is good to wait quietly for the salvation of the Lord." La 3:21-26

This is a great reminder that in the midst of our difficulties, we should call to mind God's faithfulness, and encourage ourselves with hope that He is good to us, and He will see us through.

The whole book of Lamentations is just that; it's a lament. It goes through, in mind numbing series, a whole list of terrible punishments and awful afflictions they're enduring. The prophet cries to the Lord to hear and restore them, but this is never resolved in this book. It just lists the continuous problems and hardships and predicaments and torment and crisis that they face.

In the middle of all that misery is one passage that is the basis for one of the greatest old hymns of the faith, "Great Is Thy Faithfulness." The Hymn uses these very words to proclaim the faithfulness of our God. When you're in the midst of trials and troubles, remember these words from Lamentations, and take heart. Because of the Lord's love, we are not consumed, and therefore we can't be overcome. God's compassions never fail. There's no end to them. In fact, His compassions are new each and every morning. His faithfulness is extraordinary. God is our portion. We wait for Him because He is our provider. The Lord is good to us, because our hope is in Him. We seek Him, and because we do, He's good to us. Because we can count on His love and goodness, we wait quietly for Him to save us, knowing we can trust Him to do so.

So remember to say to the Lord, "Great is thy faithfulness," and give Him praise and worship, confident He'll care for you.

Prayer: Father, bring to mind your great faithfulness whenever we face problems that seem overwhelming. Help us to walk in trust in you…

Dec 10
The Father's Gifts

"If you, then, though you are evil, know how to give good gifts to your children, how much more will your Father in heaven give good gifts to those who ask him!" Mt 7:11

We earthly fathers do know how to give good gifts to our children. We know our children, and we know what they desire, and how to please them with the kinds of gifts they'll love, appreciate, and enjoy.

Our Heavenly Father knows even better how to give good gifts. He knows us, His children, and what we need most, and what will please us and serve His good will. His gifts are the eternal kind, too, and last forever, unlike that plastic gun set my brother and I got for Christmas when we were kids. We loved those guns, and had great fun playing with them, but unfortunately, we were the epitome of 'boys' and soon broke them. But that's another story. The gifts our Heavenly Father gives us aren't temporary, soon forgotten, presents.

Number one for us is the gift of eternal life. Romans 6:23 tells us the gift of God is eternal life through Christ Jesus our Lord. The commercials tell us a diamond lasts forever. It'll last the gal's lifetime, but forever? You talk about the gift that lasts forever. Diamonds may be a girl's best friend (kind of offensive to us husbands), but they're nothing but rubble compared to eternal life in Christ.

Number two for us is the gift of the Holy Spirit. Acts 2:38-39 tells us that when we believe in Jesus, and are baptized, He gives us the gift of the Holy Spirit, and that occurs for all who put their trust in Him through all generations. This is truly the gift that keeps on giving. Not only does this gift reside within us, He continually teaches us and reminds us of what we've already learned. On top of all that, He gives us spiritual gifts, just as He wills.

So number three is the spiritual gift or gifts we've been given. I Cor 12:1-11 tells us the Holy Spirit gives us spiritual gifts, imparting them to each one as He decides. You should recognize your gift, or gifts, because you have at least one. You may have the gift of the Spirit of wisdom, or the gift of message or knowledge, or faith, or healing, or miraculous powers, or prophecy, or distinguishing between spirits, or different kinds of languages, or the interpretation of languages. Also listed in other places of the Bible are gifts of helping, administration, serving, encouraging, contributing (giving), leadership, and mercy. All these gifts are given by the Holy Spirit for the edification and encouragement of the body of Christ.

Number four for us is the gift of God's word, the Bible. II Tim 3:16-17 tells us that all the Scriptures are inspired by God, and they are the foundation of what we need to teach us, train us, rebuke us, and correct us so that we're equipped for every good work the Lord plans for us to do.

There are many more gifts the Father gives us. They're all great gifts!

Prayer: Heavenly Father, thank you for the precious gifts you've given us...

Dec 11
Heirs with the Redeemer

"But when the time had fully come, God sent his Son, born of a woman, born under law, to redeem those under law, that we might receive the full rights of sons. Because you are sons, God sent the Spirit of his Son into our hearts, the Spirit who calls out, "Abba, Father." So you are no longer a slave, but a son; and since you are a son, God has made you also an heir." Gal 4:4-7

As we celebrate that time, fully come, when God sent His son to be born of a woman, we have much to be grateful for. We've already talked about God's perfect timing, and when He deemed the time right, He sent His son. Because Christ Jesus came, we're now elevated from the status of slaves, to the position of sons and daughters. Because God has chosen to make us His children, He's also made us His heirs. In the song "The Family of God", there's a line that calls us 'joint heirs with Jesus.'

It's somewhat difficult to put this into perspective, because we're not immersed in a culture of slavery. Slavery was a relatively common practice in the days of Jesus on earth, and they understood the degradation and hopelessness inherent in being a slave more intimately than we do, being so far removed from it. But think about being taken from the lowest social standing you could possibly have, where no one looked up to you, and everyone looked down on you with contempt, and being elevated to the highest social rank possible, wherein you are now a prince or princess in the palace of the king. Then undertake to comprehend that our position in Christ Jesus is even more extreme, because we've been moved into the family of the King of Kings.

Jesus has redeemed us so that we might have the full rights of sons. Because our Heavenly Father is Spirit, we've also been given His Spirit. We can now call the Most High God, Father. What a blessing we have, what an amazing gift we've been offered! One can't help but praise the Lord because of it.

Now it's important to live as princes and princesses of the King of Kings. We no longer live as slaves; rather we live as ambassadors and diplomats for Christ Jesus. We have a message of reconciliation for the world. God wants to redeem you, too. Turn to Him through Jesus, and live as heirs with us. It's the best Christmas gift you could receive!

Prayer: God in heaven, we thank you for the gift of redemption, and the position of sons and daughters we now have…

Dec 12
Promote Love

"He who covers over an offense promotes love, but whoever repeats the matter separates close friends." Pr 17:7

Discretion is one of *the* most important virtues one can have. There is no end to the harm, pain and hard feelings created by those who gossip. From schoolgirls to crones, from young boys to codgers, this uncontrolled wagging of the tongue has probably caused more quarrels, disputes, and outright wars than any other vice ever has.

When you're talking to one who insists on keeping a squabble going, it's so disheartening to listen to the foolishness. Regardless of how the dispute began, those who are unwilling to forgive the offense and move on are on a treadmill of anger and spite that just never ends. And those who join in regurgitating the problem just add fuel to the fire. They have no interest in resolving the issue, unless they can do so in a way that proves they were right, and humiliates the other party, most preferably very publicly. They want to be able to smile down their nose and gloat. Their pride is at stake, and nothing less than complete annihilation of the other person in abject mortification and disgrace will do. It would be funny if it weren't so sad.

Contrast that with the person who gently disengages from such discussions. See the difference in the attitude and heart of one who covers over the offense by offering rational explanations that might unravel the reasons for what happened. The forgiving, nonjudgmental pursuit of reconciliation is at the heart of discretion. One who is discrete withholds storytelling that fosters misunderstanding and hurt feelings. The pleasant interaction of all involved is at the heart of discretion.

Discretion isn't just the avoidance of conflict. The one who covers over an offense may well have every justification to engage in discord, but chooses not to. The offense may be serious, but even so, he chooses not to allow it to grow to unmanageable levels. In deciding to forgive, and allow the disagreement to die away, he promotes love. And the one who covers over the offense has freed himself from the bondage of anger and spite, moving forward in a positive, healthy relationship that has been resolved and reconciled.

Prayer: Lord, help us to promote love at all times by having a forgiving heart, and covering over offenses...

Dec 13
Don't Borrow Trouble

"But seek first his kingdom and his righteousness, and all these things will be given to you as well. Therefore do not worry about tomorrow, for tomorrow will worry about itself. Each day has enough trouble of its own." Mt 6:33-34

It's noteworthy that the first phrase in these verses is pulled out and used all the time, but we rarely hear messages in the context of the whole passage. There are some who teach that if you seek God's kingdom and His righteousness first, then the Lord will bless you with great wealth and extraordinary financial prosperity. But this passage isn't actually about prosperity. It's about *worrying*, and it instructs us *not* to worry, and particularly not to worry about our basic needs of what to eat or what to wear. From verses 25 through 34 it doesn't once mention wealth.

This passage gives the example of birds and flowers. Our Heavenly Father sees all the birds, and the birds neither plant nor harvest, nor do they store away food for lean times, and yet our Father feeds them. We're much more valuable than the birds. And the flowers don't work or make clothing, and yet they're dressed more beautifully than any wealthy person possibly can.

Jesus is teaching us that, us worrying about the necessities of life, won't change a thing. We have no power in ourselves, and God knows what our needs are, and He'll provide them. Rather than running after food and drink like the pagans do, and chasing new fashionable clothes, we ought to be seeking His kingdom and His righteousness. The promise is that when we seek Him, He'll provide our needs as well.

Since God will supply our needs, why worry whether we'll have them tomorrow. There's enough to worry about today without borrowing more concerns and anxiety about what will happen tomorrow, too. Today has enough of it's own trouble, so there's no reason to add tomorrow's to it, or the next day's, or week's, or month's either.

The real crux of this passage is: Seek first His kingdom and His righteousness, and don't worry about the rest, our Heavenly Father will take care of it.

Prayer: Father, give us the mind to seek you first, and not worry about what the future holds...

Dec 14
Point to Jesus

"And this was his message: "After me will come one more powerful than I, the thongs of whose sandals I am not worthy to stoop down and untie. I baptize you in water, but he will baptize you with the Holy Spirit." Mk 1:7-8

This was the message of John the Baptist. He's a great example to anyone who has a ministry of any kind, whether it be Sunday School teacher, deacon, usher, worship leader, musician, custodian, or pastor. Whatever we do should honor and glorify Jesus Christ. It should not build a following for ourselves in any way.

As we travel in our gospel music ministry, we're very aware of what our ministry is, and what our place in the scheme of things is. We're only messengers, bringing the good news of Jesus Christ through music and teaching. We're not the point of the worship concert; Jesus is! Our responsibility is just like John's, to direct people to the One whose sandals we're not worthy to untie. We understand that we've been given a great privilege to be able to serve the Lord this way. We also are keenly aware that it is the *Lord* we serve, not ourselves.

In your service to Christ, you too, must be careful that you point people to Jesus. We don't have the answers; He does. We only pass along the answers to life problems that He gives us, to minister to their needs. Whether we're teaching a class, sharing with a friend enduring problems, or bringing a music special in church, the Holy Spirit gives us the abilities, wisdom, and message to share that will touch others for Jesus Christ and glorify His name.

Without the Lord, we would be nothing. We're sons and daughters of God Almighty through the love and grace of Christ Jesus. He is God. We are His servants. Even though He gives us a royal place in His house, we have no reason for pride, and every reason to be humble, because it's through the gift of God that we're here. So we're thankful to the one who brought us into the family of God, and we gratefully point to Him as the one to whom praise belongs.

Point to Jesus!

Prayer: Lord Jesus, we thank you for our place in God's family, and we'll be sure to point others to you, that they might know you, just as we do...

Dec 15
Offer a Sacrifice of Praise

"Through Jesus, therefore, let us continually offer to God a sacrifice of praise—the fruit of lips that confess his name. And do not forget to do good and to share with others, for with such sacrifices God is pleased." Heb 13:15-16

We don't hear too much about sacrifice any more, but it has always been an integral part of worship. In the Old Testament, they brought an array of sacrifices, from bulls to sheep to goats to pigeons, and from grain to oil. That didn't count the tithes they brought, the first fruits of all their increase, nor did it count the alms they were to bring for the poor. In certain years they brought an extra tithe, added to the normal tithe. And we think it's hard to give just ten percent of our income. Think what it would be like if you had to give twenty to thirty percent! And the tithing wasn't considered a sacrifice. It was a normal part of worship.

The sacrifices were for sin, for atonement, and for cleansing. Then the real sacrifice was made. God sacrificed His only begotten Son, Jesus, to bear the sins of the world. He was the perfect lamb, without sin, fault, or blemish, which was offered once for all time for the purification of sins. By His sacrifice, we've been freed from the bondage of sin, the bondage of the law, and the sacrifices required by it.

Now the Lord requests a different type of sacrifice from those of us who have been saved through our faith in Christ Jesus. He wants us to bring sacrifices of praise, part of which is our confessing His name. When we confess the name of Jesus, we honor and worship Him in the process. And He asks us to bring sacrifices that extend His love and mercy to others. By doing good things for those around us, by helping them when they need it, or even when we can give it unsolicited, we bring a sacrifice with which God is pleased. When we share with others, we give a portion of what God has blessed us with, and that's a sacrifice that pleases God, also, because by doing so we share His love.

Let's remember that this isn't a once in a while practice. This is a continual activity on our part, through Jesus, as we offer God our praise.

Prayer: Lord, remind us to continually give you praise, and to do good things for our neighbors, and to share with them...

Dec 16
Be a Contender

"I felt I had to write and urge you to contend for the faith that was once for all entrusted to the saints." Jud 3b

Yes, we're supposed to be fighters. Perhaps not in the normal context of the word, since we're not called to fight physically. We normally think of a contender in the realm of the boxing venue. When a boxer is good enough, and has won a number of matches against quality opponents, they're given the chance to contend for the championship. And when they get in the ring to contend for the crown, they give it all they've got. In fact, they begin training months in advance, to get themselves in peak physical condition. They study their opponent for any weaknesses they can exploit. They're mentally and physically focused on the bout so they'll win the fight.

In the same way, we have to be ready to contend for the crown of our faith, too. It's been entrusted to us, the saints, so we have to be ready at all times. We have to stay in top condition. We have to study God's word, and walk in His light. We have to spend time in prayer, fellowshipping with the Lord, and learning His will. We have to train ourselves to be godly in our habits, so we minimize any weaknesses the enemy can exploit. Not only must we learn to protect ourselves, we must learn to take the gospel to the enemy, those who don't know Jesus Christ as Lord and Savior. We win by taking the fight to our challenger, and introducing him or her to Jesus, and His saving grace.

The fact that Jude wrote this to the believers indicates some apathy might have been setting in. The saints may well have become complacent in their faith, content to coast along where they were. We know how that is. It's easy to do. The church is comfortable, the pews are cushy, the people are friendly and agreeable, and the teaching is so interesting. But we're not called to be ringside. Christianity is not a spectator sport. We're to be inside the ring, contending for the faith.

So when someone criticizes the faith, or Jesus, we have to be ready to counterpunch with truth. When someone slanders believers, we ought not stay silent; rather we have to step into the fray, and correct the misperceptions. We can't be on the sidelines. We're the ones who have to contend for the faith. Are you a contender?

Prayer: Heavenly Father, give us the courage and boldness to be contenders for the faith of Jesus Christ…

Dec 17
The Foundation

"It is by the name of Jesus Christ of Nazareth, whom you crucified but whom God raised from the dead, that this man stands before you healed. He (Jesus) is 'the stone you builders rejected, which has become the cornerstone.' Salvation is found in no one else, for there is no other name under heaven given to men by which we must be saved." Ac 4:10b-12

Can you imagine being called in front of the ruling council to defend yourself for a kindness you did that resulted in a miracle? It seems ludicrous to have to justify why you healed someone who had been crippled from birth. And Peter and John freely testified as to how this happened. It wasn't them who did it; rather, it was the power of Jesus' name that gave the man his healing. The man didn't know how it was done, either, but he knew one thing. He'd been crippled from birth, but now he could walk.

Interestingly, Peter, filled with the Holy Spirit, moved right past the miraculous healing to the main point of the gospel of Jesus Christ. The one whom they had crucified, but was raised again to new life by God, has become the cornerstone of the faith.

The cornerstone was the stone upon which the entire building was constructed. It was perfectly square, plumb, and level. The whole structure was raised from this one stone. Jesus is the stone upon which the entire structure of Christianity is based. Everything we think and believe should trace back to Jesus, and be square and level with His truth.

Then Peter comes to the heart of salvation. Only Jesus saves! You can't find salvation in anyone else. It's not found in Hare Krishna, or Mohammed, or Buddha, or Reverend Moon, or any other. The only name under heaven that can save us is Jesus. It's by faith in Jesus alone, that we are saved.

As we celebrate the coming of Christ, we look with excitement at that little baby, born of a virgin, who was sent to save us, and became the rock upon which our faith is built. May the hallelujahs ring to the skies. That little baby is the King of Kings!

Prayer: Lord Jesus, thank you for coming in the flesh, and becoming the rock we build upon…

Dec 18
A Prophecy

"But you, Bethlehem Ephrathah, though you are small among the clans of Judah, out of you will come for me one who will be ruler over Israel, whose origins are from of old, from days of eternity." Mic 5:2

Several days ago we talked about how God put everything in place so that Jesus would be born in the right place. Hundreds of years before that took place, though, the prophet Micah foretold that the town of Bethlehem would be the place from which the Messiah would come.

It doesn't matter how small you are, or your place is, God can use it. Regardless of how insignificant you may be, or your gifts are, or your resources are, God can use it for great things. We often think that because we're nobody, God won't use us. We know He can do anything, but think we're so inconsequential He wouldn't bother with us. But that's the wrong way to think. We weren't so trifling that the Lord didn't save us, so why wouldn't He use us? We need only be available, and God may do something wonderful through us.

This parallels what John tells us in his gospel, too. The prophecy speaks to the fact that the Messiah would be one whose origins were from old, who was eternal. They probably didn't even know what that meant, but in looking back we clearly see that the Messiah was God. He was always there. He wasn't confined by time and space to a thirty-three year life span on earth. He has always been, and He always will be. We don't serve a man who became God; we serve the God who became man, and who lives eternally in His glorified body.

We now know that Christ is the ruler over, not only Israel, but the entire world. And to think that the King of Kings and Lord of Lords came from a tiny little village in the smallest of the clans of Judah.

Prayer: Lord, thank you that use small things, and unimportant people to do great things for your kingdom. Use us, we pray...

Dec 19
Are You a Pretender

"One man pretends to be rich, yet has nothing; another pretends to be poor, yet has great wealth." Pr 13:7

When I was growing up on the farm, we had neighbors. One neighbor had the nicest, new machinery, and drove a new vehicle, and lived in a nice, fancy house. Another neighbor, while he had a decent amount of land, had old machinery, rarely bought a new car, and had a decent home, but nothing extraordinary. The first neighbor went out of business. He had new machinery, but no money. The second neighbor purchased some of his property. The second neighbor, while he rarely bought a new piece of equipment, took good care of his machines, and only purchased new when he had to. When he did, he didn't have to borrow money to buy it. His house was well stocked, had good furniture, and was well taken care of. It turns out the second neighbor was the wealthiest farmer in the entire area, but you wouldn't know it by looking at his lifestyle. Us? We had old machinery and we didn't have any money, either—lol.

We all have a tendency to pretend. It may be we pretend to be better off, or less well off, financially than we are, or it may have nothing to do with money. We sometimes pretend our marriage is fine when in fact it's coming apart at the seams. We pretend our spiritual life is great when we have barely a passing acquaintance with the Lord. We sometimes pretend we have expertise when we really don't. Whatever it is, this is sure. Pretending doesn't make it so.

Pride is at the heart of pretending, because in most cases we pretend to have, or be, more than we do, or are. Humility is a great virtue to have. It assists us in telling the truth. We don't have to distort anything to save face. When we're genuine in our personal and professional lives, it makes everything so easy. It takes a lot of effort and energy to put on a façade.

And it's all wasted time and exertion. That activity could be better used in productive areas that are substantive.

Don't be a pretender. You'll find life to be so much easier to handle, and far more enjoyable when you're being authentic. You don't have to work as hard, either.

Prayer: Father, keep us genuine in our walk, and remove any desire to pretend to be other than what we are…

Dec 20
Blessed and Prosperous

"Blessed is the man who does not walk in the counsel of the wicked or stand in the way of sinners or sit in the seat of mockers. But his delight is in the law of the Lord, and on his law he meditates day and night. He is like a tree planted by streams of water, which yields its fruit in season and whose leaf does not wither. Whatever he does prospers." Ps 1:1-3

It takes a conscious effort to avoid walking in the counsel of ungodly people, or going along with the world's values, or staying out of the company of those who mock what is good and pure. We're so immersed in the culture we live in that it takes real thought, and intentional living, to keep clear of the ungodly actions and attitudes. With the media telling us day in and day out that what God calls evil is good, or part of an alternate lifestyle, and that helping your neighbor is government taking what some have worked for and giving it to others, rather than people giving directly to people, it's tough to see through the barrage.

Blessed is the man who stays away from the world and it's values because he can stay clean. His thinking can be clear and godly. He can stand up for the values that God sets as the standard. We don't accept that sexual immorality is okay, or that it's just a choice. We don't believe in harming our coworkers to get ahead, or being selfish and rude. We know God's word and we generously share with others and lend a helping hand whenever we can. We give. The world takes. We share. The world hordes. We help. The world ignores.

As we seek God's will and purpose for our lives, as we meditate on His word, we're given a promise in these verses. We'll be like a tree planted by the water. That means we'll never lack for sustenance; in fact, we'll have plenty. We'll flourish in that stream of living water, and when the season comes, we'll bear a wonderful yield of fruit. We need never fear withering away, because God will sustain us. More than that, God will bless us and prosper all that we do.

We have no intention of going the way of the wicked, because they will be swept away like dust in the wind, unable to stand in the assembly of the righteous at the judgment. We'd much rather have the Lord watching over us, and prospering whatever we do.

Prayer: Lord, we do delight in your word, and in following your ways. Bless and prosper our efforts, and make all we do honoring to you…

Dec 21
A Prophecy

"Therefore the Lord himself will give you a sign: The virgin will be with child and will give birth to a son, and will call him Immanuel." Is 7:14

Why look at prophecy? Because when we look at God's prophecies, written and handed down for hundreds of years, and see those prophecies fulfilled, it proves God. It proves what He says is true, it proves He's accurate, it proves He knows the beginning from the end, it proves He knows all things, it proves He can set His will in place centuries ahead of time, so it proves God.

This prophecy concerning the Messiah is so unusual, and so specific, that it cannot be mistaken. There's never been any circumstance like it. There aren't any virgin pregnancies recorded, and no virgins giving birth. The Lord reserved this for Himself, to prove who was coming, and to give a sign that when this event occurred, Messiah had come.

Even being called Immanuel is striking. Immanuel means, 'God with us.' But this was a little human baby, complete and in the flesh. Yes, but He was also God, complete and in the Spirit. Remember? Fully man, and fully God. Astonishing!

The virgin birth is one of the core beliefs of Christianity. To come to Christ, it's necessary to know who He is. If He were born in the normal manner, following sexual relations with a normal man, then there would be no chance that He's God. That's why it's essential to understand the prophetic timetable, given approximately two thousand, seven hundred years ago, and the prophecy fulfilled in the actual event, just two thousand years ago. The foretelling and fulfilling of the virgin birth is too accurate to be dismissed, and is one of the foundational truths regarding Jesus Christ.

Because of these, and the many other prophecies concerning the Messiah that were fulfilled in Jesus, we have absolute confidence that He is who the Bible claims He is. The only begotten Son of the Heavenly Father, the Most High God himself, who by His Spirit overshadowed Mary, and gave her this child. He is the son of Mary, and the Son of God.

The virgin gave birth to a son, and called him Immanuel. What a sign!

Prayer: Father, thank you for the gift of your Son, and for the proofs of who He is. We give you praise and glory as we celebrate the first coming of Messiah...

Dec 22
A Noble Task

"Here is a trustworthy saying: If anyone sets his heart on being an overseer, he desires a noble task. Now the overseer must be above reproach, the husband of but one wife, temperate, self-controlled, respectable, hospitable, able to teach, not given to drunkenness, not violent but gentle, not quarrelsome, not a lover of money. He must manage his own family well and see that his children obey him with proper respect. He must not be a recent convert, or he may become conceited and fall under the same judgment as the devil." I Tim 3:1-4,6

First, note that it's a noble thing if you have the desire to be an overseer in the church. Second, note that there are some qualifications to become one. The third thing to think about is this; it's important to sense a clear calling from the Lord if you're moving towards engaging in a set apart ministry. Without that vision, you'll be overwhelmed by the responsibility you take on.

We should have the desire to find a place of service for the Lord. There's something all of us can do, and there is a calling that God has for you. Regardless of what area of service you're led to, it's a noble task in the kingdom of God to be fulfilled with integrity, faithfulness, and enthusiasm.

One thing we must do, though, is align our personal lives with the mandates of Scripture. It's imperative that we develop the fruit of the Spirit in our lives. We cannot effectively serve the Lord unless we have the self-control to live out the attitudes and behavior listed. We're not talking about faking it, either. We have to get these attributes down inside, so they're part and parcel of our everyday, everywhere, all the time walk with Christ.

If you're not there, move in the direction of growing in these areas. Your marriage must be stable, loving, and affectionate. You must be gentle, self-disciplined in every area of your temperament, decent, and content with your position. You have to start your spiritual service in your own family, teaching them to live obediently and respectfully.

This last part is vital. It's not worth seeking to be a spiritual leader if you're a relatively new convert. Satan's pride was his downfall, and because of his conceit he lost his place in heaven. We don't want to chance falling under judgment. Wisdom in the faith comes from time and study in the faith.

We certainly encourage you to seek the place God calls you. It's a noble task.

Prayer: Lord, show us clearly where you want us to serve, and how. Move us to line our lives up with your teaching in the word…

Dec 23
Joseph

"Because Joseph her husband was a righteous man and did not want to expose her to public disgrace, he had in mind to divorce her quietly. But after he had considered this, an angel of the Lord appeared to him in a dream and said, 'Joseph son of David, do not be afraid to take Mary home as your wife, because what is conceived in her is from the Holy Spirit. She will give birth to a son, and you are to give him the name Jesus, because he will save his people from their sins.'" Mt 1:19-21

There's a stark contrast between the kindness, gentleness, and godliness of Joseph, and the way the world reacts to what, on the surface, looks like betrayal of the worst kind. Being engaged to be married was quite different in those days than it is now. We see that in this passage when Joseph had in mind to divorce her quietly. What? Divorce? They're not even married yet! That's true, but by the laws of their time when the pledge of marriage was entered into, it was as binding as the marriage. So the unfaithfulness was just as it would have been to married couples in our age.

Most men would be seething at the unfaithful acts apparent in this situation. Who could believe the story of being with child by the power of the Holy Spirit? It's not like there was ever a precedent for this situation. So the course of action for most men would have been to publicly humiliate the disloyal, treacherous woman, and broadcast the divorce for all to see.

You have to admire Joseph. Before the angel of the Lord appeared, he showed the kind of gracious, loving, forgiving man he was. Rather than make a spectacle of Mary, he decided to effect the divorce quietly, and go on with life, unwilling to cause any more trouble for Mary than she was already in. What a gracious spirit. What tender concern for someone who didn't seem to deserve it. Joseph had the perfect heart, attitude, mind, and aptitude to raise the Son of God to learn those same godly attributes through his example.

"When Joseph woke up, he did what the angel of the Lord had commanded him and took Mary home as his wife. But he had no union with her until she gave birth to a son. And he gave him the name Jesus." Mt 1:24-25

Then Joseph was obedient. And Joseph was pure. He's a great example of a godly man.

Prayer: Heavenly Father, teach us to be the kind of godly example that Joseph was. Fill us with those same attributes...

Dec 24
The Shepherds

"And there were shepherds living out in the fields nearby, keeping watch over their flocks at night. An angel of the Lord appeared to them...and said to them, "Do not be afraid. I bring you good news of great joy that will be for all the people. Today in the town of David a Savior has been born to you; he is Messiah the Lord. This will be a sign to you: You will find a baby wrapped in cloths and lying in a manger."

The shepherds said to one another, "Let's go to Bethlehem and see this thing that has happened, which the Lord has told us about." Lk 2:8-9a,10-12,15b-d

Who? Why in the world would the announcement come to shepherds, the people on the lowest rung of the social ladder? They were unclean (by the law of Moses), dirty, unkempt, and they smelled like sheep. Rather than going to the Sanhedrin, the elite, and announcing it there, it went to the opposite end of the social spectrum. And the answer is found within the angel's message. This good news of great joy was for *all* the people. There was already enough snobbery in the hierarchy of the synagogues, and they were much too insulated from the outside, not bothering to bring Gentiles into the faith. So there was really no reason to take it where the message would be kept for their own uses and political machinations. Because the message was for all the people, it was brought to those who would spread the news to all the people. Hmmm, does that mean the shepherds were prolific gossipers?!?-lol.

There was certainly a heightened amount of angelic activity in those days. And why not? This was the most exciting, most important, most extraordinary event in eternity to date. The angels were bringing God's messages, and they were gathering to praise God. We should join with them in worship, saying, "Glory to God in the highest, and on earth peace to men on whom His favor rests." Lk 2:14

The shepherds had to have been astonished. They would likely have thought they were having delusions except they all saw and heard what the angel said, and what the choir of angels proclaimed. Picture it. You're quietly minding your sheep, watching out for predators in the still of the night, and suddenly this blinding light confronts you, and an angel appears from nowhere right in front of you. No wonder they were terrified. That would be enough to stop your heart. The adrenaline rush would have kept us awake for days!

But the shepherds received the message. They believed it, and decided to go see what the angels had told them about. What about the sheep they left behind? Who cares? They wanted to see what the angel had told them. So they headed for Bethlehem. Wouldn't you?

Prayer: Lord, thank you that your love and saving grace extends to all people, and that we've been privileged to receive it...

Dec 25
The Birth

"So Joseph also went up from the town of Nazareth in Galilee to Judea, to Bethlehem the town of David, because he belonged to the house and line of David. He went there to register with Mary, who was pledged to be married to him and was expecting a child. While they were there, the time came for the baby to be born, and she gave birth to her firstborn, a son. She wrapped him in cloths and placed him in a manger, because there was no room for them in the inn.

(The shepherds) found Mary and Joseph, and the baby, who was lying in the manger. When they had seen him, they spread the word concerning what had been told them about this child, and all who heard it were amazed at what the shepherds said to them."

Lk 2:4-7, 16b-18

We come today to commemorate the birth of our Savior. We celebrate with joy and thanksgiving. We give gifts to one another to honor the greatest gift we've ever received, our Lord Jesus Christ. And we spread the word concerning Him so that others may come and receive the greatest gift, too.

As you spend time with your family today, we encourage you to sit down with them before you open your gifts, and read the whole story of the coming of Jesus. Keep Him central to your holiday, and He'll bless you richly as you do.

May the grace of our Lord Jesus Christ, and His enduring love, be with you as you celebrate His birth today.

Have a very Blessed, and Merry Christmas,
Gary & Glenda

Prayer: Lord Jesus, we praise and glorify you for giving us the gift of yourself...

Dec 26
Rest

"There remains, then, a Sabbath-rest for the people of God; for anyone who enters God's rest also rests from his own work, just as God did from his." Heb 4:9-10

"The fear of the Lord leads to life: Then one rests content, untouched by trouble." Pr 19:23

Following the Christmas holiday, we all need to rest. There's been so much activity, effort, and energy expended in the preparation and execution of celebrating Christmas that we can end up feeling totally worn out. Well, there's a solution, a cure, if you will.

God never meant for us to work ourselves to a frazzle. He created for us a Sabbath-rest. This is the rest that we enter into with the Lord himself. This is a time when we cease from our frenetic pace, and simply stop in quiet, peaceful solitude with God. We can turn off the radio, television, and stereo. We can walk away from the work left undone, have a cup of coffee or tea, or a soda, and sit down and relax with Jesus. He's waiting for you, right over there by your most comfortable chair. So enter His rest, and spend some time fellowshipping with Him.

In Christ Jesus is life and rest. This fear of the Lord is reverence for Him. The kind of fear in which we freely, lovingly, and willingly give Him our worship, our praise, and our highest honor. We set aside a special time with Jesus to refresh ourselves in His living water, that spring of eternal life that wells up within us. When we're resting in Christ Jesus, we're content. We don't worry about the world outside. We're just spending time in the tranquil, placid place of rest with Him. When we're with Jesus, we have these serene moments untouched by trouble.

Find some time today to take a mini Sabbath-rest. Whether for a half hour, fifteen minutes, or even five or ten, create a way to step aside from the daily rush and rest in the Lord. Refresh yourself in Him. It'll be worth every moment!

Prayer: Jesus, give us some time today to enter into your rest...

Dec 27
Blameless and Holy

"Night and day we pray most earnestly that we may see you again and supply what is lacking in your faith. May the Lord make your love increase and overflow for each other and for everyone else, just as ours does for you. May he strengthen your hearts so that you will be blameless and holy in the presence of our God and Father when our Lord Jesus comes with all his holy ones." I Th 3:10,12-13

Our goal in the faith is to be able to stand with Jesus, blameless and holy, before the Father on judgment day. All we do as we walk with Christ and study and apply His word to our lives is geared toward attaining that goal.

It may surprise you to know that, like Paul, we too have been praying earnestly for you, that as you spend your time in devotions together, the Lord is supplying what is lacking in your faith through this book. We pray that you're growing in the faith, and growing together, more tightly knit than ever before in your covenant relationship. Our hope is that you're growing in your love for each other, and that your Christ-centered love is overflowing to your children, and overflowing to your friends and coworkers.

As we go through what can sometimes be the grind of life, it's easy to grow faint and weary. It can be tough to maintain your godly attitudes and your gracious love for one another. It's difficult to control your tongue on those days you're assaulted on every side. Those are times when we especially need the Lord to strengthen our hearts. We need Him to give us the self-discipline to curb our tongues. We need Him to well up His love inside so we can pass it on when we don't feel like it ourselves. We need the mind and heart of Jesus, so we ask the Holy Spirit to give us His attitudes.

Only in Christ Jesus can we be blameless and holy. Continue to fix your gaze on Him, and keep Him the central focus of your life, both in your thoughts, and in your actions. He is able to keep you from falling, and to bring you home to God the Father in the right condition. Look forward to the thrill of being amidst Jesus and all His holy ones as we stand in the presence of our Heavenly Father. Christ Jesus will bring you there, blameless and holy.

Prayer: Lord, make your love well up and overflow from us, and strengthen us in our walk with you...

Dec 28

Pick Some Flowers for Romance

"My lover has gone down to his garden, to the beds of spices, to browse in the gardens and to gather lilies. I am my lover's and my lover is mine; he browses among the lilies." SS 6:2-3

In the busyness of this season, it's easy to forget to take time for romance. You're too tired, or so focused on all that has to be done that you can overlook your special time as a couple. Do not neglect your intimate life! It's too important to the health of your relationship, so set aside time for it.

Make plans for a romantic night out. You may have to get a babysitter, but with all you've spent on Christmas, you may not be able to afford one. Make a deal with friends. You watch all the kids one night; they watch all the kids the next night, so each of you can have an evening for yourselves.

Be creative if you have to. There are many things you can do while spending little or no money. Take a walk among the Christmas lights. Or take a long leisurely drive by the lights. Go have a cup of coffee and just visit. Sit in the mall and talk about the upcoming year. Snuggle up wherever you are. Hold hands. Steal a kiss here and there (and everywhere). See a movie (not inexpensive). Go out for a quiet dinner (okay, we've past inexpensive).

Find something you can both enjoy and do it. The important thing is to set aside time for just the two of you. And make sure you end your evening with romantic intimacy. You are each other's. Act like it. Get the cheese and crackers. Don't worry about the crumbs. Bring out the chocolate and the beverage. Laugh together. A lot! You can even be Sir Laughalot! It's okay to be corny; you probably are, anyway. Just have fun!

And don't forget the flowers. Try some lilies. They're great for romance.

Prayer: Father, give us ideas to spend wonderful, romantic interludes together. Bless our time as we're intimate…

Dec 29
The Dedication

"On the eighth day, when it was time to circumcise him, he was named Jesus, the name the angel had given him before he had been conceived. When the time of their purification according to the Law of Moses had been completed, Joseph and Mary took him to Jerusalem to present him to the Lord (as it is written in the Law of the Lord, "Every firstborn male is to be consecrated to the Lord"), and to offer a sacrifice in keeping with what is said in the Law of the Lord: "a pair of doves or two young pigeons." Lk 2:21-24

If there was any doubt as to whether Jesus would be brought up in the ways of the Lord, there certainly shouldn't be. Joseph and Mary were careful to follow in obedience to the Law of the Lord, and bring Him for circumcision on the eighth day, when they also named Him, and when they came to the temple in Jerusalem to offer their purification sacrifice and consecrate Jesus to the Lord.

In effect, they were dedicating Jesus to the Lord. This must have taken on special significance, knowing what they knew. They were faithful to God, and they give us an example that we can follow, as well.

While they were at the temple, Simeon and Anna came and prophesied about Jesus, and who He was. He was proclaimed there as our salvation, a revelation to the Gentiles, glory to His people Israel, the falling and rising of many, a sign that would be spoken against, a revealer of hearts, a sword that would pierce their hearts, and the redemption of Jerusalem.

Following all this, they returned home, and the child grew in strength, wisdom, and the grace of God. Joseph and Mary brought Him up in the nurture of the Lord.

We have a responsibility, also. As they set an example of obedience, we ought to be obedient to our instructions from the Lord, too. We should bring our children to the Lord and dedicate each of them to God. We promise to bring them up in the Lord, and to introduce each of them to Jesus Christ, teaching them to put their faith and trust in Him, and making Him Lord of their lives. We teach them the precepts of God's word, and how it applies. We worship the Lord faithfully and consistently, and do our best to set a godly example of walking with Christ. Above all, we show our children we love the Lord, and we set God's standards as the benchmark for our life.

That's dedication!

Prayer: Dear Lord, move us to be completely faithful in setting an example of godly living to whoever will see us, and especially to our children...

Dec 30
Set a Higher Standard

"Everything is permissible—but not everything is beneficial. Everything is permissible—but not everything is constructive. Nobody should seek his own good, but the good of others." I Cor 10:23-24

As we look ahead to the new year, and think about areas of growth we may seek, it's important for us to set a higher standard. If you make New Year's resolutions that are lower than the standards you've already attained, they'd be pretty easy to achieve. But as believers, we ought to set godly goals that help us grow in our faith. As you look forward to some things you hope to achieve in the upcoming year, apply these standard tests to your activities.

Is our goal honorable? If it leads us to the carnal side of life, we ought to forget it.

Does our goal achieve consideration of others? In other words, do we take care to bring good things to others in the pursuit of our aims?

Does our goal produce quality? If we don't intend to invest quality into our target, it's probably not worth going after.

Will our goal glorify God? If we intend to achieve a resolution that doesn't bring praise to the Lord, we ought not bother with it.

Does our goal look good? Avoid the very appearance of evil. Be sure your destination looks holy.

Would we want to have Jesus help us with our goal? To be sure, Jesus is going to be with you, so make certain you're comfortable with Him as your companion as you strive for your objective.

Is your goal healthy for your reputation? A good name is far more important than great riches, so be sure your aim reflects well on you.

Do you have inner peace regarding you goal? If you're content that God is in this, and particularly if this is His leading, you'll know your aspiration is worthwhile, and the Lord will bless it.

If you can apply these questions to your ambitions for the upcoming year and answer positively to each one, you'll know you've set standards God is pleased with. Remember this; just because something is permissible does *not* mean it's beneficial or constructive.

Prayer: Heavenly Father, help us to set goals that are pleasing to you. Holy Spirit, guide us to the areas of growth you want for us this coming year...

Dec 31
Stay in the Word

"As the rain and the snow come down from heaven, and do not return to it without watering the earth and making it bud and flourish, so that it yields seed for the sower and bread for the eater, so is my word that goes out from my mouth: It will not return to me empty, but will accomplish what I desire and achieve the purpose for which I sent it." Is 55:10-11

There is a purpose for God's Word. The Lord has a desire that His Word is meant to accomplish. God sent His Word to us, and it won't return empty. Several times throughout the year we've stressed the importance of reading the Word, of spending at least a little time in the Scriptures each and every day. For the final time this year, how's your Bible reading streak coming along?

God designed the rain and snow to fall to earth for a reason. It waters and nourishes plants that, in turn, grow and produce seeds, or vegetables, or fruit. Those seeds of grain accomplish at least two things. They provide seeds for next years planting, and they make flour from it to bake bread, or make pasta, or even cake. We're able to eat the produce because of the rain. The rain and snow achieved its purpose.

I speak from personal experience when I say God's Word achieves the purpose for which He sent it, too. Since I began reading Scripture a little each day, it has become clear to me that the importance of this discipline cannot be overstressed. I look back at the consistency of my spiritual growth since I began and I marvel at what the Word can do for us. I'm amazed at the depth of understanding God has revealed to me. That's not to say I don't have a long journey ahead of me, because I most certainly do. But I know God's Word is not returning empty. It's accomplishing the growth in my life that the Lord intended, and for that, I'm eternally grateful. I've learned that the answers to all of life's questions are answered in this book, the Bible. I've learned that all the wisdom I need is contained within its pages. I've learned that the disciplines, examples, teaching, corrections, and training I need are all wrapped up in these Scriptures. I've learned the Bible can equip us for everything we need to walk with, and serve, Jesus Christ.

We encourage you to allow it to achieve the purpose it's meant to accomplish in your life, also. Stay in the Word!

Prayer: Lord, thank you for your Word. Teach us all we need to learn from it, and help us to grow in your wisdom and grace as we continue to read and study…

Gary & Glenda are available for Gospel concerts and family or couples conferences. To make a request to schedule them at your church or event, please contact them through their website at www.garyministries.com or email them at gbaltrusch@yahoo.com.

You can also hear a sample of their music on the website, as well as order their compact discs.

CPSIA information can be obtained at www.ICGtesting.com
Printed in the USA
LVOW112358050312

271703LV00001B/84/P